Brigham Young University
2006–2007 Speeches

Order from
Speeches
218 UPB
Brigham Young University
Provo, UT 84602
http://speeches.byu.edu

Frequently Used Abbreviations

CR—*Conference Reports of The Church of Jesus Christ of Latter-day Saints.*

DBY—Young, Brigham. *Discourses of Brigham Young.* Selected by John A. Widtsoe. Salt Lake City: Deseret Book Company, 1941.

GD—Smith, Joseph F. *Gospel Doctrine.* 5th ed. Salt Lake City: Deseret Book Company, 1939.

GI—McKay, David O. *Gospel Ideals.* 2nd printing. Salt Lake City: Improvement Era, 1954.

GS—Grant, Heber J. *Gospel Standards.* Compiled by G. Homer Durham. Salt Lake City: Improvement Era, 1941.

HC—Smith, Joseph. *History of The Church of Jesus Christ of Latter-day Saints.* 7 vols. 2nd ed. revised. Edited by B. H. Roberts. Salt Lake City: The Church of Jesus Christ of Latter-day Saints, 1932–51.

Hymns—*Hymns.* Revised and enlarged. Salt Lake City: The Church of Jesus Christ of Latter-day Saints, 1948 and 1985.

JD—*Journal of Discourses.* 26 vols. London: Latter-day Saints' Book Depot, 1854–86.

Lectures on Faith. Compiled by N. B. Lundwall. Salt Lake City: N. B. Lundwall, n.d.

MD—McConkie, Bruce R. *Mormon Doctrine.* 2nd ed. Salt Lake City: Bookcraft, 1966.

PPP—Pratt, Parley P. *Autobiography of Parley P. Pratt.* Edited by his son Parley P. Pratt. Salt Lake City: Deseret Book Company, 1973, 1985, 1994.

Sing—*Sing with Me: Songs for Children.* Salt Lake City: The Church of Jesus Christ of Latter-day Saints, 1970.

Songbook—*Children's Songbook.* Salt Lake City: The Church of Jesus Christ of Latter-day Saints, 1989, 1995.

Teachings—Smith, Joseph. *Teachings of the Prophet Joseph Smith.* Selected by Joseph Fielding Smith. Salt Lake City: Deseret Book Company, 1938.

TETB—Benson, Ezra T. *The Teachings of Ezra Taft Benson.* Salt Lake City: Bookcraft, 1988.

TGBH—Hinckley, Gordon B. *Teachings of Gordon B. Hinckley.* Salt Lake City: Deseret Book Company, 1997.

TSWK—Kimball, Spencer W. *The Teachings of Spencer W. Kimball.* Edited by Edward L. Kimball. Salt Lake City: Bookcraft, 1982.

PRINTED IN THE UNITED STATES OF AMERICA

07-801/22386 1200

CONTENTS

Seeing Through the Generations 1
Neil L. Andersen

On Being a Christian Perfectly 13
Joseph D. Parry

"Be Strong and of a Good Courage". 25
Donald L. Staheli

Learning from Our Conflicts. 39
Gerald R. Williams

The Power of One: Selfless Service 51
Jo Ann C. Abegglen

Knowing, Doing, and Being 61
William H. Baker

Exactness in Our Discipleship 75
Scott D. Sommerfeldt

"Fresh Courage Take" 89
David A. Hunt

Truth Restored 105
Dieter F. Uchtdorf

Gifts of the Spirit for Hard Times 121
Henry B. Eyring

"Even If All, Not I" 135
Sharon G. Samuelson

What Is It That We Honor? 141
Cecil O. Samuelson

Your Refined Heavenly Home. 151
Douglas L. Callister

Experiences Worth Remembering 165
Gordon B. Hinckley

Faith and Works in a Secular World. 177
Keith B. McMullin

Three Gates to Open. 193
Thomas S. Monson

Brotherly Love 205
Tom Holmoe

Peace on Earth—Some Restrictions Apply 215
Julie Franklin

Finding Answers 227
Joseph Fielding McConkie

The Still, Small Voice 239
Sharon G. Samuelson

Mixing Reason and Faith 245
Cecil O. Samuelson

Lehi's Dream and You 255
Boyd K. Packer

Pilgrimages 267
Alvin F. Sherman, Jr.

A Reservoir of Living Water 281
David A. Bednar

Faith, Family, and Friendship 297
Peter M. Johnson

Personal Ministry: Sacred and Precious 311
Bonnie D. Parkin

Hold Fast to the Words of the Prophets 325
Neil L. Andersen

Precious Precepts of Truth 343
William A. Barrett

Be a Missionary All Your Life 357
Quentin L. Cook

Live Right Now 373
Gerrit W. Gong

Preparing for That Which Is to Come 387
Richard O. Cowan

"Don't Miss the Miracle" 401
Catherine H. Black

Seeing Through the Generations

Neil L. Andersen

I feel very humbled to be with you today, realizing that each person who is here has chosen to be here. You have come with the attitude of learning by faith, and I pray that the Holy Ghost will be in abundance with us, that your faith will be rewarded, and that you can learn something that can be helpful to you.

I want to introduce my subject this morning by telling you of a very simple event that happened to me 32 years ago during the spring semester of my junior year here at BYU.

I was taking a class in a large amphitheater classroom. Entering the classroom on one of those first days of the semester, I sat in the very back, far from the professor. As he began writing on the blackboard, and as those around me began taking notes, I realized that I could not see what they could see on the chalkboard. Up until that very moment I had not imagined that I needed glasses. I had not anticipated glasses in my future.

Neil L. Andersen was a member of the Presidency of the Seventy of The Church of Jesus Christ of Latter-day Saints when this devotional address was given on 16 May 2006. © *Intellectual Reserve, Inc.*

But that experience led me to the optometrist and to a pair of glasses. Suddenly my world improved immensely. I could see many things that I had not been seeing for some time. The world became much more alive for me. I remember asking myself, "Why didn't I realize before that I needed glasses? How could I have not known that I was not seeing?"

While seeing can be a function of our eyes, we also use the word *see* to mean "understand" or "comprehend." Have you ever asked, "Don't you see what I mean?" And haven't you responded at some time, "Oh, now I see."

My objective today is to enlarge your vision in some small way that allows you to see or to understand what you have not totally seen or understood before.

As you live righteously, you will find that during your lifetime your perspective will enlarge many, many times. Usually this shift in perspective is not a dramatic one that you can see from one day to the next, but over time the advances are significant.

The most important perspective we want to gain was described beautifully by the Savior: "And this is life eternal, that they might know thee the only true God, and Jesus Christ, whom thou hast sent" (John 17:3).

I will start with two rather academic examples and then move to a more spiritual principle.

First, a perspective on time.

THE PERSPECTIVE OF TIME

In the same year that I first put on a pair of glasses—1974— I attended a large fireside held in the Marriott Center, where the speaker was Elder Neal A. Maxwell, then a new member of the Quorum of the Seventy. I have never forgotten the talk he shared. It helped me to view my own mortality in a slightly different way. He read from the writing of Brother A. Lester Allen, a former dean and scientist of the Department of Biology and Agriculture on this campus. Let me read you this analogy and see if it expands, just a little, your view of time. Listen closely.

Suppose, for instance, that we imagine a "being" moving onto our earth whose entire life-span is only 1/100 of a second. Ten thousand "years" for him, generation after generation, would be only one second of our time. Suppose this imaginary being comes up to a quiet pond in the forest where you are seated. You have just tossed in a rock and are watching the ripples. A leaf is fluttering from the sky and a bird is swooping over the water. He would find everything absolutely motionless. Looking at you, he would say: "In all recorded history nothing has changed. My father and his father before him have seen that everything is absolutely still. This creature called man has never had a heartbeat and has never breathed. The water is standing in stationary waves as if someone had thrown a rock into it; it seems frozen. A leaf is suspended in air, and a bird has stopped right over the middle of the pond. There is no movement. Gravity is suspended." The concept of time in this imaginary being, so different from ours, would give him an entirely different perspective of what we call reality.

On the other hand, picture another imaginary creature for whom one "second" of his time is 10,000 years of our time. What would the pond be like to him? By the time he sat down beside it, taking 15,000 of our years to do so, the pond would have vanished. Individual human beings would be invisible, since our entire life-span would be only 1/100 of his "seconds." The surface of the earth would be undulating as mountains are built up and worn down. The forest would persist but a few minutes and then disappear. His concept of "reality" would be much different than our own. [A. Lester Allen, quoted in Neal A. Maxwell, "But for a Small Moment," 1 September 1974, in *Speeches of the Year, 1974* (Provo: BYU, 1975), 454]

When I first heard this analogy—with time moving so very quickly or moving so very slowly—I thought of the words of Alma: "All is as one day with God, and time only is measured unto men" (Alma 40:8). I also thought of Nephi's words: "As well in these times as in times of old, and as well in times of old as in times to come; wherefore, the course of the Lord is one eternal round" (1 Nephi 10:19). Somehow I sensed that my "reality" as an individual walking through earthly time could be very limited without some perspective greater than my own.

Now I switch perspectives—to a perspective of space.

THE PERSPECTIVE OF SPACE

To help illustrate this perspective, let's examine a leaf on a plant that sits in the V part of the Y on Y Mountain. If we move far, far away from the plant—10 million light years away—can you see the leaf? To help you understand this distance, one light year is approximately 6 trillion miles. After traveling for 27 years, the Voyager I space probe had only covered a distance of 13 light hours. So 10 million light years is a very, very long way. If we look at the leaf 10 times closer—from 1 million light years away—we see the spiral of the Milky Way galaxy. Then 10 times closer than that is only 100,000 light years away. As we come again 1,000 times closer, we still see nothing but stars. At 1 trillion kilometers—1,000 times closer still— we can begin to identify our sun. Another 1,000 times closer—at 10 billion kilometers—we can see our solar system. This is 10 billion times closer to the leaf than where we started at 10 million light years away. As we continue to move even closer—at 1 million kilometers— we see the earth and the orbit of the moon. At 100 times closer than that—at 10,000 kilometers—we see the Western Hemisphere of the earth. And, finally, from 10 kilometers we can see Y Mountain with Provo below. From 10 meters away we can easily see the Y and the plant in front of us, and, then, at 10 centimeters, we see the leaf we have been following from so far away.

But now that we are here, there is still much more to see. Moving into the leaf we get quite another view. At 1 millimeter we see the leaf magnified 100 times. Looking 1,000 times closer, at 1 micrometer, the nucleus of the leaf cell is visible. At 100 nanometers— 10 times closer than that—the chromatin of the leaf cell nucleus is visible. From 10 nanometers we can see or we can imagine the individual DNA strands. Still 100 times closer, at 100 picometers, the outer electron cloud of a carbon atom is visible. This is 1 billion times closer than when we were seeing the leaf from 10 centimeters.

Going 100 times closer still, we see the empty space between the inner shell and the nucleus of the atom. As we magnify 100 times more at 10 femtometers, we can see the nucleus of the carbon atom. Finally, magnified 100 times more at 100 attometers, we are looking at quarks within the single proton. (The idea of this demonstration was taken from a Florida State University Web site at micro.magnet.fsu.edu/ primer/java/scienceopticsu/powersof10.) This is quite a journey to view a simple leaf on Y Mountain.

When I see the immensity of space and the intricacies and complexity of objects on earth, I think of the words of Moses:

And were it possible that man could number the particles of the earth, yea, millions of earths like this, it would not be a beginning to the number of thy creations. [Moses 7:30]

Remember also the words of the Psalmist:

When I consider thy heavens, and the work of thy fingers, the moon and the stars, which thou hast ordained;
What is man, that thou art mindful of him? [Psalm 8:3–4]

And in that glorious hymn we sing, "There is no end to matter; There is no end to space" ("If You Could Hie to Kolob," *Hymns,* 1985, no. 284).

In the powerful words of the prophet Alma to the deceiver Korihor, we read:

All things denote there is a God; yea, even the earth, and all things that are upon the face of it, yea, and its motion, yea, and also all the planets which move in their regular form do witness that there is a Supreme Creator. [Alma 30:44]

I bear witness that He lives, that this Supreme Creator is He who we call our Heavenly Father and His Son Jesus Christ. A developed perspective of space helps us to see the greatness of our Heavenly

Father and also that we would be wise to learn of Him and to conform our lives to His eternal plan.

Let us now look more closely at His plan for us—a plan He has called "the great plan of happiness" (Alma 42:8). For this we must speak of His words to both ancient and modern prophets.

You have been who you are for a very, very long time. We are sons and daughters of heavenly parents who love us and who have sent us on a course to become more like Them. We lived in the premortal existence prior to our coming to earth. We were taught of our Heavenly Father's plan. We would receive a physical body; we would learn to choose good over evil. The Only Begotten Son of the Father offered Himself as the Savior of the world, allowing us a way to return to our heavenly home. We rejoiced in the plan, and we "fought for it. Many of us also made covenants with the Father concerning what we would do in mortality. In ways that have not been revealed, our actions in the spirit world influence us in mortality" (Dallin H. Oaks, "The Great Plan of Happiness," *Ensign*, November 1993, 72).

We do not have all the answers, but it is very clear that our life is not a coincidence—and that it is not by chance that we find ourselves here at this time in human history.

The Restoration scriptures explain a beautiful linking of the generations that, once understood, opens our view, and we see our lives in a more complete way.

Three thousand years ago the Lord covenanted with a righteous man named Abraham, promising him that "in thy seed shall all the nations of the earth be blessed" (Genesis 22:18). There was a covenant made, a people established, and a promise that through this people many great things would come to pass in the latter days.

When the Savior visited the Nephites following His Resurrection, He said to them:

Ye are the children of the prophets; and ye are of the house of Israel; and ye are of the covenant which the Father made with your fathers, saying unto Abraham: And in thy seed shall all the kindreds of the earth be blessed.

. . . Ye are the children of the covenant. [3 Nephi 20:25–26]

You and I are "children of the covenant." The Savior has declared it, and I confirm it to you. As we come to understand what it means, we see more clearly. Mortality comes more into focus. Just like putting on glasses and seeing the blackboard of our mortality, our understanding grows.

The Apostle Peter described members of the Church as "a chosen generation, a royal priesthood, an holy nation, a peculiar people" (1 Peter 2:9).

I repeat: It is not by chance that we find ourselves within this holy lineage, the blood of Israel, with a promise and a destiny that through our lives and the lives of our posterity all the peoples of the earth will be blessed (see 1 Nephi 15:18; 3 Nephi 16:5–7; D&C 39:11).

When we see ourselves in the perspective of this holy family, those who came before us and those who come after us become very important to us. I have heard President Gordon B. Hinckley say on more than one occasion, "I have been thinking a lot about my grandfather and grandmother. I have been thinking a lot about my father and my mother. I have been thinking just a little about myself and my dear wife. And I have been thinking a lot about my children, about my grandchildren, and about my great-grandchildren." And then he has concluded with this phrase: "And I have been thinking a lot about this wonderful link that binds us all together" (President Hinckley speaking at Vernal, Utah, and Campinas, Brazil, temple dedications).

Now you might say, "But my parents and grandparents were not like President Hinckley's; they were not members of the Church." Or, "They were not faithful in the Church." Or, as a man in Argentina who I called to be a stake president said to me: "I don't even know who my father is." He had been given the family name of his mother. He had not heard the name of the Church until he was 18 years old. How could he be part of this royal family?

Through miraculous circumstances—that we will one day appreciate more than we can now explain—each of us has been brought into this covenant family and we have become children of the covenant. It is not necessary that we be able to explain every detail. Here is where we reverse "seeing is believing" to "believing is the beginning of seeing." I confirm to you that it is not by chance that we are here and that we are who we are.

Notice in President Hinckley's words that he looked both *back* through his generations—his parents, grandparents, great-grandparents—and *forward* through his generations—his children, grandchildren, and great-grandchildren.

This is the major point I want to make to you today: As we see through our generations, both backward and forward, we see who we are, and we see more clearly what we must become. Let me give you an example.

Let me show you the engagement picture of our son, Derek Andersen, with his fiancée, Erica Wible. They met here at BYU and fell in love. Three weeks ago, in their caps and gowns, they graduated together. Three days ago, kneeling at the altar in the San Diego Temple, they were sealed by the holy priesthood for time and for all eternity. They look to the future with great hope and anticipation.

Their lives will be like all of our lives: filled with challenges, tests, happiness, and satisfactions—and moments where they must exhibit the character and strength that is in them. If they look back and look forward and see their role in the generations, it will strengthen and fortify them.

Now let me show you two people in their lives from the past. Daniel Henry Arline was born in 1841 in northern Florida. He is Derek's great-great-grandfather. One day in 1898 he heard the missionaries speak in the town square. He felt something inside. Although there was great persecution against the Church and against the missionaries as well, he took the missionaries to his home, fed them, and watched over them. He was then 57 years old, but he told his wife, "For the first time in my life I have heard the truth." He and all his family were baptized. Though it was not easy to be a pioneer and a member of The Church of Jesus Christ of Latter-day Saints at the turn of the century in the southern United States, Daniel Arline remained true to the gospel and to his covenants. Part of who Derek is comes because of the goodness and righteousness of this man whom Derek has never met.

Marva Olson Prior is the great-grandmother of Erica. Her life did not take every turn as she expected. She reared her four children righteously in the Church without her husband being a member. She once said: "If we keep His commandments, we will be blessed and find peace of mind and true joy, but not without trials, for we learn so much from our challenges." Her husband joined the Church after they had been married 46 years. Part of who Erica Wible is comes because of the noble life of this great-grandmother. I have a picture of Erica with her great-grandmother when Erica was younger. Sister Prior passed away four years ago.

In the world in which we live there is a great focus on "me," "I," "my world," "my style," "my satisfactions," and "my things." In the popular recent book *Generation Me*, author Jean M. Twenge leads with these words on the cover: "Why Today's Young Americans Are More Confident, Assertive, Entitled—and More Miserable Than Ever Before."

Here is a paragraph from the book describing some of those in your generation:

Born after self-focus entered the cultural mainstream, this generation has never known a world that put duty before self. Linda's youngest child, Jessica, was born in 1985. When Jessica was a toddler, Whitney Houston's No. 1 hit song declared that "The Greatest Love of All" was loving yourself. Jessica's elementary school teachers believed that their most important job was helping Jessica feel good about herself. Jessica scribbled in a coloring book called We Are All Special, *got a sticker on her work sheet just for filling it out, and did a sixth-grade project called "All About Me." When she wondered how to act on her first date, her mother told her, "Just be yourself." Eventually, Jessica got her lower lip pierced and obtained a large tattoo on her lower back because, she said, she wanted to express herself. She dreams of being a model or a singer. She does not expect to marry until she is in her late twenties, and neither she nor her older sisters have any children yet. "You have to love yourself before you can love someone else," she says. This is a generation unapologetically focused on the individual, a true Generation Me.* [Jean M. Twenge, *Generation Me: Why Today's Young Americans Are More Confident, Assertive, Entitled—and More Miserable Than Ever Before* (New York: Free Press, 2006), 1–2]

Now this does not describe you, but it describes a part of your generation.

If we can look back through the generations, we see those who helped us to get where we are now—those who forged the way before us, whether they were members of the Church or not. And in the restored gospel we realize even more deeply our responsibility to link them to us through the ordinances of the temple.

In a letter from the Prophet Joseph Smith to the members of the Church, we read:

These are principles in relation to the dead and the living that cannot be lightly passed over. . . . *For their salvation is necessary and essential to our salvation,* . . . *they without us cannot be made perfect—neither can we without our dead be made perfect.* [D&C 128:15; see also verse 18]

Now let's see through our generations forward. Who will be your children and your grandchildren? Or, if by chance you do not marry, who will be those you influence in the generations ahead?

Looking ahead through the generations, what kind of care and example will Derek and Erica's great-grandchildren receive from their parents? Will Derek and Erica teach their children in such a way that their grandchildren will believe that they are "children of the covenant"? When we look at our own lives, we must be prepared to look forward into the generations that will follow us, for our footprints will be seen in homes and on paths where we will never walk.

As we are righteous, there is a power in the priesthood that passes through us into our posterity, shaping their eternity as it shapes ours.

Let me share with you the words of a blessing pronounced by the Prophet Joseph Smith upon Bishop Newel K. Whitney in Kirtland on October 7, 1835:

He shall be blessed with a fullness of the good things of this earth, and his seed after him from generation to generation. . . . Angels shall guard his house, and shall guard the lives of his posterity, and they shall become very great and very numerous on the earth. [HC 2:288]

I close by giving you a promise. As you can learn to see through the generations—by looking back and by looking forward—you will see more clearly who you are and what you must become. You will better see that your place in this vast, beautiful plan of happiness is no small place. And you will come to love the Savior and depend on Him—as His great gift to us makes this all possible. Your influence will continue generation after generation throughout all eternity.

I bear witness of these things: Jesus is the Christ, the Only Begotten of the Father. He lives. He is resurrected. One day everyone from all nations, all generations, all times, and all places will kneel and confess Him to be who we claim and know Him to be: the Savior of the world. He restored the priesthood to the earth. That priesthood and that power is found in The Church of Jesus Christ of Latter-day Saints. He guides His prophets. I bear witness that you are a child of the covenant and pray that you may through your generations see the power that is in you, in the name of Jesus Christ, amen.

On Being a Christian Perfectly

Joseph D. Parry

I want to think with you today about what it means to be a Christian. And, since, ultimately, what it means to be a Christian is to "be perfect even as [Jesus], or [our] Father who is in heaven is perfect" (3 Nephi 12:48; see Matthew 5:48), I want to think with you about being a Christian perfectly, rather than doing Christianity perfectly. Perfection, we tell ourselves, is a process, but I want to take the Lord at His word, and His word when He issued this command is that we "be perfect" with no additional words of comforting qualification. The word *be* is an important word in this statement. To be perfect is to be complete, whole—though we mean to lose the self in the service of others so we can find it again. Our modern lives have a way of scattering us into the many sectors of our responsibilities, each with its own list of tasks to be performed, superiors to be satisfied, substances or situations to be avoided, and people to be loved. Something tells me that the wholeness the Lord is talking about is

Joseph D. Parry was an associate professor in the BYU Department of Humanities, Classics, and Comparative Literature when this devotional address was given on 6 June 2006. © *Brigham Young University.*

not the sum of the items on these lists, especially because the lists contain so many "to don'ts" as well as "to dos."

One of the striking things about sin is that it is not an opposite form of completing the self but rather a way of dividing and dislocating a bit of oneself from the whole. We often refer to this phenomenon as compartmentalizing our lives and ourselves. I think that what we might call "Internet sin" is particularly effective in exploiting this vulnerability in us as well as in the world that we usually try to distinguish ourselves from. Certainly pornography, plagiarism, and gambling on the Internet are the problems they are for us because the chance to indulge the powerful temptations that have always been with us is now just a few clicks away. And it doesn't help us that these temptations often find us, rather than our having to go out and look for them at a store, theater, or party.

But the basic challenge the Internet poses is that it's more than just an easily accessible storehouse of images and information. The Web, with its many entrances into labyrinths of virtual experience and relationships, makes it easy for a part of oneself to wander off and slip into another room unnoticed by others and barely noticed by the rest of oneself. The appeal of restaging one's life on another stage where it can enter in and exit from some contained adventure and stimulation is very strong, especially when one constitutes one's world as a place of denials, deferrals, and dangers, and when envy of others' worlds of popularity and possessions is inverted into configuring a good world as one that *deprives* its inhabitants of such things. Is that what we think righteousness is—a life of privation we endure on the promise that we'll get more and better versions of the stuff and the station we've always wanted? If so, is it any wonder that when technology gives us the chance to privately make our envious fantasies more real, we seize the opportunity to reinvent ourselves as someone more daring and sophisticated on a personal-space site?

I don't mean to preach a Luddite sermon on the evils of modern technology. In fact, if anything, this technology has revealed some problems and weaknesses in us that we need to address; it didn't exactly cause them. And, dear friends, it is urgent that we all address them now. Far, far too many of us of all ages are depositing small portions of our soul in scattered electronic closets. The answer is ultimately not to try to search out and lock the door to every closet. It is in affirmation—not merely in avoidance—in doing good, not just resisting evil, that one takes up Christianity as a way of being in the world. If mortal life for us is simply a time of doing without, then we're probably spending most of our time thinking about what we're doing without—like me on a diet, constantly thinking about the food I wish I could have. Being a Christian in this world means living in our own and others' inabilities, disabilities, and fallibilities. Our limitations don't keep us from who we really are; they are the conditions in which we are who we are.

I am so very grateful that the Lord Jesus Christ lived in this world as well as atoned for it. I don't know what limitations He actually had as part of His mortal way of being. Did He have bad days, perfect recall, and hormonal spikes? Were there foods He turned up His nose at? Was He neat and orderly? Could He have been both a computer and a poetry nerd or gone out for any sport He wanted to and been the best at everything? Consequently, I don't know what it means that the Lord Himself, in Paul's words, "suffered being tempted" (Hebrews 2:18). But I do know there is no temptation, no form of suffering, loneliness, or injustice we experience that the Lord through His life and Atonement did not Himself experience or comprehend. Whatever existential pluses and minuses were His mortal lot, the Redeemer implicitly chose in His thoughts, actions, and words to be for others and for His Father. Whether or not He felt like it, He did not withdraw—as we often do—into being for self through indulging the kind of longings and passions that spring from insecurity, impatience, and fear of failure.

To be like Jesus—and we must be like Him if we want to be with Him and the Father—we must strive for a deeper knowledge of who the Son of God is, since it is by Him we come to know the Father (see John 14:6ff.). To that end the Lord talked a great deal about what it means to be like Him. In fact, the way He talked about Himself during His mortal ministry constantly reminded His audience that the Jewish concept of God was about being.

You and I know that the Lord Jesus Christ, who walked and talked with the remnant of Israel left in Palestine, was also the great Jehovah, who had brought the descendants of Abraham, Isaac, and Jacob out of Egypt and into the promised land with a mighty hand. To His disciples and His detractors, the Lord often declared who He was by referring to the meaning embedded in the name Jehovah, or "I am." You easily remember many of these that John, in particular, recorded: "I am the way, the truth, and the life" (John 14:6); "I am the good shepherd" (John 10:11); and "I am the true vine" (John 15:1). Now, I'll spare you the complexities associated with the meaning and usage of the word *Jehovah*, or *Yahweh*, except to acknowledge that many scholars think a better translation of this word is "I will be" or "I cause to be." But the concept expressed in the name of the Lord talking about Himself as, for instance, the "bread of life" (John 6:48) or "the light of the world" (John 8:12) was a direct way of reintroducing Himself to His people as their God and of teaching them and us that keeping the law meant taking upon us His name. As the Lord told the Nephites after His resurrection, "I am the law" (3 Nephi 15:9).

One of the most powerful of the Lord's "I am" self-declarations gives us a special insight into what it means to be a Christian. On a few rather ominous occasions—when the Lord first spoke to the Nephites embalmed in darkness after the great destruction that marked His death on this continent (see 3 Nephi 9:18); at the beginning and the end of the Revelation of St. John (see Revelation 1:8; 22:13); and twice in Joseph Smith's initial revelations to Martin Harris (see D&C 19:1) and Sidney Rigdon (see D&C 35:1)—the Lord declared: "I am Alpha and Omega, the beginning and the end" (3 Nephi 9:18; Revelation 22:13). There is a world of meaning in this name. It declares that the Lord is the Lord absolutely. Whatever it means to be a joint heir with Christ of all the Father hath—a startling and, at first glance, an even brash idea—this name indicates that, in an eternity that is without beginning or end, He is nevertheless for us the beginning and the end of our immortality and eternal life.

I don't know what our relationship to the Son of God will be in the eternities. But the fact that the Son still bears in His resurrected body—"restored to [its] proper and perfect frame" (Alma 40:23)—the scars of the Atonement suggests to me that He will always be our Redeemer, that He didn't live a mortal life just to get it over with but rather to be able to live it with us over and over again. That's what it means, by the way, to be an eternal parent.

In any event, what is clear to me in this life is that as the Beginning and, especially, the End, the Lord is not a means to another end. With His Father and our Father He *is* the end, the target, the audience, the culmination of all we try to do and be individually and collectively, just as He is the source of all we are able to do or be. But don't you find yourself, as I find myself, treating the Lord and His gospel as a means to another end—that is, yourself as the end? Don't you, like I, slip in prayer into seeing God as the giver of gifts in which, truth be told, we have really invested our thoughts and hearts—good grades, jobs, marriage, protection—thus making the gifts rather than the Gift-giver the object of our desires?

Don't we spend most of our time working out *our* eternal salvation, *our* happiness, when Jesus Himself spends all of His time worrying about our eternal salvation and happiness? Is God an instrument and His gospel a program we use for our personal development? Are His commandments a set of strategies for us to avoid misfortune, bad health, and punishment?

Keeping commandments like paying tithing does yield tangible, substantial temporal blessings, but do we treat the idea of giving "our" material substance to the Being whose substance it really is in the first place as an investment for a bigger heavenly mansion? Do we give simply to get? Do we perform service to others as a way of obligating God to bless us and in the meantime to give us good, warm feelings about ourselves? Do we treat obedience like a kind of reality TV show, a race, a series of ordeals or obstacle courses, a form of public humiliation we're willing to endure in this life for the celestial fame and fortune it brings the winners in the next?

When we take the sacrament or confess something to the bishop, does the Atonement serve as a software application that scans and cleans our hard drives that we need to insert into ourselves once a week or so and then put back in its case to be used again next time? The things we talk about doing, dear brothers and sisters, like prayer and repentance, should become our way of being and bearing ourselves in this world—not something we do just to get through the world. Scripture study and church service should be a chosen lifestyle, not just an accepted assignment. Faith, hope, and charity must become the thoughts we think and the language we speak. Mormon promised his son Moroni and us that if we are "filled with [charity]; . . . when [the Lord] shall appear we shall *be* like him, for we shall see him as he *is*" (Moroni 7:48; emphasis added). Look at the list Mormon gave just before he issued this promise: charity is long-suffering, not self-serving, not easily provoked, bears all things, believes all things, hopes all things, and endures all things (see Moroni 7:45; 1 Corinthians 13:4–7).

None of these characteristics by itself represents charity. One must endure all things, but one also hopes and believes them as well. In fact, I wonder what the difference is between "bearing" all things and "enduring" all things. The words don't function like synonyms here, although they can in common usage. It sounds to me like bearing things means to take up the burden of living as an affirmative choice rather than weathering a storm, hunkered down for however long it rages. In any event, this particular list is not an itemized menu of techniques for success that can be taught in a class or at a convention but is instead an articulation of a fundamental orientation toward being in this world that will continue into the next.

Now, I'm not saying we don't need particular techniques or therapies, especially those revealed by prophets and apostles, as well as those discovered by good, smart people who have studied their fellow human beings to help them. It's just that when I hear the Lord giving instruction—especially in the full expression of the law and the gospel that the Lord delivered in that most elegant and profound Sermon on the Mount—I hear Him saying things in such a way as to make us think past technique in order to rethink our conception of both sin and righteousness. In this amazing document the Lord breathed life back into the laws He wrote on tables of stone with His own finger by offering to write the law in the "fleshy tables" of our hearts (see 2 Corinthians 3:3; Jeremiah 31:33; Hebrews 8:10, 10:16). Indeed, He reminded us throughout the Sermon on the Mount that the purpose of a law of ordinances and performances that directed the very motions of our bodies to enact the Atonement in practice and ritual was not just to train but to transform our hearts so that the Atonement would be the spark that ignites that heart's each and every beat. This is why Jesus could say in the sermon that He came to fulfill the law, not to destroy it, because He came to resuscitate, to restore, to resurrect the law.

Take, for example, the passages that lead up to the Lord's astonishing command to us to be perfect. As you remember, the actual statement the Lord made is: "Be ye therefore perfect, even as your Father which is in heaven is perfect" (Matthew 5:48). The *therefore* seems to me to refer to what has just preceded this statement, and what immediately comes before it is a list of six revisions to the law of Moses, the six "Ye have heard it said . . . but I say unto you" statements. Look, for instance, at the famous "adultery" passage. After the Lord talked about anger and made us already nervous about, say, something as harmless as calling another driver on the road an idiot, He said this:

> *Ye have heard that it was said by them of old time, Thou shalt not commit adultery:*
> *But I say unto you, That whosoever looketh on a woman to lust after her hath committed adultery with her already in his heart.* [Matthew 5:27–28]

The Lord began by quoting the very statement He Himself gave in the Ten Commandments, then He rephrased and broadened it on His own authority to make adultery a sin not only as a committed act but also as a contemplated one. Did He revise Himself to show us that we all need to do this? This is where the Lord starts to pound the chisel into our hearts, because that is where the seat of sin really is. In fact, the *already* seems to suggest that the kind of looking He was talking about is a symptom, not a cause. But, thus far, we are still talking about what we should not do. So the Lord's next move was to tell us what we should do:

> *And if thy right eye offend thee, pluck it out, and cast it from thee: for it is profitable for thee that one of thy members should perish, and not that thy whole body should be cast into hell.*
>
> *And if thy right hand offend thee, cut it off, and cast it from thee: for it is profitable for thee that one of thy members should perish, and not that thy whole body should be cast into hell.* [Matthew 5:29–30]

Surely the crowd must have gasped at this point. I have this mental image of Peter hearing the Lord utter verse 29, looking confusedly over at John and whispering, "Did He just say . . . ?" while John holds a hand up, listens to verse 30, then turns to Peter, nodding his head slowly, his eyes wide with amazement and a touch of fear. It's a good thing Matthew or somebody else was taking notes that day, because I imagine that many in the crowd did what many of us do when we hear this same passage: we rush in and start interpreting what He "really" meant to say.

Interpretation is called for here, but it ought to stay connected to the way He said it. Why did He say it the way He did, and could He really have meant exactly what He said? Now, before you start writing yourself a note like "Having trouble with lust in swimming class; leave right eye in locker," let's think about a way of keeping our limbs but still taking up the Lord's amputate-to-repent program. (And you thought being stoned was bad.)

The Lord made a conditional if/then statement, and maybe the "if" part doesn't happen very much: for the most part, if my right hand does something bad, I bear at least some responsibility for what it does. So then what could the statement mean? Let's not leave the statement as it is worded just yet. The Lord says that if a part of my body—part of my physical wholeness (but something I could live without if I had to)—is giving me problems, I should cut it off. The Lord is telling us that if we wish to be perfect, complete, in our observance of the law of sexual morality, our bodies, our thoughts, and our lives should have no part that works against the good of the whole. If it were an eye that was the root of our sexual sin, we should be willing to give it up and take on that disability, even though we'd really like to keep it. It should be that important to us.

But since it doesn't seem like a good idea to jump into penitent self-mutilation just yet, how does this sound: Men, if you can't keep the eye away from, say, pornography on the Internet or cable TV, would you be willing to cut off the Internet or the cable service? If you've gotten into this stuff; have tried to change; talked to your bishop; broken off from it for a week, a month, six months, but keep coming back to it; at what point are you willing to cut it off?

I can hear some of you saying, "But the computer is my life. The Internet is central to my schoolwork and will be central to my career. Plus, it's great for genealogy." Fair enough. But if you're not winning the war, if you're not going to be able to have a healthy marriage now and a marriage at all in the eternities, if you can't, as Moroni said, "come unto Christ, and be perfected in him" (Moroni 10:32), do you really think your career ought to be your chief consideration, the end of your existence?

I don't want to pick on just the guys. Women, are you willing to pull the plug on your service if you find yourselves getting and look-ing for a buzz from having titillating chats with often-anonymous virtual "friends"? Both genders: Are you willing to sever yourself from a TV show or a DVD that doesn't necessarily show forbidden skin or actions but simply assumes and builds its skin-deep plot around the notion that people try out their crushes and infatuations in the bed-room before they commit themselves to another? If silently rooting for a couple to have premarital or extramarital sex with each other on the screen—no matter what you actually see or don't see—is not look-ing at another person to lust after him or her, I don't know what is.

But this isn't the place to stop our thinking, because we can't remove all of the TVs and computers in all of the places we might be in this world. You will be alone in a hotel room on a business trip, and you'll have to make the choice not to even turn to the wrong channel rather than playing the self-deceiving game we play of just flipping through all the channels to see what's on, hoping in willed ignorance to be flashed.

The Lord asks us in this particular section of the Sermon on the Mount to think honestly about what we're looking for. While we're being honest with ourselves about this, it is also an occasion to think about what it means to look at another human being in any context. Do we look to detach some part of another's being to use or consume it—not just in the sexual context we've been talking about but, for example, with a server at a restaurant? Despite that person's complexity, humanity, and, thus, potential divinity, do we turn them into an extension of our own will for power or pleasure? The Lord might be suggesting that doing so is a form of maiming someone. Is that why the Lord tells us to give up a part of ourselves—that a severed arm would be just recompense for looking at anyone to *do* anything with them?

If we are to do something, it ought to be *for* the other, not with or to them. This imperative to do and to be for others is why the Lord finished His discussion of the law in Matthew 5 with two breathtaking revisions of the law. Because it's about time to conclude, we don't have time to consider fully what the Lord is saying in these passages. For that matter, a talk of any length is inadequate to this task. Let me just say this in closing: When the Lord tells us to "turn the other cheek," He's not just asking us to take responsibility for our own actions and responses and to accept our responsibility to the other who stands before us, be they impoverished or threatening. He's also inviting us to acknowledge the other's humanity and capacity to be responsible for what he or she does.

There are lots of problems with answering aggression with aggression, not the least of which is that we imitate the aggressor in such a response. We allow the aggressor to set the terms in which our interaction with them takes place and, indeed, let the act, not the actor, govern the interaction. Offering our cloak when our coat is required is a way of imputing a reasonable motive to another's action, allowing the action to define itself as a statement of need or fear that we might actually be able to do something about. Moreover, in asking us to give what they would take from us, He is asking us to extend to them the right to rethink what they wanted and why they wanted it; to acknowledge their right and capacity to change without being compelled to do so, just as we would prefer not to be compelled to do or give something—the Golden Rule, in other words.

The Lord isn't trying to cover every possible aggressive or passive-aggressive situation here. Surely He isn't asking us to respond to a child abuser or someone who has just shot someone else by cheerfully offering the person another victim. But when the Lord tells us to love, bless, and pray for those who do us wrong or are fundamentally set against us—an enemy—He is offering Himself to us, isn't He, to do for them what we would do for them if we could? Isn't that why the Lord got so excited over Nephi, son of Helaman, because he arrived at the point that he wouldn't ask for anything for himself or others that the Lord, in His perfection, wouldn't Himself want to do (see Helaman 10:4–10)?

The Lord wants us to be instruments in His hands, agents for His work, but it sounds to me that if we became much like Him in this life, He wouldn't mind too much if we asked Him—nicely, like Nephi did—to be a means for us to conduct His work and His glory: the immortality and eternal life of our fellow humans. That we be more like Him in doing His work is my prayer in the name of Jesus Christ, amen.

"Be Strong and of a Good Courage"

Donald L. Staheli

Thank you, President Samuelson. BYU is blessed to have you serve as its president. It is an honor to be here today with this outstanding assembly of students. President Gordon B. Hinckley has spoken about how "you represent a great generation in the history of the world and in the history of this Church." He has described you as "part of the greatest generation we have ever had" ("True to the Faith," *Ensign*, June 1996, 2).

As students here at BYU you represent one of the great centers of strength in the Church. Along with the future leadership you will provide to the Church, many of you will make significant contributions to our communities across the nation and the world. You have so much to give and so much to do in the years that lie ahead. The challenge of your professors and leaders is to help you be prepared both spiritually and temporally for the world of opportunities and challenges that awaits you. I trust you are preparing now to make the most of those future opportunities.

Donald L. Staheli was a member of the Second Quorum of the Seventy of The Church of Jesus Christ of Latter-day Saints when this devotional address was given on 13 June 2006. © *Intellectual Reserve, Inc.*

They are a team. {

Interestingly, it was 50 years ago about this very week that we graduated from the University of Illinois with my PhD degree. I say "we" because Sister Staheli earned her share of that degree as she worked to help pay the rent and food bills during our three years of graduate school.

Over the ensuing 40 years we lived in the suburban areas of Chicago and New York City, where we worked and raised our family. We were blessed with a rewarding career as we traveled the world of business. We were blessed with opportunities for service in the Church, as well as in organizations in various areas of the world. For the past nine-plus years I have served as a member of the Quorum of the Seventy. That, too, has been a special experience and blessing.

The Lord's hand has truly been in our lives. But with these blessings have come tests and challenges—just as most of you periodically experience and will continue to experience in the years ahead.

This is a special time in your life when choices are made and patterns and habits are formed that will have a major impact on who you will become.

Your enrollment here at BYU is a significant step in preparing for your future. In addition to your educational pursuits, your future happiness, personal righteousness, and relationship with the Lord will depend in large part on the habits you embrace and the choices and commitments you make over these next few years.

As you think about your preparation for the next steps in your life, ponder with me for a moment how the Lord transferred responsibility from Moses to Joshua. He gave Joshua an extraordinary promise, followed by some strong counsel. Listen to a few excerpts of what the Lord said:

As I was with Moses, so I will be with thee: I will not fail thee, nor forsake thee.

Be strong and of a good courage. . . .

Only be thou strong and very courageous, that thou mayest observe to do according to all the law . . . : turn not from it to the right hand or to the left, that thou mayest prosper whithersoever thou goest. [Joshua 1:5–7]

After reminding Joshua of the importance of obedience, the Lord promised: "For then thou shalt make thy way prosperous, and then thou shalt have good success" (verse 8). This is a great promise.

And then, for the third time, the Lord repeated in verse 9: "Have not I commanded thee? Be strong and of a good courage; be not afraid, neither be thou dismayed: for the Lord thy God is with thee whithersoever thou goest."

The Lord's message to Joshua—"I will not fail thee, nor forsake thee"—has been repeated through the ages in the scriptures and through the prophets of the Restoration. It applies to each of us today—conditioned, of course, upon our obedience to His commandments and the covenants we make in the temples.

Some of you know exactly what you want to do with your life. Others are still pondering and discovering opportunities for the future. In either case, it is essential to your future success and happiness that you keep your minds and your hearts open to the promptings of the Spirit. As you live to be worthy of those spiritual promptings, the Lord has promised that He will be with you.

Joshua later made his own choice clear to his people when he said, "Choose you this day whom ye will serve . . . : but as for me and my house, we will serve the Lord" (Joshua 24:15).

A philosopher once gave good counsel regarding choices:

Choose well; your choice is
Brief, and yet endless.
[Johann Wolfgang von Goethe, "Symbolum" or "Mason Lodge," trans. Thomas Carlyle]

As you acknowledge that the Lord "will not fail thee," as long as you are obedient to His teachings, then I would ask, Are you happy with the present conduct of your life? What changes or course corrections should you make in order to take full advantage of your daily opportunities for learning and personal spiritual growth? *[handwritten: more focused scripture study, more time serving others.]*

Now is the time to set the course for what you want to be—five or 10 years or even 50 years from now.

During our few minutes together today, it would be my prayer that something might be said or felt that will help you crystallize your thoughts as to who you are and what you have the potential to become.

It has been said that one of the greatest tragedies of our time is that so many people live so far below their potential.

President Spencer W. Kimball frequently encouraged us to "lengthen our stride" and to "enlarge our vision" ("When the World Will Be Converted," *Ensign*, October 1974, 5).

President Gordon B. Hinckley continually counsels, "Do your best." And then he has added: "But I want to emphasize that it be the very best. We are too prone to be satisfied with mediocre performance. We are capable of doing so much better" ("Standing Strong and Immovable," World Leadership Training Meeting, 10 January 2004 [Salt Lake City: The Church of Jesus Christ of Latter-day Saints, 2004], 21).

The late Elder Neal A. Maxwell said it another way: "The Lord loves each of us too much to merely let us go on being what we now are, for he knows what we have the possibility to become!" ("In Him All Things Hold Together," *BYU 1990–91 Devotional and Fireside Speeches* [Provo: BYU, 1991], 107).

Implicit in the statements from each of these distinguished leaders is the message that each of us can and should do more to meet the Lord's expectations of us.

Let's talk about a few principles that are essential for success and happiness as you develop your careers, families, and service to the Lord. As you further refine your plans for the future, you will not only find success in a temporal sense but you will be moving toward achieving a relationship with your Father in Heaven and Savior that prepares you for an eternal relationship in the celestial kingdom.

First and foremost in your pursuit is the development and nurturing of a strong personal testimony. I assume that each of you has a basic testimony of the gospel. Some periodically struggle. Many are strong as you have returned from missions or have focused on prayer and study that have brought you to an undeniable testimony of the truth. Presumably that was a major factor in motivating you to come to BYU.

Hopefully you feel that your testimony is vibrant and growing stronger each day. Yet, even though you are in a special environment here at BYU, I would suspect that many of you are being challenged by the "things of the world" with which you periodically deal. I am referring to the daily bombardment of worldly messages and entice-ments from the media of TV, movies, and the Internet that tend to tempt or distract you from keeping your testimony strong and staying completely true to gospel principles and covenants. Certain kinds of peer pressures can also be challenging.

Let me tell you about a young friend I met while serving as presi-dent of a stake that included West Point Academy in the state of New York. He was a bright 4.0 student at the academy. He had been given a leave of absence from West Point to serve a mission and was read-mitted on completion of his mission—not a common occurrence. On one of my visits to the West Point Branch he requested some time to talk.

As we talked he told me of how he had deepened his conversion to the gospel as he served his mission. He remembered the feelings and strength of his testimony when he returned to West Point fol-lowing his mission. Then he said: "In the two years since my mission I have gradually felt the Spirit slipping away from me. Every day I am associating with other cadets with different values. Their whole focus in life is successfully graduating from the academy. Periodically the honor code is compromised. Nearly every weekend is party time—alcohol and young women. I am hazed and ridiculed when I refuse to join with them.

"President Staheli, I need help. I feel like I am being tossed to and fro on the seas of life, and I have lost my mooring. My gospel anchor of the past seems to be giving way to the life of fun and pleasures enjoyed by my colleagues at the academy."

As we talked it became clear that the magnet of the adversary was gradually but surely drawing him into Satan's grasp. My young friend had lost his mooring—not because Satan had become stronger but because my friend had not been nurturing and tending to his testimony. He was in the process of losing what he had previously so deeply cherished.

I realize you are in a very different environment here at BYU, yet I relate this experience because even here at BYU you are not immune to the adversary's many wiles that look attractive on the surface and may appear harmless only because you feel you can resist.

Just claiming to know the gospel is true is not always enough. My young friend at West Point knew. He had developed a testimony, but it had slipped away from him because he failed to nourish it. As he had begun to respond to and engage in the activities of his peers, he gradually lost the promptings of the Spirit.

I cannot think of a greater loss to anyone than the loss of the promptings of the Spirit.

Our testimonies grow through faith, prayer, scripture study, and obedience to the commandments. The daily exercise and nurturing of these principles is key to a strong and resilient testimony and commitment to gospel principles. Let me comment on each of these principles.

President Gordon B. Hinckley speaks often about our need for faith. I had the privilege of returning with President Hinckley from Nauvoo on the plane following the cornerstone ceremony at the Nauvoo Temple. As we flew over the rich farmland of Iowa, I was commenting on the unbelievable faith and commitment of those early Saints. I was musing that I was not sure I would have had sufficient faith to keep company with those faithful Saints.

In his usual optimistic response, President Hinckley said, "Sure you would, Don." And then he made his real point with me as he reminded me that some of the most faithful Saints faltered, lost faith, and fell by the wayside. His response strongly suggests that our testimonies are vulnerable if we do not stay on course in keeping God's commandments.

President Gordon B. Hinckley frequently encourages us to have "the kind of faith that moves one to get on his knees and plead with the Lord and then get on his feet and go to work" ("God Shall Give unto You Knowledge by His Holy Spirit," *Speeches of the Year, 1973* [Provo: BYU, 1974], 109; see also *TGBH*, 186).

That is sound advice for every one of us. As we follow his counsel, our testimonies and our commitments to make right choices will grow.

When I reflect on my youth and the initial development of my testimony, I realize nothing had a greater impact on its development than the faith of my mother and father and their daily application of that faith in their prayers. The Lord responded to their faith and prayers, and as children we witnessed the hand of the Lord in our family. We came to know the meaning of what Moroni meant when he said: "I would show unto the world that faith is things which are hoped for and not seen; wherefore, dispute not because ye see not, for ye receive no witness until after the trial of your faith" (Ether 12:6).

The faith of our family was tried time and again. And, periodically, special spiritual experiences too tender to tell followed. I bear testimony that the Lord does hear and answer prayers—prayers from the hearts of His faithful children.

When your lives become crowded with other activities, it is easy to periodically skip a prayer or to use an abbreviated version of your prayers. *Don't shortchange the Lord on your prayers.* Nothing you will do during any day of your life will be more important to your temporal success or your eternal progress than consistent, humble, sincere prayers offered at least morning and night of every day.

As I visited with my young friend from West Point, it became clear that his faith had wavered and the consistency and sincerity of his prayers had waned. The joshing of his peers and the seeming attractiveness of Satan's alternatives had begun to overshadow his commitment to exercise his faith and prayers.

Equally important in our pursuit of happiness and a secure testimony is the daily habit of reading and pondering the scriptures. The reading and study habits you are forming in your religion classes will have a lasting impact on your personal commitment to the scriptures. The busier life becomes, the more difficult it is to stay connected to this important part of our spiritual growth. Yet making the scriptures a part of your daily life is another foundation stone of your testimony.

King Benjamin sternly admonished his people, "If you believe all these things see that ye do them" (Mosiah 4:10).

Living to be worthy of the Spirit and then responding to its promptings is an essential ingredient to a strong and vibrant testimony.

To be worthy of the Spirit embodies the bottom line of obedient living. To truly accomplish this is the quest of a lifetime.

Nephi's early example of obedience has been taught to us from our youth. Likewise, we know how Laman and Lemuel developed into the "murmurers" of the family. They played the role of the "natural man" that King Benjamin described.

Conversely, Nephi made his commitment to the Lord early on when he said, "I will go and do the things which the Lord hath commanded" (1 Nephi 3:7). And then he did, with unwavering faith.

The important point is that Nephi had made the decision as to how he was going to respond to the Lord's commandments. From that point forward he was steadfast. I suspect Satan worked on him, just as he does each of us today, yet the scriptures indicate that Satan was totally unsuccessful in affecting Nephi's decision to do the Lord's will.

The prototype of Lehi's family has played out through the centuries. The world is replete with the Lamans and Lemuels. They are some of Satan's best students. Great blessings come to those who follow Nephi's example.

Understanding and responding to the principle of obedience has singular importance in preparing us for success and eternal happiness. As the Lord promised Joshua, He "will not fail thee, nor forsake thee" as long as you are striving daily to obey His commandments.

As you progress through your education here at BYU, you have some electives or choices in what you pursue in your education. You also have some "required" subjects.

The same is true of the gospel of Jesus Christ. It gives us agency and ample freedom of choices, but the ultimate success of those choices depends on our diligence in keeping the commandments and covenants we have made with the Lord.

As you pursue your educational goals, it is essential that you keep focused on your spiritual commitments. The challenge with most of us is the tendency to become casual or to lose focus on those non-negotiable or non-compromising commandments from which promised blessings flow. Let me give you an example.

When Sister Staheli and I left Utah, en route to the University of Illinois with everything we owned contained in our little car, we were excited about embarking upon a new adventure. We had tried to be diligent in keeping the covenants we had made in the temple as a part of our marriage of about one year.

As we became fully engaged in our new life as a happily married but financially struggling couple, we lost focus on one important—in fact, essential—commandment of the gospel. As we approached the end of the year and tithing settlement, we had not only slipped on paying our tithing but were literally without food money for the last week of the year.

As we sheepishly and humbly approached our branch president at tithing settlement, he taught us an important lesson in financial management. More important, he gave us a phenomenal promise.

He promised that if we would make up the tithing owed to the Lord and then faithfully pay it each month before we addressed our other needs and wants, the Lord would bless us as promised. In fact, he promised us that as future faithful tithe payers we would have an increase in income each year thereafter. That came true—and stayed so, until my call as a Seventy. The Lord truly did open the windows of heaven and pour out blessings to us.

My wife and I had been raised by faithful tithe-paying parents. We had been full-tithe payers throughout our youthful years. Yet this came as a poignant lesson of how becoming casual on important principles can cause one to lose focus on what is really essential to the Lord.

Satan works constantly on this principle of blurring our focus relating to gospel principles. He seductively encourages our casualness by helping us feel secure that "this won't matter" or "that won't taint my mind." This is especially true as he casually leads young people down the slippery slope of immorality.

I believe Satan has a dominant influence on the media—television, movies, and the Internet. Each becomes seductive in its own way. As young adults you may feel you can handle the sexually explicit programs on television without affecting your spiritual well-being.

Even more pernicious are the R-rated movies that carry you into the even more explicit. It is clear that frequent exposure tends to legitimize that which we see and hear. It dulls our sense of conscience between the acceptable and unacceptable. It is Satan's way of leading you down the slippery slope toward immoral thoughts and actions.

And those parts of the Internet that move you into pornography serve as the devil's trump card. It only takes a few viewings of pornography and he has you hooked. Then he begins to work his evil power, because what you have seen and heard becomes paramount in your thought processes. And the more you see, the more addicted you become.

You young people, especially you young men, have become Satan's target audience. It is his way of leading you into the abyss of immorality. Let me hasten to add that neither are you married students immune to Satan's attractions. Pornography can become one of the most destructive elements of your marriage.

We plead with any of you who are in any way involved in pornography to see your bishop so that he can help you find your way out of the cesspool of filth that is designed to destroy you.

Be careful that you don't let Satan use his influence to control your thoughts and actions, and ultimately your future.

When you are able to recognize and overcome any personal irritants you may have toward certain principles of obedience, you will feel God endowing you with the power of the Spirit to resist the inappropriate things of the world that Satan would have you enjoy.

When we are able to declare as the people did to King Benjamin that there has been "a mighty change in us, or in our hearts, that we have no more disposition to do evil, but to do good continually" (Mosiah 5:2), then we will be well on the road to success and eternal happiness.

The companionship of the Spirit and the strength of your testimonies will depend on daily nurturing of your faith, praying, studying the scriptures, and obeying the commandments. As you do so, you will be moving toward achieving the spiritual and temporal blessings the Lord has in store for you.

You will realize the blessing promised to Joshua: "For then thou shalt make thy way prosperous, and then thou shalt have good success" (Joshua 1:8).

The Lord wants each of you to find joy and happiness and success in your professional and vocational pursuits. But He wants you to do it in a way that your ambitions for success do not supersede your priority for living gospel principles.

President Thomas S. Monson painted the picture as follows: "We have been provided divine attributes to guide our journey. We enter mortality not to float with the moving currents of life, but with the power to think, to reason, and to achieve" ("Invitation to Exaltation," *Ensign*, June 1993, 5).

These are the years when you must take responsibility for who you now are and what you want to become.

Think carefully about where you are. Remember, education is the key to the door of opportunity.

The Savior's parable of the talents is so applicable to you at this stage in your lives. Jesus knows there are differences between you— intellectually, emotionally, and physically. Therefore He only expects you to magnify and develop whatever talents and abilities you have.

But He expects you to be accountable for your actions in so doing. He will not measure your progress against others. He does not grade on the curve! Rather He blesses you for what you are doing to magnify whatever gifts and talents you have been given.

At all costs do not allow yourself to "float with the moving currents of life," as President Monson has counseled. Take control of your actions and prepare to succeed at whatever you are capable of doing.

Remember President Hinckley's counsel: "Just do the best you can, but be sure it is your very best" ("A Challenging Time—A Wonderful Time," An Evening with President Gordon B. Hinckley, seminary and institute broadcast, 7 February 2003, 5).

This is also a time in your life when counsel from others can help you decide what you should be doing that will move you toward achieving your full potential.

It is the wise counsel and mentoring of a few special teachers, priesthood leaders, parents, and a loving wife that helped me make some course corrections in preparation for what has turned out to be a wonderfully challenging and happy pursuit of life.

As you recall, the Lord counseled Joshua to "be strong and of a good courage" as he took on his new responsibilities. That same counsel applies to you as you prepare to pursue careers that will take you to different parts of the world.

Periodically you will be placed in situations that will require you to "be strong and of a good courage" in order to stay true and faithful to gospel principles. As President David O. McKay has said, paraphrasing William George Jordan, "There is one responsibility which no man can evade, and that responsibility is personal influence" ("The Mission of Brigham Young University," address given at BYU, 27 April 1948, 3; also *CR*, October 1969, 87; see William George Jordan, "The Power of Personal Influence," chapter 3 of *The Majesty of Calmness* [New York: Fleming H. Revell Company, 1900], 19).

Worldly standards will always be in a state of flux. The only true and unchanging standards are those set by the Savior and His teachings and principles of the restored gospel.

My wife and I have lived all our married life in the mission field. We have traveled the world as part of our business career. In the earlier years of our career, to live by LDS standards was an oddity—and not a generally accepted one either. Yet, with a few exceptions, once people understood our principles and standards and our desire to stay true to them, they respected us for them.

As you have the courage to be true to your beliefs, your exemplary conduct will not go unnoticed. While you will be tried and tested, your faithful adherence to the Lord's standards will be seen as a beacon in the night to those around you.

I could recite dozens of examples of my personal experiences on this subject, but let me conclude with a reference to President Hinckley.

President Hinckley is an impeccable example of courageous leadership. He is steadfast and true to principle and courageously forthright in his convictions. Yet with unwavering courage he has the ability to express his commitments to gospel principles in clear but acceptable terms to those not of our faith.

Hopefully his example will help you to "be strong and of a good courage" when pushed to compromise your standards. You will be respected for your integrity. And if occasionally you are not, you need not worry, because that is not the kind of association you will want or need in your future.

"As the finest generation in the history of the Church," much is expected of you (Gordon B. Hinckley, *CR*, April 1992, 96; or "A Chosen Generation," *Ensign*, May 1992, 69). And we have confidence you will live up to those expectations.

I bear testimony, brothers and sisters, of the divinity of Heavenly Father's plan for each of you. Jesus is truly our Savior, and He very much loves and cares for you. As you keep His commandments and follow the counsel of the prophets and your leaders, He will be there to guide you through the challenges that lie ahead. He "will not fail thee, nor forsake thee."

May His choicest blessings be with each of you, I pray in the name of Jesus Christ, amen.

Learning from Our Conflicts

———◆———

Gerald R. Williams

Some months ago, when I was invited to speak today, I asked what
I should talk about. After a long pause the voice said, "Well,
people usually talk about things they're good at." So my topic today
is conflict.

I used to think other people had conflicts but that I was immune.
Then I came upon two incidents in the life of the Prophet Joseph
Smith that completely changed my understanding of conflicts and
forced me to admit I probably have as many as anybody else.

What is a conflict? For our purposes today, a conflict is any situation in which both sides feel the other is in the wrong.

I'll begin with seven propositions about conflicts.

1. It is strange, but unless we had a conflict in the last few hours,
most of us don't remember our conflicts. This may be good, because
it saves us pain, but it creates a problem. If we don't remember our
conflicts, we can't learn anything from them.

*Gerald R. Williams was a professor of law at the BYU J. Reuben Clark Law School
when this devotional address was given on 27 June 2006. © Brigham Young
University.*

2. We probably experience conflicts differently—depending on our personalities, our prior experiences (such as the way conflicts were handled in the home where we grew up), and perhaps other factors such as gender and culture.

3. In Mormon culture most people are conflict avoiders. However, some of us are neutral about conflict, and some of us actually enjoy a good conflict.

4. If we are in relationships with others, there will be conflicts. They may be small or they may be large, but there will surely be conflicts. Can you think of any conflicts in your life right now? Perhaps a few hints will help. If you do think of a conflict or two, I hope you will jot them down.

a. Conflicts with family, such as father, mother, siblings, spouse, children, or in-laws.

b. Conflicts with people you see often who are *not* family: neighbors, landlords, merchants, even people at church. President Brigham Young summed it up in rhyme:

To live with Saints in Heaven is bliss and glory
To live with Saints on Earth is another story.[1]

5. It takes two sides to create a conflict. More important, there is almost always fault on *both* sides. As someone said, "It's a mighty thin pancake that only has one side."

6. During a conflict we are usually blind to our own fault and we blame the other side.

7. A final proposition introduces my theme. When we remember our conflicts and reflect on them, they are like mirrors that can teach us things about ourselves that are otherwise difficult to discover. If we permit them, our conflicts will show us where we are weak, defensive, prideful, or otherwise in need of repair.

FIRST EXAMPLE

I'll illustrate the value of conflicts with three examples. Two are from the life of the Prophet Joseph Smith. These both involve Oliver

Cowdery, who, at the time, was Joseph's most trusted associate. These conflicts occurred very close to each other in the summer of 1830, just after the Church was organized. Joseph was 24 years old, and Oliver was 23.

Joseph was busy copying and arranging revelations for publication. Oliver was staying with the Whitmer family in Fayette, 80 miles to the north. Out of the blue, Joseph received a letter from Oliver.

Joseph recorded:

[Oliver] *wrote to inform me that he had discovered an error in one of the commandments—Book of Doctrine and Covenants: "And truly manifest by their works that they have received of the Spirit of Christ unto a remission of their sins"* [D&C 20:37].

The above quotation, [Oliver] *said, was erroneous, and added: "I command you in the name of God to erase those words, that no priestcraft be amongst us!"*

The Prophet continued:

I immediately wrote to him in reply, in which I asked him by what authority he took upon him to command me to alter or erase, to add to or diminish from, a revelation or commandment from Almighty God.[2]

Doctrinally, Oliver was wrong and Joseph was right. But knowing that doesn't solve the problem. These two trusted friends were now in a conflict—both felt the other was in the wrong. The doctrinal issue could be solved, but what about the bad feelings that had arisen between them?

Realizing his letter had not really answered the doctrinal question and had made the interpersonal problem worse, Joseph traveled 80 miles to the Whitmer home to meet with Oliver and the Whitmers.

Joseph reported:

I found the [Whitmer] *family in general of* [Oliver's] *opinion concerning the words above quoted, and it was not without both labor and perseverance that I could prevail with any of them to reason calmly on the subject. . . . Finally, with [Christian Whitmer's] assistance, I succeeded in bringing, not only the Whitmer family, but also Oliver Cowdery to acknowledge that they had been in error, and that the sentence in dispute was in accordance with the rest of the commandment.*

Joseph then reflected on what he learned from this experience. His conclusions are the centerpiece of my message today:

And thus was this error rooted out, which having its rise in presumption and rash judgment, was . . . particularly calculated (when once fairly understood) to teach each and all of us the necessity of humility and meekness before the Lord, that He might teach us of His ways.[3]

Judging from his emphasis on humility and meekness, Joseph was commenting not only on Oliver's doctrinal error but also on the interpersonal conflict between them and, I think, on the nature of conflicts in general. With prophetic insight he taught two important lessons. His first point was that conflicts arise "in presumption and rash judgment." *Presumptuous* means overconfident or even offensive. *Rash* means hasty or impetuous. With these definitions in mind, let us look again at Oliver's message to Joseph. He said: "I command you in the name of God to erase those words, that no priestcraft be amongst us!"[4]

Do you see any ways in which Oliver's statement might be considered rash or presumptuous? Certainly commanding another person risks being offensive, especially if it is your ecclesiastical leader. Commanding "in the name of God" would raise offensiveness a degree or two. Accusing your leader of priestcraft would undoubtedly qualify.

I move to the next statement with trepidation, but Joseph invited us to consider the effect of his reply as well. Joseph "immediately wrote to [Oliver]," asking: "By what authority he took upon him to command me to alter or erase, to add to or diminish from, a revelation or commandment from Almighty God."

Are there ways in which Joseph's words might have lacked "humility and meekness"? At a minimum he might have responded with a comment and a question such as, "Oliver, I love you and I value your opinion. Would you help me understand your objection to this passage?"

Joseph's second point added power to the first. He concluded that "[conflicts are] particularly calculated (when once fairly understood) to teach each and all of us."

Three ideas stand out in this statement. First, conflicts are particularly calculated to teach us something. Second, we can't learn from them until they are fairly understood, until we can see both sides—meaning we need to cool off before we can learn from them. Third, in a marvelous illustration of his own humility, Joseph included himself as one who learned something important from this conflict.

If our conflicts are particularly calculated to teach us something, what are we supposed to learn? Joseph's answer goes deep: Conflicts are particularly calculated to teach us "the necessity of humility and meekness before the Lord, that He might teach us of His ways."

Why did Joseph say humility "before the Lord"? Why didn't he say "before the person on the other side"? To learn from our conflicts we must be willing to see our own faults, and we need the Lord's help to do that. Only then can He begin to "teach us of *His* ways" (emphasis added).

We come to the ultimate question: What *are* the Lord's ways for dealing with conflict? They are illustrated in a second conflict between Joseph and Oliver.

SECOND EXAMPLE

Just a month after the first conflict, to escape persecution, Joseph and Emma moved 80 miles north to the Whitmer home in Fayette— the home Joseph had so recently visited to resolve the first conflict. Arriving at the Whitmer home, Joseph was grieved to learn that Hiram Page, one of the eight witnesses to the Book of Mormon, had been receiving revelations through a "seer stone" that purported to

give instructions on how the Church should operate. Newel Knight
was with Joseph, and he described the seriousness of the problem:

[Hiram Page] *had managed to get up some dissension of feeling among the
brethren by giving revelations concerning the government of the Church
. . . , which he claimed to have received through the medium of a stone he
possessed. . . . Even Oliver Cowdery and the Whitmer family had given
heed to them.*[5]

What could have been more painful and frustrating to Joseph
than this? If Joseph had followed his earlier pattern, he would have
demanded of Hiram Page by what authority he presumed to receive
revelations for the Church, and he would have demanded of Oliver
what on earth he was thinking to believe in such things. But Joseph
was more aware that a hasty and intemperate response would not
solve the problem. Joseph knew what *not* to do, but he wasn't sure
what he *ought* to do.

Newel Knight wrote:

*Joseph was perplexed and scarcely knew how to meet this new exigency.
That night I occupied the same room that he did and the greater part of
the night was spent in prayer and supplication.*[6]

Rather than react defensively, Joseph patiently sought counsel
from the Lord. He was soon granted an answer in the form of a
revelation, which is now section 28 of the Doctrine and Covenants.

DOCTRINE AND COVENANTS, SECTION 28

Section 28 is well known for answering the question of who *can*—
and who *cannot*—receive revelation for the Church. It is also a model
of the Lord's willingness to see wrongdoers in the larger context of
their lives and to show divine confidence in them while reproving or
correcting them.

The Lord spoke in the first person directly to Oliver: "Behold,
I say unto thee, Oliver, that it shall be given unto thee that thou shalt

be heard by the church in all things whatsoever thou shalt teach them . . ." The Lord's first words were an affirmation of Oliver's good standing in the Lord's eyes. Then He added this stipulation: ". . . by the Comforter, concerning the revelations and commandments which I have given."[7]

After clarifying that only the prophet can receive revelation for the Church, the Lord reaffirmed His divine confidence in Oliver: "And if thou art led at any time by the Comforter to *speak* . . . by the way of commandment unto the church, thou mayest do it."[8] And then, again, He outlined the limits on Oliver's authority: "But thou shalt not *write* by way of commandment, but by wisdom; And thou shalt not command him who is at thy head, and at the head of the church."[9]

The Lord then turned to the source of the problem: Hiram Page. I am struck that He spoke with the same concern for Hiram's feelings as He had shown for Oliver's. This exemplifies the Lord's way, and it makes it much easier for Hiram to accept correction: "Take thy brother, Hiram Page, between him and thee alone, and tell him that those things which he hath written from that stone are not of me."[10]

Instructed and corrected in this loving and reaffirming way, both Oliver Cowdery and Hiram Page recognized their error and continued in full fellowship in the Church for a long while.

THIRD EXAMPLE

These two events in the life of the Prophet Joseph prepare us for one other scriptural example—the painful misunderstanding between Moroni and Pahoran in Alma 59 through 62. I wonder if this is where the Prophet Joseph gained his own understanding that conflicts are meaningful and we must learn from them.

Moroni is one of the great military leaders in all of scripture. At the early age of 25 he was made captain over all the Nephite armies. As you will recall, when the prophet Mormon abridged the records of Moroni's military leadership, he called him "a man of a perfect understanding"[11] and honored him with this remarkable endorsement:

If all men had been, and were, and ever would be, like unto Moroni, behold, the very powers of hell would have been shaken forever; yea, the devil would never have power over the hearts of the children of men.

Behold, he was a man like unto Ammon . . . , and even the other sons of Mosiah, yea, and also Alma and his sons, for they were all men of God.[12]

It has always astonished me that this same Mormon included, as part of his abridged record, a vivid account of Moroni's conflict with Pahoran, the chief judge and governor of the Nephites.

As we learn in Alma 59, Moroni's army was caught in a dangerous situation. Lamanite armies were rapidly gaining ground against them. As chief military leader, Moroni wrote Pahoran for reinforcements. Receiving none, the scripture reports, "Moroni was angry with the government, because of their indifference concerning the freedom of their country."[13]

When no help came from the government, Moroni wrote Pahoran again. He began with the facts: the suffering of his men, the slaughter of thousands of the Nephite people, and other atrocities of war. But Moroni didn't realize that Pahoran had been driven from his throne by the king-men and forced to take refuge in Gideon, and Moroni wrongly accused Pahoran of being a traitor to his own country. Moroni concluded with these challenging words: "Behold, the Lord saith unto me: If those whom ye have appointed your governors do not repent of their sins and iniquities, ye shall go up to battle against them."[14]

We are treading sacred ground here. Is there any question whether the Lord had inspired Moroni to know there were problems at the government level that called for military help? Not at all. However, in his abridgment, Mormon made it clear that Moroni mistakenly assumed Pahoran was part of the problem and threatened to remove him as head of the government.

I have puzzled many years why Mormon would include a detailed account of this uncharacteristic error by the great Captain Moroni. I expect it was for at least two reasons.

One would be to show us that none of us, not even the great Captain Moroni, is immune from presumption and rash judgment. What a comfort it is to me, and I hope to you, that we are in the best of company when we make errors of this kind. This is not to excuse them but to give us permission to admit our mistakes and to learn from them.

The second reason is to show us one of the best examples in all of scripture of how to respond to an unjust accusation. We know very little about Pahoran except that he was an upright ruler committed to standing "fast in that liberty in . . . which God . . . made us free."[15] In chapter 61, Mormon, as editor, gave us Pahoran's entire response to Captain Moroni. I will quote only two of the 20 verses included in his answer:

> *I, Pahoran, who am the chief governor of this land, do send these words. . . . Behold, I say unto you, Moroni, that I do not joy in your great afflictions, yea, it grieves my soul. . . .*
>
> *And now, in your epistle you have censured me, but it mattereth not; I am not angry, but* do rejoice in the greatness of your heart.[16]

How did Pahoran do it? How could he respond in such humility and meekness before the Lord? He probably sat right down and wrote an angry reply, venting his injured feelings against Moroni. If so, when he was finished, he did what we all must do—he tore it up and threw it away. Then he must have spent long hours in supplication to the Lord to find the strength to overlook the unjust accusations and to reply with such compassion and love.

In Proverbs we read that "grievous words stir up anger" and "a soft answer turneth away wrath."[17] Pahoran's soft answer is a beautiful example of what the Prophet Joseph said about "the necessity of humility and meekness before the Lord, that He might teach us of *His* ways."[18]

Even in this misjudgment Moroni is also our model. When he learned of his error, he was not prideful. He immediately marched to the aid of Pahoran, and with their combined forces they overthrew the king-men and the Lamanites, and peace was restored in the land.

As you reflect on these examples, do they call to mind any other gospel principles? I'm thinking in particular of that favorite scripture, Ether 12:27:

And if men come unto me I will show unto them their weakness. I give unto men weakness that they may be humble; and my grace is sufficient for all men that humble themselves before me; for if they humble themselves before me, and have faith in me, then will I make weak things become strong unto them.

President Kimball taught this gospel principle in terms of mirrors. He said, "Our vision is completely obscured when we have no mirror to [show us] our own faults and [we] look only for the foibles of others."[19]

Edward Edinger, a wise psychologist, wrote this about mirrors:

[A mirror] *shows us what we otherwise cannot see for ourselves because we are too close to it. Without a mirror, for instance, we would never even know what our face looks like; since we are inside looking out, there can be no self-knowledge, even the elementary self-knowledge of what we look like, unless there is some device that can turn the light back on us.*[20]

FINAL OBSERVATIONS

I conclude with a few final observations about conflicts. Again, more could be said, but you will understand.

1. Conflicts are easy to get into but difficult to get out of. If we have the courage to face them early, they are easier to resolve and to learn from.

2. Conflicts can be dangerous, because they easily fly out of control. They need good containers—such as good friendships and solid marriages—to hold them in. Early detection helps.

3. There are plenty of conflicts. They are also cyclical. If we don't learn from one, that's okay; wait a while, and, sure enough, the conflict will come around again and again until it either destroys a relationship or we learn from it. (If we learn from it, we move on to the next level of conflict, higher up on the plane of progression.)

4. Things often get worse before they get better. But it is generally better to face the problem now than to wait for the next time around.

5. It's cruel that it should be this way, but the thing we're supposed to learn about ourselves is usually obvious to the person we're in conflict with.

6. Even when we are right, we may be wrong. Even when we are right—or *especially* when we are right—if we are presumptuous and rash, we will give offense and become a stumbling block to others.

7. We learn by experience; but experience is not a very good teacher *unless* we remember our conflicts. It is a mark of greatness to remember and to learn from our conflicts.

CONCLUSION

We should think of our conflicts as mirrors that reflect back upon us things about ourselves we would rather not know. As we learn in Ether 12:27, it is a gift from heaven to be shown our weakness. If we will reflect upon *our* weakness, as the Prophet Joseph did upon his, the Lord will make us strong where we are weak.

I pray we may learn from our conflicts, that the Lord may teach us of *His* ways. In the name of Jesus Christ, amen.

NOTES

1. Barbara Neff Autograph Book, LDS Church Historical Department, Salt Lake City; quoted in Richard Neitzel Holzapfel and Jeni Broberg Holzapfel, *Women of Nauvoo* (Salt Lake City: Bookcraft, 1992), 68.

2. *HC* 1:105.

3. *HC* 1:105.

4. *HC* 1:105.

5. Newel Knight's Journal, in *Scraps of Biography* (Salt Lake City: Juvenile Instructor Office, 1883), 64; also in *They Knew the Prophet*, comp. Hyrum L. Andrus and Helen Mae Andrus (Salt Lake City: Bookcraft, 1974), 13.

6. In *Scraps of Biography*, 65; also *They Knew*, 13.

7. D&C 28:1.

8. D&C 28:4; emphasis added.

9. D&C 28:5–6; emphasis added.

10. D&C 28:11.

11. Alma 48:11.

12. Alma 48:17–18.

13. Alma 59:13.

14. Alma 60:33.

15. Alma 61:9.

16. Alma 61:2, 9; emphasis added.

17. Proverbs 15:1.

18. *HC* 1:105; emphasis added.

19. Spencer W. Kimball, *The Miracle of Forgiveness* (Salt Lake City: Bookcraft, 1969), 269.

20. Edward F. Edinger, *The Eternal Drama: The Inner Meaning of Greek Mythology* (Boston: Shambhala, 1994), 85.

The Power of One: Selfless Service

Jo Ann C. Abegglen

Mavis sat in her comfortable rocking chair as she listened to the evening news. Toward the end of the news she heard the reporter mention that in South America many newborns were being sent home wrapped in newspaper.

"Wrapped in newspaper?" said Mavis out loud. "That's terrible!"

So Mavis went to her sewing room and went to work. Over the next few weeks she made more than 200 quilts and receiving blankets. As she finished each blanket, she gave it an affectionate hug before placing it in one of the boxes to be taken to the Church's Humanitarian Services Center.

There's something you should know about Mavis: she was 91 years old and legally blind. But Mavis was an amazing individual. She said, "There is something I can do," and she wanted to exert herself to make a difference to the newborns around the world.

Elder H. Burke Peterson stated:

Jo Ann C. Abegglen was a BYU associate professor in the College of Nursing when this devotional address was given on 11 July 2006. © Brigham Young University.

In the day-to-day process of living, with all of its trials, challenges, and discouragements, we often underestimate our own God-given attributes and abilities which make it possible for each of us to pattern his or her life after that of the Savior and, in fact, do some of the things he did as he lived here among men. We may never personally experience the miracle of raising the dead, or be one to turn water into wine. We may not be one of thousands who may be fed from a few loaves and fishes, or be a part of the miraculous experience of walking on a stormy sea. But, for each one of us, there are a number of Christlike patterns of living we can be a part of in our mortal sojourn. [H. Burke Peterson, "Selflessness: A Pattern for Happiness," *Ensign,* May 1985, 66]

So what is it to be a selfless person? As Elder Peterson described:

A selfless person is one who is more concerned about the happiness and well-being of another than about his or her own convenience or comfort, one who is willing to serve another when it is neither sought for nor appreciated, or one who is willing to serve even those whom he or she dislikes. A selfless person displays a willingness to sacrifice, a willingness to [put aside] *personal wants, and needs, and feelings.* [Peterson, "Selflessness," 66]

A few years ago my son served in the Ukraine Donetsk Mission. About a year and a half into his mission, I received a letter from two sister missionaries serving in that same area. While attending fast and testimony meeting one Sunday, they had heard a touching story shared by a recent convert that involved my son and his companion. The sister missionaries were sure my son would never share this incident, so they took it upon themselves to write and tell me the story. This is the story they shared in their letter:

A brother who was a recent convert in a small branch in eastern Ukraine was a hardworking father who made very little income from his job but tried diligently to provide for his family. All of his income went to buy food and to pay rent, utilities, and tithing. There was nothing left over for extras. But the one thing this dear brother wanted most of all was a tie to wear to church when he could bless the sacrament.

During the preceding couple of months he had saved a few pennies from each of his paychecks and put the money in a small leather coin purse with the hope that one day he would finally be able to purchase a tie to wear to church. By the week before fast and testimony meeting he had gathered sufficient funds to purchase his tie. He was so excited! Then, in the middle of the week, a family member became ill, and the saved tie funds were needed to purchase medicine. This dear brother was quite disappointed that another Sunday would go by without a tie. The days preceding church he silently prayed that somehow he could acquire a tie—not an expensive tie, just a simple, plain tie—so he could respectfully administer the sacrament of the Lord.

Late Saturday afternoon there was a knock at his apartment door, and when he opened the door there stood Elder Abegglen and his companion. As he gazed down at Elder Abegglen's hands, his eyes locked on a tie the missionary was holding.

"I understand you can use this tie," said Elder Abegglen.

With tears in his eyes, this good brother said, "I am here today to tell you God knows the simple desires of our hearts, and He sends forth His servants to answer our prayers."

In his address to his people in the Book of Mormon, King Benjamin said, "I tell you these things . . . that ye may learn that when ye are in the service of your fellow beings ye are only in the service of your God" (Mosiah 2:17). Whether it's a tie, a baby blanket, a smile, or a thoughtful note, there is something each of us can do to improve another's life.

Over the last two years I have had a wonderful opportunity to accompany nursing students to Ghana for a global health and diversity course. While in Ghana the students engage in wonderful opportunities to provide service. Ghana is inhabited by amazing, loving, poor people. Their village homes are simple—many made of mud with tin or thatched roofs. Furnishings consist of a few mats on the floor and wooden benches to sit on.

The nightly news pays little attention to the fact that in this day and age in the world there are 10 million children under the age of five that die from preventable causes every year. Out of those 10 million that die, four million are under the age of one. And of these four million children, one million die in the first few days of life (see Joy E Lawn, Simon Cousens, and Jelka Zupan, "4 Million Neonatal Deaths: When? Where? Why?" [Neonatal Survival 1], *The Lancet* 365, no. 9462 [March 5–11, 2005]: 891–900). Poverty, malnutrition, unskilled birth attendants, infection, and unclean water all contribute to this sad death statistic. But despite their poverty and lack of many material things, the Ghanaian people are happy; they are cheerful people, and they go forth every day with bright smiles.

Osu Children's Home in Accra is a wonderful, emotionally exhausting place for students to provide service. It is a simple place that needs painting, but it is a place that many abandoned children call home. Infants are housed in one area, toddlers in another, and primary-school–age children in another. Each year as we prepare to depart for Ghana, it is amazing how our students and their families get involved in gathering toys, new and used clothing, books, and sums of money to be given to struggling individuals and families. Because of our own experience with our children and our grandchildren, you would think that little children in Ghana would be so excited by toys, new clothes, socks, and shoes. But at the Osu Children's Home, we found that the children would bypass the toys and the pretty clothing. What the children wanted most from our students was to be held. They just wanted to experience a human touch, to snuggle in someone's arms, to hear a heartbeat.

How much time does it take to hold a hand, to offer a comforting word, to snuggle a child? In Proverbs 31:20 we read, "She stretcheth out her hand to the poor; yea, she reacheth forth her hands to the needy." I'd like you to remember that love is never wasted.

Sister Acquah is the president of the Cape Coast Relief Society. We were very busy this spring e-mailing back and forth to plan a health fair for the Relief Society sisters to be held on the first Saturday after we arrived in Ghana. As part of the health fair, this warm, caring person wanted the sisters in her stake to assemble hygiene kits and donate them to the children at a local school for the deaf and blind. She told me that for the last few years the Ghanaian Saints have been on the receiving end of many humanitarian efforts. It was time for the sisters to reach beyond themselves and give to someone else in need. What a moment of growth when people who have little learn to give to others. Selfless caring has a giving and a receiving component. We give that we might receive, and we receive that we might give again.

At the end of the health fair, the plan was that a small group of sisters would take the hygiene kits to the designated school. As the sisters were slowly leaving the health fair, Sister Acquah came over to me with a big smile and gave me a hug. Her statement to me in the blunt style of the Ghanaian people was that the health fair had turned out better than she had thought it would. I was not sure if she lacked confidence in our ability to present classes or if she was surprised that 262 sisters were willing to walk from distant villages, come by car, come by tro-tro, or come any way they could to the health fair that day.

As we sat and rested from the warm summer heat and the busy morning activities, Sister Acquah asked, "Of course you and your students are coming with us to deliver the hygiene kits to the school for the deaf and blind?

"Oh," I said, "you should really take the sisters who prepared the hygiene kits. They should experience the reward of their service project."

"Some will come," Sister Acquah said, "but I really want you and your students to come."

So we did. What a heart-changing experience followed for us that afternoon.

We all grumbled a little as we got on the bus to ride from the stake center to the school for the deaf and blind on the outskirts of Cape Coast, Ghana. I was thinking, it's a four-hour ride back to Accra, and it's late in the afternoon. There were giant rain clouds gathering on the horizon, and dirt roads and rain don't mix well.

We turned off the main road and bounced our way down a dirt road toward the school. As we pulled into the school yard, the school seemed very deserted. I was thinking that somehow we had gotten the day or maybe the time of day wrong. But as the bus stopped and we started getting out, we saw smiling, squealing children appearing in the open windows of the assembly hall.

The Cape Coast sisters and the students helped arrange the hygiene kits on the table in the front of the assembly hall as restless children wiggled on their benches. They would wave and smile. The blind children's choir sang the opening song—"I Have God in My Heart." We were asked to respond, and in turn we sang to them "I Am a Child of God," and then the deaf and partially deaf children responded in sign language and voices singing a song called "Heavenly Father Loves Me." The Spirit was so tender in that bare room as these songs were exchanged. We knew why we had come. We had been fed by the Spirit in that room. Each one of our students helped to hand out the hygiene kits. These beautiful children greeted our students with hugs and squeals as they received their plastic bag containing soap, a toothbrush, a towel, toothpaste, and two combs. To them it was like Christmas. After hugs and many unexpected tears, we loaded up the bus and started on our trip home.

No one complained about how long it took to return to Accra or how scary the thunder and muddy roads were. They were so grateful to have been a part of delivering the hygiene kits to the school for the deaf and blind. In her reflective writing assignment related to her experience that day, one of the students shared the following quote: "She went to minister to them and found then ministering to her. She went to teach and was transformed by what she learned" (author unknown).

For 30 years I have had the opportunity to live in a wonderful neighborhood. I won't tell you where it is, because you'd probably like to move there. Every day I witness in this neighborhood selfless acts of service: friendly greetings, hot loaves of bread being exchanged, a widower being invited for Sunday dinner, a forgotten garbage can being pulled to the curb on garbage collection day, a thoughtful note left on the door, a ride to the hospital, and sack lunches prepared and delivered to the Food and Care Coalition. In times of sadness people gather to comfort. In times of celebration they are there to celebrate. We are never too young or too old to engage in selfless service.

In the BYU Museum of Art there is a large painting of the Savior healing a man by the pool of Bethesda. Historians believe the pool was most likely a natural spring rich in dissolved solids and gases. Today we would call it a mineral spring. These waters were reputed to possess curative powers, and many afflicted folks came there to bathe. The spring was a pulsating variety, where at intervals the water rose with bubbling and then receded to normal levels. It was believed that whoever was the first to enter the waters after the bubbling was made whole.

I love to sit in front of this picture. We are fortunate enough in the College of Nursing to have a smaller version of the painting. I sit on one side and see the perspective in the painting. Then sometimes I move to the other side to determine if there is something else I can see. Sometimes as I gaze at the picture I see myself as a spectator, someone who blends into the crowd and watches as others do. Sometimes I look at myself in this picture and try to think of myself as the Savior—patiently listening, focusing on the needs of the individual. The Savior always focused on individuals face-to-face, eye to eye, voice to ear, heart to heart, spirit to spirit, and hand to hand. His approach was and is loving, His voice soft and gentle. Sometimes as I look at this painting I picture myself as the suffering individual waiting by the pool to be healed, waiting for someone to help me into the pool of healing waters.

Quietly, with a soft voice, the Savior looked at the helpless man and said, "Wilt thou be made whole?" Of course the man wanted to be made whole. He was eagerly waiting for his moment in the pool.

"Sir," said the man to the Savior, "I have no man, when the water is troubled, to put me into the pool."

With tenderness in His eyes, the Savior replied, "Rise, take up thy bed, and walk."

The man obeyed. He took up his pallet and walked away. (See John 5:5–9.) Many present at the pool that day missed the whole marvelous interaction.

I often hear the Savior's words in my ear: "Wilt thou be made whole? Then serve thy brothers and sisters."

To be like the Savior is to be whole, which implies that we are engaged in acts of selfless service. Selfless service requires personal action, a desire to pick up our beds and walk. It is easy to give away excess money, used equipment, and used clothing. It is more difficult to give of our time, to give of our personal presence to help others. There is much beauty and goodness in the world today if we look for it. The evening news tells us that things are not very good and that there is a great deal of sadness. But there is a great deal of beauty in the world.

For those of you who this summer are at this university for the very first time, you need to know that there is a great tradition of service here. You have entered to learn and to serve. We want you to stretch and enlighten your minds and enrich your hearts while you are here. There are many wonderful faculty members who serve as examples of selfless service in the local community and in the extended global community. Find them. Work with them. Your loneliness from being away from home for the first time will be less if you use your power of one and engage in serving another person.

In the Gospel of Matthew the Savior conversed with the righteous people gathered around Him. They asked Him:

Lord, when saw we thee an hungred, and fed thee? or thirsty, and gave thee drink?

When saw we thee a stranger, and took thee in? or naked, and clothed thee?

Or when saw we thee sick, or in prison, and came unto thee?

And the King shall answer and say unto them, Verily I say unto you, Inasmuch as ye have done it unto one of the least of these my brethren, ye have done it unto me. [Matthew 25:37–40]

We all need caring people in our lives, and we likewise need to care for others. May we humbly recognize our individual ability to have an impact on other lives for good and have the courage to do so, I humbly pray in the name of Jesus Christ, amen.

Knowing, Doing, and Being

———◆———

William H. Baker

I am grateful to be joined by my wife, Jeannie, and a number of our children and grandchildren today. In two months Jeannie and I will celebrate our 40th wedding anniversary. She has been a wonderful companion. She and my family are the source of my greatest joys. They are also the source of some of my greatest humor.

A few years ago, in a joint family home evening, my daughter Julie gave a lesson, and then I started making a few concluding comments, as grandpas often do. My little grandson, Ethan, then aged three, had had enough, and he shouted out, "Just say amen, Grandpa!" Even though he was quite young, he had learned that there is a direct correlation between when speakers say amen and when they stop talking. Ethan is here with us this morning, and I hope he will show a little restraint with his comments as I speak.

During the years I have taught at BYU, I have enjoyed hearing from a wide range of speakers on a great variety of topics. One story shared by Elder Oaks when he was president of BYU has stuck with me. Given from this very pulpit, the story went something like this:

———

William H. Baker was a BYU professor of management communication when this devotional address was given on 25 July 2006. © *Brigham Young University.*

Many years ago the federal government placed county agents throughout the country to help farmers learn to be more productive. One county agent in the South went to visit an old farmer in his area, but he found that convincing the farmer to change proved rather difficult.

He asked the farmer, "Wouldn't you like to know how to get your cows to give more milk?"

"Nope," the farmer replied.

"Well, wouldn't you like your pigs to have larger litters of baby pigs?"

Again the farmer answered, "Nope."

"Well, wouldn't you like to learn how to get more corn per acre?"

The same answer was given as before: "Nope."

Exasperated, the county agent asked, "Well, why not?"

The farmer replied simply, "I already knows more than I does."

In other words, his knowledge was greater than his application of that knowledge, so why make matters worse by obtaining even more knowledge!

This story highlights two great challenges of mortality: first, the need to constantly increase our knowledge and, second, the need to continually improve our behavior to keep up with that greater knowledge. But there's also a third challenge the county agent might have uncovered if he had asked a second "why" question: "Why don't you do as much as you know?" This question gets closer to the core of the problem—the farmer's level of love for his work, or what he was in his heart. In addition to increasing what we know and improving how we apply that knowledge, we must refine who we are deep down in our heart.

In a general conference address a few years ago, Elder Dallin H. Oaks stated, "In contrast to the institutions of the world, which teach us to *know* something, the gospel of Jesus Christ challenges us to *become* something" ("The Challenge to Become," *Ensign*, November 2000, 32; emphasis in original).

As we move along the path of life, each of us, as members of the Church, must address these three areas of knowing, doing, and being.

INCREASING OUR KNOWING

First, we must increase our level of knowledge, or what we know. In our search for truth, however, we have to be selective, because we have an overwhelming amount of information available to us. It seems to me that information can be classified into four categories.

The first consists of that which is harmful and destructive. Much of today's media falls into this category. Pornography is especially dangerous, for it will drive away the Spirit and destroy us.

The second category includes information that isn't necessarily destructive but is not of much use. Pursuing it is largely a waste of time.

The third category includes information that is good and useful and offers much practical benefit. Most of our university learning falls into this category.

The fourth category includes vital information—specifically gospel knowledge. The truthfulness and value of the information in this fourth category will be confirmed to us by the Holy Spirit.

How important it is for us to shun the harmful, avoid wasting time on the useless, and, instead, focus on the useful and vital—that which gives eternal perspective, helps develop wisdom, and teaches us the mind and nature of God. The 13th article of faith says that we, as Latter-day Saints, seek after things that are "virtuous, lovely, or of good report or praiseworthy" (Articles of Faith 1:13). That's a good standard for us to keep in mind as we choose what to read, what to listen to, and what to view.

Where do we find the vital information for our lives? Three major sources, I believe, are the temple, Church magazines, and the scriptures. In the temple we come into the Lord's house, dedicated as "a house of learning" (D&C 109:8), where we are taught eternal truths through verbal, visual, and symbolic instruction and where we may seek inspiration for specific personal concerns. President Gordon B. Hinckley has said:

Every temple, large or small, has its beautiful celestial room. . . . It is our privilege, unique and exclusive, while dressed in white, to sit at the conclusion of our ordinance work in the beautiful celestial room and ponder, meditate, and silently pray. ["Closing Remarks," *Ensign,* November 2004, 105]

We all need to make the temple an important and frequent part of our learning.

We also need the *Ensign* and its messages of wisdom and inspiration to come into our homes and into our lives each month. Just as the early Saints looked to their prophet Brigham Young to guide them along a literal path from the Midwest to the Rocky Mountains, so must we look to our prophets to guide us along a spiritual path. I hope each student apartment receives the *Ensign* each month and is blessed by its influence.

In addition to learning from the temple and from the *Ensign,* we need daily scripture study. Just as helium slowly escapes from an inflated balloon, allowing it to shrink and fall after a few days, so do we slowly lose the power and memory of the scriptures without daily reading. President Gordon B. Hinckley has said:

I hope that for you [studying the scriptures] *will become something far more enjoyable than a duty; that, rather, it will become a love affair with the word of God. I promise you that as you read, your minds will be enlightened and your spirits will be lifted.* ["The Light Within You," *Ensign,* May 1995, 99]

In August 2005 President Gordon B. Hinckley asked all of us to reread the Book of Mormon by the end of that year. He promised us "an added measure of the Spirit of the Lord, a strengthened resolution to walk in obedience to His commandments, and a stronger testimony of the living reality of the Son of God" ("A Testimony Vibrant and True," *Ensign,* August 2005, 6). Faithful Saints from all over the world responded to the call.

Regarding this challenge, a member of my BYU stake shared the following special experience with me. To the best of my recollection, he said:

I was flying back from a trip to the Far East. It was the middle of the night, and most of the passengers were asleep. I, however, had my reading light on and was reading the Book of Mormon so I could finish by the end of the year as the prophet had asked.

Suddenly I was interrupted by a flight attendant who was walking down the aisle. She whispered, "Where are you?"

I responded, "I'm in Helaman."

She replied, "I'm in Ether." Then she said, "Turn around and look."

I turned and looked toward the back of the plane and saw several other reading lights on. She whispered, "All reading the Book of Mormon."

Although our lives are filled with countless demands and distractions, I think we all learned from our prophet that we can find the time to study the scriptures if we are determined enough, each in our own way and place and time. He has told us the *what;* individually we work out the *how.*

In addition to giving spiritual strength, the scriptures contain counsel to help address life's practical challenges. Some years ago I served as a branch president at the Missionary Training Center. I often told the missionaries that the scriptures could help them solve all their missionary challenges.

One Sunday, in priesthood meeting, we listed on the chalkboard several typical missionary challenges. Then I assigned small groups of elders to look up scriptures to address each of the challenges. After a few minutes I asked them to report their findings. One group had tackled the problem of dealing with girlfriends back home. The verse they found to solve the problem came from John 2:4: "Jesus saith unto her, Woman, what have I to do with thee? mine hour is not yet come."

IMPROVING OUR DOING

Building on the first area—increasing our knowing—we move on to the second area: improving our doing. Although increased knowledge is vital, it is not enough. The Apostle James stated that we must "be . . . doers of the word, and not hearers only" (James 1:22). Just as reading and pondering the words of God are accompanied by the Spirit, so will the doing aspect of the gospel be accompanied by the Spirit. The Savior said, "If any man will do his will, he shall know of the doctrine, whether it be of God, or whether I speak of myself" (John 7:17).

The Lord expects each step upward in knowledge to be followed by a step upward in performance. The Apostle James added, "To him that knoweth to do good, and doeth it not, to him it is sin" (James 4:17). In other words, sin is the difference between our knowing and our doing. The greater the gap between the two, the greater the sin, and, as section 82 of the Doctrine and Covenants instructs, "For of him unto whom much is given much is required; and he who sins against the greater light shall receive the greater condemnation" (D&C 82:3).

Elder Neal A. Maxwell highlighted the tight linkage between knowing and doing as follows:

So it is that discipleship requires all of us to translate doctrines, covenants, ordinances, and teachings into improved personal behavior. Otherwise we may be doctrinally rich but end up developmentally poor. ["Becoming a Disciple," *Ensign*, June 1996, 14]

Why does our doing so often lag behind our knowing, whether with home teaching, family home evening, or a wide range of other areas? I suppose that busy schedules, distractions, wrong priorities, lack of commitment, and just poor time management contribute to the problem. In statements regarding attendance at the temple, President Heber J. Grant addressed the typical excuses we make:

We can generally do that which we wish to do. A young man can find an immense amount of time to spend with his sweetheart. . . . We can arrange our affairs to get exercise in the shape of golf and otherwise. We can arrange our affairs to have amusements. And if we make up our minds to do so we can arrange our affairs to do temple work, judging from my own experience. [*GS*, 33–34; see *CR*, April 1928, 8–9]

I do not know of any one that is any busier than I am, and if I can do it they can, if they will only get the spirit in their hearts and souls of wanting to do it. [*Power from on High: A Lesson Book for Fourth Year Junior Genealogical Classes* (Salt Lake City: Genealogical Society of Utah, 1937), 26]

There is the key: get the spirit in our hearts so we want to do it. Improvement in the doing arena takes great dedication. New habits can be hard to establish, and old habits can be hard to break. As my son Steve concluded his mission in England, my wife and a daughter and I joined him to travel and to visit some of the people he had baptized or helped to activate. One faithful sister talked of her growth in the Church since her baptism. She spoke of the dedicated effort required to stay on the path and then said, "It is so easy to backslide."

It is indeed easy to backslide, but we can avoid it or overcome it with enough determination. One of the people I baptized on my mission in Canada showed incredible determination to break a cigarette habit. He and his family lived on a small farm northwest of Calgary, Alberta, and a few months after they were baptized, he was out in the barn moving some bales of hay. Under one of the bales he discovered a partially smoked cigarette. Without thinking he picked it up and ran toward the house to get a match so he could smoke it. But halfway there he stopped, looked at the cigarette, and asked himself, "Am I going to be in charge of my life or is this cigarette going to rule over me?" After a crucial moment of intense internal battle, he dropped the cigarette to the ground and walked slowly back to the barn.

For he will give unto the faithful line upon line, precept upon precept; and I will try you and prove you herewith. . . .

. . . I will prove you in all things, whether you will abide in my covenant, even unto death. [D&C 98:12, 14]

Let me share two additional doing examples that highlight the importance of establishing and maintaining good spiritual habits.

First, a member of my BYU stake recently told me that at one time in her life she had been mistreated at Church, so she stayed away for a few weeks. Even after just a few weeks of absence this wonderful returned missionary found it difficult to come back. "Looking back on it now," she said, "I realize how important it is to stick with good spiritual habits."

The second example comes from my own family. Our daughter Amy married into a family that has had daily scripture study for more than 20 years without a single miss. And Amy and her family have carried on that pattern for the seven years they have been married. Even when she is in the hospital with a new baby, their daily scripture study is carried on by telephone. How gratifying it is for Jeannie and me as parents to visit the homes of our other children as well and see a similar pattern of faithfulness—including our family's habit of weekly family home evenings, which now spans nearly 40 years.

Just as our gaining of knowledge should expand from basic principles to deeper doctrine, so should our doing go beyond minimal compliance with specific "thou shalt" and "thou shalt not" commandments. The Lord said:

It is not meet that I should command in all things. . . .

. . . Men should be anxiously engaged in a good cause, and do many things of their own free will, and bring to pass much righteousness;

For the power is in them, wherein they are agents unto themselves.
[D&C 58:26–28]

Just as there are harmful and useless materials that can occupy our reading and learning, so are there harmful and useless activities that can occupy our time. We should avoid filling our days with these activities and instead spend our time doing that which is useful and essential. As someone once stated, that which matters most must never be at the mercy of that which matters least. Giving service—such as that which we give in the Church, in our communities, and especially in our families—is central to this useful and essential work. By losing ourselves in doing good for others, we come to understand what the Lord meant when He said: "He that findeth his life shall lose it: and he that loseth his life for my sake shall find it" (Matthew 10:39).

PURIFYING OUR BEING

Moving from increasing our knowing and improving our doing, we come to the third and most important part of our progress: purifying our being, or refining who and what we are deep down in our hearts.

Elder Henry B. Eyring clarified that although doing is important, it is not our ultimate goal. In our last general conference he said, "The things we do are the means, not the end we seek. What we *do* allows the Atonement of Jesus Christ to change us into what we must *be*" ("As a Child," *Ensign*, May 2006, 16; emphasis added). Elder David A. Bednar added, "People of integrity and honesty not only practice what they preach, they are what they preach" ("Be Honest," *New Era*, October 2005, 7).

Elder Dallin H. Oaks has taught:

The Final Judgment is not just an evaluation of a sum total of good and evil acts—what we have done. *It is an acknowledgment of the final effect of our acts and thoughts—what we have* become. *It is not enough for anyone just to go through the motions. The commandments, ordinances, and covenants of the gospel are not a list of deposits required to be made in some heavenly account. The gospel of Jesus Christ is a plan that shows us how to become what our Heavenly Father desires us to become.* ["The Challenge to Become," 32; emphasis in original]

And what is it that we must become? The Savior answered very simply: "Even as I am" (3 Nephi 27:27). He is the mark we must always look to. He is our supreme example. He was chosen as our Savior not just because of His perfect obedience but because of His perfect love—love that encompasses perfect knowledge and that motivates perfect obedience.

The Savior also used the example of a child to teach us what we must become. Matthew recorded:

> And Jesus called a little child unto him, and set him in the midst of them,
> And said, Verily I say unto you, Except ye be converted, and become as little children, ye shall not enter into the kingdom of heaven. [Matthew 18:2–3]

Numerous verses of scripture give additional detail as to the type of people we must become. For example:

"We believe in being honest, true, chaste, benevolent, virtuous" (Articles of Faith 1:13).

"Be humble, and be submissive and gentle; easy to be entreated; full of patience and long-suffering; being temperate in all things" (Alma 7:23).

"Becometh as a child, submissive, meek, humble, patient, full of love, willing to submit to all things [from] the Lord" (Mosiah 3:19).

"Faith, hope, charity and love, . . . virtue, knowledge, temperance, patience, brotherly kindness, godliness, charity, humility, diligence" (D&C 4:5–6).

And, finally: "Long-suffering, . . . gentleness and meekness, . . . love . . . ; [and] kindness" (D&C 121:41–42).

That, to me, is an exciting list. Imagine yourself when all those Christlike attributes are yours! Obviously, we are in for a lifetime of effort and then some. The Prophet Joseph Smith stated:

> When you climb up a ladder, you must begin at the bottom, and ascend step by step, until you arrive at the top; and so it is with the principles of the gospel—you must begin with the first, and go on until you learn all the principles of exaltation. But it will be a great while after you have passed through the veil before you will have learned them. It is not all to be com-

prehended in this world; it will be a great work to learn our salvation and
exaltation even beyond the grave. [*HC* 6:306–7]

The family proclamation also highlighted the long-term process of becoming like Christ, saying that we are here in mortality
to "obtain a physical body and gain earthly experience to progress
toward perfection" ("The Family: A Proclamation to the World,"
Ensign, November 1995, 102; emphasis added).

Some of us become too self-critical in the process. We want
patience, and we want it now! Sooner or later we have to learn that
becoming patient includes learning patience with ourselves as well
as with others. Things take time. Those who become perfectionistic
and overzealous often find that the gospel isn't much fun anymore.
It is more stressful than satisfying. We can fall off both sides of the
path, and we must strive to stay in the middle where we are making
reasonable progress, given our life's circumstances. The Lord told the
Prophet Joseph Smith, "Do not run faster or labor more than you
have strength and means" (D&C 10:4). That is good counsel. We all
need to learn to do our very best and then to be at peace.

Two specific temple recommend interview questions set a nice
standard for us. They don't ask if we are perfect but rather if we are
"striving" to keep the commandments and if we consider ourselves to
be "worthy." Without becoming anxious and obsessive overachievers,
we can *strive* to keep the commandments and we can be *worthy.* Elder
Neal A. Maxwell reminded us, "All of us are in the process of becoming—including prophets and General Authorities" (Neal A. Maxwell,
All These Things Shall Give Thee Experience [Salt Lake City: Deseret
Book, 1979], 105.

Because of differences in opportunity, talent, and circumstance,
how we become Christlike varies somewhat from person to person.
But common elements in our spiritual progress include gospel study,
service and activity in the Church, and obedience to the commandments. But, above all, it is the cleansing effect of the Atonement and
the Spirit that purify and change our hearts. As King Benjamin's
people learned, it was "the Spirit of the Lord [that] wrought a mighty

change in [them], that [they had] no more disposition to do evil, but to do good continually" (Mosiah 5:2).

The many trials and challenges of life also help us become more Christlike. For some people, life's trials seem to be relatively small. But even many little trials over a period of years can help us learn patience, meekness, and love if we will be humble and teachable students. In our last general conference, President Gordon B. Hinckley, at age 96, said, "When a man grows old he develops a softer touch, a kindlier manner" ("The Need for Greater Kindness," *Ensign*, May 2006, 58). Someone once told me, "It's not your fault if you're not beautiful by age 18, but it is your fault if you're not beautiful by age 80."

One of the special older and beautiful people in my life was my mother. After my father died, at almost 99 years of age, my mother, also in her nineties, lived with my family from time to time. Through her sweet example she taught us always to look on the bright side of life and to see the good in others. One day Jeannie was telling her of one of our sons whose bedroom was a disaster, with clothes, schoolbooks, and other "stuff" strewn about on the bed and floor. My mother listened patiently and then said lovingly, "Well, just tell him he has a clean ceiling." This grandmother with her pure and loving heart was able to overlook the mess on the floor and look upward to the ceiling to find something to compliment.

For some people the trials of life can be much more challenging. A month ago my son Steve and his wife, Amy, were saddened to learn that their little five-month-old daughter, their first child, has a 17th-chromosome disorder that presents to her and to her parents a very uncertain future. Since then, the Primary Children's Medical Center in Salt Lake City has become their home as the medical staff monitors little Brooklyn's rare problems. Remembering that Robby Hammond, my teaching assistant from two years ago, has a daughter with an 18th-chromosome problem, I wrote to Robby and told him of Steve and Amy's situation. In his e-mail reply regarding my granddaughter, this young father revealed the tenderness of his heart as he talked of his own daughter Emily, now two years old:

It's always a difficult time when you learn something like this, but believe me when I tell you that there is so much joy that comes from situations like these. Camille and I have never been through anything as joyful, or as painful at times, as with Emily. But it's the painful times that make the joyful times so indescribable. For example, when Emily was born, we were told a fairly "doom and gloom" story about what Emily would be like as she grew up. If those doctors could only see Emily now . . .

Her most recent trick is rolling onto her stomach and getting up on her hands and knees and rocking back and forth. Because she is blind, she hasn't quite figured out that crawling can get her where she wants to go. I mention this because of how incredible I feel when I see her learn to do something as simple as get on her hands and knees and rock back and forth. It has almost brought me to tears of joy sometimes just watching her progress.

Please let your son know that while there are certainly difficulties, the joys are unimaginable. Emily brings a very strong spiritual presence to my life. [Robby Hammond, e-mail to author, June 2006]

Trials were certainly no stranger to the Prophet Joseph Smith. While suffering in Liberty Jail, he was told by the Lord, "All these things shall give thee experience, and shall be for thy good" (D&C 122:7). At the end of his life, just before riding off to Carthage, where he would meet his death, Sister Mary Ellen Kimball overheard him say to her neighbor, "If I never see you again, or if I *never come back*, remember that I love you." Sister Kimball wrote that the Prophet's "enemies had ripened in wickedness and he in goodness." (In Mark L. McConkie, *Remembering Joseph: Personal Recollections of Those Who Knew the Prophet Joseph Smith* [Salt Lake City: Deseret Book, 2003], 75, 76; emphasis in original.)

That is also our challenge—to ripen in goodness even in the midst of a world ripening in wickedness, to develop a Christlike heart filled with love for God and all mankind. Without a heart filled with love for what we do and for those whom we serve, none of us will ever fully achieve what we could or should.

CONCLUSION

I pray that the Lord will bless us throughout our lives as we strive to progress in all three areas of knowing, doing, and being. I pray that we will be diligent and do our very best, but I also pray that we will be patient as we improve line upon line, learning upon learning, repentance upon repentance, onward and upward, with the Lord trying us and proving us as we go.

At times we will learn first and be tried later; at other times the Lord will try us first and then teach us from the trials. But in spite of the sequence, I pray that we will move forward with faith in and love for the Lord—even while not knowing beforehand what lies ahead. Later in life we'll be able to look back on the *what* of our lives and understand the *why*. If we have been true and faithful, these backward glances will reveal to us a clear path of progress toward perfection guided by an all-wise, patient, and loving Heavenly Father. I testify that He lives, that His Son Jesus Christ is our Savior and Redeemer, and that They know and love each one of us beyond our present capacity to comprehend. In the name of Jesus Christ, amen.

Exactness in Our Discipleship

Scott D. Sommerfeldt

I am grateful and humbled to be with you here this morning. During my time here at BYU I have had the opportunity to listen to numerous devotional addresses, and, frankly, I have never considered myself to be in the category of those who deliver these addresses. So I pray that I may be able to speak through the Spirit today and deliver a message that will be worthwhile to you.

Let me begin by talking for a minute about my professional work. My discipline of training is in the area of acoustics, and for much of my career I have been involved with research on what is referred to as active noise control. With this technology you can in essence cancel noise with noise. Sound waves are created in the air as molecules oscillate, thereby making the pressure in the air oscillate up and down.

We can represent this oscillating pressure graphically with peaks on the graph representing points in time when the pressure is high and dips representing points in time when the pressure is low. Our

Scott D. Sommerfeldt was chair of the BYU Department of Physics and Astronomy when this devotional address was given on 1 August 2006. © Brigham Young University.

ears detect this oscillating pressure and perceive it as sound. Another important concept is that multiple waves can add together—much as numbers add together. So if one sound wave makes the pressure in the air go up and a second sound wave makes the pressure in the air go down by the same amount, the two waves will add like positive and negative numbers and cancel each other, thereby eliminating the sound.

On a graph, we could show three sounds where the upper line would schematically represent the oscillating pressure that exists before we decide we want to cancel it. The middle line on the graph would represent the pressure that we are going to create by turning our control on to try to cancel the original sound. With the control turned on, the middle line would represent a wave that is close to being the mirror opposite of the original sound wave, which should lead to significant cancellation. The bottom line would show the result of our effort, as the amplitude, or height, of the sound wave goes down noticeably—thus we would expect an audible difference.

In my first example we were not able to completely cancel the original sound. This is because we did not create a completely exact mirror image of the original sound. The middle line on the graph would have what we call a "phase error." This means that the peaks of one wave do not line up exactly in time with the dips in the other wave. This time relation of one point on a wave to another point on the wave is referred to as *phase*. As you follow the oscillation through a complete cycle from a peak through a dip and back to the next peak, that is represented by a change in phase of 360 degrees, analogous to going around a circle. The ideal phase of our cancelling wave for active control is 180 degrees, as that would exactly line up the peaks of the original wave with the dips of our control wave. In my first example we were off by 5 degrees of phase from the ideal of 180 degrees.

What if we are a little sloppier? My second example shows a similar result, but in this result we are even less careful and we have a phase error of 45 degrees. In this case the results do not appear to be nearly as impressive, though the 45-degree phase error still appears to produce a cancelling wave that is close to what we want. As you heard in my second example, this result was not very impressive, and you would be highly unlikely to invest significantly in this technology if this result was the best that could be obtained.

Let's look at one last example. In this case we have been careful and have reduced the phase error to half a degree, which is quite close to the perfect solution. As a result, in this example the sound is essentially completely cancelled. If you were in business, this represents a result you might be much more willing to invest in.

Well, at this point I suspect many of you are thinking, "I thought I was attending a devotional and not one of those dreaded physics classes." Let me assure you that you can relax—we are pretty much finished with the physics lecture. Just why have I taken the time to explain all this to you? In my mind there is a strong analogy that can be drawn from these active noise control results we have heard and our discipleship of the Savior. As we become exact in getting the right phase for implementing active noise control, the results become very impressive. Similarly, as we become more exact in our discipleship of the Savior, there is an impressive power that comes into our lives that aids us in our spiritual growth. As we look at people we may be acquainted with, as well as individuals in the scriptures, I am sure that we can identify numerous examples representing various levels of commitment in our discipleship.

Consider one of the earliest examples that we have record of. Adam and Eve had two sons: Cain and Abel. They were commanded to make offerings unto the Lord:

> And in process of time it came to pass, that Cain brought of the fruit of the ground an offering unto the Lord.
> And Abel, he also brought of the firstlings of his flock and of the fat thereof. And the Lord had respect unto Abel and to his offering:
> But unto Cain and to his offering he had not respect. And Cain was very wroth, and his countenance fell. [Genesis 4:3–5]

You know the ending of this tragic story from there.

But what was it that led the Lord to accept Abel's offering and not accept Cain's offering? Didn't they both give offerings as they were commanded? We gain additional insight to this question from the Pearl of Great Price. When Adam and Eve were cast out of the Garden of Eden, they were commanded "that they should . . . offer the firstlings of their flocks, for an offering unto the Lord" (Moses 5:5). In this sense Cain was close to doing what he had been commanded, having brought of the fruit of the ground, but he wasn't exact in following the commandment given. Furthermore, we find that "Satan commanded [Cain], saying: Make an offering unto the Lord" (Moses 5:18), after which Cain made his offering. Thus Cain was sort of doing the right thing, but for all the wrong reasons, as he was really following Satan rather than the Savior.

Let's move forward to the New Testament. After the Resurrection of the Savior, we find the Saints striving to live the law of consecration, having implemented a form of the united order. In the book of Acts we read of Ananias and his wife, who sold one of their possessions. They then proceeded to almost live the law of consecration by bringing a portion of the money they received to the Apostles; however, they kept back a portion of it for themselves. We read of how Peter through the Spirit detected their dishonesty, first on the part of Ananias and then later with his wife. Both were stricken and died as a result of not being completely honest in their offering to the Lord (see Acts 5:1–10).

Examples are not restricted to the Old World. Let's move to the Book of Mormon record. We find Lehi and his family leaving Jerusalem, only to receive direction from the Lord that they should return to get the brass plates. You know how Laman and Lemuel grumbled. Sam and Nephi were much more willing to follow the commandments of the Lord. In spite of this, Laman and Lemuel sort of followed the commandment in that they did go up to Jerusalem with Nephi. As you recall, Laman first went in to Laban to request the plates. However, Laban became angry, thrust Laman out, and tried to kill him. Nephi was successful in persuading his brothers to return with him to try again. This time they essentially offered to buy the plates from Laban. Laban thrust them out again, and their riches fell into the hands of Laban. (See 1 Nephi 1–3.)

At this point Laman and Lemuel had had enough. I can almost hear them saying to Nephi, "Look, this was completely crazy to have us come back here to get these useless plates. The Lord can't really expect us to do this. It's time for us to clear out of here and at least save our lives." They even said to Nephi, "How is it possible that the Lord will deliver Laban into our hands?" (1 Nephi 3:31).

However, we read of the commitment of Nephi as he replied, "Let us be faithful in keeping the commandments of the Lord" (1 Nephi 4:1). As you know, Nephi went back to Jerusalem, where he "was led by the Spirit, not knowing beforehand the things which [he] should do" (1 Nephi 4:6). Laman and Lemuel sort of followed the commandments they had received, but not precisely, and as a result missed out on the blessings that came to Nephi because of his commitment to do all that the Lord commanded.

We have another example in the two thousand stripling warriors who Helaman led into battle. These young men were described as "men who were true at all times in whatsoever thing they were entrusted" (Alma 53:20). The Nephite army marveled that not a single one of these young men was killed. In explaining this miracle, Helaman observed:

> *Yea, and they did obey and observe to perform every word of command with exactness; yea, and even according to their faith it was done unto them; and I did remember the words which they said unto me that their mothers had taught them.* [Alma 57:21]

There is a principle we can learn from these examples in the scriptures. As we are obedient and try to follow the direction we receive from the Lord to the best of our ability, we are blessed and receive further spiritual insights and strength to live the gospel. The Lord put it this way:

For behold, thus saith the Lord God: I will give unto the children of men line upon line, precept upon precept, here a little and there a little; and blessed are those who hearken unto my precepts, and lend an ear unto my counsel, for they shall learn wisdom; for unto him that receiveth I will give more; *and from them that shall say, We have enough, from them shall be taken away even that which they have.* [2 Nephi 28:30; emphasis added]

Or, put another way:

It is given unto many to know the mysteries of God; nevertheless they are laid under a strict command that they shall not impart only according to the portion of his word which he doth grant unto the children of men, according to the heed and diligence which they give unto him. [Alma 12:9; emphasis added]

So how does this correspond to our everyday lives? Let me illustrate with a personal example. You may recall that one year ago we received some guidance from our living prophet, President Gordon B. Hinckley. In the August 2005 *Ensign,* as part of the First Presidency message, he said:

We studied the Book of Mormon in Sunday School this past year. Nonetheless I offer a challenge to members of the Church throughout the world and to our friends everywhere to read or reread the Book of Mormon. If you will read a bit more than one and one-half chapters a day, you will be able to finish the book before the end of this year. . . .

Without reservation I promise you that if each of you will observe this simple program, regardless of how many times you previously may have read the Book of Mormon, there will come into your lives and into your homes an added measure of the Spirit of the Lord, a strengthened resolution to walk in obedience to His commandments, and a stronger testimony of the living reality of the Son of God. [Gordon B. Hinckley, "A Testimony Vibrant and True, *Ensign,* August 2005, 5–6]

I am sure you remember this challenge. How did you respond to it? Let me tell you of my experience. I remember that when the challenge came out, I was going strong with a personal study of the Doctrine and Covenants. I remember distinctly going through a thought process something like "I'm doing really well with my Doctrine and Covenants study right now. I've read the Book of Mormon many times, and, if I read it now before the end of the year, it will take enough time that I know it will mess up my current study. Maybe I can come back early next year and study the Book of Mormon." Do you see the fallacy of my reasoning? I was sort of being a disciple of Christ and more or less striving to live the gospel, but I wasn't following the counsel received through His prophet with exactness. I was rationalizing, saying I had read the Book of Mormon many times, when a prophet of God had said, "Regardless of how many times you previously may have read the Book of Mormon, there will come into your lives and into your homes an added measure of the Spirit of the Lord."

After a few days of fighting this challenge, it finally sunk into me that I had been asked by a prophet to do something, and it was time to stop moaning about my Doctrine and Covenants study and get with the program. So I did start studying the Book of Mormon, and some interesting things happened in our family. My wife, who is always ahead of me in spiritual things, had already embraced the challenge and was studying the Book of Mormon. As we went forward accepting this challenge, we noticed that each of our five children, without any urging from us, had also accepted the challenge, and each was regularly studying the Book of Mormon. One or two of our children had a nontraditional New Year's Eve last year as they finished up the last few chapters, but each member of our family was able to finish reading the Book of Mormon, including our youngest son, who finished a personal reading of the entire book for the first time. That in and of itself was enough blessing for me as a father, but I also observed, as President Hinckley had promised, that an added measure of the Spirit came into our home, and my testimony of Jesus Christ and His gospel was strengthened.

There is a difference in our spiritual strength that results when we are actively striving to live the gospel to the best of our ability. It is often seemingly small things that can make such a difference in our lives. I recall another experience I had while serving as a bishop. I had felt impressed that there were some things we needed to be aware of and to work on to help strengthen the youth in our ward. In a combined priesthood/Relief Society meeting I outlined some of my concerns and feelings regarding what I felt we needed to do as a ward. A discussion period followed, and I remember one brother in my ward who raised his hand and said, "Bishop, if this is what you feel we need to do as a ward, I want you to know that I support it and will do whatever I can." How gratifying that was to see this member committed to following the counsel he had received. That type of commitment to do whatever the Lord asks of us generates a spiritual strength and awareness that will bring us closer to the Savior and help us to continue to progress in our lives.

Contrast this with an experience an elders quorum president had. He told me he had felt inspired to challenge his elders quorum to do some specific things to prepare for general conference. He met with his quorum and outlined several things he wanted them to do before, during, and after conference and promised them that if they would follow his counsel, they would have a spiritually uplifting and enlightening experience. He presented his proposal to the quorum as a priesthood assignment and indicated he would ask for feedback after conference. He told me that after general conference he asked for a report from his quorum members. What was the result? Two people, one of whom was himself, had accepted the assignment, and both had a wonderful and rewarding experience while listening to conference. A number of others reported that they had gone home and simply thrown the assignment into the garbage. Think of the blessings that were forfeited by those who decided that it was not important to be exact in their discipleship of the Savior and to follow counsel and direction received through priesthood leaders.

I think I am safe in saying that all of us look to our living prophet as one who is fully committed to following the Savior. As we look at the life of President Hinckley, we see abundant evidence of him deciding at an early age that he would do all that was asked of him by the Lord. He tells the story about a time during his mission in England when three or four of the London papers carried some negative reviews of a reprint of an old book purporting to be a history of the Mormons.

His mission president said to then Elder Hinckley, "I want you to go down to the publisher and protest this."

Elder Hinckley was about to say, "Surely not me," but instead meekly said, "Yes, sir."

President Hinckley talked about the fear that he felt, but he offered a prayer and then, with stomach churning, went down to meet with the president of the publishing company. He presented his card to the receptionist, who took it into the inner office and then returned to indicate that the president was too busy to meet with him. Elder Hinckley replied that he had come five thousand miles and would wait. Over the next hour the receptionist went into the office several times and then finally invited Elder Hinckley in. As he entered, he noticed that the president was smoking a long cigar and had a look that seemed to say, "Don't bother me."

President Hinckley doesn't recall what he said, but another power seemed to speak through him. At first the company president was defensive and belligerent. Then he began to soften. By the end of their conversation he promised to do something, and he sent word out to every book dealer in England to return the books to the publisher. At great expense he printed in the front of each volume a statement to the effect that the book was not to be considered as history but only as fiction. President Hinckley concluded his telling of this story by saying, "I came to know that when we try in faith to walk in obedience to the requests of the priesthood, the Lord opens the way, even when there appears to be no way" (Gordon B. Hinckley, "If Ye Be Willing and Obedient," *Ensign*, July 1995, 5).

Many times, the difference between being fully committed to the gospel and being sort of committed to the gospel can be fairly small, just as the differences were small in our active noise control examples.

Nonetheless, these differences can result in a huge contrast. With the Liahona, Lehi and his family had a visual indicator of how they were doing. Nephi observed:

The pointers . . . did work according to the faith and diligence and heed which [they] *did give unto them.*

And there was also written upon them a new writing . . . ; and it was written and changed from time to time, according to the faith and diligence which [they] *gave unto it. And thus we see that by small means the Lord can bring about great things.* [1 Nephi 16:28–29]

We have various Liahonas in our lives today. Are we being diligent in giving heed to them? Are we faithfully studying the scriptures as we have been counseled to do? Do we earnestly strive to follow the guidance we receive from our living prophets, our stake president, bishop, elders quorum president, Relief Society president, and other Church leaders? Are we striving to be as exact as we can in our discipleship of the Savior? In doing this, we need to be aware that we are not perfect and we will not be perfect anytime soon. As King Benjamin counseled his people, "It is not requisite that a man should run faster than he has strength. And again, it is expedient that he should be diligent, that thereby he might win the prize" (Mosiah 4:27). We need to maintain a balance in our lives between being able to accept ourselves with our weaknesses and current limitations and being committed to progressing and becoming more exact disciples of the Savior. If you recall, the phase matching of the control wave in the last active noise control example was still not completely exact. Nonetheless, as the match becomes closer and closer, the results become more and more impressive. So it is with our spiritual lives.

There is one other concept that I would like to mention briefly. Going back to my active noise control analogy, if things get out of alignment with our control system, we can lose the control effect we are striving for. To deal with this problem, we generally use digital control systems that are adaptive in nature and can correct for those errors that may creep in over time. This is not unlike our spiritual lives. Due to our mortal natures, we do things in our lives that can degrade our spiritual strength. Uncorrected, this will lead to spiritual illness and eventually spiritual death. So how do we correct for these spiritual errors as we go through our lives? The answer, of course, is repentance, but I want to emphasize that we need repentance that is centered on the Savior. If we make mistakes in our lives, we can sometimes correct them on our own—but, generally, it is the hard way to do it. The Savior offered a much easier and more effective way when He said:

And if men come unto me I will show unto them their weakness. I give unto men weakness that they may be humble; and my grace is sufficient for all men that humble themselves before me; for if they humble themselves before me, and have faith in me, then will I make weak things become strong unto them. [Ether 12:27; emphasis added]

Although it may be difficult for us to completely understand the inner workings of the Atonement of the Savior, we nonetheless know everything we need to know to be recipients of its power. The Atonement brings an enabling power into our lives—cleansing us, strengthening us, and buoying us up through the challenges of life that would derail us from the path we are striving to follow. The Atonement is not only important if we have committed a major transgression. It is also there to strengthen us in all aspects of our lives.

In speaking of the coming of Jesus Christ, Alma taught his people:

And [Christ] shall go forth, suffering pains and afflictions and temptations of every kind; and this that the word might be fulfilled which saith he will take upon him the pains and the sicknesses of his people.

And he will take upon him death, that he may loose the bands of death which bind his people; and he will take upon him their infirmities, that his bowels may be filled with mercy, according to the flesh, that he may know according to the flesh how to succor his people according to their infirmities. [Alma 7:11–12]

The Savior understands you and He understands me. He knows the challenges we face and understands our feelings when we get down because life isn't going as well as we would like it to. These things can often be precursors to straying off from the path that we are striving to follow, but as we focus on the Savior and His Atonement, He can succor us, buoy us up, and give us strength and resolve to do what we should.

Nephi was one of the great prophets of the Book of Mormon. But it is apparent that life got him down on occasion as well. Shortly after the death of Lehi, Nephi was struggling some with life—Laman and Lemuel were yet again angry with him, and perhaps he was still feeling the loss of his father, Lehi. In this frame of mind, he wrote:

My heart sorroweth because of my flesh; my soul grieveth because of mine iniquities.

I am encompassed about, because of the temptations and the sins which do so easily beset me.

And when I desire to rejoice, my heart groaneth because of my sins; nevertheless, I know in whom I have trusted. [2 Nephi 4:17–19]

Now, I don't know about you, but I have a difficult time believing that Nephi was talking about any sins here that we might categorize as being major. In fact, I wouldn't be surprised if the sins he was referring to were his frustration with his bullheaded brothers and perhaps feelings of wanting to beat them over the head with a two-by-four. Whatever the case, there is a great lesson that we can learn from Nephi as he dealt with these feelings in going to the Lord. As he prayed, he said:

O Lord, wilt thou redeem my soul? Wilt thou deliver me out of the hands of mine enemies? Wilt thou make me that I may shake at the appearance of sin? . . .

O Lord, wilt thou encircle me around in the robe of thy righteousness! . . . Wilt thou make my path straight before me! . . .

*O Lord, I have trusted in thee, and I will trust in thee forever. I will
not put my trust in the arm of flesh; for I know that cursed is he that
putteth his trust in the arm of flesh.* [2 Nephi 4:31, 33–34]

Through his desire to be fully committed and exact in his discipleship, Nephi received strength to move forward and be the person our
Father in Heaven wanted him to be. So can it be with us.

As Moroni finished the Book of Mormon, his last words of
counsel for each of us were:

*Yea, come unto Christ, and be perfected in him, and deny yourselves of
all ungodliness; and if ye shall deny yourselves of all ungodliness, and love
God with all your might, mind and strength, then is his grace sufficient for
you, that by his grace ye may be perfect in Christ. . . .*

*And again, if ye by the grace of God are perfect in Christ, and deny
not his power, then are ye sanctified in Christ by the grace of God, through
the shedding of the blood of Christ, which is in the covenant of the Father
unto the remission of your sins, that ye become holy, without spot.* [Moroni
10:32–33]

May each of us follow this counsel to come unto Christ, to be His
disciples with all our might, mind, and strength and thereby enjoy the
sanctifying power of the Atonement in our lives. I know through a
personal witness of the Spirit that Jesus Christ is the Son of God, that
He was resurrected, and that He lives today. Because of His love for
us, He carried out the Atonement for me and for you, making it possible for each of us to return to our Father in Heaven as we become
the disciples He would have us be. Of this I bear testimony in the
name of Jesus Christ, amen.

"Fresh Courage Take"

David A. Hunt

My dear brothers and sisters, I express my gratitude for the privilege of sharing this devotional hour with you and pray that my words will help to invite the Spirit to touch our hearts and minds.

During my career here at the university, I have had numerous opportunities to witness the magnitude of struggles students can face. I admire and applaud those who pursue their academic goals while overcoming great difficulties and seemingly insurmountable challenges. The plight of a student overwhelmed by studies, financial burdens, health concerns, homesickness, and social relationships—just to name a few—is not uncommon. At best these may be difficult to bear; other times they seem impossible. I have often found that in the midst of these seemingly impossible circumstances, great relief and even joy can come as our understanding is deepened by spiritual encouragement and continued obedience to Heavenly Father's commandments.

David A. Hunt was assistant administrative vice president of Student Auxiliary Services when this devotional address was given on 8 August 2006. © *Brigham Young University.*

On April 15, 1846, William Clayton was asked by President Brigham Young to compose the hymn "Come, Come, Ye Saints."[1] The purpose of this hymn was to give encouragement and support to the early pioneers as they would gather around their campfires at the end of the day. It was meant to help them forget the many difficulties and trials of their journey.[2] Even today the singing of this hymn lends comfort in our trials and inspires us to "gird up [our] loins" and "fresh courage take."[3]

"THOUGH HARD TO YOU THIS JOURNEY MAY APPEAR"

I wonder if we had such thoughts when we sat in the Grand Council in Heaven as spirit children of our heavenly parents before this earth was formed. In that great gathering we each had the privilege of hearing our Heavenly Father's plan for this mortal existence. We learned that through this earth-life experience we would have the opportunity to become like our exalted parents. The prophets have revealed that we all sang together and "shouted for joy"[4] at this glorious news.

We were taught that this life would be a time of probation in which we would be faced with trials and tests, but if we were found true and faithful and *thankful* in all things, we would inherit all that our Heavenly Father had prepared for us. I feel confident that in spite of the challenges we knew we would face, we were still eager to experience this mortal state.

As a result of the Fall of Adam and Eve, the Lord declared that the *ground* would be cursed for Adam's sake. It is important to note that the scriptures specify that "the ground"—not Adam—was cursed and that it would be for his "sake," meaning for his benefit as well as for that of all his posterity.[5] This would mean that Adam and his children would need to labor all their days, overcoming challenges and obstacles to obtain even the basic necessities of life.

Adam and Eve were later instructed by an angel of the Lord who taught them the gospel and explained the plan of redemption and exaltation. They were told:

*It must needs be that the devil should tempt the children of men, or they
could not be agents unto themselves; for if they never should have bitter
they could not know the sweet.*[6]

They were also told that a Savior would come to redeem all mankind,
so that all Adam's children would have an opportunity to return to
our Heavenly Father.

Imagine Adam and Eve's joy as they received this eternal truth.
Eve exclaimed:

*Were it not for our transgression we never should have had seed, and never
should have known good and evil, and the joy of our redemption, and the
eternal life which God giveth unto all the obedient.*[7]

"'TIS BETTER FAR FOR US TO STRIVE"

A primary reason for coming to this mortal life was to prove our
ability to make choices in the face of opposition. Overcoming opposition in this mortal probation is essential to our eternal progress. The
prophet Lehi said to his son Jacob:

*For it must needs be, that there is an opposition in all things. If not so
. . . , righteousness could not be brought to pass, neither wickedness, neither
holiness nor misery, neither good nor bad.*[8]

This life and its accompanying pain, temptation, sickness, and
sorrow is part of the plan for our eternal progress. "Adam fell that
men might be; and men are, that they might have joy."[9] This law of
opposition makes it possible for us to recognize goodness, virtue, and
joy, along with having an appreciation for well-being. This law makes
freedom of choice possible, and if we humbly submit to the will of
our Heavenly Father and follow His counsel to yield to His Spirit and
resist temptation, God promises to "consecrate thine afflictions for thy
gain."[10]

When going through a difficult trial in our life, which one of us
has not asked the Lord: "Why me?" As the trial continues or grows

more intense, we may even wonder: "How long can I endure this before I am overcome?" It is in the midst of such questioning that we can be led to greater empathy for others who have endured life's trials and persecution. In a small way we gain a greater appreciation for the suffering the Savior bore for our sake:

Which suffering caused [Him], *even God, the greatest of all, to tremble because of pain, and to bleed at every pore, and to suffer both body and spirit—and would that* [He] *might not drink the bitter cup, and shrink.*[11]

In his moments of greatest struggle, the Prophet Joseph Smith pleaded with the Lord to respond to these questions in a way that would give him understanding. Out of the depths of his suffering and heartache, the Lord answered his cry as recorded in section 121 of the Doctrine and Covenants:

My son, peace be unto thy soul; thine adversity and thine afflictions shall be but a small moment;
And then, if thou endure it well, God shall exalt thee on high; thou shalt triumph over all thy foes.[12]

The Prophet later stated: "I think I never could have felt as I now do, if I had not suffered the wrongs that I have suffered. All things shall work together for good to them that love God."[13]

Elder Russell M. Nelson shared with us: "The precise challenge you regard now as 'impossible' may be the very refinement you need, in His eye."[14]

"AND SHOULD WE DIE BEFORE OUR JOURNEY'S THROUGH"

Physical suffering and death are part of the challenges we face in this mortal existence. They will visit all of us sometime.

In February 1837, Noah Rogers and his wife, Eda Hollister, joined the Church in New York. Noah gave up his practice as a physician, and with his wife and eight children, he set out to become part of the gathering Saints in Missouri. A ninth child was born to them the following year.

Noah and his family endured many hardships on their journey to Missouri, even being threatened by hostile mobs who demanded that they turn back or be killed. Undaunted in their desire to participate more fully in the blessings of the restored gospel, Noah and Eda continued onward until they were able to join a body of Saints in Commerce, Illinois, which later became know as Nauvoo the Beautiful.

While working in his field one day, Noah was kidnapped by a party of mobsters and taken across the state line into Missouri. In the hands of the mobsters he was dragged into the woods, bound, brutally beaten, and then confined in chains in a small shed for several months simply because he was a "Mormon." Noah eventually regained his strength and was able to escape back to his family.

In April conference of 1843, Noah Rogers was called on a mission to Vermont. Soon after this, a new mission call was extended to preach the gospel among the people of the islands of French Polynesia in the region known as the Society Islands. He was to be accompanied by Addison Pratt, Benjamin F. Grouard, and Knowlton Hanks. The small group of missionaries quickly prepared for their journey and bid farewell to their families, trusting that they would be taken care of amidst the ever-increasing storm of hatred and bigotry aimed at the early Saints. Their missionary journals and letters home describe the many trials and hardships they endured as they made their way to the islands over the next nine months.

Their missionary companion Elder Hanks had been sick before leaving Nauvoo and progressively got worse. He refused to turn back. He was fearful that he would not be able to fulfill his mission and kept hoping that the long sea voyage and priesthood administrations would restore his health. He insisted that if he must die, at least it would be as near his mission field as possible. Elder Hanks' condition continued to worsen until he died on November 3, 1843. It was a sad and mournful event as his companions watched his body be wrapped in "a bit of old sail"[15] and dropped into the sea.

The remaining three missionaries continued their journey, finally arriving in Tahiti to begin the work of preaching the restored gospel throughout the surrounding Polynesian islands. Not all their efforts were met with great success. Noah encountered major opposition from the established churches on the islands he visited. After many months and many miles traveling from island to island, he was given a release to return home.

His journey back to Nauvoo again proved to be extremely difficult. He returned via the Orient, becoming the first missionary to circumnavigate the globe. Letters and communication from his wife and family were essentially nonexistent for his entire absence of two and a half years. He had heard rumors of the Martyrdom of the Prophet Joseph Smith, but, beyond that, news was only hearsay, and he feared greatly for the safety of his loved ones.

Noah arrived back in Nauvoo on December 29, 1845, finding his family, along with the majority of the Saints, driven out of the city and living on the outskirts. Nevertheless, it was a joyful reunion, and shortly thereafter he and Eda were able to receive their endowments in the newly completed temple. They were among the last Saints to receive this sacred ordinance before being forced to flee across the frozen Mississippi River and eventually set up camp on the windswept prairie at Mount Pisgah, Iowa. There Noah became ill and passed away within a matter of days. A couple of his sons fashioned a coffin out of a wagon box and buried him in a small cemetery that was to become the resting place for hundreds of other Saints who likewise perished along the trail.

Eda Rogers had lost her beloved husband. Other family members soon followed him in death. Eda and her sister Amanda recorded:

Our afflictions seemingly were greater than we could bear, yet we trust in God and feel that He will support and comfort the widow and the fatherless.

. . . We feel not to complain nor murmur but to go ahead in the things of the Lord.[16]

Many critics could say that Noah Rogers' life ended without his having accomplished much—that his sacrifice to answer the call to serve a mission resulted in little success and robbed him of precious time with his family. Of what worth were his struggles? His death and burial were unheralded events and were marked by a simple journal entry and a wooden grave marker. His grieving widow was left to move on with her children to the Salt Lake Valley. Yet who among us can question the designs of our Heavenly Father?

Noah and Eda Rogers' example of quietly submitting themselves to the will of the Lord set a sure foundation for their posterity. I am honored to be numbered in that lineage.

The records of our collective pioneer ancestry as well as scriptural documentation teach us that when resistance and opposition are greatest, we also have the greatest potential for growth in our faith, our commitment, and our advancement. As witnessed in the Book of Mormon, complacency and eventual loss of faith result when opposition is minimal. Alma lamented, "Thus we see how quick the children of men do forget the Lord their God, yea, how quick to do iniquity, and to be led away by the evil one."[17]

As we look back on the past 176 years of Church history, we can testify that our progress today has been made possible because of the early Saints who were able to faithfully encounter and overcome opposition. I trust that future generations will likewise be able to look back on our generation and attribute their progress to our own faithfulness and courage.

"WHY SHOULD WE THINK TO EARN A GREAT REWARD IF WE NOW SHUN THE FIGHT?"

How can we expect to receive the fullness of the blessings the Lord has prepared for us if we quit the battle because the fight is difficult and the odds seem against us? Truly, we cannot expect to gain the reward our Heavenly Father has prepared for us if we "shun the fight" or surrender partway through the battle.

In the Old Testament we find another exemplar of great faith and obedience. The prophet Gideon, of ancient Israel, found himself facing a seemingly impossible obstacle. The book of Judges relates, "All the Midianites and the Amalekites and the children of the east were gathered together,"[18] prepared to give battle to the Israelites under Gideon's command. Like many of us in overwhelming situations, Gideon seriously doubted the odds of winning such a conflict. He pleaded with the Lord to confirm that he was the right one to lead Israel into triumph and devised a couple of tests by which the Lord could do so.

And Gideon said unto God, If thou wilt save Israel by mine hand, as thou hast said,

Behold, I will put a fleece of wool in the floor; and if the dew be on the fleece only, and it be dry upon all the earth beside, then shall I know that thou wilt save Israel by mine hand, as thou hast said.

And it was so: for he rose up early on the morrow, and thrust the fleece together, and wringed the dew out of the fleece, a bowl full of water.[19]

Gideon, wanting not to mistake the Lord's answer and continuing to doubt his own ability to conquer such a mighty foe, approached Him once again and prayed:

Let not thine anger be hot against me, and I will speak but this once: let me prove, I pray thee, but this once with the fleece; let it now be dry only upon the fleece, and upon all the ground let there be dew.

And God did so that night: for it was dry upon the fleece only, and there was dew on all the ground.[20]

With this miraculous confirmation Gideon must have been feeling reassured, but it was now the Lord's turn to prove Gideon and to teach the host of Israel that they must always look to Him for salvation rather than rely upon their own strength. Gideon was commanded to dismiss any of the warriors who were fearful of going into battle. Twenty-two thousand departed, leaving only 10 thousand.[21]

The Lord then informed Gideon that he still had too many soldiers, and another reduction was made, leaving only 300 men to deliver Israel from the Midianites, who were in numbers "like grasshoppers for multitude."[22] With this unlikely army the Lord proceeded to deliver a victory to the outnumbered Israelites.

We each have occasions in our lives when we feel overwhelmed and far outnumbered with life's battles. We can be put in the midst of trials that shake us to the very core and test our ability to hang on. President Gordon B. Hinckley encourages us to remain true even when the odds seem against us. He challenges us: "Be true to yourselves and the best you have within you"; likewise, "Be true to our Eternal Father and His Beloved Son."[23]

I sincerely believe that if we are humble and obedient to the Lord, we will find His helping hand even in the worst of circumstances. I also testify that many of the choicest instructions the Lord would have us receive will come in the midst of our greatest trials.

"FRESH COURAGE TAKE"

Often our struggles and challenges are accompanied by feelings of isolation and loneliness. Our initial suffering can make us feel that we are alone and that no one can possibly understand the depth of our pain or comprehend the magnitude of our trial. We seek consolation from others who can share our burden—those who can care about us and understand the nature of our burden.

In a peaceful cemetery located south of the BYU campus, there is a section of graves specifically set apart for the burial of infants and small children. This particular place is surrounded by the graves of others of all ages who have been laid to rest by loving family and friends. My wife and I cannot visit this particular area in the cemetery without thinking of similar mothers and fathers who had such wonderful expectations and hopes for their child, only to have them laid to rest in an untimely season.

If you visit this particular section of the cemetery on certain days of the year, you will find a small flower or decoration placed on every infant's grave. No grave is forgotten. This small token represents the expression of love and understanding by another mother and father who faced a similar trial and who now reach out to console others.

Fresh courage is received when such selfless acts of service and compassion are freely given. Not only does our compassionate service help another, it provides the vehicle to lift us from our own sorrow and misery. We are commanded to bear one another's burdens, and, as Latter-day Saints, we truly understand the importance the Savior has put on selfless service to others. The Lord does not place any restrictions upon us in our participation in good works. As brothers and sisters in the gospel, helping one another, giving comfort and support, and sacrificing on behalf of those in need should be second nature to us. Our own trials and tribulations cannot justify withholding our love and service to others.

"OUR GOD WILL NEVER US FORSAKE"

Elder Eldred G. Smith admonished us:

> *Remember that this world was created and all the development and the progress on this earth from Adam till now have been primarily for* you *as much as anyone else.*
> *Christ came to atone for* you.
> *The gospel was restored for* you.
> *The Lord will answer* your *prayers.*
> *God is mindful of* you, *for* you *are* [His child].
> *It is true—each has a different life to live and a different task to fill. Some tasks may be more important than others, but you—a son or daughter of God—are just as important to God as anyone else.*[24]

With faith in the Lord, you can even do hard things, for "with God all things are possible."[25] Power to overcome our trials, as well as protection from the adversary, will come as we obey the commandments and live according to the counsel we receive from the prophets. The Lord has promised:

> *For I will go before your face. I will be on your right hand and on your left, and my Spirit shall be in your hearts, and mine angels round about you, to bear you up.*[26]

"WITH THE JUST WE SHALL DWELL!"

I feel quite confident that if we look closely, with a sensitive heart, each of us can recognize someone who is an example of the teachings of the Savior—someone who "cleave[s] unto charity" while bearing all things and enduring all things.

We are taught in Moroni in the Book of Mormon:

> *And charity* suffereth long, *and is kind, and envieth not, and is not puffed up, seeketh not her own, is not easily provoked, thinketh no evil, and rejoiceth not in iniquity but rejoiceth in the truth,* beareth all things, *believeth all things, hopeth all things,* endureth all things.
> . . . *For charity never faileth. Wherefore, cleave unto charity, which is the greatest of all, for all things must fail—*
> *But charity is the pure love of Christ.*[27]

One of the choicest examples in my personal life of "charity [that] never faileth" was manifest in the life of a close friend known to my family as Grandma Gardner. Muriel Gardner recently passed away after a courageous fight with cancer.

While this sweet lady was not directly related to us, her example of the pure love of Christ made me and my family feel that we were her own. We were prayed over, watched over, and blessed by her faith throughout the past 30 years of our lives. She always seemed to know when we were at a challenging crossroad and needed additional help or encouragement.

She would not be considered as anyone of great acclaim or importance. She did not change the world, nor was she instrumental in making any remarkable contribution to her community. Grandma Gardner was just an ordinary individual trying to live the best she knew how. It was through the latter refining months of her life that she exclaimed that she finally "got it"—meaning that she finally understood the purpose of the Atonement and Christ's love for each of us.

Her own life was filled with trials and challenges. She bore them with dignity and thankfulness to the Lord for allowing her to be an instrument in His hands. Always a vibrant and lively person, she refused to let cancer destroy her love of the Lord. Never did she blame the Lord for the afflictions she bore. She continued to express her testimony and faith in writing—even when the cancerous growth took away her ability to speak and bear testimony vocally. She hoped that by doing so, her family and friends would be led to say that they also got it. I am grateful that the Lord placed this dear sister along my life's path as an example to me.

"BUT WITH JOY WEND YOUR WAY"

President Hinckley reminds us that even in the midst of opposition and turmoil, "life is to be enjoyed, not just endured."[28] In the gospel sense, enduring to the end is more than just physically abiding. The greatest victory comes to those who endure with joy and gratitude, with a deep abiding faith in the divine purpose of life's mortal existence. This was affirmed by the Lord when He stated to the early Saints through the Prophet Joseph Smith:

> *Verily, verily, I say unto you, ye are little children, and ye have not as yet understood how great blessings the Father hath in his own hands and prepared for you;*
>
> *And ye cannot bear all things now; nevertheless, be of good cheer, for I will lead you along. The kingdom is yours and the blessings thereof are yours, and the riches of eternity are yours.*
>
> *And he who receiveth all things with thankfulness shall be made glorious; and the things of this earth shall be added unto him, even an hundred fold, yea more.*[29]

I have shared with you some thoughts on the need for opposition in all things. I do not pretend to know all the reasons that the Lord has for giving us trials and obstacles, but let me review some of the reasons that I would like to leave with you today by way of the examples I have just given.

First, I believe the Lord provides opportunities for us to be tested because He wants to know on whom He can depend and trust. The

Lord found that He could trust Noah and Eda Rogers to be faithful in whatever circumstances they were given. He knew He could trust Gideon because he was willing to follow His counsel even in the midst of incredible odds. The Lord uses trials to help us grow in faithfulness and obedience.

Second, the Lord tells us in section 122 of the Doctrine and Covenants that adversity came to the Prophet Joseph Smith to give him experience and to be for his good.[30] Opposition and adversity are necessary experiences in the course of our eternal progression. The great plan of happiness demands that we experience trial and sorrow as we strive to overcome, "for if they never should have bitter they could not know the sweet."[31] President James E. Faust stated: "The suffering of the Savior in Gethsemane was without question the greatest that has ever come to mankind, yet out of it came the greatest good in the promise of eternal life."[32]

Third, our individual struggles and suffering teach us to relate to the Atonement of Christ in a deep and profound way that cannot be learned through any other experience. As exemplified by Sister Gardner, our capacity to show empathy and compassion for another is heightened by our own endurance and suffering. My personal witness is that only through such experiences can a person develop true charity—the pure love of Christ.

Please be assured that there is purpose in it all. The Lord has promised to give us His power and protection as we live righteous lives. I pray that we can each take fresh courage and truly find the refuge that God has prepared for us in our personal lives, where we will be blessed with those who overcome the trials of this life, where we too can exclaim: "All is well! All is well!" I humbly pray in the name of Jesus Christ, amen.

NOTES

1. William Clayton journal entry of 15 April 1846.

2. See "Guide Lessons for March," Lesson III: Literature, *Relief Society Magazine*, January 1921, 58.

3. "Come, Come, Ye Saints," *Hymns*, 1985, no. 30; and for all subsequent quotations from this hymn.

4. Job 38:7.

5. Moses 4:23.

6. D&C 29:39.

7. Moses 5:11.

8. 2 Nephi 2:11.

9. 2 Nephi 2:25.

10. 2 Nephi 2:2.

11. D&C 19:18.

12. D&C 121:7–8.

13. *HC* 3:286.

14. Russell M. Nelson, "With God Nothing Shall Be Impossible," *Ensign*, May 1988, 35.

15. Inez Smith Davis, "A Mission to the South Sea Islands," in *The Story of the Church*, 3rd ed. (Independence, Missouri: Herald Publishing House, 1943), 288.

16. *Sketch of the Life of Noah Rogers and His Wife, Eda Hollister*, comp. Julia Fellows Rogers; www.timeforitnow.knotsindeed.com/genealogy/NoahRogersEdaHollister.html.

17. Alma 46:8.

18. Judges 6:33.

19. Judges 6:36–38.

20. Judges 6:39–40.

21. See Judges 7:2–3.

22. Judges 7:12.

23. Gordon B. Hinckley, "Stand True and Faithful," *Ensign*, May 1996, 92, 93.

24. Eldred G. Smith, "Opposition in Order to Strengthen Us," *Ensign*, January 1974, 63; emphasis in original.

25. Matthew 19:26.

26. D&C 84:88.

27. Moroni 7:45–47; emphasis added.

28. Hinckley, "Stand True," 94.

29. D&C 78:17–19.

30. See D&C 122:5–7.

31. D&C 29:39.

32. James E. Faust, "The Blessings of Adversity," *Ensign*, February 1998, 4.

Truth Restored

———◆———

Dieter F. Uchtdorf

M y dear brothers and sisters, Brigham Young University has always been a very special place to our family. When our children were teenagers, they attended the different summer programs on the BYU campus. And my wife, Harriet, and I went to a course called Especially for Parents, aimed to improve parenting. We never dared ask our children whether this class really improved our parenting. I have to admit, however, that they turned out to be great kids anyhow. I account this to the goodness of their mother and the tender mercies of God.

In those younger years my wife and I enjoyed very much the opportunities to occasionally come all the way from Germany to attend BYU Campus Education Week. Back then we stayed at Helaman Halls, and for this short period of time we felt like real BYU students. We met great people and had a wonderful time. My wife was super-perfect in planning our days. Since we wanted to learn as much as possible, she scheduled each of us for different lectures.

Dieter F. Uchtdorf was a member of the Quorum of the Twelve Apostles of The Church of Jesus Christ of Latter-day Saints when this devotional address was given on 22 August 2006 during Campus Education Week. © *Intellectual Reserve, Inc.*

Then, during lunch breaks and in the evenings, we exchanged notes and shared our impressions. We still have many books filled with notes—unfortunately never again to be looked at after we had left the campus. But, make no mistake, it was a great experience, and we will always treasure these wonderful memories very close to our hearts.

Sister Uchtdorf and I are so happy to be with you today and feel of your wonderful spirit. We are grateful for your testimonies and for your dedication as members of The Church of Jesus Christ of Latter-day Saints. You are living witnesses of the truth restored. We thank you for your exemplary lives as mothers and fathers, single adults, single parents, and grandparents. We know that many of you have come from far away and at a significant sacrifice. I also would like to thank all who have organized this education week and all who will teach and are teaching.

I am especially grateful for this year's theme—Seek Learning—which is taken from the Lord's injunction to "seek learning, even by study and also by faith" (D&C 88:118).

The restored Church of Jesus Christ has always encouraged its members to pursue knowledge and education through study and also by faith—line upon line and precept upon precept.

For us, knowledge is understood to be an active, motivating force rather than simply a passive awareness of facts. Indeed, certain truths must be understood and applied because they are essential for salvation and eternal life (see John 17:3; 1 John 4:7–8). The Prophet Joseph Smith taught that "a man is saved no faster than he gets knowledge, for if he does not get knowledge, he will be brought into captivity" (*HC* 4:588). His words build on the Savior's commandment: "Ye shall know the truth, and the truth shall make you free" (John 8:32).

It is knowledge of truth that makes us free to exercise our moral agency and freedom of choice (see Helaman 14:30–31). God Himself defines His glory in terms of light and truth. In modern-day revelation we read, "The glory of God is intelligence, or, in other words, light and truth" (D&C 93:36). Perhaps this is why "pure knowledge

. . . shall greatly enlarge the soul" (D&C 121:42). The more knowledge of truth we have, the better we can progress spiritually.

The scriptures encourage us to seek deeply and broadly to gain knowledge of both heavenly and earthly things (see D&C 88:77–80).

What is this knowledge, this intelligence, this light and truth that our Heavenly Father would have us receive? Certainly it is found in the scriptures and in the words of the living prophets. But it also includes what we consider to be secular. Some of the early apostles had little secular learning, while others were highly educated in the eyes of the world. Regardless of their different backgrounds in secular education, all of the apostles knew the weightier matters of life; all of them knew the path to eternal life.

It is wise, therefore, to keep a balanced and eternal perspective when seeking and studying all knowledge—revealed and secular. If we proceed on this path, we will learn to master ourselves, which in turn enables us to master this beautiful earth and its vast opportunities. And it will help us to become a more effective tool in the hands of the Lord. It will help us to become peacemakers in a world of wars and rumors of war.

My dear brothers and sisters, let us remember that all truth, all pure knowledge, can be circumscribed by the restored gospel of Jesus Christ. Of all the treasures of knowledge, the most vital is the knowledge of God—of His existence, His powers, His love, and His promises.

This is why the Restoration of the gospel is such a tremendous blessing and of such great importance for each and every one of us. Every gift and power and grace of God that was available when Jesus Christ walked the earth has been restored in our time.

Through the knowledge of the Restoration we learn that God has a plan for us that will enable us to both enjoy the beauties of life and cope with its sorrows and disappointments. This divine plan was established before the foundation of the earth and can enable us to return to our Heavenly Father one day. The sacred knowledge of this plan brought us joy when we accepted it in our premortal life, and it gives us an eternal vision as we follow it in this life.

The Restoration of the gospel opens doors to glorious sources of knowledge and wisdom. Jesus taught, "The Spirit of truth . . . will guide you into all truth" (John 16:13). And the Book of Mormon, a tangible witness of this Restoration, speaks to us through the prophet Moroni, that "by the power of the Holy Ghost [we] may know the truth of all things" (Moroni 10:5).

Secular knowledge alone can never save a soul nor open the celestial kingdom to anyone. Life itself, the gospel, and God cannot be understood through research alone. For that understanding we must be taught from on high. Jacob reminded us: "To be learned is good if [we] hearken unto the counsels of God" (2 Nephi 9:29). The ancient word *hearken* means to listen and to pay attention to God's words given through the scriptures and by the living prophets. Faithful application of gospel principles is the key. Applying knowledge of divine truth leads to wisdom.

Our learning, even by study and also by faith, when directed toward the Restoration, will give us supernal knowledge and wisdom to cope with the challenges of daily life and prepare us to receive all the blessings of eternity.

Therefore, I would like to make this message my testimony of the "restitution of all things" (Acts 3:21)—meaning, of course, the restoration of all things. God lives, and He speaks today as He did anciently. This is the message and the testimony we as Church members need to have in our hearts and in our minds and carry into all the world.

As we share our testimony with others, I hope that we will have the same convincing power and enthusiasm the members had who brought the message to Brigham Young. He said:

The brethren who came to preach the Gospel to me, I could easily out-talk them . . . ; but their testimony was like fire in my bones; I understood the spirit of their preaching; I received that spirit; it was light, intelligence, power, and truth, and it bore witness to my spirit, and that was enough for me. [Remarks by Brigham Young, 28 July 1861; *JD* 9:141; also reported in *Deseret News Weekly*, 2 October 1861, 177]

Please allow me at this point to give special thanks to my wife, Harriet, for her witness and testimony of the Restoration of the gospel of Jesus Christ. And let me share with you the story of how my wife's family became converted to the gospel many years ago.

One Sunday when I was a teenager attending the Frankfurt Branch in Germany, the missionaries brought a young mother and her two beautiful daughters to our church meetings. At that age I had no real interest in girls; however, I still remember the impressions I had when I saw those two young girls walking into our chapel. The older daughter, especially, with her large brown eyes and beautiful black hair, immediately caught my attention. I thought, "These missionaries are doing a really great job!" Little did I know that this young lady would later bless my life forever.

But I'm getting ahead of the story. Let me go back and start with how this young family met the missionaries.

In the fall of 1954, two missionaries were ringing the doorbells inside of an apartment building in the city of Frankfurt. Beginning with the doors on the main level, they gradually worked their way up the floors without any success. No one invited them in or wanted to listen to their message. But these were dedicated and faithful missionaries, and they did not give up or try another, perhaps more fruitful, apartment building. Finally they rang the bell of the last door on the fourth floor. It was opened by young Harriet Reich, who immediately asked her mother to invite them in. Sister Carmen Reich initially hesitated, but after some additional pleading by Harriet, she finally invited Elder Gary Jenkins from California and his companion into their home.

These two missionaries were truly guided by the Spirit, not only in where to go but also in what to say. After briefly explaining who they were and what the message was they wanted to share, the missionaries left a Book of Mormon with the mother, asked her to read the marked scriptures, and departed with a prayer and a blessing. Two days later they returned. This time the missionaries received a friendly welcome and were invited in quickly. When they asked Sister Reich if she had read the marked scriptures in the Book of Mormon, she answered without hesitation, "I read the whole book, and I feel that it is true."

Sister Carmen Reich was only 36 at the time, a widow with two daughters. Only eight months before she had lost her husband, a renowned musician, to cancer. The family had always lived in good circumstances and had no need for financial help even after the loss of their husband and father. But after his unexpected death, they struggled with a number of unanswered questions: Is there a purpose in life? Is there anything after death? And, if so, what? Why are we born? Did we live before this life?

Representatives of a number of different religions approached them, trying to be of help. However, Sister Reich never felt a need for their assistance. The answers they offered were not new to her and not very helpful.

Let me make it clear that Sister Reich was a religious person. She loved to read, and the Bible was one of her favorite books. She was always seeking truth, even by study and faith. She believed firmly that Jesus is the Christ, and she taught her family to follow His teachings. They accepted Peter, Paul, Matthew, Mark, Luke, James, and John as apostles and regarded their teachings highly. This family had always been happy. They were good, honest people, and even the loss of their husband and father could not take away their strong feeling of family.

However, when Sister Carmen Reich read the Book of Mormon cover to cover in two days, she felt something she had never before experienced. By her own account, it was "the spirit of revelation." Her experience was consistent with Joseph Smith's description of personal revelation; she said she could "feel pure intelligence flowing" into her, giving her "sudden strokes of ideas" about the things of the Spirit of God (*HC* 3:381). These ideas related to her special circumstances. The Spirit was able to teach her, for she was open and receptive to truth and light. As the missionaries taught her the plan of salvation and the other doctrines of the Restoration, she continued to grow in the principle of personal revelation. All the good things she had learned in her Lutheran faith received a new and a deeper meaning, and all of a sudden life itself had a totally different and divine eternal perspective.

It was not that she felt any disdain for what she had believed for so many years. She still loved many of the hymns she had sung at church. One of her favorites was (and continues to be in our family) "A Mighty Fortress Is Our God," by Martin Luther (*Hymns*, 1985, no. 68). She was also glad that she had learned to quote and internalize many key scriptures of the New Testament. But when she heard the message of the Restoration, a door was opened into a world flooded with light and filled with love and hope. Looking back, she described her experience this way: It was as if something of great importance had been lifeless and inert but was now resurrected to life, beauty, and activity.

Sister Reich, my dear mother-in-law, represents in many ways the multitude of converts who are coming into the Church every day from other religions—both Christian and non-Christian, and even from no religion at all. One characteristic is true of all of them—they are willing and pure enough to believe when God speaks.

Sister Reich was baptized on November 7, 1954. In December, only a few weeks after her baptism, the missionary who baptized her asked if she would write down her testimony. Elder Jenkins wanted to use her testimony to help others feel the true spirit of conversion. Fortunately, he kept her handwritten original for more than 40 years and then returned it to my mother-in-law as a very special gift of love. Sister Carmen Reich passed away in 2000 at age 83.

Let me read to you parts of her written testimony. It shows what she saw, at this time of her life, as the key points of the Restoration. Please bear in mind that you are listening to a sister who was taught and had accepted the restored gospel only a few weeks earlier. Before the missionaries came, she had never heard anything about the Book of Mormon, and she knew nothing about Joseph Smith or Mormons in general. Also keep in mind that in 1954 there were no temples outside the United States except in Canada. And remember that Sister Reich had recently lost her husband. This is the English translation of her handwritten testimony:

*Special characteristics of The Church of Jesus Christ of Latter-day
Saints that are not present in other religious communities include, above all:
Modern revelation given through the Prophet Joseph Smith.
Sacred priesthood authority as in the time of Christ, with a living
prophet today.*

*Next, the Book of Mormon in its clear and pure language, with all its
instructions and promises for the Church of Jesus Christ—truly a second
witness with the Bible that Jesus Christ lives.*

Faith in a personal God—that is, God the Father; God the Son [Jesus
Christ]; *and the Holy Ghost, who facilitates prayer and guides us personally.*

*Belief in a premortal life, the premortal existence. Knowledge of the
purpose of our earthly life and of our life after death. The plan of salvation
is so clearly laid out in the restored gospel that our lives receive new meaning
and direction.*

*The Word of Wisdom as a guide to help us to keep our body and spirit
healthy and improve them. This is our goal because we know that we will
take our body up again after death.*

*Temple work, with its many sacred ordinances enabling families to
be together forever. This doctrine, totally new to me, was given through
revelation to the Prophet Joseph Smith.*

How grateful I am for Sister Reich. How grateful I am for the
missionaries. How grateful I am for the families who had prepared
these missionaries. How grateful I am for the Restoration.

The key messages of the Restoration have the power to bring
divine feelings to the heart and mind of the earnest seeker of truth,
irrespective of the person's cultural or religious background. There
are no geographic or cultural boundaries for the Holy Ghost. The
Holy Ghost is not restricted by space, neither is the Spirit restricted
by time. We all have witnessed the power of the Spirit, and the scriptures testify of it: "[Jesus Christ] manifesteth himself unto all those
who believe in him, by the power of the Holy Ghost; yea, unto every
nation, kindred, tongue, and people" (2 Nephi 26:13).

My dear brothers and sisters, many of you have served as missionaries or have sent sons and daughters to lands and missions with

names you might have never heard before and geographic locations you may have had a hard time finding on the world map. Thank you for this wonderful service of love. At the same time, may I invite you to take a good look into the future. Your children, grandchildren, and great-grandchildren may be serving in countries and areas of the world with cultural and religious backgrounds totally different from your traditional mission fields. Your firm belief in and your willingness to testify of the Restoration today will prepare the ground for the successful service of future generations of missionaries. These future missionaries, prepared by you, will be a great blessing to individuals, to families, and to the peoples of the world.

As members of the Church of Jesus Christ, we have a responsibility to extend the message of the restored gospel of Jesus Christ, as guided by the Spirit, to every corner of the world. Sometimes this corner may be located in our own home—perhaps in our own family. And we have a special privilege and responsibility to prepare our youth for this service of love by building their personal testimonies. That responsibility should not overwhelm us. Let us be humbled by it, but not overwhelmed.

It may be helpful to recall the Savior's charge and the promises He gave to His disciples. They are still applicable to us today. Jesus said:

> *Go ye therefore, and teach* all nations, *baptizing them in the name of the Father, and of the Son, and of the Holy Ghost:*
> *Teaching them to observe all things whatsoever I have commanded you: and, lo, I am with you alway, even unto* the end of the world. [Matthew 28:19–20; emphasis added]

> *Ye shall receive power, after that the Holy Ghost is come upon you: and ye shall be witnesses unto me both in Jerusalem . . . and unto* the uttermost part of the earth. [Acts 1:8; emphasis added]

You and I have the same responsibility and promise today. Members of the Church live in all parts of the world—sometimes in the uttermost parts of the earth. To one person Germany may be the uttermost part. To someone from New York City, the uttermost part of the earth—*the farthest away*—may be the town of Preston, Idaho. Or New York City may qualify as the uttermost part of the earth for those who have lived all their lives in Manti, Utah. Wherever we may be, we are expected to invite our neighbors, friends, and acquaintances to come, see, and experience what the restored gospel is all about. We can invite them to our homes and to our church meetings.

As members of The Church of Jesus Christ of Latter-day Saints, we invite people of all backgrounds—many of which are very different from our own—to come unto Christ. We should not hesitate to invite those of other religions. Many of these good people have been seeking for the truth, even by study and also by faith, for a long time. We need to reach out to them in a courageous way with a sweet boldness, with love, and with a pure desire to share the truth from which they have been kept "because they know not where to find it" (D&C 123:12).

President Gordon B. Hinckley said:

We do not stand out in opposition to other churches. We respect all men for all the good that they do, and we say to those of all churches, we honor the good that you do and we invite you to come and see what further good we can do for you. [*TGBH*, 667]

The Prophet Joseph Smith explained:

We don't ask any people to throw away any good they have got; we only ask them to come and get more. [*HC* 5:259]

President Howard W. Hunter quoted President George Albert Smith and then expanded on his words:

In our humble efforts to build brotherhood and to teach revealed truth, we say to the people of the world what President George Albert Smith so lovingly suggested:

"We have come not to take away from you the truth and virtue you possess. We have come not to find fault with you nor to criticize you. We have not come here to berate you because of things you have not done; but we have come here as your brethren . . . and to say to you: 'Keep all the good that you have, and let us bring to you more good, in order that you may be happier and in order that you may be prepared to enter into the presence of our Heavenly Father.'" (Sharing the Gospel with Others, *comp. Preston Nibley [Salt Lake City: Deseret News Press, 1948], pp. 12–13). . . .*

Ours is a perennial religion based on eternal, saving truth. Its message of love and brotherhood is lodged in scripture and in the revelations of the Lord to his living prophet. It embraces all truth. It circumscribes all wisdom—all that God has revealed to man, and all that he will yet reveal. [Howard W. Hunter, "The Gospel—A Global Faith," *Ensign*, November 1991, 19]

The Restoration in its fulness completes and enhances the truths found in the religions of the world.

Latter-day Saints are occasionally accused of being narrow-minded or unwilling to consider the beliefs of others. Such accusations may be true of Latter-day Saints who do not understand their own religion, but those who know the position of the Church regarding the beliefs of other people willingly allow all to "worship how, where, or what they may" (Articles of Faith 1:11).

In a conference address in 1921, Elder Orson F. Whitney described many religious leaders as being inspired. He said:

[God] *is using not only his covenant people, but other peoples as well, to consummate a work, stupendous, magnificent, and altogether too arduous for this little handful of Saints to accomplish by and of themselves. . . .*

All down the ages men bearing the authority of the Holy Priesthood— patriarchs, prophets, apostles and others, have officiated in the name of the Lord, doing the things that he required of them; and outside the [limits] *of their activities other good and great men, not bearing the Priesthood, but possessing* [depth] *of thought, great wisdom, and a desire to uplift their fellows, have been sent by the Almighty into many nations, to give them, not the fulness of the Gospel, but that portion of truth that they were able to receive and wisely use.* [*CR*, April 1921, 32–33]

The First Presidency has clearly stated:

The great religious leaders of the world such as Mohammed, Confucius, and the Reformers, as well as philosophers including Socrates, Plato, and others, received a portion of God's light. Moral truths were given to them by God to enlighten whole nations and to bring a higher level of understanding to individuals. [Statement of the First Presidency regarding God's Love for All Mankind, 15 February 1978; included in James E. Faust, "Communion with the Holy Spirit," *Ensign*, May 1980, 12]

The religion into which a person is born may be incomplete, but it can still serve as a foundation for the reception of the fulness of the gospel. We are wise when we show respect for the beliefs of others.

Just as we recognize and support the privilege of others to worship God Almighty according to their conscience, so we claim the right to declare our faith and our testimony of the restored gospel of Jesus Christ according to our beliefs:

We talk of Christ, we rejoice in Christ, we preach of Christ, we prophesy of Christ, and we write according to our prophecies, that our children may know to what source they may look for a remission of their sins. [2 Nephi 25:26]

To share the message and the redemptive power of Christ and His Atonement with our friends and neighbors all over the world, we need to declare with courage and with clarity the events of 1820 and thereafter. These events, and the revelation that attended them, are what distinguish us from other religions and from any people with good intent.

The Restoration was foreseen by those with priesthood power and keys at the meridian of time. They understood why a restoration of truth and priesthood power would be necessary.

The Apostle Paul, writing from Corinth to the Saints in
Thessalonica, prophesied:

*Now we beseech you, brethren, by the coming of our Lord Jesus Christ,
and by our gathering together unto him,*
*That ye be not soon shaken in mind, or be troubled, neither by spirit,
nor by word, nor by letter as from us, as that the day of Christ is at hand.*
*Let no man deceive you by any means: for that day shall not come,
except there come a falling away first.* [2 Thessalonians 2:1–3]

If Paul knew that there would be a falling away, surely Jesus
knew. But while Jesus knew that the church He established during
His mortal ministry would be lost, He still established a divine
pattern because He also knew that future generations would be able
to recognize the very same priesthood authority and structure when
it was restored centuries later.

Eusebius, a historian of the Christian church in the fourth
century, wrote about this divine pattern:

*Our Lord and Saviour Jesus Christ, not very long after the commencement
of his public ministry, elected the twelve, whom he called Apostles, by way
of eminence over the rest of his disciples. He also appointed seventy others
beside these, whom he sent, two and two, before him into every place and city
whither he himself was about to go.* [Eusebius Pamphilus, *Ecclesiastical
History*, trans. Christian Frederick Crusé (Grand Rapids, Michigan:
Baker Book House, 1955), 40; book 1, chapter 10]

And Eusebius, quoting Hegesippus, also wrote about a falling
away:

*When the sacred choir of apostles became extinct, and the generation of those
that had been privileged to hear their inspired wisdom had passed away,
then also the combinations of* [immoral] *error arose by the fraud and delu-
sions of false teachers. . . . As there was none of the apostles left, henceforth*

[they] *attempted, without shame, to preach their false doctrine against the gospel of truth.* [Eusebius, *Ecclesiastical History,* 118; book 3, chapter 32]

Without the Prophet Joseph, we would still be in this same state of confusion and darkness. Some 1,500 years after Eusebius, Joseph found himself in the midst of a "war of words and tumult of opinions" about religion. He asked himself, "Who of all these parties are right?" "If any one of them be right, which is it, and how shall I know it?" (JS—H 1:10). Then he read James 1:5. And Joseph, this courageous 14-year-old, chose to "do as James directs, that is, ask of God" (JS—H 1:13).

Joseph went into the woods near his family home to offer his first vocal prayer to God. He had barely begun to offer up the desires of his heart when a power of darkness so overcame him that he could not speak (see JS—H 1:15). This was not an imaginary power but the power of some actual being from an unseen world trying to destroy him.

Joseph later testified:

[After] *exerting all my powers to call upon God . . . , I saw a pillar of light exactly over my head, above the brightness of the sun, which descended gradually until it fell upon me.*
*. . . When the light rested upon me I saw two Personages, whose brightness and glory defy all description, standing above me in the air. One of them spake unto me, calling me by name and said, pointing to the other—*This is My Beloved Son. Hear Him! [JS—H 1:16–17; emphasis in original]

From that day forward the heavens were open again. Joseph learned line upon line, precept upon precept. He studied the scriptures and he communed with angels. Apostles and prophets from ancient times came to confer on him sacred priesthood authority and keys. Heavenly messengers taught him the ordinances of everlasting life and the mysteries of the kingdom of God. Revelation flowed from on high.

Evidences of this revelation are many. Among them is the Book of Mormon, which Joseph Smith translated by the gift and power of God. Through him the Church of Jesus Christ was established again on the earth with the same structure and the same priesthood authority the Lord's Church had anciently.

In a revelation given in 1831 the Lord stated the reasons for this Restoration:

Wherefore, I the Lord, knowing the calamity which should come upon the inhabitants of the earth, called upon my servant Joseph Smith, Jun., and spake unto him from heaven, and gave him commandments;

And also gave commandments to others, that they should proclaim these things unto the world. . . .

That faith also might increase in the earth;

That mine everlasting covenant might be established;

That the fulness of my gospel might be proclaimed by the weak and the simple unto the ends of the world. [D&C 1:17–18, 21–23]

Having the fulness of the gospel should not lead any of us to feel arrogant or harbor a holier-than-thou attitude. We should simply be grateful with all our heart for the truth restored and for the privilege of bringing this truth and these eternal blessings to our brothers and sisters.

What a great time to live in. We are living in the dispensation of the fulness of times. The gospel of Jesus Christ has been restored. Future generations will look upon you with gratitude and appreciation for how you used your opportunities.

Do not fear! Trust the Lord! Be courageous! Seek learning! Have faith!

Brothers and sisters, let us never be ashamed to testify of this wonderful Restoration, the restored gospel of Jesus Christ, "for it is the power of God unto salvation to every one that believeth" (Romans 1:16).

Let us never be ashamed to testify that Joseph Smith was a true prophet of God and that we have a living prophet today.

The keys of the kingdom of God have been restored again, and they are held by apostles of the Lord Jesus Christ. The president of The Church of Jesus Christ of Latter-day Saints, who is the senior apostle, holds all the keys necessary to preside over all the organizational and ordinance work of the Church. President Gordon B. Hinckley has this authority today. He stands as the prophet of God—the most recent in an unbroken succession of prophets and apostles from Joseph Smith to our own day. This is my apostolic witness of the reality of the Restoration and the truthfulness of this great work.

May God bless you and your loved ones, today and always, I pray, in the name of Jesus Christ, amen.

Gifts of the Spirit for Hard Times

———◆———

Henry B. Eyring

I am grateful for the lovely music and for the Spirit that it has brought. I am grateful for this opportunity to be with you this evening. Many of you are here in the Marriott Center at Brigham Young University. There are thousands more listening and watching at locations across the world. I cannot see all of you, but your Heavenly Father can. He knows your name and your needs. He knows your heart. Each of you has unique challenges. I pray that I may be inspired to say the words He would have you hear.

BLESSINGS AND CHALLENGES OF THE LAST DAYS

With all of our uniqueness, we all have some things in common. We are all in the probationary test of mortality. And, wherever we live, that test will become increasingly difficult. We are in the last dispensation of time. God's prophets have seen these times for millennia. They saw that wonderful things were to happen. There was to be a restoration of the gospel of Jesus Christ. The true Church was to be

Henry B. Eyring was a member of the Quorum of the Twelve Apostles of The Church of Jesus Christ of Latter-day Saints when this fireside address was given on 10 September 2006. © *Intellectual Reserve, Inc.*

brought back with prophets and apostles. The gospel was to be taken to every nation, kindred, tongue, and people. Most marvelous of all, the true Church and its members are to become worthy for the coming of the Savior to His Church and to His purified disciples.

But the true prophets also saw that in the last days Satan would rage. There would be wars and rumors of wars. That would inspire fear. The courage of many would fail. There would be great wickedness. And Satan would deceive many.

Yet, happily, many would not be overcome. And many would not be deceived. The fact that you are here listening tonight is evidence that you want to be among those who will not be overcome and will not be deceived. My purpose is to teach you how you can reach that happy and glorious goal.

THE HOLY GHOST IS THE KEY

The key for each of us will be to accept and hold the gift we have been promised by God. You who are members of the true Church of Jesus Christ will remember that, after you were baptized, authorized servants of God promised you that you could receive the Holy Ghost. Some of you may have felt something happen when that ordinance was performed. Most of you have felt the effects of that promise being fulfilled in your lives. I will tell you tonight how to recognize that gift, how to receive it every day in your life, and how it will bless you in the days ahead.

You have felt the quiet confirmation in your heart and mind that something was true. And you knew that it was inspiration from God. For some of you it may have come as the missionaries taught you before your baptism. It may have come during a talk or lesson in church. It may have come already tonight when something that was true was said or sung, as I felt when I heard the singing, as some of you did. The Holy Ghost is the Spirit of Truth. You feel peace, hope, and joy when it speaks to your heart and mind that something is true. Almost always I have also felt a sensation of light. Any feeling I may have had of darkness is dispelled. And the desire to do right grows.

The Lord promised that having those experiences would be true for you. Here are His words, recorded in the Doctrine and Covenants:

> *And now, verily, verily, I say unto thee, put your trust in that Spirit which leadeth to do good—yea, to do justly, to walk humbly, to judge righteously; and this is my Spirit.*
>
> *Verily, verily, I say unto you, I will impart unto you of my Spirit, which shall enlighten your mind, which shall fill your soul with joy.* [D&C 11:12–13]

The Lord also promised that those who have accepted the gift of the Holy Ghost in their lives would not be deceived. He spoke reassuringly to you and to me, who live in the times when the Church is being made ready for the time when He comes again. Here is the promise from the Doctrine and Covenants:

> *And at that day, when I shall come in my glory, shall the parable be fulfilled which I spake concerning the ten virgins.*
>
> *For they that are wise and have received the truth, and have taken the Holy Spirit for their guide, and have not been deceived—verily I say unto you, they shall not be hewn down and cast into the fire, but shall abide the day.*
>
> *And the earth shall be given unto them for an inheritance; and they shall multiply and wax strong, and their children shall grow up without sin unto salvation.*
>
> *For the Lord shall be in their midst, and his glory shall be upon them, and he will be their king and their lawgiver.* [D&C 45:56–59]

MANIFESTATIONS OF THE SPIRIT

As you heard those words just now, you may have felt another instance of receiving a manifestation of the Spirit that you have been promised. Those words paint a picture of the day when we may be with the Savior, who spoke of the ten virgins and of His coming again—only this time in glory. And they describe a day when we might be with Him and have His glory upon us. Of all the things to which the Holy Ghost testifies, and which you may have just felt, none is more precious to us than that Jesus is the Christ, the living Son of God. And nothing is so likely to make us feel light, hope, and joy. Then it is not surprising that when we feel the influence of the Holy Ghost, we also can feel that our natures are being changed because of the Atonement of Jesus Christ. We feel an increased desire to keep His commandments, to do good, and to deal justly.

Many of you have felt that effect from your frequent experiences with the Holy Ghost. For instance, in the mission field some of you had to rely on the Spirit to have the words to teach what the people needed. More than once, and perhaps every day, you had the blessing that Nephi and Lehi had among the people in their mission, described in Helaman:

> *And it came to pass that Nephi and Lehi did preach unto the Lamanites with such great power and authority, for they had power and authority given unto them that they might speak, and they also had what they should speak given unto them—*
>
> *Therefore they did speak unto the great astonishment of the Lamanites, to the convincing them, insomuch that there were eight thousand of the Lamanites who were in the land of Zarahemla and round about baptized unto repentance, and were convinced of the wickedness of the traditions of their fathers.* [Helaman 5:18–19]

Although you may not have been blessed with so miraculous a harvest, you have been given words by the Holy Ghost when you surrendered your heart to the Lord's service. At certain periods of your mission, such an experience came often. If you will think back on those times and ponder, you will also remember that the increase in your desire to obey the commandments came over you gradually. You felt less and less the tug of temptation. You felt more and more the desire to be obedient and to serve others. You felt a greater love for the people.

One of the effects of receiving a manifestation of the Holy Ghost repeatedly was that your nature changed. And so, from that faithful service to the Master, you had not only the witness of the Holy Ghost that Jesus is the Christ but you saw evidence in your own life that the Atonement is real. Such service, which brings the influence of the Holy Ghost, is an example of planting the seed, which Alma described:

And now, behold, because ye have tried the experiment, and planted the seed, and it swelleth and sprouteth, and beginneth to grow, ye must needs know that the seed is good.

And now, behold, is your knowledge perfect? Yea, your knowledge is perfect in that thing, and your faith is dormant; and this because you know, for ye know that the word hath swelled your souls, and ye also know that it hath sprouted up, that your understanding doth begin to be enlightened, and your mind doth begin to expand.

O then, is not this real? I say unto you, Yea, because it is light; and whatsoever is light, is good, because it is discernible, therefore ye must know that it is good; and now behold, after ye have tasted this light is your knowledge perfect?

Behold I say unto you, Nay; neither must ye lay aside your faith, for ye have only exercised your faith to plant the seed that ye might try the experiment to know if the seed was good.

And behold, as the tree beginneth to grow, ye will say: Let us nourish it with great care, that it may get root, that it may grow up, and bring forth fruit unto us. And now behold, if ye nourish it with much care it will get root, and grow up, and bring forth fruit. [Alma 32:33–37]

RECEIVING REVELATIONS DAILY

Now, if you and I were visiting alone (I wish we could be), where you felt free to ask whatever you wanted to ask, I can imagine your saying something like this: "Oh, Brother Eyring, I've felt some of the things you have described. The Holy Ghost has touched my heart and mind from time to time. But I will need it consistently if I am not to be overcome or deceived. Is that possible? Is it possible, and, if it is, what will it take to receive that blessing?"

Well, let's start with the first part of your question. Yes, it is possible. Whenever I need that reassurance—and I need it from time to time too—I remember two brothers. Nephi and Lehi, and the other servants of the Lord laboring with them, faced fierce opposition. They were serving in an increasingly wicked world. They had to deal with terrible deceptions. So I take courage—and so can you—from the words in this one verse of Helaman. The reassurance is tucked into the account of all that happened in an entire year, almost as if to the writer it was not surprising. Listen:

And in the seventy and ninth year there began to be much strife. But it came to pass that Nephi and Lehi, and many of their brethren who knew concerning the true points of doctrine, having many revelations daily, therefore they did preach unto the people, insomuch that they did put an end to their strife in that same year. [Helaman 11:23]

They had "many revelations daily." So, for you and for me, that answers your first question. Yes, it is possible to have the companionship of the Holy Ghost sufficiently to have many revelations daily. It will not be easy. But it is possible. What it will require will be different for each person because we start from where we are in our unique set of experiences in life. For all of us there will be at least three requirements. None of them can be gained and retained from a single experience. All of them must be constantly renewed.

FAITH IN GOD

First, receiving the Holy Ghost takes faith in our Heavenly Father and in His Beloved Son, Jesus Christ. A memory of a great spiritual experience some time ago, where you had confirmed to you that truth, won't be sufficient. You will need to be sure of your faith in the moment of crisis, which may come at any time day or night, when you plead for the influence of the Spirit. You must then be unshaken in your confidence that God lives, that He hears your cry for help, and that the resurrected Savior will do for you what He promised to do for His servants in His mortal ministry. You remember:

> *But when the Comforter is come, whom I will send unto you from the Father, even the Spirit of truth, which proceedeth from the Father, he shall testify of me.* [John 15:26]

The brothers Nephi and Lehi received many revelations daily. The record shows that they knew concerning the true points of doctrine. Of all the true doctrine, nothing is more important to you and me than the true nature of God the Father and His Son, Jesus Christ. For that I return again and again to the scriptures. For that I return again and again to prayer. For that I return again and again to partaking of the sacrament. And, above all, I come to know God and Jesus Christ best by keeping the commandments and serving in the Church. By diligent service in the Church we come not only to know the character of God but to love Him. If we follow His commands, our faith in Him will grow and we may then qualify to have His Spirit to be with us.

Vibrant faith in God comes best from serving Him regularly. Not all of us have received callings to offices in the Church. Some of you may not yet be called to something in a formal way, yet every member has a multitude of opportunities to serve God. For instance, for years we have heard the phrase "every member a missionary." That is not a choice. It is a fact of our membership. Our choice is to speak to others about the gospel or not. Similarly, each member is to care for the poor among us and around us. Some of that we do privately and alone. Some we do together with other members. That is why we have fast offerings and service projects. Our choice is to decide whether to join with the Lord and His other disciples in our day as He and His disciples did during His mortal ministry.

Most of us have or may have callings as home and visiting teachers. There is in those callings great opportunity to grow in faith that the Lord sends the Holy Ghost to His humble servants. That builds faith and renews our faith in Him. I've seen it and so have many of you.

I received a phone call from a distraught mother in a state far away
from where I was. She told me that her unmarried daughter had moved
to another city far from her home. She sensed from the little contact
she had with her daughter that something was terribly wrong. The
mother feared for the moral safety of her daughter. She pleaded with
me to help her daughter.

I found out who the daughter's home teacher was. I called him.
He was young. And yet he and his companion both had been awak-
ened in the night with not only concern for the girl but with inspiration that she was about to make choices that would bring sadness and
misery. With only the inspiration of the Spirit, they went to see her.
She did not at first want to tell them anything about her situation.
They pleaded with her to repent and to choose to follow the path
that the Lord had set out for her and that her mother and father had
taught her to follow. She realized as she listened that the only way
they could have known what they knew about her life was from God.
A mother's prayer had gone to Heavenly Father, and the Holy Ghost
had been sent to home teachers with an errand.

More than once I have heard priesthood leaders say that they
had been inspired to go to someone in need, only to find the visiting
teacher or the home teacher had already been there. My wife, who is
here with me tonight, is an example. We had a bishop once who said
to me, "You know, it bothers me—when I get an inspiration to go to
someone, your wife has already been there." Your faith will grow as
you serve the Lord in caring for Heavenly Father's children as the
Lord's teacher to their home. You will have your prayers answered.
You will come to know for yourself that He lives, that He loves us,
and that He sends inspiration to those with even the beginnings of
faith in Him and with the desire to serve Him in His Church. Stay
close to the Church if you want your faith in God to grow. And as it
grows, so will your ability to claim the promise you were given that
you can receive the gifts of the Spirit.

REQUIREMENT TO BE CLEAN

The first requirement was faith in the Lord Jesus Christ and in our Heavenly Father. A second requirement for frequent companionship and direction from the Holy Ghost is to be clean. The Spirit must withdraw from those who are not clean. You remember the sad illustration of that in the history of the people in the Book of Mormon:

And because of their iniquity the church had begun to dwindle; and they began to disbelieve in the spirit of prophecy and in the spirit of revelation; and the judgments of God did stare them in the face.

And they saw that they had become weak, like unto their brethren, the Lamanites, and that the Spirit of the Lord did no more preserve them; yea, it had withdrawn from them because the Spirit of the Lord doth not dwell in unholy temples. [Helaman 4:23–24]

The path to receiving the Holy Ghost is to exercise faith in Christ unto repentance. We can become clean through qualifying for the effects of the Savior's Atonement. The covenants offered in baptism by authorized servants of God bring that cleansing. We renew our pledge to keep those covenants each time we partake of the sacrament. And the peace we all seek is the assurance that we have received forgiveness for our sins of omission or commission.

The Savior is the one who has been given the right to grant that forgiveness and to give that assurance. I have learned that the Lord gives that assurance at the time He chooses, and He does it in His own way. And I have learned to ask for it in prayer. One way He grants that assurance is through the Holy Ghost. If you have difficulty in feeling the Holy Ghost, you might wisely ponder whether there is anything for which you need to repent and receive forgiveness.

If you have felt the influence of the Holy Ghost during this day, or even this evening, you may take it as evidence that the Atonement is working in your life. For that reason and many others, you would do well to put yourself in places and in tasks that invite the promptings of the Holy Ghost. Feeling the influence of the Holy Ghost works both ways: the Holy Ghost only dwells in a clean temple, and the reception of the Holy Ghost cleanses us through the Atonement of Jesus Christ. You can pray with faith to know what to do to be cleansed and thus qualified for the companionship of the Holy Ghost and the service of the Lord. And with that companionship you will be strengthened against temptation and empowered to detect deception.

PURE MOTIVE

A third requirement for the companionship of the Holy Ghost is pure motive. If you want to receive the gifts of the Spirit, you have to want them for the right reasons. Your purposes must be the Lord's purposes. To the degree your motives are selfish, you will find it difficult to receive those gifts of the Spirit that have been promised to you.

That fact serves both as a warning and as helpful instruction. First, the warning: God is offended when we seek the gifts of the Spirit for our own purposes rather than for His. Our selfish motives may not be obvious to us. But few of us would be so blind as the man who sought to purchase the right to the gifts of the Spirit. You remember the sad story of a man named Simon and of Peter's rebuke:

And when Simon saw that through laying on of the apostles' hands the Holy Ghost was given, he offered them money,

Saying, Give me also this power, that on whomsoever I lay hands, he may receive the Holy Ghost.

But Peter said unto him, Thy money perish with thee, because thou hast thought that the gift of God may be purchased with money.

Thou hast neither part nor lot in this matter: for thy heart is not right in the sight of God.

Repent therefore of this thy wickedness, and pray God, if perhaps the thought of thine heart may be forgiven thee.

For I perceive that thou art in the gall of bitterness, and in the bond of iniquity.

Then answered Simon, and said, Pray ye to the Lord for me, that none of these things which ye have spoken come upon me. [Acts 8:18–24]

Apparently Simon recognized his own corrupt motives. It may not be so easy for each of us. We almost always have more than one motive at a time. And some may be mixtures of what God wants as well as what we want. It is not easy to pull them apart.

For instance, consider yourself on the eve of a school examination or an interview for a new job. You know that the direction of the Holy Ghost could be of great help. I know from my own experience, for example, that the Holy Ghost knows some of the mathematical equations used to solve problems in thermodynamics, a branch of the sciences. I was a struggling physics student studying in a book that I still own. I keep it for historical and spiritual reasons. Halfway down a page (I could even show you where it is on the page), in the middle of some mathematics, I had a clear confirmation that what I was reading was true. It was exactly the feeling I had had come to me before as I pondered the Lord's scriptures and that I have had many times since. So I knew that the Holy Ghost understood whatever was true in what I might be asked on an examination in thermodynamics.

You can imagine that I was tempted to ask God to send me the Holy Ghost during the examination so I wouldn't need to study further. I knew that He could do it, but I did not ask Him. I felt that He would rather have me learn to pay a price in effort. He may well have sent help in the examination, but I was afraid that my motive might not be His. You have had that same choice to make often. It may have been when you were to be interviewed for a job. It may even have been when you were preparing for a talk or to teach a missionary discussion. Always there is the possibility that you may have a selfish purpose for yourself that is less important to the Lord.

For instance, I may want a good grade in a course, when He prefers that I learn how to work hard in the service of others. I may want a job because of the salary or the prestige, when He wants me to work somewhere else to bless the life of someone I don't even know yet. He surely will have purposes for your hearing me speak tonight.

He knows you. I might have a desire to entertain or impress you. But I have tried to suppress my desire and surrender to His.

I saw a man do that once. It changed my life. A member of the General Authorities came to speak to a conference where I was sitting on the stand. I was in the local priesthood presidency. I knew personally the struggles of the local families and the members. He, the General Authority, had just flown in from a long assignment in Europe. He was obviously tired. He stood to speak in the meeting. It seemed to me that he rambled from one subject to another. At first I felt sorry for him. I thought he was failing to give a polished sermon of the kind I knew he had delivered many times.

After a while I was thrilled to recognize that as he moved from one apparently unrelated topic to another, he was touching the need of every poor struggling member and family we were trying to help. He did not know them and their needs. But God did.

How grateful I am that his motive was not to give a great sermon or to be seen as a powerful prophet. He must have done what I hope you and I will always do. He must have prayed something like this: "Father, I need Thy help. I am tired. Please guide me with the Holy Ghost. Bless these people. I love them. I ask only that I can do Thy will to help them."

The Holy Ghost came that night. And the Lord's will was done. The General Authority had spent a lifetime feeding himself and others on the good word of God. He had served the Master faithfully. He was a special witness of Jesus Christ because he had paid the price to be one. All of that came from keeping his motives as closely tied as he could to what the Lord wanted. That made it possible for the Lord to send the whisperings of the Holy Ghost to His servant and so bless the people.

PURE LOVE OF CHRIST

I surely don't understand all the meaning of the scriptural words "the pure love of Christ." But one meaning I do know is this: It is a gift we are promised when the Atonement of Jesus Christ has worked in us. The gift is to want what He wants. When our love is the love

He feels, it is pure because He is pure. And when we feel our desire for people is moving toward being in line with His, that is one of the ways that we can know that we are being purified. When we pray for the gifts of the Spirit—and we should—one for which I pray is that I might have pure motives, to want what He wants for our Father's children and for me and to feel, as well as to say, that what I want is His will to be done.

That is what these words from Moroni mean to me:

Wherefore, my beloved brethren, if ye have not charity, ye are nothing, for charity never faileth. Wherefore, cleave unto charity, which is the greatest of all, for all things must fail—

But charity is the pure love of Christ, and it endureth forever; and whoso is found possessed of it at the last day, it shall be well with him.

Wherefore, my beloved brethren, pray unto the Father with all the energy of heart, that ye may be filled with this love, which he hath bestowed upon all who are true followers of his Son, Jesus Christ; that ye may become the sons of God; that when he shall appear we shall be like him, for we shall see him as he is; that we may have this hope; that we may be purified even as he is pure. Amen. [Moroni 7:46–48]

I bear you my witness that God the Father lives, a glorified and exalted Man. He is the Father of our spirits. He and His Beloved Son, both resurrected and glorified, appeared to the boy Joseph Smith in a grove of trees in New York. They were there. The Father spoke to Joseph, first calling him by name and then introducing His Son. Heavenly messengers came to restore all the priesthood keys of authority. Joseph translated the Book of Mormon by the gift and power of God. It had been written on plates by ancient prophets, one of whom gave them to Joseph and took them back when the translation was done. The keys of the priesthood are on the earth today. As a witness of Jesus Christ, I testify to you that I know He lives and that He leads His Church.

I pray with all the energy of my heart that you will have your prayers answered to meet the requirements to receive the Holy

Ghost. And I pray that you will endure faithful to the end and that, for you, it will be glorious.

I leave you my blessing that your pleadings for the gifts of the Spirit to serve the Lord will be granted. And I leave you my love. In the name of Jesus Christ, amen.

"Even If All, Not I"

Sharon G. Samuelson

The Lord has said to all of us, "Seek ye out of the best books words of wisdom; seek learning, even by study and also by faith."[1] Welcome to all of you wonderful young men and women who are moving forward in your lives to acquire knowledge and to use it to enhance your futures, both intellectually and spiritually. Our prophet, President Gordon B. Hinckley, has said, "We live in a world where knowledge is developing at an ever-accelerating rate. Drink deeply from this ever-springing well of wisdom and human experience."[2]

My dear friends, these schooling years pass quickly. I can attest to that fact. Having the wonderful opportunity to be in your midst often gives me many opportunities reminiscent of my university experiences. They seem like a long time ago, but the time between then and now seems to have just whizzed by so rapidly.

Your education is the road to many wonderful opportunities. This is a defining and refining time of your lives. Plato said, "The direction in which education starts a man [or woman], will determine

Sharon G. Samuelson, wife of BYU president Cecil O. Samuelson, delivered this devotional address on 12 September 2006. © Brigham Young University.

his [or her] future life."[3] Your Brigham Young University education can bless your lives as well as those of your immediate family,
descendants, church, and community. My experiences in university
life—now and in the past—have influenced my life in so many different ways. Yours will do likewise. It is also true that friendships made
at these times will last a lifetime.

About four months ago my husband and I were having dinner
with such friends. I noticed that above an archway in their home
they had placed some printed words. They were in Latin, and I did
not know what they meant. These were the words: "Et si omnes
ego non."

I was curious as to what they meant and why they had them in
such a prominent place in their home. I was told that their translation
was, roughly: "Even if all, not I." In other words, "Even if everybody does it, I will not." They proceeded to explain to me that the
saying was the motto of the Barons von Boeselager, an old German
noble family. Two descendants in the family, Philipp and Georg
von Boeselager, were members of the resistance group that had
planned the failed assassination attempt on Adolph Hitler on July 20,
1944. Their involvement in the operation went undetected, and they
were not executed along with the majority of the other conspirators.
The saying is carved in a timber beam on the outside of Philipp's
family home in Germany.[4]

Our friends explained that they used this quote as a motto for
their family and that it was a reminder to them that they are members
of a chosen generation and must be different in the world of today.
As members of The Church of Jesus Christ of Latter-day Saints, they
should make choices consistent with the teachings of the gospel and
shun the negative, misleading, and evil messages of the world that
surround them.

How many of you can remember when you were a small child?
For some of us here it is a stretch, but for you it should be relatively
easy. Can you recall when you and your friends wanted to do something and you had to ask permission of your parents? If they hesitated
in the least in saying your desired response of yes, did you ever say,

"But, Mom (or Dad), everybody else gets to do it"? I tried that ploy quite often. Or I might have said, "Sally's mom is letting her go."

I love the story told by President Hinckley of the time he learned about having the courage to make his own decisions and not "follow the crowd." The year that he started junior high school, the building was not large enough to accommodate all the students, and his class had to return to the elementary school. He and his friends were not very happy, so the boys decided that they would go on strike and not attend school the next day—and they didn't. They had no place to go, so they just wandered around wasting time.

The next morning, the principal, Mr. Stearns, met the boys at the front door and told them that they had to have a note from their parents to be able to return to school. Young Gordon went home and reluctantly approached his mother, who knew something was wrong. He told her the situation.

She did write him a note, which read, "Dear Mr. Sterns, Please excuse Gordon's absence yesterday. His action was simply an impulse to follow the crowd."[5] President Hinckley stated, "I determined then and there that I would make my own decisions on the basis of their merits and my standards and not be pushed in one direction or another by those around me. That decision has blessed my life many times."[6]

During the last general conference in April we were warned many times concerning the fact that the world of today is shifting in its values and standards. We cannot nor should we live secluded from the world around us. It is indeed an exciting time to be alive, but it is also one that is fraught with danger both physically and spiritually. The adversary is very subtle and deceitful and will entice you any way possible to get you to "follow the crowd" or succumb to the evil ways of the world. He would have you ignore and not understand the blessings and promises available to you because of the Lord's great love for you.

What are some of the messages we hear from many of the "world crowd"? You who are students here today live in a very different world from that experienced by your parents and many others of us here.

From all types of media we are shown and told that chastity before marriage and fidelity afterward is not the norm in dating and marriage today. However, the Lord tells us: "Be thou an example of the believers . . . in purity."[7]

You are given many examples of how to dress and look. There are examples for both men and women. The pressure can be strong to "be in style." However, we are constantly taught by our Church leaders that "modesty in dress is a quality of mind and heart, born of respect for oneself, one's fellowmen, and the Creator of us all. Modesty reflects an attitude of humility, decency and propriety."[8]

We live in a world where success seems largely measured by possessions and professional status. To many the manner of obtaining these often seems to be of no consequence. This can also apply to university experiences and studies as you strive to achieve high grades, earn degrees, and gain desired employment positions. Qualities such as integrity, charity, honesty, and spirituality often are thought to be of less value than the means of obtaining what is assumed to be outward signs of success.

There may be the pressure and desire to have the largest house, the best car, expensive clothes, and so forth. Our Church leaders have warned us against unnecessary buying and cumbersome debt. It may be necessary to borrow for an education and, at appropriate times, an affordable home and other necessary items. However, we are constantly counseled to stay out of debt by purchasing wisely and living within our means. Do not be unduly swayed or influenced by those around you to do otherwise.

My dear friends, in the world today our voices can be heard as we speak of and stand for our convictions of truth and righteousness. I love the example in the Book of Mormon of Captain Moroni, of whom it was said:

If all men had been, and were, and ever would be, like unto Moroni, behold, the very powers of hell would have been shaken forever; yea, the devil would never have power over the hearts of the children of men.[9]

Oh that such could be written of us as we stand for and speak of our beliefs!

As I see you here today and around the campus, my heart is filled with admiration for the wonderful lives you live and the examples you are to the world. I would love to know each one of you personally. However, you are 33,000 strong; therefore that is impossible. I do, however, have a testimony that you can stand up to worldly influences that would draw you away from your beliefs and say, in mighty voices, "Even if all, not I." Those who see and hear you can know of your testimonies of the Savior and our Father in Heaven.

Elder David B. Haight said it this way:

You need not look just like the world; you need not entertain like the world; your personal habits should be different; your recreation will be different; your concern for your family will be vastly different. If you establish this distinctiveness firmly in your life pattern, only blessings await you for doing what is right.[10]

It would be the desire of those who love and lead you in many areas of your lives that you follow the admonition of the 13th article of faith, which reads:

We believe in being honest, true, chaste, benevolent, virtuous, and in doing good to all men; indeed, we may say that we follow the admonition of Paul—We believe all things, we hope all things, we have endured many things, and hope to be able to endure all things. If there is anything virtuous, lovely, or of good report or praiseworthy, we seek after these things.[11]

That we may all do so would be my prayer in the name of Jesus Christ, amen.

NOTES

1. D&C 88:118.

2. Gordon B. Hinckley, "A Three-Point Challenge," BYU commencement address, 27 April 1995; excerpt in *TGBH*, 171.

3. Plato, *The Republic*, trans. Benjamin Jowett, book 4 (Adeimantus).

4. See www.answers.com/topic/philipp-von-boeselager.

5. Gordon B. Hinckley, "Some Lessons I Learned as a Boy," *Ensign*, May 1993, 53.

6. "Some Lessons," 53.

7. 1 Timothy 4:12.

8. *Priesthood Bulletin*, September 1970, 2.

9. Alma 48:17.

10. David B. Haight, "You Are Different," *Ensign*, January 1974, 42.

11. Articles of Faith 1:13.

What Is It That We Honor?

Cecil O. Samuelson

As always at this time of year, I look forward to welcoming each of you to campus and the start of what we anticipate will be a wonderful, productive, and enriching new academic year. We are grateful to have each of you: those who are here for the first time, those who are continuing, and those who are returning after missions or other endeavors elsewhere. It is good to be in your company.

If I were a student, which I try to be, I would now be entering my senior year at BYU. I have been generally delighted by my experiences and hope that this is your lot as well. BYU is wonderful. It is also a big, complicated, and sometimes intimidating place. I am grateful to so many who go out of their way to be friendly and extend greetings as we pass each other on the campus. I hope that all of you will make special efforts to reach out and befriend your new associates. Some of you come with already made friends and previous contacts. While these relationships will and should continue, I hope and ask that all of you will consciously seek to broaden your circles, meet

Cecil O. Samuelson was president of Brigham Young University when this devotional address was delivered on 12 September 2006. © *Intellectual Reserve, Inc.*

new friends, and always be friendly and courteous to everyone you encounter. This is part of what BYU is and should be.

We must never forget that BYU is not just another "good" university. It was established by the Lord's servants and continues to be blessed with the direction and support of prophets, seers, and revelators. While we may not understand all of the details, we do know that Brigham Young University occupies a key place in the Lord's plans for the completion of His work in these last days.

Because there is so much that is good and praiseworthy here at BYU, and because almost all of you are so good and praiseworthy, it is a great temptation to spend our limited time together in complimentary expressions. These are in order, and I do express my deep and profound appreciation and admiration for so much and to so many of you, especially those who make the BYU experience possible: the faithful tithe payers of the Church, your loyal families and supporting friends, our generous supporters and donors, and others who contribute in so many ways.

As I do so, however, I also feel impressed to share with you some reflections of admonition that accompany my appreciation and admiration. I listen to and read with deep interest the comments that many in our community make and those that are shared by people who mainly love and care about BYU and you. You would not be surprised that in my responsibilities I receive significant input. My e-mail and letter boxes are often quite full, and in my meetings and question-and-answer sessions with students, faculty, staff, and administrative colleagues, as well as with alumni, community groups, university supporters, and Church leaders, I am provided with volumes of feedback, suggestions, and occasional criticisms. Almost all are constructive and well-meaning, although there is occasional evidence of a little carping, lack of charity, or limited understanding of issues being addressed.

While not a universal theme, it continues to impress me that so much of the dialogue at BYU and about BYU seems to focus on our Honor Code in one way or another. It is typically not so much that individuals are overtly opposed to the Honor Code as it is they are

concerned about the perceived understandings or applications that
other individuals have about what the Honor Code really means and
what it really is or should be.

As I have tried to think seriously and ponder all of the dimensions of this issue, I have repeatedly been reminded of the words of
the Savior. I hope you will consider them carefully and see if there
are applications to the Honor Code that you can identify and use to
deepen your own understanding and commitment.

As we know, Jesus was rich in His praise and encouragement
when conditions allowed Him to do so, but He was also crisp and
clear in His corrections and criticisms when such was necessary.
I hope we can avoid being selective in our attention to His correc-
tives, just as I hope we can find joy in considering that many of His
compliments are directed to us when we live as we should.

Think of that terrible night, just prior to the Atonement, when
Jesus met with His apostles to keep the Passover with them. As He
opened the curtain for them about the events to occur shortly, He
announced that one of their quorum would betray Him. Listen to
Matthew's account of their reaction to this distressing announcement:
"And they were exceeding sorrowful, and began every one of them to
say unto him, Lord, is it I?" (Matthew 26:22).

Note that Peter didn't say, "Is it Andrew?" Nor did James say,
"Is it John?" I don't know what any of them really thought of or
about Judas Iscariot. Their reflections and concerns were upon themselves and their own weaknesses and limitations. Although we know
that they were perceptive and undoubtedly aware of the shortcomings
of others, at that sacred moment they were most anxious that their
own lives were in order and, however their actions, thoughts, weaknesses, or failings might be afflicting themselves and others, they did
not want to be involved in any way in the betrayal of the Lord. In
my judgment, this is an attitude and approach worthy of our emulation and application generally and in particular with respect to the
Honor Code.

With the question "Lord, is it I?" at the forefront of our minds
and hearts, think about Jesus' description and condemnation of

the scribes and Pharisees. I don't believe we have a single scribe or Pharisee among us, but I do fear that, on occasion, some of their characteristics and attitudes find their way into our circle. The entire 23rd chapter of Matthew is worthy of our careful study and consideration. Rarely has a recorded rebuke by the Master been so lengthy, specific, and scathing. In a similar vein, in modern revelation, the Savior drew searing attention to those who neglected or omitted "the weightier matters of the law" (Matthew 23:23; see also D&C 117:8).

Like those mentioned in the meridian of time and in the early days of the Restoration, we in our day continue to be tempted to be selective in our discipleship and choosy about which conventions and commandments we will observe and which we might justify in ignoring.

Jesus Himself suggested a hierarchy of importance in the things we have been asked to do and to observe. Most would agree that murder is more vile than is cheating on our taxes and that physical assault is more vexing than a lack of common courtesy. Likewise, violation of sacred temple covenants should trouble us more than a missed day of scripture study, and disappointing a friend or loved one by an act of dishonesty is more distressing than is a hurt engendered only by thoughtless forgetfulness.

Nevertheless, we must be clear that an emphasis on the seemingly "weightier matters" does not excuse us "to leave the other undone" (Matthew 23:23). Because we consider the mandate never to cheat on examinations, plagiarize in writing our papers, steal from our associates or the university, or commit any immoral act absolute, it does not excuse us from seemingly lesser requirements having to do with proper parking on campus or requirements with respect to dress and grooming. Yes, some things are more important than others. Yes, we can agree to disagree individually on the place in the hierarchy of importance a particular standard explicated in the Honor Code should have.

What we must agree on—and have agreed on as we signed the appropriate document of acceptance when we came to BYU—is that we will abide by the Honor Code. Is our Honor Code all-inclusive? It is a remarkably broad and detailed description of things deemed to be important institutionally to us. We need to remember that, like all important documents, it has constituents that are implicit as well as those obviously explicit. Remember the words of King Benjamin as he completed his remarkable benedictory sermon:

And finally, I cannot tell you all the things whereby ye may commit sin; for there are divers ways and means, even so many that I cannot number them.

But this much I can tell you, that if ye do not watch yourselves, and your thoughts, and your words, and your deeds, and observe the commandments of God, and continue in the faith of what ye have heard concerning the coming of our Lord, even unto the end of your lives, ye must perish. And now, O man [BYU students, faculty, staff, administrators, friends, families, supporters, and visitors], *remember, and perish not.* [Mosiah 4:29–30]

Some have suggested that because Jesus was so concerned about the importance of what goes on inside of us, we should be less concerned about external appearances or observances. Make no mistake, who we are in private and what we value most at our core are of supreme importance and are "weightier matters." However, it is also true that what we project externally should reflect who we really are.

In a recent tribute to President James E. Faust, his daughter, Janna F. Coombs, remarked that even when performing priesthood ordinances for members of his family in the privacy of their own home, he would be dressed appropriately as a representative of the priesthood he was exercising. President Faust is not stuffy; he is not pretentious. He makes no efforts to impress anyone unduly. He is meek, humble, and self-effacing. But he is fearless in his defense of the Lord and all things sacred. He is scrupulous in his devotion and honor to those things serious and fundamental. In other words, he lives the Honor Code with exactness.

I would suggest that you men who hold the priesthood have the same responsibility to honor the priesthood. President Faust did not become honest, honorable, and respectful when he was called to the First Presidency. It did not begin when he was ordained as an apostle or called as a bishop, stake president, or General Authority. He did not suddenly become a man of honor when he was called as a missionary or when he graduated from law school. He made all of these decisions and commitments when about your age and before—and all that has transpired since has been made possible because he has always taken the matter of honor seriously.

Likewise, you sisters who know that you "are daughters of our Heavenly Father" who loves you (Young Women theme) have a similar obligation and opportunity to demonstrate what you really understand and value by how you follow the Honor Code—to which you have attached your own name and personal honor.

All of us are beset with ideas, temptations, and distractions that have the potential to lead us to places we do not wish to go and to consequences we would not choose. The Word of Wisdom was given "in consequence of evils and designs which do and will exist in the hearts of conspiring men [and women] in the last days [our days]" (D&C 89:4). It is my judgment that this is also a major reason for the development of the Honor Code at Brigham Young University.

Similarly, the BYU Honor Code—not a canonized revelation but "adapted to the capacity of the weak and the weakest of all [BYU students]—is associated with promised blessings (D&C 89:3).

Included in the many blessings that a BYU education and experience may provide is the opportunity to understand and reflect carefully on what things in life are most important to us. This occurs in an environment where sacred things are held sacred and where we are committed to helping each other understand and apply eternal truths as we strive and grow in the quest for academic and scholarly excellence.

In addition, like the Word of Wisdom, the Honor Code is not primarily a law of health or blind conformity. It is a principle of obedience. It is an outward manifestation of our inner appreciation for and understanding of the privilege of being at BYU.

As we do our best to live the Honor Code in this light, we are assisted by focusing on "the weightier matters" ourselves and by not distracting others by our carelessness or neglect of those things "not to [be left] undone" (Matthew 23:23).

I like the attitude and approach of the Apostle Paul. In a discourse that has many applications to our current Honor Code dialogue, Paul makes some observations that I suggest for your consideration. The specifics of his attention had to do with the eating of meat and offerings made to idols. Our doctrine has not changed, although many other dimensions of life have. Listen to Paul's words and try to grasp the Honor Code implications of things that you might have considered to be of little importance or consequence:

> *But meat commendeth us not to God: for neither, if we eat, are we the better; neither, if we eat not, are we the worse.*
>
> *But take heed lest by any means this liberty of yours become a stumblingblock to them that are weak.* . . .
>
> *Wherefore, if meat make my brother to offend, I will eat no flesh while the world standeth, lest I make my brother to offend.* [1 Corinthians 8:8–9, 13]

If you do not care enough to shave for yourselves, do it for your associates and friends. If you do not respect yourselves enough to dress modestly and appropriately, do it for others.

If you are ambivalent about the importance of the little things as they apply to you, do them anyway out of respect for those who have sacrificed and do sacrifice in order that you might have the remarkable experience of a BYU education. Is the Honor Code a small thing? I do not accord it as such. Is compliance with the Honor Code to which you have attached your signature and pledged your personal honor really that significant? I judge it to be.

Now, I have been direct and, hopefully, clear as I have expressed my concerns and observations. I hope that I have not given offense to anyone, but I also hope that I have added clarity to some matters that may have been blurry in the thinking of some. I feel somewhat as Jacob may have felt as he attempted to be helpful to the people of Nephi. Said he:

O, my beloved brethren, give ear to my words. Remember the greatness of the Holy One of Israel. Do not say that I have spoken hard things against you; for if ye do, ye will revile against the truth. . . . I know that the words of truth are hard against all uncleanness; but the righteous fear them not, for they love the truth and are not shaken. [2 Nephi 9:40]

I am convinced that what I have said is true and consistent with the statements and teachings of the Savior and the prophets. Some years ago, in a BYU devotional, President Gordon B. Hinckley said the following:

Every one of us who is here has accepted a sacred and compelling trust. With that trust, there must be accountability. That trust involves standards of behavior as well as standards of academic excellence. For each of us it carries with it a larger interest than our own interest. It carries with it the interest of the university, and the interest of the Church, which must be the interest of each and all of us.

Some few students resent the fact that the board has imposed a code of honor and a code of dress and behavior to which all are expected to subscribe. . . .

I think I can hear a student, perhaps a number of them, saying to a bishop, "Why do we have to sign these codes? Don't they trust us?"

I am reminded of what I heard from a man—a great, strong, and wise man—who served in the presidency of this Church years ago. His daughter was going out on a date, and her father said to her, "Be careful. Be careful of how you act and what you say."

She replied, "Daddy, don't you trust me?"

He responded, "I don't entirely trust myself. One never gets too old nor too high in the Church that the adversary gives up on him."

And so, my friends, we ask you to subscribe to these codes and to have the endorsement of your respective bishops and stake presidents in doing so. It is not that we do not trust you. But we feel that you need reminding of the elements of your contract with those responsible for this institution and that you may be the stronger in observing that trust because of the commitment you have made. With every trust there must be accountability, and this is a reminder of that accountability. [Gordon B. Hinckley, "Trust and Accountability" (13 October 1992), *BYU 1992–93 Devotional and Fireside Speeches* (Provo: BYU, 1993), 24]

Might we truly recognize what it is and who it is that we really honor. Might we understand the trust that has been bestowed upon us and the accountability that is ours is my prayer in the name of Jesus Christ, amen.

Your Refined Heavenly Home

Douglas L. Callister

Half a century ago Elder Adam S. Bennion of the Quorum of the Twelve was the assigned speaker at this devotional. His address was preceded by a stirring passage from *Cavalleria Rusticana* by Mascagni, performed by one of the university's fine choral groups. Elder Bennion was so touched that he began his message with these words: "I will shorten my remarks today so that this musical masterpiece may be performed for us a second time at the close of this assembly."

The nearer we get to God, the more easily our spirits are touched by refined and beautiful things. If we could part the veil and observe our heavenly home, we would be impressed with the cultivated minds and hearts of those who so happily live there. I imagine that our heavenly parents are exquisitely refined. In this great gospel of emulation, one of the purposes of our earthly probation is to become like them in every conceivable way so that we may be comfortable in the presence of heavenly parentage and, in the language of Enos, see their faces "with pleasure."[1]

Douglas L. Callister was a member of the Second Quorum of the Seventy of The Church of Jesus Christ of Latter-day Saints when this devotional address was given on 19 September 2006. © *Intellectual Reserve, Inc.*

Brigham Young said: "We are trying to be the image of those who live in heaven; we are trying to pattern after them, to look like them, to walk and talk like them."[2] To prepare us to do this, the 13th article of faith encourages: "If there is anything virtuous, lovely, or of good report or praiseworthy, we seek after these things."[3] Refinement is a companion to developed spirituality. Refinement and spirituality are two strings drawn by the same bow.

Today I would like to peek behind the veil that temporarily separates us from our heavenly home and paint a word picture of the virtuous, lovely, and refined circumstances that exist there. I will speak of the language, literature, music, and art of heaven, as well as the immaculate appearance of heavenly beings, for I believe that in heaven we will find each of these in pure and perfected form.

God speaks all languages, and He speaks them properly. He is restrained and modest of speech. When God described the grand creational process of this earth, He said in measured tones that "it was good."[4] We would be disappointed if God had to use "awesome" or other exaggerated phrases in every paragraph.

Britain's Ben Jonson said: "Language most shows a man: Speak, that I may see thee."[5] Our language reveals our thoughts, our virtues, our insecurities, our doubts, even the homes from which we come. We will feel more comfortable in Heavenly Father's presence if we have developed proper habits of speech. We not only wish to see God's face "with pleasure," we want to open our mouths with confidence that our speech harmonizes with the refinement of heaven.

We will thrill to hear exalted beings express their sublime thoughts in perfectly chosen words. I suppose that the language of heaven, properly spoken, may approach a form of music. Did C. S. Lewis have this in mind when he wrote: "Isn't it funny the way some combinations of words can give you—almost apart from their meaning—a thrill like music?"[6] At Jesus' birth the angels appeared and spoke, not sang, "Glory to God in the highest, and on earth peace, good will toward men."[7] We now try to capture that beauty in song, but the original angelic utterance was in spoken words, which thrilled like music.

Van Wyck Brooks, in his biography *The Life of Emerson*, told us that Ralph Waldo Emerson was invited to speak at the commemoration of the 300th anniversary of Shakespeare's birth. After proper introduction Emerson presented himself at the pulpit and then sat down. He had forgotten his notes. He preferred to say nothing rather than words not well measured. For some, it was Emerson in one of his most eloquent hours.[8]

A few years ago I overheard a Church leader lament the fact that he never had time for anything except to read the scriptures and other works of literature and to prepare talks. His wife admiringly responded, "I know, dear. We all know. We know every time you stand up to speak." As he spoke, listeners saw. The unremitting preparation through a lifetime of reading great literature naturally produced messages eloquent in both phrase and substance.

Refinement in speech is more than polished elocution. It results from purity of thought and sincerity of expression. A child's prayer on occasion may reflect the language of heaven more nearly than a Shakespearean soliloquy.

Refinement in speech is reflected not only in our choice of words but also in the things we talk about. There are those who always speak of themselves, and they are either insecure or proud. There are those who always speak of others. They are usually very boring. There are those who speak of stirring ideas, compelling books, and inspiring doctrine. These are the few who make their mark in this world. The subjects discussed in heaven are not trifling or mundane. They are sublime beyond our most extended imagination. We will feel at home there if we are rehearsed on this earth in conversing about the refined and noble, clothing our expressions in well-measured words.

I grew up in a home in which the Sunday afternoon meal was an institution. We remained in our church attire. My parents almost always invited a special guest to join us at the dinner table. Several times it was the then president of this university. We were expected to remain at the table and converse about worthwhile things. In later years, as a student at this school, we attempted to do the same, often gathering in one of the Heritage Halls' kitchens on a Sabbath afternoon for a reverie of uplifting conversation.

Is there a generation today that needs to be superficially entertained? What is the prospect of a young man sitting in a dorm on Friday evening to read a great book and be thrilled by the music of the masters? Is Friday evening a frenetic flight to see where the entertainment and action will be? Could our society produce a Newton or a Mozart? Can 85 channels and uncountable DVDs ever fill our insatiable appetite to be entertained? Do any unwisely become addicted to computer games or Internet surfing, thereby missing the richer experiences of great reading, conversations, and music enjoyment?

One wrote: "We need the slower and more lasting stimulus of solitary reading as a relief from the pressure on eye, ear and nerves of the torrent of information and entertainment pouring from ever-open electronic jaws."[9] This solitary reading should evidence our spiritual and refined taste in selection of the reading materials.

Another said: "[Education] has produced a vast population able to read but unable to distinguish what is worth reading."[10] This happy chapter of your lives at Brigham Young University will help you focus on reading materials of greatest worth.

I don't know whether our heavenly home has a television set or a DVD machine, but in my mind's imagery it surely has a grand piano and a magnificent library. There was a fine library in the home of President Hinckley's youth. It was not an ostentatious home, but the library contained about 1,000 volumes of the rich literature of the world, and President Hinckley spent his early years immersed in these books. When President Hinckley once came to my home, he spent time perusing the library. He observed the 50-volume collection of the Harvard Classics, commented that he has the same collection in his home, and said he had read much of it. To be well read, however, it is not necessary to possess expensive collections of literature, for they are available to rich and poor alike in the libraries of the world.

President David O. McKay was inclined to awaken at 4:00 a.m., skim read up to two books each day, and then commence his labors at

6:00 a.m. He could quote 1,000 poems from memory. We knew that whenever he stood at the pulpit. He referred to the grand masters of literature as the "minor prophets." He was a living embodiment of the scriptural admonition to "seek ye out of the best books words of wisdom."[11]

My wife and I recently spent four years on Church assignment in Eastern Europe, residing in Moscow, Russia. We often traveled on the Moscow underground subway called the Metro. We noticed the bowed heads of the Russian passengers, for they were reading Tolstoy, Chekhov, Dostoyevsky, or Pushkin—and, sometimes, Mark Twain. The people were poor, but they were not obsessed with their poverty. They possessed the rich tradition of Russian literature, art, and music.

Elder James E. Talmage, before his call to the Twelve, was a mining geologist. He once spoke of the features of certain geology he had observed during a field trip more than a year before. He explained that he could not with certainty recall the terrain until after he developed a photograph he had made of the location. The photographic plate had been laid away in darkness for an extended time. It had only been exposed to the light for one-fiftieth of a second—but the image was indelibly impressed on the negative, awaiting a future date to reveal its message.[12]

The lesson does not escape us. The images to which our minds are exposed are held in store, seemingly forgotten, even for years. But at the crucial moment they re-present themselves to influence our thoughts and lives. And so it is with the music, literature, art, media, and other images to which we are exposed. The pamphlet *For the Strength of Youth* states: "Whatever you read, listen to, or look at has an effect on you. Therefore, choose only entertainment and media that uplift you."[13]

These are the words of President McKay:

As with companions so with books. We may choose those which will make us better, more intelligent, more appreciative of the good and the beautiful in

the world, or we may choose the trashy, the vulgar, the obscene, which will
make us feel as though we've been "wallowing in the mire."[14]

If we know the books located at the bedside, we know much
about the man.

A good book, such as the scriptures, becomes a lifelong
companion. A thoughtful man wrote:

An unliterary man may be defined as one who reads books once only.[15]

I can't imagine a man really enjoying a book and reading it only once.[16]

Clearly one must read every good book at least once every ten years.[17]

The sure mark of an unliterary man is that he considers "I've read it
already" to be a conclusive argument against reading a work. . . . Those who
read great works, on the other hand, will read the same work ten, twenty or
thirty times during the course of their life.[18]

Of all the works worthy of repetitive reading, the scriptures stand
paramount, for they are not founded in the opinions of men. Over
the years I have oft remembered the counsel of the late Hugh Nibley:
"If you pray for an angel to visit you, you know what he'll do if he
comes. He'll just quote the scriptures to you—so you're wasting your
time waiting for what we already have."[19]

Many years ago, while living in another part of the country,
I became acquainted with a fine Latter-day Saint young man. He
was a superior athlete, but he had never attended a cultural event.
Living in the same community was a lovely young LDS sister. She
spoke French as well as English. She played the violin. She presented
herself as a refined daughter of God. One day the American Ballet
Theatre came to our town. A group of us decided to attend, including
this young man and young woman.

Now and then I glanced at the young man during the ballet. His
eyes were riveted on the stage. Windows of new appreciation were

opened. After the performance he approached me privately and said, in reference to the refined young sister, "Where have I been all of my life? This is what I want in my home. This is what I want as the mother of my children. Until now I thought only physical appearance mattered." I gently reminded him that she would likely be drawn to one of refined nature, like herself, and it was time for him to look within.

Dear daughters of God, you are the crown jewels of all of His creations. There has never been a sunset, symphony, or work of art as lovely as you. May you catch the vision that you are destined to be a refined and regal queen, honored by an uncountable posterity, worlds without end.

If we could peek behind the heavenly veil we would likely be inspired by the music of heaven, perhaps more glorious than any music we have heard on this earth.

When some music has passed the tests of time and been cherished by the noble and refined, our failure to appreciate it is not an indictment of grand music. The omission is within. If a young person grows up on a steady diet of hamburgers and french fries, he is not likely to become a gourmet. But the fault is not with fine food. He just grew up on something less. Some have grown up on a steady diet of musical french fries.

Elder Neal A. Maxwell said:

We . . . live in a world that is too prone to the tasteless, and we need to provide an opportunity to cultivate a taste for the finest music. And, likewise, we're in a world that's so attuned to the now. We need to permit people to be more attuned to the best music of all the ages.[20]

A few years ago I made my way to the bedroom of one of my sons to say good night. He was a junior in high school. As I approached his room, I heard the strains of Tchaikovsky's sixth symphony. I was surprised. I knew the boy loved sports, but I didn't know he loved Tchaikovsky. Months later, as my wife and I were listening to a videotape of three tenors singing, our son came in and sat down.

He listened and saw, and a new appreciation developed. He said: "You never told me about opera." He took the videotape to his room, and I never saw it again. Appreciation of the finest in music does not depend upon your age.

President J. Reuben Clark of the First Presidency, one of our greatest Christ scholars, used to listen to inspirational music in the evening before he began his insightful writings concerning the life of the Savior. The music opened his spiritual pores, as it does for all of us.

Recognizing the penetrating influence of great music, Oscar Wilde had one of his characters say: "After playing Chopin, I feel as if I had been weeping over sins that I had never committed, and mourning over tragedies that were not my own."[21] After the first performance of *Messiah*, Handel said: "My lord, I should be sorry if I only entertained them; I wish to make them better."[22] Haydn "dressed in his best clothes to compose because he said he was going before his maker."[23]

There are events of life so sublime that they cannot be imagined without the companionship of beautiful music. We could not have a Christmas without carols or a general conference without sacred anthems. And there could not be a heaven without music of surpassing beauty. Brigham Young said: "There is no music in hell, for all good music belongs to heaven."[24] It would be punishment enough to go to hell and not hear a note of music for all eternity.

This would be a good time to sift through your music library and choose primarily that which uplifts and inspires. It is part of the maturing process of your eternal journey. This would also be a fine time to learn a musical instrument or improve musical skills now partially possessed.

On the eve of his release, one of my fine missionaries during my tenure as a mission president spoke of a girl at home with whom he intended to renew association.

He inquired, "How will I know if she is the right one?"

I suggested, among other things, that he invite her to a cultural event. If she responded that this would be of no interest to her, then maybe he should pursue other alternatives. But if she had compelling spiritual qualities and could be enthralled by culture on Friday and love the athletic contest on Saturday, she might be the type of young lady he could choose as the mother for his children. It might be balanced and rewarding to be paired with her for eternity.

That which has been said about bringing great language, music, and literature into the home may be said with equal truth of great art—perhaps tastefully displayed in our heavenly home. It may also be said of our physical appearance and manners, as well as the order of the place in which we live, the way we offer our prayers, and the way we read God's word.

I once had opportunity to visit briefly with Audrey Hepburn, the great actress of days gone by, at the time she was making the movie *My Fair Lady.* She spoke of the opening scene in the movie in which she depicted a modest, unpolished flower girl. Her face had been besmirched with charcoal to make her seem part of her surroundings. "But," she said, with a twinkle in her eye, "I was wearing my Chanel perfume. Inside I still knew I was a lady." It doesn't take expensive perfume to make a lady, but it does require cleanliness, modesty, self-respect, and pride in one's appearance.

Many years ago an associate of mine decided he would please his wife by sharing with her a very specific compliment each night as he arrived home. One night he praised her cooking. A second night he thanked her for excellence in housekeeping. A third night he acknowledged her fine influence on the children. The fourth night, before he could speak, she said: "I know what you are doing. I thank you for it. But don't say any of those things. Just tell me you think I am beautiful."

She expressed an important need that she had. Women ought to be praised for all the gifts they possess that so unselfishly add to the richness of our lives, including their attentiveness to their personal appearance. We must not "let ourselves go" and become so casual— even sloppy—in our appearance that we distance ourselves from the beauty heaven has given us. Every man has the right to be married to a woman who makes herself as beautiful as she can be and who looks in the mirror to tidy herself up before he comes home. Every woman has a right to be married to a man who keeps himself clean, physically as well as morally, and takes pride in his appearance. A husband should hurry home because of the angel who awaits him, and that angel should be watching the clock awaiting his arrival.

Occasionally a young man comes home from his mission and hastens to distance himself in appearance from everything associated with missionary service. He becomes slovenly. Heaven blushes. The young man who wants an exemplary spouse needs to look in the mirror and ask why she would want him. Then he should shave and press his clothes.

Years ago I attended a stake conference in California at which the wife of the stake president shared this story: She had been born considerably after the other children in the family, and her father was unusually protective of her. When a suitor would stop by to pick her up for a date, the father would look him over very carefully and then say: "Do you want to date my princess? Go home and wash your car and shine your shoes. Then I will give my permission." I sometimes wonder if our Heavenly Father whispers the same when we date His precious daughters. The Book of Mormon speaks of a people who "did not wear costly apparel, yet they were neat and comely."[25]

There are those who flippantly say: "How I look has nothing to do with how God feels about me." But it is possible for both earthly and heavenly parents to have unspoken disappointment in their offspring without diminished love. I say it again: Sometimes heaven blushes but loves on.

President Joseph F. Smith, the sixth president of the Church, owned few things, but he took care of them. He was fastidious in his appearance. He pressed his dollar bills to remove the wrinkles. He allowed none but himself to pack his overnight bag. He knew where every article, nut, and bolt of the household was, and each had its place.

Would this be true of the environment in which you live? Is it a house of order? Need you dust, clean, and rearrange before you invite the Spirit of the Lord into your apartment? President Lorenzo Snow said: "The Lord does not intend that the Saints shall live always in dens and caves of the earth, but that they shall build fine houses. When the Lord comes he will not expect to meet a dirty people, but a people of refinement."[26]

David Starr Jordan, a former president of Stanford University, wrote:

To be vulgar is to do that which is not the best of its kind. It is to do poor things in poor ways, and to be satisfied with that. . . . It is vulgar to wear dirty linen when one is not engaged in dirty work. It is vulgar to like poor music, to read weak books, to feed on sensational newspapers, . . . to find amusement in trashy novels, to enjoy vulgar theatres, to find pleasure in cheap jokes.[27]

I once heard a story about an imaginary king whose wife gave birth to a baby boy. The parents knew that the lad would someday inherit the kingdom. Desiring that their son be a wise king, fully familiar with the needs of the people over whom he would reign, the king and queen took the infant into the country to be raised as part of a peasant family. He was to be told nothing of his secret destiny until he became a man.

At the appropriate time the king and queen returned to the country to confer on their son the kingdom. They were greatly disappointed. Having been told nothing of his appointed destiny, he was exactly that which life had prepared him to be. He understood the proper care of animals and the gathering of crops, but he knew nothing of armies and palaces and courtyards and presiding. He had lost his vision.

It should not be difficult for you to glean the truth in this story. Another King, your Father in Heaven, has sent you away from His presence to have experiences you would not have had in your heavenly home—all in preparation for the conferral of a kingdom. He doesn't want you to lose your vision. You are children of an exalted being. You are foreordained to preside as kings and queens. You will live in a home and environment of infinite refinement and beauty, as reflected in the language, literature, art, music, and order of heaven.

I close with the words of President Brigham Young: "Let us . . . show to the world that we have talent and taste, and prove to the heavens that our minds are set on beauty and true excellence, so that we can become worthy to enjoy the society of angels."[28] Even more, that we may enjoy the refined society of heavenly parentage, for we are of the race of the gods, being children of the Most High.

This is my testimony and my humble supplication for you, in the name of Jesus Christ, amen.

NOTES

1. Enos 1:27.

2. *JD* 9:170.

3. Articles of Faith 1:13.

4. Genesis 1:4.

5. Ben Jonson, *Timber; or, Discoveries Made upon Men and Matter* (1640).

6. C. S. Lewis, letter of 21 March 1916, paragraph 3, in *The Letters of C. S. Lewis to Arthur Greeves* (New York: Collier Books, 1986), 96.

7. Luke 2:14.

8. See Van Wyck Brooks, *The Life of Emerson* (New York: The Literary Guild, 1932), 297.

9. Storm Jameson, *Parthian Words* (New York: Harper and Row, 1970), 123.

10. George Macaulay Trevelyan, *English Social History: A Survey of Six Centuries, Chaucer to Queen Victoria* (London: Longmans, Green and Company, 1942), 582.

11. D&C 88:118.

12. See James E. Talmage, "The Parable of the Photographic Plate: An Episode in Field Work," *Improvement Era*, April 1914, 503–505.

13. *For the Strength of Youth: Fulfilling Our Duty to God* (Salt Lake City: The Church of Jesus Christ of Latter-day Saints, 2001), 17.

14. David O. McKay, *Pathways to Happiness* (Salt Lake City: Bookcraft, 1957), 15.

15. C. S. Lewis, paragraph 24 of "On Stories," in *On Stories: and Other Essays on Literature* (New York: Harcourt Brace Jovanovich, 1982), 16.

16. C. S. Lewis, letter of February 1932, in *Letters to Greeves*, 439.

17. Lewis, letter of 17 August 1933, in *Letters to Greeves*, 458.

18. C. S. Lewis, chapter 1, paragraph 4, in *An Experiment in Criticism* (New York: Harcourt Brace Jovanovich, 1982), 2.

19. Hugh Nibley, "Gifts," BYU lecture, 13 March 1979, in *Approaching Zion*, vol. 9 of *The Collected Works of Hugh Nibley* (Salt Lake City and Provo: Deseret Book Company and Foundation for Ancient Research and Mormon Studies, 1989), 87.

20. Neal A. Maxwell, remarks at the inauguration of KRIC-FM, Ricks College, May 1984.

21. In Oscar Wilde, "The Critic as Artist," part 1 (1891).

22. In George Hogarth, *Musical History, Biography, and Criticism* (New York: J. S. Redfield, 1848), 67; see "A Tribute to Handel," *Improvement Era*, May 1929, 574.

23. Reid Nibley, in Hal Williams, "Dr. Reid Nibley on Acquiring a Taste for Classical Music," *BYU Today*, April 1980, 14.

24. *JD* 9:244.

25. Alma 1:27.

26. Lorenzo Snow, in *Wilford Woodruff, Fourth President of the Church of Jesus Christ of Latter-Day Saints: History of His Life and Labors as Recorded in His Daily Journals*, prep. Matthias F. Cowley (Salt Lake City: Bookcraft, 1964), 468.

27. David Starr Jordan, *The Strength of Being Clean: A Study of the Quest for Unearned Happiness* (New York: H. M. Caldwell Co., 1900), 25.

28. *JD* 11:305.

Experiences Worth Remembering

———◆———

Gordon B. Hinckley

M y dear friends, over the years I have spoken many times to generations of students who have assembled in this great Marriott Center. Today, if you will bear with me, I think I shall change the pattern of those previous addresses. Whether that change will be acceptable or not will depend on you. Furthermore, it is Halloween, and that calls for something a little different, though I don't know why it should.

As all of you recognize, I am now an old man who has weathered many seasons and been touched and affected by many experiences. Emerson was once asked what books he had read that had most influenced his life. He replied that he could no more remember the books he had read than the meals he had eaten, but they had made him.

And so, in the spirit of what Emerson said, rather than giving a speech I have thought to offer several brief cameos or vignettes or seemingly little experiences that I remember from out of the past and that have touched my life in an unforgettable manner. They have all

Gordon B. Hinckley was president of The Church of Jesus Christ of Latter-day Saints when this devotional address was delivered on 31 October 2006. © *Intellectual Reserve, Inc.*

been published, and some of you may be familiar with them. They will not be in chronological order.

I begin with number one.

I was in the city of Torreón, Mexico, and was being driven about in a beautiful and expensive automobile. It belonged to a man named David Casteñeda. At one time he and his wife and their children lived on a little rundown farm. They owned 30 chickens, two pigs, and one skinny horse. They walked in poverty.

Then one day two missionaries called on them. Sister Casteñeda said, "The elders took the blinders from our eyes and brought light into our lives. We knew nothing of Jesus Christ. We knew nothing of God until they came."

They moved into the little town of Bermejillo. Circumstances led them to the junk business. They bought wrecked automobiles. This led to association with insurance companies. They gradually built a prosperous business in which the father and his five sons worked. With simple faith they paid their tithing. They lived the gospel. They served wherever they were called. Four of their sons and three of their daughters filled missions.

Through their influence some 200 of their family and friends have joined the Church. More than 30 sons and daughters of family and friends have served missions. They donated the land on which a chapel now stands. At the time I met them, the children—now grown to maturity—and the parents were taking turns going to Mexico City each month to work in the temple. They are a shining and inspirational example of the miraculous power of missionary work. Think of the wonderful consequences of their being taught and receiving the teachings of the gospel from two humble missionaries. Such miracles are occurring today all across the world.

Now, vignette number two.

I have stood at the tomb of Napoleon in Paris, at the tomb of Lenin in Moscow, and before the burial places of many others of the mighty leaders of the earth. In their time they commanded armies, they ruled with near omnipotence, and their very words brought terror into the hearts of people.

I have reverently walked through some of the great cemeteries of the world. I have reflected quietly and thoughtfully as I have stood in the military cemetery in Manila in the Philippines. There, laid out in perfect symmetry, are marble crosses marking the graves of 17,000 Americans who gave their lives in the Second World War. Encircling this burial ground are beautiful marble colonnades, where are remembered another 35,000 who died in the terrible battles of the Pacific and whose remains were never found.

I have walked with reverence through the British cemetery on the outskirts of Rangoon, Burma (now known as Myanmar), and noted the names of hundreds and thousands of young men who came from the villages, towns, and great cities of the British Isles and who gave their lives in hot and distant places. I have strolled through old cemeteries in Asia and Europe and yet other places, and I have reflected on the lives of those who were once buoyant and happy, who were creative and distinguished, who gave much to the world in which they lived. They have all passed into the darkness of the grave.

All who have lived upon the earth before us are now gone. They have left all behind as they have stepped over the threshold of silent death. As I have visited these various cemeteries I have reflected, first, on the terrible cost of war. What a fruitless thing it so often is, and what a terrible price it exacts.

I have thought further of the oblivion of the grave. What would we do without the atoning sacrifice of Jesus Christ, the Son of God, our Savior and our Redeemer? He has given us the assurance that life goes on beyond the veil, that it is purposeful and productive, and that each of us shall go on living after we depart this life.

Number three, the next item in my chronicle of significant events, is the great and deadly plague of the 14th century, followed by the Renaissance, and eventually followed by the Restoration of the gospel.

Following the death of the Savior the centuries rolled on. A cloud of darkness settled over the earth. Isaiah described it: "For, behold, the darkness shall cover the earth, and gross darkness the people" (Isaiah 60:2).

It was a season of plunder and suffering, marked by long and bloody conflict. Charlemagne was crowned emperor of the Romans in the year 800.

It was an age of hopelessness, a time of masters and serfs.

The first thousand years passed, and the second millennium dawned. Its earlier centuries were a continuation of the former. It was a time fraught with fear and suffering. In the 14th century the great plague began in Asia. It spread to Europe and on up to England. Everywhere it went there was sudden death. Boccaccio said of its victims, "At noon [they] dined with their relatives and friends, and at night [they] supped with their ancestors in the next world!" (Giovanni Boccaccio, *The Decameron*, trans. Richard Aldington [1930 trans.; Garden City, New York: Garden City Books, 1949], 7).

The plague struck terror in the hearts of people. In five years it took the lives of 25 million—one-third the population of Europe. Periodically it reappeared, with its dark and ghoulish hand striking indiscriminately.

But this was also a season of growing enlightenment, the dawning of the Renaissance. As the years continued their relentless march, the sunlight of a new day began to break over the earth. There was a magnificent flowering of art, architecture, and literature.

Reformers worked to change the church—notably such men as Luther, Melanchthon, Hus, Zwingli, and Tyndale. These were men of great courage, some of whom suffered cruel deaths because of their beliefs. Protestantism was born with its cry for reformation.

While this great ferment was stirring across the Christian world, political forces were also at work.

There came the American Revolutionary War, resulting in the birth of a nation whose constitution declared that government should not reach its grasping hand into matters of religion. A new day had dawned—a glorious day. Here there was no longer a state church. No one faith was favored above another.

All of the history of the past had pointed to this season. The centuries, with all of their suffering and all of their hope, had come and gone. The Almighty Judge of the nations, the Living God, determined that the times of which the prophets had spoken had arrived. Daniel had foreseen a stone that was cut out of the mountain without hands and that rolled forth and filled the whole earth (see Daniel 2:34–35).

Then occurred that most wonderful event, the revealing of the Father and the Son to the 14-year-old Joseph Smith. There followed in orderly procession the coming forth of the Book of Mormon and the restoration of the priesthood with keys to unlock the door of eternal life. How thankful we should be for these marvelous and wonderful things that so richly bless our lives, including the privilege of attending this university.

And now, number four is a cameo of a little different nature.

Joseph Anderson was a Seventy. He lived to be 102, the oldest General Authority ever.

He served as secretary to President Heber J. Grant, beginning way back in 1922. In his old age, President Grant became seriously ill. When Joseph visited with him, President Grant said, "Joseph, have I ever been unkind to you? Have I ever abused you in any way?"

Joseph said, "No, President Grant, you have never been unkind to me in all these many years."

Tears rolled down President Grant's cheeks, and he said, "Joseph, I am glad that you can say that I have never been unkind to you."

President Grant died the next day. Joseph Anderson, through the remainder of his life, had reason to rejoice in the kindness, the civility, the decency, the honesty, and the integrity on the part of a most remarkable and wonderful man—President Heber J. Grant.

Number five is a touch on the lighter side. My father used to tell this story:

A boy came down to breakfast one morning and said to his father, "Dad, I was dreaming about you last night."

"You were?"

"Yes."

"What were you dreaming?"

"I was dreaming that I was climbing a ladder to heaven, and on each rung of the ladder as I went up, I had to write one of my sins."

His father said, "Yes, where do I come into your dream?"

The boy said, "As I was going up, I met you coming down for more chalk."

Now for number six:

I have always loved this piece of poetry by Rosemary and Stephen Benét. It is entitled "Nancy Hanks" and speaks the thoughts of the mother of Abraham Lincoln. It reads as follows:

If Nancy Hanks
Came back as a ghost,
Seeking news
Of what she loved most,
She'd ask first
"Where's my son?
What's happened to Abe?
What's he done?

"Poor little Abe,
Left all alone
Except for Tom,
Who's a rolling stone;
He was only nine
The year I died.
I remember still
How hard he cried.

"Scraping along
In a little shack,
With hardly a shirt
To cover his back,
And a prairie wind
To blow him down,
Or pinching times
If he went to town.

"You wouldn't know
About my son?
Did he grow tall?
Did he have fun?
Did he learn to read?
Did he get to town?
Do you know his name?
Did he get on?"
[Rosemary and Stephen Vincent Benét, "Nancy Hanks," in *A Book of Americans* (New York: Farrar and Rinehart, 1933), 65]

You know the answer. He became America's most-admired president.

Number seven:

No series of vignettes drawn from Church history would be complete without reference to the handcart pioneers of 1856—150 years ago at this very season.

My wife's great-grandmother, Mary Penfold Goble, was baptized in England. The family joined the Hunt Wagon Company, which accompanied the Martin Handcart Company. Her daughter's account is written in the simple, matter-of-fact manner of a young girl, but behind those plain words is stark tragedy. She wrote:

We traveled from 15 to 25 miles a day. . . .

We traveled on till we got to the Platte River. . . . We caught up with the handcart companies that day. We watched them cross the river. There were great lumps of ice floating down the river. It was bitter cold. The next morning there were fourteen dead. . . . We went back to camp and went to prayers. We sang the song "Come, Come, Ye Saints, No Toil Nor Labor Fear." I wondered what made my mother cry. . . . The next morning my little sister was born. It was the 23rd of September. We named her Edith, and she lived six weeks and died. . . . [She was buried at the last crossing of the Sweetwater.]

When we arrived at Devil's Gate it was bitter cold. . . . My brother James . . . was as well as he ever was when he went to bed. In the morning he was dead.

My feet were frozen [also my brother's and sister's]. *It was nothing but snow. We could not drive the pegs . . . for our tents. . . .*

. . . We did not know what would become of us. One night a man came to our camp and told us . . . [Brigham] *Young had sent men and teams to help us. . . . We sang songs, some danced and some cried. . . .*

. . . My mother . . . never got well. . . . She died between the Little and Big Mountains. . . . She was 43 years old. . . .

We arrived in Salt Lake City [at] *nine o'clock at night the 11th of December 1856. Three out of* [the] *four that were living were frozen. My mother was dead in the wagon. . . .*

Early next morning . . . Brigham Young . . . came. . . . When he saw our condition—our feet frozen and our mother dead—tears rolled down his cheeks.

The doctor amputated my toes . . . [while] *the sisters were dressing mother* [for her grave]. *. . . . That afternoon she was buried.* [Life of Mary Ann Goble Pay, autobiographical sketch, typescript, LDS Church Archives, Salt Lake City; also, "Mary Goble Pay Autobiography," in Arthur D. Coleman, comp., *Pay-Goble Pioneers of Nephi, Juab County, Utah* (Salt Lake City: n.p., 1968), 78–81; text modernized]

What a story in a few brief words.

Number eight:

In 1966, while the Vietnam War was raging, I went to that land. When we landed at Tan Son Nhut Airport, Colonel Rosza put a piece of paper in front of me and said, "Sign this."

I said, "What is it?"

He said, "It's a release relieving the United States government of any responsibility for you while you are in Vietnam."

I signed the release, and we climbed aboard an old "goony bird" airplane and went down the runway. The sergeant had left the door open. When we got up in the air I said, "Aren't you going to close the door?"

And he said, "It's too hot."

And so we flew up to Da Nang, and I'll never forget that meeting as long as I live. Men came in from the battle areas and stacked their rifles at the door of the building. Three of their number had been killed that previous week, and we held a memorial service for them and had a meeting. Soldiers of the Jewish faith were to have had the building that night—it was Saturday—and when they saw how many of us there were (there were only about a dozen of them), they generously said, "You go back in and use the building."

When the meeting was over, we were loaded into an army ambulance and taken to stay the night in an unfinished field hospital. It was made of components that were being bolted together—produced in the States and shipped to Vietnam. The windows were all sealed and the air-conditioning wasn't working, so it was like an oven. To take a shower we had a big barrel of water with a dipper. All through the night fighter aircraft were flying north, and we wondered how many of them would come back.

We went down to Nha Trang on Sunday morning and held a wonderful meeting there. We had the sacrament with men who hadn't had the sacrament in months.

For me that was a great and significant and unforgettable experience.

Number nine:

I had a long-remembered meeting with Mr. Shimon Peres of Israel. He was a former prime minister. He had seen much of conflict and trouble in his time.

I asked him whether there was any solution to the great problems that constantly seem to divide the people of Israel and the Palestinians. He replied, "Of course there is."

As I recall, he said, "When we were Adam and Eve, we were all one. Is there any need for us now to be divided into segments with hatred for one another?"

He told a very interesting story that he said he had heard from a Muslim. The Muslim told of a Jewish rabbi who was conversing with two of his friends. The rabbi asked one of the men, "How do you know when the night is over and a new day has begun?"

His friend replied, "When you look into the east and can distinguish a sheep from a goat, then you know the night is over and the day has begun."

The second was asked the same question. He replied, "When you look into the distance and can distinguish an olive tree from a fig tree, then you know morning has come."

They then asked the rabbi how he could tell when the night is over and the day has begun. He thought for a time and then said, "When you look into the east and see the face of a woman and you can say, 'She is my sister.' And when you look into the east and see the face of a man and can say, 'He is my brother.' Then you know the light of a new day has come."

Think of that for a few moments, my dear friends. How eloquently it speaks of the true meaning of brotherhood.

And so, my brothers and sisters, I might go on. I have given you a sampling of significant occasions that have forever touched my life.

They have influenced my thinking and my behavior. They have affected my life in an unforgettable manner.

You likewise will have significant experiences. I hope that you will write them down and keep a record of them, that you will read them from time to time and refresh your memory of these meaningful and significant things.

Some of them may be funny. Some may be of significance only to you. Some of them may be sacred and quietly beautiful. Some may build one upon another until they represent a lifetime of special experience. So it was with the girl I married nearly 70 years ago. My experiences with her stand out vividly in my memory. I cannot forget them. When she was young I was bewitched and in love. That love strengthened through the years. She came to be a woman of recognized capacity. She traveled across the world with me and spoke on every continent, giving encouragement and bearing her testimony. She authored books. She was once honored here as the woman of the year. A chair at this university carries her name.

She left me two and a half years ago. The resulting loneliness never entirely disappears. On the granite marker at her grave site are inscribed the words "Beloved Eternal Companion." Such she is and such she always will be.

I remind you that the association you now enjoy as students is probably the best time of your lives to find your own "Beloved Eternal Companion." Do so with a prayer in your heart. It will be the most important decision you will ever make. It will influence your life from now through all eternity.

God bless you, my beloved friends. May this be a wonderful season in your lives as you attend this great Church-sponsored university is my humble prayer, in the name of Jesus Christ, amen.

Faith and Works in a Secular World

Keith B. McMullin

Ｍy dear brothers and sisters, what a sobering sight you are, coming from various walks of life and various parts of the country. And to think this evening we are assembled across the breadth of the earth. Between now and the rebroadcast of these proceedings, young adults throughout the Church will gather together and participate in such an event as this. It is truly marvelous.

A glorious thing happened at general conference last month. For most of the world it went unnoticed, but for those who know and love the truth it was as unforgettable as the clap of 10,000 thunders.

Think back to the closing session. From the Tabernacle Choir came the familiar strains:

We thank thee, O God, for a prophet
To guide us in these latter days.
We thank thee for sending the gospel
To lighten our minds with its rays.[1]

Keith B. McMullin was Second Counselor in the Presiding Bishopric of The Church of Jesus Christ of Latter-day Saints when this fireside address was delivered on 5 November 2006. © Intellectual Reserve, Inc.

Of a sudden, men and women, boys and girls assembled in the Conference Center arose in reverence and gratitude for the blessings spoken of in this hymn. We stood in grateful acknowledgment that the gospel of Jesus Christ has been restored, that God the Father and His Beloved Son have spoken from the heavens, that Joseph Smith was a prophet, and that President Gordon B. Hinckley is the Lord's prophet on the earth today.

It was a spiritually moving experience. It was a time when citizens of God's kingdom, acting under the influence of the Holy Ghost, *stood up for their faith!*

Earlier that day President Hinckley had spoken tenderly and gratefully about his advanced years and attendant health. Always an example of faithfulness, he pledged anew his life to the Lord's purposes. Said he:

> *The Lord has permitted me to live; I do not know for how long. But whatever the time, I shall continue to give my best to the task at hand. . . .*
>
> *. . . We shall carry on as long as the Lord wishes. . . . When it is time for a successor, the transition will be smooth and according to the will of Him whose Church this is. And so, we go forward in faith*—and faith is the theme I wish to discuss this morning.[2]

His message was timely and inspired. It came as a spiritual reminder of what life is really about and how Heavenly Father's children can overcome every obstacle. It came to a world steeped in secularism, unbelief, and sin.

SECULARISM

Education in secular subjects contributes much to the betterment of our world. Secular learning of the highest level blossoms in an atmosphere of virtue, moral responsibility, spiritual truth, and faith.

Much is touted today about secular societies. People and nations pride themselves in being *secular,* in focusing on "worldly things or [on] things that are not regarded as religious, spiritual, or sacred."[3]

Much of the world today views secularism as vital to a balanced, just, and ordered government. Hence, religious expression is discouraged in public forums, civil rights are dependent on the courts and legislative processes, and men and women readily seek solutions and redress through litigious means. In the extreme, society's secularism overlooks the concept of eternal life, places all things in the context of the natural world, and consequently is prone to *works without faith.*

It requires watchfulness and great effort to be men and women of faith in a secular world. When inundated by worldliness, it is the nature of man to "first endure, then pity, then embrace."[4] Secularism is inundating people today with such results.

Unchecked by faith in Christ as the Redeemer of mankind, this secular or natural world produces men and women who are

proud, obsessed with self, overly competitive, reactionary, fiercely independent, driven by desires, appetites, [and] *worldly acclaim. . . . In general, the natural man is an unredeemed creature, a being who walks . . . in the light of his own fire . . .* [see 2 Nephi 7:10–11]. *Such a one is acclimated to the nature of things about him, taking his cues and bearings from a fallen world.*[5]

Succinctly stated, "Men that are in a state of nature . . . are without God in the world" (Alma 41:11).

Because secularism typically ignores the eternal perspective, it can in time lead to unbelief. In the words of Wolfhart Pannenberg, a professor of theology at the University of Munich:

A public climate of secularism undermines the confidence of Christians in the truth of what they believe. . . .

In a secular milieu, even an elementary knowledge of Christianity . . . dwindles. It is no longer a matter of rejecting Christian teachings; large numbers of people have not the vaguest knowledge of what those teachings are. . . . The more widespread the ignorance of Christianity, the greater the prejudice against Christianity. . . .

. . . The difficulty is exacerbated by the cultural relativizing of the very idea of truth. . . . In the view of many, . . . Christian doctrines are merely opinions that may or may not be affirmed according to individual preference, or depending on whether they speak to personally felt needs. . . .

. . . The thoroughly secularized social order gives rise to a feeling of meaninglessness.[6]

Faith in Christ is replaced by faith in man. In public discourse and private thought, the questions of where we came from, where we go when life is over, and what ultimately governs the here and now not only go unaddressed but are also considered irrelevant. This state of unbelief is becoming a calamity of colossal proportions.

Heavenly Father knew this would happen. The Restoration of the gospel rekindled faith in Jesus Christ as Creator, Savior, and Redeemer. It brought again the correct understanding of life's purposes. In 1831 Heavenly Father's children were told:

Wherefore, I the Lord, knowing the calamity which should come upon the inhabitants of the earth, called upon my servant Joseph Smith, Jun., and spake unto him from heaven, and gave him commandments; . . .

That faith . . . might increase in the earth. [D&C 1:17, 21]

Before the foundations of this world were laid, before the orbs of the universe received their place, men and women lived and moved and had their being (see Acts 17:28). The secular thought that life is nothing more than biology denies the fundamental truth, the subconscious awareness residing in the recesses of every living soul, that "man *was* also in the beginning *with God*" (D&C 93:29; emphasis added). This fact is immutable and irrefutable.

Paradisiacal Eden with our first parents, Adam and Eve, came thereafter so that man, through mortal life's experiences and Christ's Redemption, might become a complete, fully developed, and perfected being. The ages of the patriarchs, the supernal advent of our Savior and His incomparable Atonement in the meridian of time, and "the times of restitution of all things" (Acts 3:21), which began in 1820, set the framework by which men and women, boys and girls could once more govern their lives and surroundings by "faith in the Lord Jesus Christ" (Articles of Faith 1:4).

My dear young friends, you stand at the confluence of these world events. "What is past is prologue, and what has been is yet to be."[7] What can happen—what must happen—is that your faith and accompanying works will stem the tide of unbelief. This is your lot in life. This is your sacred duty.

BENCHMARKS OF FAITH

Our Master said, "If ye have faith as a grain of mustard seed, . . . nothing shall be impossible unto you" (Matthew 17:20). President Hinckley reminded us: "When all is said and done, the only real wealth of the Church is in the faith of its people."[8]

He also said: "In the on-working of this great cause, increased faith is what we most need. Without it, the work would stagnate. With it, no one can stop its progress."[9]

Such faith is more than attitude, more than belief, more than testimony of what one knows or feels. Real faith, the faith spoken of by our beloved prophet, begets righteousness in this life and salvation in the life to come. It is centered in the true and living God and in Jesus Christ whom He has sent (see John 17:3). It is founded on truth, preceded by knowledge, and perfected by works. It causes mortals to understand and behave as Heavenly Father's children should. This faith "is the first great governing principle which [enables us to have] power, dominion, and authority over"[10] how we think, how we act, and what manner of men and women we are.

The Apostle James gave us the formula for such faith:

What profit is it . . . for a man to say he hath faith, and hath not works? . . .

Yea, a man may say, I will show thee I have faith without works; but I say, Show me thy faith without works, and I will show thee my faith by my works. . . .

. . . Faith, if it have not works is dead, being alone. . . .

Seest thou how works [are] *wrought with . . . faith, and by works* [is] *faith made perfect?* [JST, James 2:14–15, 17, 21]

We hear much about *benchmarks.* A benchmark is "a standard of excellence [or] achievement . . . against which similar things [are] measured or judged."[11]

There are four benchmarks that can help each of us know if our personal faith in Christ is being "made perfect" by our works. These benchmarks are (1) the choices we make, (2) the devotion we exhibit, (3) the obedience we practice, and (4) the service we give. Permit me to explain.

THE CHOICES WE MAKE

First, the benchmark of choice. Latter-day Saints "believe in *being* honest, true, chaste, benevolent, virtuous. . . . If there is anything virtuous, lovely, or of good report or praiseworthy, *we seek after* these things" (Articles of Faith 1:13; emphasis added).

Imagine a young elder, whom we will call Bill. He learned this in Primary. He believed it then; he believes it now. For some time, however, Bill has been plagued with pornography. He has found its allurements powerful and addictive. After each encounter with this sleazy stuff, Bill has felt sickened, ashamed, and worthless inside.

Bill attended general conference a few weeks ago. In the priesthood session, he heard President Hinckley say:

There is not a man or boy in this vast congregation tonight who cannot improve his life. And that needs to happen. After all, we hold the priesthood of God. . . .

With this priesthood comes a great obligation to be worthy of it. We cannot indulge in unclean thoughts. We must not partake of pornography. We must never be guilty of abuse of any kind. We must rise up above such things. "Rise up, O men of God!" and put these things behind you, and the Lord will be your guide and stay.[12]

Bill decided, "It is time for me to stand up for my faith!"

He went to that secret place, retrieved the filthy pictures, the vulgar films and literature, and destroyed them. He purged his library of the hard, raucous music and sordid lyrics. He deleted from his computer all references to pornographic sites, installed a protective filter, and placed his computer in a more public place so as to fortify himself against repeating his sin.

Bill acknowledged his transgressions before God. He prayed fervently for the strength to repent, to expel this evil from his life. He sought help from his bishop and loved ones. In his extremity, Bill has felt the quiet assurance "My son, you are on the right path." His faith, because of his works, is being affirmed and strengthened.

Much remains to be done. There will be fasting, prayer, scripture study, and many tears. A good bishop will provide indispensable help. The faithfulness and prayers of parents and loved ones will provide needed support. Nevertheless, *the benchmark shows: Bill is beginning to exercise faith unto repentance—he has made the right choice!*

THE DEVOTION WE EXHIBIT

Second, the benchmark of devotion. Latter-day Saints

believe all that God has revealed, all that He does now reveal, and we believe that He will yet reveal many great and important things pertaining to the Kingdom of God.

We believe in the literal gathering of Israel and in the restoration of the Ten Tribes; that Zion (the New Jerusalem) will be built upon the American continent. [Articles of Faith 1:9–10]

And Latter-day Saints believe that men and women are "called of God, by prophecy" and divine authority to bring this about (Articles of Faith 1:5).

True devotion is tied to divine causes set in motion before the foundations of this world. Righteous ancestors enlisted in them and gave their lives to the furtherance of Heavenly Father's purposes. We have been entrusted to carry on, to build upon their consecrated labors.

Now a story, one familiar to some of you:

In 1856 Robert and Ann Parker, with their four children, embarked from England to join the Saints in Utah. A prophet had spoken, and theirs was the charge to gather to the Great Basin and help build Zion. As members of the McArthur Handcart Company, each in their family bore a share of the work. Father and Mother pulled the heavy cart, Maxie (12 years of age) pushed, and Martha (10 years old) tended little Arthur (six years of age). Baby Ada (one year old) toddled, was carried, and rode in the cart.

Somewhere in Nebraska little Arthur sat down to rest and fell asleep. A sudden storm arose. The company hurried on and made camp. It was then they discovered that Arthur was not with the other children.

Days of searching were in vain. The company had to press on. This was the time for Robert and Ann Parker to act in accordance with their faith. Archer Walters recorded in his diary under July 2, 1856: "Brother Parker's little boy . . . was lost, and the father went back to hunt him."

As Robert departed, Ann pinned a bright red shawl about his shoulders and said: "If you find him dead, wrap him in the shawl to bury him. If you find him alive, you could use this as a flag to signal us." She, with the other children, took up the handcart and struggled on with the company.

Robert retraced the miles of forest trail, calling, searching, and praying for their helpless little son. At last he reached a mail and trading station where he learned that their child had been cared for by a woodsman and his wife. Little Arthur had been ill from exposure and fright, but God had heard the prayers of his loving parents.

On the trail each night, Ann and her children kept watch. On the third night, as the rays of the setting sun caught the glimmer of a bright red shawl, this brave mother sank in a pitiful heap in the sand. Completely exhausted, Ann slept for the first time in six long days and nights.[13] God indeed was kind and merciful; their works had rewarded their devotion and sanctified their faith, and in the gladness of their hearts the Saints sang, "All is well!"[14]

Baby Ada, my grandmother, grew to womanhood and married my grandfather, Brigham Young McMullin. Now here is the moral. She never allowed her children to forget that she and her family came across the plains with the Daniel D. McArthur Handcart Company. The story of the red shawl became our story—the legacy of their faith became ours as well. And so we all "carry on,"[15] and great obstacles fade as the dew before the morning sun.

About these early Saints, *the benchmark shows: Their works were a hallmark of faith, their devotion a standard for their posterity to live by.*

THE OBEDIENCE WE PRACTICE

Third, the benchmark of obedience. Latter-day Saints "believe that through the Atonement of Christ, all mankind may be saved, by *obedience to the laws and ordinances of the Gospel*" (Articles of Faith 1:3; emphasis added).

Here we imagine a young couple representative of those living in this secular world. David and Michelle knew this article of faith long before they knew each other. Even so, they deal with concerns facing many participating in this broadcast. You see, David and Michelle are in their mid-to-late twenties. They have known one another for some time, they "hang out" together, and they are in love. Nevertheless, they are indecisive about marriage and family. Should they postpone marriage until they have completed their schooling, until they have more money, until some of their personal ambitions are realized?

They also wonder about the escalating trends of divorce, the wars and tumults around the world, and overpopulation. Would their marriage survive? Should they bring children into such a world?

Oh, David and Michelle, exercise your faith! Remember: "Marriage between a man and a woman is ordained of God."[16] "What . . . God hath joined together, let not man put asunder" (Matthew 19:6; see also D&C 132:19–20). "Children are an heritage of the Lord" (Psalm 127:3). "The earth is full, . . . there is enough and to spare" (D&C 104:17).

Act upon what you know to be true and your righteous works will perfect your faith. Your lives will be full and wonderful. Follow the good example of your parents. They could not afford to get married, but they did. They too worried about war and tumult, but they exercised their faith and had you! The demands of marriage and family did not deter their education; they enriched it. As for their personal ambitions, they are completely and happily entwined in the well-being of each other and of you, your brothers and sisters, and the grandchildren.

Life was not easy for your parents. They had to scrimp and save, make do with what they had. They too faced questions and circumstances they could not answer, but they knew that the pathway ordained by Almighty God decreed that they move ahead. And you are so much "richer" because of it.

From the stories they have told you over and over again, you know that everything for them has been uphill, "both ways." But their works have sanctified their faith.

They are older, to be sure. Their step is not as spry, their manner not as intense, their appearance not something advertisers typically clamor for. But their love for God and for each other reflects deep reverence and adoration. The scars of life have afforded them wisdom, patience, and gratitude. In small but important ways they have become "the substance of things hoped for, the evidence of things not seen" (Hebrews 11:1)—things they could not see earlier in life. But they obeyed. Exercising their faith, they were sealed in the temple, were blessed with children, and now know the true sources of happiness. *The benchmark shows: Obedience calls forth the blessings of heaven—it did so for your parents and it will do so for you.*

THE SERVICE WE GIVE

Fourth, the benchmark of service. Latter-day Saints

believe in God, the Eternal Father, and in His Son, Jesus Christ, and in the Holy Ghost. . . .

We believe . . . that Christ will reign personally upon the earth; and, that the earth will be renewed and receive its paradisiacal glory. [Articles of Faith 1:1, 10]

We know more about the Godhead than all the minds of men have ever conceived—and what we know is true. Furthermore, we know the purposes of Deity for this earth and all of its creatures. Because of what we know and because the Lord has placed upon our shoulders the sacred duty to help bring it to pass, we must not be casual about our Church membership.

Some are enticed into being less committed for fear of appearing to be too religious. They view "the Church as an institution, but not as a kingdom."[17] "O youth of the noble birthright,"[18] make the work of the Church and kingdom of God the center of your life. When called to serve, say, "Yes," and do your very best. Listen to this charge from the Lord:

> *Wherefore, seek not the things of this world but seek ye first to build up the kingdom of God, and to establish his righteousness, and all these things shall be added unto you.* [JST, Matthew 6:38]

In just four days from now, on November 9, it will be 150 years since the ill-fated Willie Handcart Company pioneers struggled into the Salt Lake Valley. They had waded through much suffering and death. The storms and their weakened condition had claimed many— the rescuers had saved many more.

Levi Savage was among those arriving that day. History records his faithful and dogged labors to save the Saints and bring them safely to the valley. But his noble service did not begin on the snow-bound plains of Wyoming. This was but another chapter, perhaps the crowning one, in a consecrated life of service.

Levi was baptized in June 1846 at 26 years of age. Answering the prophet's call to move west, he noted that

> *we prepared as well as we could for a long journey into a strange and to us wholly unknown country. . . . We bid adieu to the old homestead . . . and directed our course westward, not knowing the place of destination, only we expected to locate somewhere in the western wilds of the Rocky Mountains.*[19]

On July 16, 1846, he, with other valiant men, again responded to the prophet's urging, enlisted in the Mormon Battalion, and marched approximately 2,000 miles from Council Bluffs, Iowa, to San Diego, California, and then on to Los Angeles. Here they were discharged from government service. Though they knew nothing of the whereabouts of their homes and families, they began their trek to the valley of the Great Salt Lake. The route Levi Savage traveled was an additional 1,300 miles over rugged and hostile terrain, but he finally arrived in the Salt Lake Valley.

Here Levi pioneered, fought crickets, married, had a son, and buried his wife some months following the child's birth. Ten months after his wife's death, in the October conference of 1852, he and several other faithful brethren were called by the prophet to open a gospel mission to Siam (today's Thailand).

This time they journeyed by team and wagon back to lower California and the Pacific Ocean. In time, they sailed from San Francisco to Calcutta, bound for their mission to Siam. Levi's journal entry of January 29, 1853, provides us a glimpse into the hearts of these early missionaries. He wrote:

Our gallant ship, propelled by a gentle breeze, steered her course across the boisterous deep for our places of destination; leaving behind us our much loved native land. . . . Each sought his own place for meditation, and there reflected upon the comforts of his home, the affections of his beloved wife and children or friends. . . . But now he was called to take up his abode in the remote parts of the earth, and for what? For the sake of heaping up gold and silver, or to secure for himself the honors, pomp and splendor of this world? No, verily no! But in obedience to the commands of the Lord to carry the message of truth and . . . salvation to the benighted and superstitious nations. *Soon after, each retired to his cot for rest and repose. But whether asleep or awake, his mind continued to wander upon the realities of the past, and the prospects of the future.*[20]

Following his mission, Levi sailed home by way of Boston, Massachusetts, made his way to his place of birth in Greenfield,

Ohio, and noted upon his arrival there, "I have circled the globe."[21] He joined the Willie Handcart Company in Iowa City, Iowa, which began a saga of eternal importance to him, his family, and the entire Church. His works in that epic crowned a life of sacrifice and service. Of these pioneers, *the benchmark shows: Their faith and works were a beacon in an unbelieving world, their service a pattern for each of us to follow.*

We are moved by the words from the clergyman Frederick W. Faber:

Faith of our fathers, living still,
In spite of dungeon, fire, and sword;
Oh, how our hearts beat high with joy
Whene'er we hear that glorious word.

Faith of our fathers, we will strive
To win all nations unto thee,
And thru the truth that comes from God,
Mankind shall then be truly free.

Faith of our fathers, we will love
Both friend and foe in all our strife,
And preach thee, too, as love knows how,
By kindly words and virtuous life.

Faith of our fathers, holy faith,
We will be true to thee till death![22]

I bear you my witness, my dear brothers and sisters—God is in His heavens, His name is Elohim, and He knows all of His children, irrespective of from whence they come or where they dwell. Jesus, the Holy One of Israel, is His Beloved Son, the Redeemer of all mankind. Joseph Smith, a young lad, was called by the voice of God and His Holy Son as a prophet, and ensuing from that call the true Church and kingdom of God was restored on the earth. How blessed we are to know these things, and you, my dear brothers and sisters, you stand at the confluence of history. You came from realms of glory. It is your singular privilege to be true to the faith, to press forward in good works. Do what the prophets say. Generations past expect it, generations present are saved by it, generations future depend upon it, and the Holy Spirit will guide you every step of your way.

In the name of Jesus Christ, amen.

NOTES

1. "We Thank Thee, O God, for a Prophet," *Hymns*, 1985, no. 19.

2. Gordon B. Hinckley, *CR*, September–October 2006, 87; or "The Faith to Move Mountains," *Ensign*, November 2006, 82; emphasis added.

3. *Random House Webster's Unabridged Dictionary*, 2nd ed. (2001), s.v. "secular," 1731.

4. Alexander Pope, *An Essay on Man* (1733–1734), Epistle 2, line 220.

5. *Book of Mormon Reference Companion*, ed. Dennis L. Largey (Salt Lake City: Deseret Book, 2003), s.v. "natural man," 582.

6. Wolfhart Pannenberg, "How to Think About Secularism," *First Things*, no. 64 (June–July 1996): 27, 30; www.firstthings.com/ftissues/ft9606/articles/pannenberg.html.

7. Boyd K. Packer, General Authority training meeting, October 2006; see William Shakespeare, *The Tempest*, act 2, scene 1, line 261.

8. Gordon B. Hinckley, *CR*, April 1991, 74; or "The State of the Church," *Ensign*, May 1991, 54.

9. Gordon B. Hinckley, *CR*, September–October 2006, 90; or "Faith to Move Mountains," 85.

10. Joseph Smith, comp., *Lectures on Faith* (Salt Lake City: Deseret Book, 1985), 5, 8 [1:24].

11. *Random House Webster's Unabridged Dictionary*, s.v. "benchmark," 193.

12. Gordon B. Hinckley, *CR*, September–October 2006, 66; or "Rise Up, O Men of God," *Ensign*, November 2006, 60.

13. See Boyd K. Packer, "Bringing in the Lost," *Memorable Stories and Parables by Boyd K. Packer* (Salt Lake City: Bookcraft, 1997), 4–6; LeRoy R. Hafen and Ann W. Hafen, *Handcarts to Zion* (Glendale, California: Arthur H. Clark Co., 1960), 60–64.

14. "Come, Come, Ye Saints," *Hymns*, 1985, no. 30.

15. "Carry On," *Hymns*, 1985, no. 255.

16. "The Family: A Proclamation to the World," *Ensign*, November 1995, 102.

17. Neal A. Maxwell, *CR*, October 1992, 89; or "Settle This in Your Hearts," *Ensign*, November 1992, 66.

18. "Carry On," *Hymns*, 1985, no. 255.

19. In *Levi Savage Jr. Journal*, comp. Lynn M. Hilton (Salt Lake City: John Savage Family Organization, 1966), xii.

20. In *Savage Journal*, 5; emphasis added.

21. Entry of 19 June 1856 in *Savage Journal*, 59.

22. "Faith of Our Fathers," *Hymns*, 1985, no. 84.

Three Gates to Open

Thomas S. Monson

It's humbling to sit here and gaze from left to right and see how many people are assembled here waiting for what they might hear from their speaker. It reminds me of a little boy in our fast and testimony meeting a couple of months ago. I watched him from the stand, and I could tell he was fidgeting, trying to get up enough courage to come up and bear his testimony. He was just a little fellow. Finally he made the move. He stood up, walked solemnly up that long aisle, passed in front of me and smiled, stepped over to the pulpit, put his hands down, looked at the audience, removed his hands, and turned around and walked back to his parents.

All I could do today would be to turn around and walk back to the arms of President Samuelson. I think he would rather I speak now than have to take over. You're my friends. I feel close to you, and it is a privilege to be with you and to speak to you today.

What a wonderful opportunity you have to attend Brigham Young University and to be taught by the fine faculty we have here.

Thomas S. Monson was First Counselor in the First Presidency of The Church of Jesus Christ of Latter-day Saints when this devotional talk was given on 14 November 2006. © Intellectual Reserve, Inc.

As I think of learning, I am reminded of a father and his son who went fishing one day. After a couple of hours in the boat, the boy suddenly began asking questions about their surroundings.

"How does this boat float?" he asked his father.

His father thought for a moment and then replied, "I don't rightly know, son."

The boy returned to his contemplation, then looked again at his father. "How do fish breathe underwater?" he asked.

Once again the father replied, "Don't rightly know, son."

Next the boy asked, "Why is the sky blue?"

Again, the father replied, "Don't rightly know, son."

Worried he would annoy his father, the boy said, "Dad, do you mind my asking you all of these questions?"

"Of course not, son. If you don't ask questions, you'll never learn anything."

As I have pondered what message I would wish to leave with you today, I have thought of the scripture from Ecclesiastes, or the Preacher: "To every thing there is a season, and a time to every purpose under the heaven."[1] This is your time. What will you do with it? Are you where you want to be with your life? If not, what are you going to do about it?

The Prophet Joseph Smith counseled:

> *Happiness is the object and design of our existence; and will be the end thereof, if we pursue the path that leads to it; and this path is virtue, uprightness, faithfulness, holiness, and keeping all the commandments of God.*[2]

I have devoted considerable time reflecting on years gone by, when I was your age and facing your challenges, your objectives, your opportunities, your futures.

During my high school years, and into my first year at the University of Utah, World War II was raging in full conflict. The daily newspapers carried the news of men dying, cities being obliterated, hospitals filled with grievously burned and maimed servicemen. They faced futures altered, dreams shattered, home-comings ruined.

It didn't seem to matter that gasoline was severely rationed. This was a catalyst for double dating and carpooling. Textbooks were delayed due to paper shortages. They weren't available until midway through our courses, and yet we were expected to know everything in them by final exams.

It was the era of the big bands, and everyone enjoyed a date to the dance, although dancing then was quite different from dancing now.

Looming in the background of every thought for each young man was the inevitable call to serve one's country. Left behind were the comforts of family and home, the teachings of classrooms, and, of course, a special girlfriend. (By the way, she and I have now been married for 58 years!)

Whether speaking of your generation or of mine, there are some constancies amid the changes of the times. The past is behind—we must learn from it. The future is ahead—we must prepare for it. The present is now—we must live in it.

Years ago, I discovered a thought which is true and, in a way, prophetic. It is this: The gate of history swings on small hinges, and so do people's lives.

Today I have chosen to discuss three gates which you alone can open. You must pass through each gate if you are to be successful in your journey through mortality:

- Gate Number 1: The Gate of Preparation
- Gate Number 2: The Gate of Performance
- Gate Number 3: The Gate of Service

THE GATE OF PREPARATION

First, let us speak of the Gate of Preparation. The Lord has counseled, "If ye are prepared ye shall not fear."[3] Fear is the enemy of growth and accomplishment.

It is necessary to prepare and to plan so that we don't fritter away our lives. Without a goal, there can be no real success. The best definition of success I have ever found goes something like this: "Success is the progressive realization of a worthy ideal." Someone has said that the trouble with not having a goal is that you can spend your life running up and down the field and never crossing the goal line.

Years ago there was a romantic and fanciful ballad that contained the words "Wishing will make it so; Just keep on wishing and cares will go."[4] I want to state here and now that wishing will not replace thorough preparation to meet the trials of life. Preparation is hard work, but it is absolutely essential for our progress.

Concerning your preparation, let me share with you this time-honored advice, which has never been more applicable than it is right now: It is not the number of hours you put in but what you put in the hours that counts.

Have discipline in your preparations. Have checkpoints where you can determine if you're on course. Study something you like and which will make it possible for you to support a family. While this counsel would apply almost certainly to every young man, it also has relevance to young women. There are situations in life which we cannot predict which will require employable skills. You can't get the jobs of tomorrow until you have the skills of today. Business in the new economy, where the only guarantee is change, brings us to serious preparation.

Make certain as you prepare that you do not procrastinate. Someone has said that procrastination is the thief of time. Actually, procrastination is much more. It is the thief of our self-respect. It nags at us and spoils our fun. It deprives us of the fullest realization of our ambitions and our hopes.

In academic preparation, I found it a good practice to read a text with the idea that I would be asked to explain that which the author wrote and its application to the subject it covered. Also, I tried to be attentive in any lecture in the classroom and to pretend that I would be called upon to present the same lecture to others. While this practice is very hard work, it certainly helps during test week!

It is hazardous in the extreme to count on a situation typical of one I read about some years ago pertaining to a large, ecclesiastically oriented college in the eastern part of America, where every student had to enroll in a class called Religion 101. The professor of that particular class had been there many years and loved the writings and teachings of the Apostle Paul. He loved them with such vigor that that is about all he taught in Religion 101. Consequently, he would tell the class at the beginning of the semester, "I will not give any examinations during the semester except the final. The result of the final examination will determine your grade for the course."

Now, that would be kind of overwhelming, except that every semester for 21 years he had given the same examination in every class of Religion 101. The examination consisted of one question. And for all those years, the question had been the same. Can you believe it? What a snap class! The question had always been: *Describe the travels and teachings of the Apostle Paul.*

Some young people would come to class the first day and get their name on the record. That was about it until the final examination. Then they would come, having boned up on an answer to that question.

One particular semester, three young men who had followed that practice of registering and then absenting themselves until the end of the semester sat with their pencils poised as the professor went to the chalkboard and said, "I shall place on the board the question on which your entire grade will depend." To their great astonishment he did not write the usual question. Instead, he wrote, "Criticize the Sermon on the Mount."

One of the three young men said, "I don't even know what book it is in." He closed his test book and left the room.

The second young man thought for a moment. He didn't know anything about the Sermon on the Mount because he had prepared for a different test question. He left the room, anticipating a failing grade.

The third one of this trio stayed in the class. He wrote line after line and page after page. His friends were outside in the hallway, looking through the door window, wondering what he was writing. They knew that he had no more knowledge of the Sermon on the Mount than did they, that he had prepared for the question that was not asked. They wondered what he was writing in that test book.

He didn't tell them until the day the papers were examined and returned. They all huddled around to see what grade he had received. He had an A on the test and therefore an A in the course. As he opened the cover of the exam book, there was the question: "Criticize the Sermon on the Mount." And here is what this enterprising young man had written: "I will leave it to someone far more knowledgeable and experienced than I am to criticize the greatest sermon from the greatest life ever lived. As for me, I would prefer to describe the travels and teachings of the Apostle Paul."

May I now turn to the Gate of Performance. Like the Gate of Preparation, you alone can open it.

THE GATE OF PERFORMANCE

The Apostle Paul provided sound counsel to guide our performance: "Let no man despise thy youth; but be thou an example of the believers, in word, in conversation, in charity, in spirit, in faith, in purity."[5]

Remember that the mantle of leadership, my brothers and sisters, is not the cloak of comfort but the robe of responsibility. Accountability is not for the intention but for the deed. You must continue to refuse to compromise with expediency. You must maintain the courage to defy the consensus. You must continue to choose the harder right, instead of the easier wrong. The poet John Greenleaf Whittier expressed this truth when he wrote these lines:

For of all sad words of tongue or pen,
The saddest are these: "It might have been!"[6]

Don't forget: One of the saddest things in life is wasted talent.

It is a good idea to be ambitious, to have goals, to want to be good at what you do, but it is a terrible mistake to let drive and ambition get in the way of treating people with kindness and decency. The point is not that they will then be nice to you. It is that you will feel better about yourself.[7]

Whenever we are inclined to feel burdened down with the blows of life, let us remember that others have passed the same way, have endured, and then have overcome. When we have done all that we are able, we can rely on God's promised help.

You, my brothers and sisters, have access to the lighthouse of the Lord. There is no fog so dense, no night so dark, no mariner so lost, no gale so strong as to render useless the lighthouse of the Lord. It beckons through the storms of life. It seems to call, "This way to safety; this way to home."

Will you remember to select your friends carefully, for you will tend to be like them and to be found where they choose to go. Consider the love your parents have for you and that you have for them. Instead of simply asking them, "Where are the keys to your car?" you might add, "I'll be a bit late tonight." Often the clock ticks more loudly and the hands move more slowly when the night is dark, the hour is late, and a son or a daughter has not yet come home. A telephone call—"We're okay; we just stopped for something to eat. Don't worry; we're fine"—is an indication of true love of parents and of the training of a Latter-day Saint home.

Let me relate another example. At the funeral service of a noble General Authority, H. Verlan Andersen, a tribute was expressed by a son. He related that, years earlier, he had a special school date on a Saturday night. He borrowed from his father the family car. As he obtained the car keys and headed for the door, his father said, "Remember, tomorrow is Sunday. The car will need more gas before then. Be sure to fill the tank before coming home."

Elder Andersen's son then related that the evening activity was wonderful. Friends met, refreshments were served, and all had a good time. In his exuberance, however, he failed to follow his father's instruction and add fuel to the car's tank before returning home. He simply forgot.

Sunday morning dawned. Elder Andersen discovered the gas gauge showed empty. The son saw his father put the car keys on the table. In the Andersen family the Sabbath day was a day for worship and thanksgiving, and not for purchases.

As the funeral message continued, Elder Andersen's son declared, "I saw my father put on his coat, bid us good-bye, and walk the long distance to the chapel, that he might attend an early meeting." Duty called. Truth was not held hostage to expedience.

In concluding his funeral message, Elder Andersen's son said, "No son ever was taught more effectively by his father than I was on that occasion. My father not only knew the truth, but he also taught the truth and lived the truth."

Youth need fewer critics and more models to follow. Your own personal performance in all aspects of your life, including reading the scriptures regularly and following their teachings, will help you to become such models. Then the Gate of Performance will open before you as you proceed to Gate Number 3—the Gate of Service.

THE GATE OF SERVICE

Albert Schweitzer, the noted theologian and missionary physician, declared: "I don't know what your destiny will be, but one thing I know: the only ones among you who will be really happy are those who have sought and found how to serve."

May I share with you an experience I had with a dear friend of mine, Louis McDonald. Louis never married. Because of a crippling disease, he had never known a day without pain nor many days without loneliness. One winter's day, as I visited him, he was slow in answering the doorbell's ring. I entered his well-kept home; the temperature in save but one room—the kitchen—was a chilly 40 degrees. The reason? Insufficient money to heat any other room. The walls needed papering, the ceilings needed to be lowered, the cupboards needed to be filled.

I was troubled by Louis's needs. A bishop was consulted, and a miracle of love, prompted by testimony, took place. The members of the ward—particularly the young adults—were organized and the labor of love begun.

A month later, my friend Louis called and asked if I would come and see what had happened to him. I did and indeed beheld a miracle. The sidewalks which had been uprooted by large poplar trees had been replaced, the porch of the home rebuilt, a new door with glistening hardware installed, the ceilings lowered, the walls papered, the woodwork painted, the roof replaced, and the cupboards filled. No longer was the home chilly and uninviting. It now seemed to whisper a warm welcome.

Louis saved until last showing me his pride and joy: there on his bed was a beautiful plaid quilt bearing the crest of his McDonald family clan. It had been made with loving care by the women of the Relief Society. Before leaving, I discovered that each week the Young Adults would bring in a hot dinner and share a home evening. Warmth had replaced the cold, repairs had transformed the wear of years, but, more significantly, hope had dispelled despair, and now love reigned triumphant.

All who participated in this moving drama of real life had discovered a new and personal appreciation of the Master's teaching "It is more blessed to give than to receive."[8]

The holy scriptures are replete with examples of service by the servants of the Lord and by Jesus Himself. Of Him it is recorded: "[He] went about doing good, . . . for God was with him."[9] He caused lame beggars to walk and blind men to see. He cleansed the lepers and healed the centurion's servant. He restored to the widow at Nain her dead son, who through Him now lived. He raised Lazarus from the tomb. He forgave the woman taken in adultery. He atoned for the sins of all of us. He died that we might eternally live.

As we go about our daily lives, we discover countless opportunities to follow the example of the Savior. When our hearts are in tune with His teachings, we discover the unmistakable nearness of His divine help. We are on the Lord's errand, and when we are on the Lord's errand, we are entitled to the Lord's help.

Through the years, the offices I have occupied have been decorated with lovely paintings of peaceful and pastoral scenes. However, there is one picture that always hangs on the wall which I face when seated behind my desk. It is a constant reminder of Him whom I serve, for it is a picture of our Lord and Savior, Jesus Christ. When confronted with a vexing problem or difficult decision, I always gaze at that picture of the Master and silently ask myself the question "What would He have me do?" No longer does doubt linger, nor does indecision prevail. The way to go is clear, and the pathway before me beckons. Such will also work for each of you as you focus on what the Lord would have you do.

The noble King Benjamin counseled his many subjects, after a lengthy but powerful sermon on the subject of service: "When ye are in the service of your fellow beings ye are only in the service of your God."[10]

At times we may think that no one cares—but someone *always* cares! Your Heavenly Father will not leave you to struggle alone but stands ever ready to help. Most often such assistance comes quietly, at other times with dramatic impact. Elder Marion D. Hanks, some years ago, related an account of one who received such assistance. He told of a young divorced woman, the mother of seven children then ranging in ages from five to 16. One evening she went across the street to deliver something to a neighbor. She indicated later that as she turned to walk back home, she could see her house lighted up. She could hear echoes of her children as she had walked out of the door a few minutes earlier: "Mom, what are we going to have for dinner?" "Can you take me to the library?" "Mom, I have to get some poster paper tonight." Tired and weary, she thought of all of those children who were home waiting for her to come home and meet their needs. She said that at that moment her burdens felt very heavy on her shoulders.

She recalled looking through tears toward the sky, and she said, "O my Father, I just can't handle things tonight. I'm too tired. I can't face it. I can't go home and take care of all those children alone. Could I come to You and stay with You for just one night? I'll come back in the morning."

She didn't really hear the words of reply, but she heard them in her mind. The answer was, "No, little one, you can't come to me now, for you would never wish to return. But I can come to you."

Seek heavenly guidance one day at a time. The help you need may not come just as you envision, but it will come. When we remember that each of us is literally a child of God, we will not find it difficult to approach Him.

Seek heavenly help also to know how to serve others. There is no feeling so gratifying nor knowledge so comforting as knowing that our Father has answered the prayer of another through you.

I close with a tender yet simple experience. Each time I would visit Mattie, a dear friend and an older widow whom I had known for many years and whose bishop I had been, my heart grieved at her utter loneliness. One of her sons lived many miles away, halfway across the country, but he rarely visited her. He would come to Salt Lake, take care of business matters, see his brothers and sisters, and leave for his own home without visiting his mother. When I would call to see this mother, she would make an excuse for her boy and tell me just how busy he was. Her words did not carry power or conviction. They simply masked her disappointment and grief.

The years passed. The loneliness deepened. Then one afternoon I received a telephone call. That special son was in Salt Lake City. A change had occurred in his life. He had become imbued with a desire to help others, to adhere more faithfully to God's commandments. He was proud of his newfound ability to cast off the old man and become new and useful. He wanted to come immediately to my office that he might share with me the joy in service that he now felt. With all my heart I wanted to welcome him and to extend my personal congratulations. Then I thought of his grieving mother, that lonely widow, and suggested, "Dick, I can see you at four o'clock this afternoon, provided you visit your dear mother before coming here." He agreed.

Just before our appointment, a call came to me. It was that same mother. There was an excitement in her voice that words cannot adequately describe. She exuded enthusiasm even over the phone and declared proudly, "Bishop, you'll never guess who has just visited me." Before I could answer, she exclaimed, "Dick was here! My son Dick has spent the past hour with me. He is a new man. He has found himself. I'm the happiest mother in the world!" Then she paused and quietly spoke: "I just knew he would not really forget me."

Years later, at Mattie's funeral, Dick and I spoke tenderly of that experience. We had witnessed a glimpse of God's healing power through the window of a mother's faith in her son.

Today I pray earnestly that all of us may open wide the three gates of which I have spoken—the Gate of Preparation, the Gate of Performance, and the Gate of Service—and walk through them to our exaltation. In the name of Jesus Christ, amen.

NOTES

1. Ecclesiastes 3:1.
2. *Teachings*, 255–56.
3. D&C 38:30.
4. "Wishing (Will Make It So)," words and music by Buddy DeSylva.
5. 1 Timothy 4:12.
6. John Greenleaf Whittier, *Maud Muller* (1856), stanza 53.
7. Robert Solow.
8. Acts 20:35.
9. Acts 10:38.
10. Mosiah 2:17.

Brotherly Love

—◆—

Tom Holmoe

My dear brothers and sisters, do we really mean what we say when we address each other as brother and sister?

These are rather peculiar titles for many people not familiar with our Mormon culture. Names such as Brother Jim or Sister Smith are used fondly and respectfully when addressing each other to express our kinship in the family of God. Why do we use these affectionate titles?

Let me quote from the missionary guide *Preach My Gospel:*

God is the Father of our spirits. We are literally His children, and He loves us. We lived as spirit children of our Father in Heaven before we were born on this earth. We were not, however, like our Heavenly Father, nor could we ever become like Him and enjoy all the blessings that He enjoys without the experience of living in mortality with a physical body.

God's whole purpose—His work and His glory—is to enable each of us to enjoy all His blessings. He has provided a perfect plan to accomplish His

Tom Holmoe was BYU athletic director when this devotional talk was delivered on 28 November 2006. © *Brigham Young University.*

purpose. We understood and accepted this plan before we came to the earth. [*Preach My Gospel: A Guide to Missionary Service* (Salt Lake City: The Church of Jesus Christ of Latter-day Saints, 2004), 48]

When I was a small boy growing up, my older brother was bigger than life to me. He was nine years older and the best player on every team he played on. He always looked out for his little brother and spent many hours teaching me the skills of various sports. Since we shared a bedroom—much to his chagrin—I oftentimes would hear him awake late at night and slip out to the backyard to lift weights to get stronger. I spent many nights peering out the window at his example of extra effort and dreamed I one day could be like him. He truly was, and still remains, a great brother. He continues to influence my life for good as my big brother.

Elder Henry B. Eyring taught: "Your responsibility is to touch people so that they will make the choices that will take them toward eternal life. And eternal life is the greatest of all the gifts of God" ("To Touch a Life with Faith," *Ensign*, November 1995, 37–38).

Perhaps one of the more thought-provoking questions asked in the scriptures is the one asked by Cain when questioned by the Lord on the whereabouts of his brother Abel: "Am I my brother's keeper?" (Genesis 4:9). Cain had slain his younger brother because God had accepted Abel's offering and rejected his. Cain's words have come to symbolize man's unwillingness to accept responsibility for the welfare of his "brothers" on this earth. In our present-day situations, we would all do well, as children of our Heavenly Father, to contemplate our answer to that same question: "Am I my brother's keeper?"

To be able to answer in the affirmative, "Yes, I am my brother's keeper!" we must be obedient to the command given us by Jesus when He said:

> *A new commandment I give unto you, That ye love one another; as I have loved you, that ye also love one another.*
>
> *By this shall all men know that ye are my disciples, if ye have love one to another.* [John 13:34–35]

Just how do we determine who our brothers and sisters are? The Apostle Paul stated on Mars Hill that God "hath made of *one blood all nations* of men for to dwell on all the face of the earth" (Acts 17:26; emphasis added). All mankind have chosen to come to this earth in obedience to the plan of salvation and are indeed the sons and daughters of God—and thus brothers and sisters in His heavenly family.

Modern revelation further describes the familial relationship that we are granted through the Atonement of our Savior. We learn from King Benjamin of our place in the family of Christ:

And now, because of the covenant which ye have made ye shall be called the children of Christ, his sons, and his daughters; for behold, this day he hath spiritually begotten you; for ye say that your hearts are changed through faith on his name; therefore, ye are born of him and have become his sons and his daughters. [Mosiah 5:7]

We catch a further glimpse of who Jesus considers His brothers and sisters from this exchange found in Matthew:

While he yet talked to the people, behold, his mother and his brethren stood without, desiring to speak with him.

Then one said unto him, Behold, thy mother and thy brethren stand without, desiring to speak with thee.

But he answered and said unto him that told him, Who is my mother? and who are my brethren?

And he stretched forth his hand toward his disciples, and said, Behold my mother and my brethren!

For whosoever shall do the will of my Father which is in heaven, the same is my brother, and sister, and mother. [Matthew 12:46–50]

The hoped-for result of this knowledge of our heavenly family was described by Paul in his letter to the Romans:

Let love be without dissimulation. Abhor that which is evil; cleave to that which is good.

Be kindly affectioned one to another with brotherly love; in honor preferring one another. [Romans 12:9–10]

Furthermore, we are instructed in Timothy:

Rebuke not an elder, but intreat him as a father; and the younger men as brethren;
The elder women as mothers; the younger as sisters, with all purity.
[1 Timothy 5:1–2]

Brothers and sisters, love one another. Serve each other. I would think that most of you here today have followed and accepted the premise of brotherhood and sisterhood as taught from the scriptures. The issue is not so much that you don't accept a stranger as a brother or sister as much as it is you simply have not conditioned yourself to serve them. Serving those who we love and who love us—those who think like us or look like us or speak like us, or even worship like us—is good. However, we must learn to reach out to those we don't know: to the discarded, the sick, those less fortunate, the inflicted, the lonely, and those we don't necessarily understand.

The story of the dramatic rescue of the members of the Martin and Willie Handcart Companies—a group of our early pioneer Saints trapped and frozen on the plains—is one that inspires me today to listen for the call to action and GO! Elder Jeffrey R. Holland reminded us that being our brother's keeper is a theme we need oft remember. Quoting from Elder Holland's most recent general conference address:

As surely as the rescue of those in need was the general conference theme of October 1856, so too is it the theme of this conference and last conference and the one to come next spring. . . . The needy . . . can be rescued only by those who have more and know more and can help more. And don't worry about asking, "Where are they?" They are everywhere, on our right hand and on our left, in our neighborhoods and in the workplace, in every community and county and nation of this world. Take your team and wagon;

load it with your love, your testimony, and a spiritual sack of flour; then drive in any direction. The Lord will lead you to those in need if you will but embrace the gospel of Jesus Christ. ["Prophets in the Land Again," *Ensign*, November 2006, 106]

President Thomas S. Monson, speaking of our call to service, stated:

This is the service that counts, the service to which all of us have been called: the service of the Lord Jesus Christ.

Along your pathway of life you will observe that you are not the only traveler. There are others who need your help. There are feet to steady, hands to grasp, minds to encourage, hearts to inspire, and souls to save. ["How Firm a Foundation," *Ensign*, November 2006, 68]

The Prophet Joseph Smith—oft referred to by the people of his day as Brother Joseph—was the epitome of selflessness. He reached out to strangers in many ways to assist them and bless their lives. We need not look far to find excellent examples of brotherly and sisterly love. The Lord's chosen servants of today emulate their predecessors and shine a light on all that is good, devoting their lives to serving others.

A story is told of a man having a conversation with the Lord one day. He said, "Lord, I would like to know what heaven and hell are like."

The Lord led the man to two doors. He opened one of the doors, and the man looked in. In the middle of the room was a large round table. In the middle of the table was a large pot of stew, which smelled delicious and made the man's mouth water.

The people sitting around the table were thin and sickly. They appeared to be famished. They were holding spoons with very long handles that were strapped to their arms. Each found it possible to reach into the pot of stew and take a spoonful, but because the handle was longer than their arms, they could not get the spoons back into their mouths.

The man shuddered at the sight of their misery and suffering. The Lord said, "You have seen hell."

They went to the next room and opened the door. It was exactly the same as the first one. There was the large round table with the large pot of stew that made the man's mouth water. The people were equipped with the same long-handled spoons strapped to their arms, but here the people were well nourished and plump, laughing and talking.

The man said, "I don't understand!"

"It is simple," said the Lord. "It requires but one skill. You see, they have learned to feed each other, while the greedy think only of themselves."

Dr. Martin Luther King, Jr., wondered why men do not treat each other like brothers and sisters. Let me quote Dr. King:

Modern man has brought this whole world to an awe-inspiring threshold of the future. . . .

Yet . . . something basic is missing. There is a sort of poverty of the spirit which stands in glaring contrast to our scientific and technological abundance. The richer we have become materially, the poorer we have become morally and spiritually. We have learned to fly the air like birds and swim the sea like fish, but we have not learned the simple art of living together as brothers. [Speech accepting the Nobel Peace Prize (11 December 1964)]

I believe Dr. King would be pleased with the response from people all over the world to our brothers and sisters in Indonesia who were suffering from the devastation of last year's tsunami. Millions of people came to the aid of brothers and sisters they didn't even know. They acted on the impression of loving our neighbors as ourselves (see Matthew 19:19).

Brothers and sisters, the business of making a living, raising a family, receiving an education, and any other worthy endeavor we are involved in truly tests how we answer the question "Am I my brother's keeper?" God works miracles in the lives of His children through the Christlike service rendered by their brothers and sisters. A warm smile, a friendly greeting, a door held open, any good deed—however simple it may be—can turn a bad day into a good one.

I enjoy singing the words of a favorite Church hymn:

Have I done any good in the world today?
Have I helped anyone in need?
Have I cheered up the sad and made someone feel glad?
If not, I have failed indeed.
["Have I Done Any Good?" *Hymns,* 1985, no. 223]

It will be a long time before I forget the special kindness expressed by my friend Verl Rasband, an older gentleman who attended my ward. Verl served well in many capacities throughout his life and still finds the time and makes the effort today to continue to make a difference in the lives of others. Verl learns the first names of many of the children in our ward and goes out of his way to greet and talk with them regularly. At first the children are surprised that an older man would even know their name. But his warm greeting makes them feel good. As a result of his kind heart and sweet spirit, all my children respect, admire, and love Brother Rasband. From his fine example my children now go out of their way to greet Verl before he can find them. His love is contagious.

It is unlikely that any of us will be honored for our service, but recognition is not the reward. Our reward is blessing lives. Loving one another is not merely a suggestion or a good recommendation. It is a commandment. When we are obedient to this command, our lives and the lives of our brothers and sisters are richly blessed. As we express our love through actions on behalf of our brothers and sisters, we set a good example to others of Christlike service.

BYU is a *big* place with *many* people moving in *all* directions. It sometimes may seem a difficult task to make a difference in the life of one of your fellow students, faculty, or staff members. I often enjoy looking for examples of good works here on campus and seeing acts of brotherly kindness. Two years ago, when I was appointed director of athletics, I was touched by the many helping hands extended to my associates and me by brothers and sisters across campus. Words of encouragement, free time spent assisting us with our plans, and other extra effort enabled us to lighten our load and ensure us a good start. As a result of their service to us, I feel a strong camaraderie and a greater desire to do more to further build up our campus.

One group of BYU students I admire—our own BYU football team—refers to each other affectionately as the Band of Brothers.

The team's motto was inspired from the lines of Shakespeare's play *Henry V*:

We few, we happy few, we band of brothers;
For he to-day that sheds his blood with me
Shall be my brother.
[William Shakespeare, *Henry V*, act 4, scene 3, lines 60–62]

This year's members of the BYU football team have bonded to the cause of restoring tradition, being honorable, and living by the Spirit. Skeptics were cynical concerning the rare approach of this team and their leader. How can there be enough time to prepare for game day when weekly firesides are held on the eve of each game? Rough and tumble football players will get soft focusing on things of the Spirit instead of visualizing on-field violence.

This Band of Brothers strives toward holding each other accountable for the good of the whole. Selfish motives are shelved in place of team objectives. The duty to represent not only each other but also BYU and The Church of Jesus Christ of Latter-day Saints is not just a part-time thing. When one falters, all are affected. When one succeeds, all benefit!

Coach Bronco Mendenhall and the team's leadership council have instituted what they call the Big Brother Program. Each younger player on the team is paired up with one of the upperclassmen. Each week the "big brother" conducts an interview with his "younger brother." They address such topics as academics, football, family, girlfriends, spirituality, and any other issue the two care to discuss.

Then the big brother writes a letter to Coach Mendenhall sharing any thoughts, experiences or concerns the two might have concerning each other, the team, or their teammates. The letters are confidential—some are even sacred to Bronco. Privately, Coach Mendenhall is able to assist his boys based on their communication. What has developed within this year's team goes way beyond what is witnessed on the field of play, as can be seen in such activities as the Band of Brothers performing a team hymn at a recent pre-game fireside in Fort Collins, Colorado, the night before the Cougars played the Colorado State Rams.

Like many of you here today, my life took further shape through my experiences as a student at BYU. Not only was I challenged physically and emotionally through athletics, but I also grew mentally and emotionally through the rigors of academics and was changed forever by the ever-present Spirit that is often expressed through many brothers and sisters on campus.

I will be eternally grateful for the wonderful example of the best teacher I ever had: Joe Wood—a man more affectionately referred to by his students as Uncle Joe. Uncle Joe taught religion and history here. When I arrived at BYU, I was not a member of The Church of Jesus Christ of Latter-day Saints. I was way out of my element: in a very different culture, homesick for my family, and feeling like a fish out of water. As weeks went by during my first semester, I considered abandoning my hopes and dreams for BYU and returning to the friendly confines of home. Somehow, Uncle Joe saw something missing in me. He went out of his way to approach me after class and encourage me to stay strong. He reached out a hand of friendship, which I gladly accepted. He continued to look after me, and soon I looked forward to his class as the highlight of my day. He laughed and smiled and even shed tears of gratitude. He called his students by their first name and often shook our hand or put his arm around our shoulders. I grew to realize that he hadn't just taken a special interest in *me*. He made *everyone* in class feel special. The sweet spirit that radiated from Uncle Joe was what first softened my heart to the gospel of Jesus Christ. I am grateful for all people on our campus like

Uncle Joe who care enough to make a difference in the lives of their brothers and sisters.

I love the spirit of our BYU students. Your desire to be the best you can be—to educate and train yourselves toward becoming future family, community, and national leaders—is impressive. Many of you have made the worthy choice to pause from your college education to serve full-time missions for the Lord. Truly this is brotherly love in action: to seek out your brothers and sisters from all walks of life and from the four corners of the earth, to find all those who have been separated from the truth, and then to help lead them back to their Father in Heaven and remind them of the one great plan of salvation that leads to eternal life.

Ask yourself this question: Have I done any good in the world today?

Then wake up and do something more
Than dream of your mansions above.
Doing good is a pleasure, a joy beyond measure,
A blessing of duty and love.
["Have I Done Any Good?" *Hymns*, 1985, no. 223]

It is my hope and prayer that we may serve our Lord by being actively engaged in blessing the lives of *all* our brothers and sisters and being an instrument in the hands of our Heavenly Father, in the name of Jesus Christ, amen.

Peace on Earth—Some Restrictions Apply

Julie Franklin

During an exceptionally hectic morning my mind was full to overflowing as I thought about the stress of my day at work, family responsibilities, and additional large assignments I had at the time. I was trying to work out the physical and emotional commitment to each and was overwhelmed, knowing that one person with two hands and 24 hours in a day couldn't possibly do it all. I turned on the car radio only to hear the kind of news that makes you want to cry. As all these things swirled through my brain, the thought came to mind: "So much for peace on earth, good will to men." I wondered how the heavenly host at the birth of Christ could have possibly pronounced peace on earth and good will to men when normal people like me can be distracted by chaos, feel a lack of peace, and find a lack of evidence of good will.

Because of that little experience and the musing I did, I decided to prepare this talk about peace and good will. I began my preparation with the scriptures and read the account of the angels' appearance to the shepherds. I imagined how the shepherds must have felt, how startled they must have been, what the angel might have looked

Julie Franklin was director of Residence Life at BYU when this devotional talk was given on 5 December 2006. © *Brigham Young University.*

like, and how the heavenly host appeared. As I imagined the heavenly host, I saw a group of beautiful angels illuminated by heavenly light and expressing exquisite joy through song. My children are young, and in our home the expressions of happiness and joy are full-body experiences, so the angels in my thoughts were not standing still; in my imagination they were dancing for joy. Then I got to the verse in Luke from which I believe Henry Wadsworth Longfellow took his familiar phrase "peace on earth, good will to men." The heavenly host sang out, "Glory to God in the highest, and on earth peace, good will toward men."[1]

I used the tools available to me on the Web and several commentaries in the Harold B. Lee Library to learn as much as I could about this scripture. I found that all of the conference addresses that quote this particular verse speak primarily of peace. Peace is mentioned in the scriptures multiple times and good will only a small handful of times. The two ideas of peace and good will are found together only once, in Luke 2:14. Through all of my reading and studying I decided that from a purely cerebral standpoint I think I understand the "glory to God in the highest" part and the "on earth peace" part, but when it came to "good will toward men" I was stumped. My dictionary defines *good will* as "a desire for the well-being of others; benevolence,"[2] but I couldn't quite figure out how it fit into the verse. It had never occurred to me that I didn't really understand the scripture I had read literally hundreds of times.

I questioned if the angels commanded the people on earth to have "good will toward men" at the same time they pronounced peace on earth—that is, to have peace and be men of good will. I wondered if perhaps the good will mentioned was a reference to the good will of our Father expressed to us by the coming of His Only Begotten Son, the source of peace to the earth. Then I considered if perhaps the mention of good will could possibly be a condition that has to exist in order for peace to be experienced on earth.

I read several passages from books—and there are a couple of different opinions by very convincing authors, some of them learned LDS scholars and other qualified sources. I do not claim to be an expert on this subject, nor to be worthy to declare the one true way to interpret the scripture. I will leave that to each of you to discover through your own investigation. In the end, all of the different possibilities may be true, and I don't believe one interpretation contradicts the others sufficiently to cause anyone to have heartburn—unless that person happens to be writing a devotional address. For the purpose of today's discussion I have chosen to assume "good will toward men" refers to a condition that must exist in the hearts of men in order for peace to be felt on earth. In other words, the scripture could be read, "Glory in the highest to God and on earth peace among men of good will."[3] Another way to state this, consistent with messages we receive in the media today, is "Glory to God in the highest and on earth peace—some restrictions apply." Some may assume this is proof that in heaven there is a legal office—I personally won't go that far.

One reason I believe that peace comes to earth with restrictions in place is based on the fact that I have experienced that phenomenon in my own life. The times I have felt the greatest peace were times when I was striving to be an instrument in the Lord's hands and was purposefully reaching out to others. We read "there is no peace, saith my God, to the wicked"[4] in the scriptures and sing "there is peace in righteous doing"[5] from the hymnbook.

The restrictions that apply to the ability to have peace on earth are somewhat specific and have nothing to do with the circumstances we find ourselves in: We can be unprepared for final exams, papers, or projects; have minimal financial resources; still have no idea what we should get for the hard-to-shop-for person in our life; have an undeclared major; be a graduate without a job offer or graduate school acceptance; have health concerns, relationship issues, acne, or a bad haircut; or live in areas where there are wars, rumors of wars, religious intolerance, oppressive leaders, or obnoxious radio talk show hosts and still have the peace the angels promised.

Henry Wadsworth Longfellow probably understood this when he penned the poem "Christmas Bells" that would be set to music and become a favorite Christmas carol—the refrain of which I mentioned earlier.

Mr. Longfellow used church bells ringing on Christmas Day as the setting for a poem he wrote during the Civil War. The fighting had been fierce and touched the lives of the Longfellow family personally. Mr. Longfellow's son Charles, who had enlisted in the Union Army at 17 years of age, had arrived home about two weeks prior to Christmas 1863 after being critically injured in a battle.[6] While Charles eventually recovered from his wounds, his father was likely concerned about the long-term health of his son and of his country. In addition to these concerns, Mr. Longfellow continued to feel the grave loss of his beloved wife, Francis Appleton Longfellow, also known as Fanny. In 1861, the same year the Civil War broke out, Fanny died from injuries she sustained when her light summer dress ignited in their home. The light weight of the fabric and the hoops she wore allowed ample oxygen to feed the flames, and Mrs. Longfellow was quickly engulfed. Mr. Longfellow attempted to extinguish the fire and was himself burned in the process. With her death he was left to raise five children and manage the affairs of his home as a single parent.[7] The death of his wife and his son's critical injuries were not the only tragedies in Mr. Longfellow's life. Fanny was Henry Wadsworth Longfellow's second wife, and together they had a daughter also named Frances who died when she was 17 months old.[8] His first wife, Mary Potter Longfellow, died just over a month after she miscarried during her sixth month of pregnancy.[9] This was a man who had every reason to pity himself and feel cranky about his condition, and yet he declared in beautiful verse:

Then pealed the bells more loud and deep:
"God is not dead, nor doth he sleep;
The wrong shall fail, the right prevail,
With peace on earth, good will to men."

Till, ringing, singing, on its way,
The world revolved from night to day,
A voice, a chime, a chant sublime,
Of peace on earth, good will to men![10]

Jesus Christ, that highly anticipated infant whose birth has been celebrated with the ringing of Christmas bells, is a perfect example for us of how to feel peace and good will. The circumstances of His life were anything but tranquil. His world was politically unstable. He and His family experienced life under Roman rule and a Jewish king who wanted Jesus dead. Jesus was challenged and criticized. He felt hunger, fatigue, sorrow, temptation, and frustration. He was mocked, abandoned, and betrayed. In the world where Jesus lived there were problems in families and people had severe illness, injuries, and tragic losses. Neighbors were not always kind to one another, at times business was bad, salt lost its savor, and occasionally folks ran out of refreshments during wedding receptions; and yet every incident we have recorded of the Savior's life points to a life of peace.

When Christ was in situations where He was challenged, confronted, or pestered, we read of a man who stood firm and unshaken. When He rebuked individuals who needed correction, His words were measured and delivered with the precise level of emotion to bring about the desired result. During the events leading to the Crucifixion, Jesus Christ did not shrink. I love the account where Christ was taken into custody and Peter, the loyal Apostle, drew his sword and cut off the ear of one of the high priest's servants. Jesus did not use the opportunity to run, nor to feel smug that someone else might suffer a fraction of what He had and would endure. He also did not criticize Peter. With a few of what I would characterize gentle words to Peter, He simply touched the servant's ear and healed him.[11] We have no evidence Jesus was ever out of control; instead, in all things He displayed peace.

As for finding evidence of a person who possessed good will, there has never been another person whose entire life reflected benevolence more completely than Jesus Christ. At the lowest level of good will, I believe we simply think kindly or hope the best for others. At the highest level of good will, I believe we have charity. At some point in the middle I think we are service oriented. It appears Jesus never acted without considering the impact of His behavior on others. He comforted, gave hope, taught, healed the sick, and raised the dead. We know the Savior possessed charity; He provided us with the Atonement. In fact, He possessed charity so perfectly that when Mormon defined the word *charity* as "the pure love of Christ,"[12] he listed Jesus in the definition.

Having peace all of the time sounds like a noble project. Knowing that restrictions apply to having peace, though, means that you and I, who could use an additional measure of it in our lives, need to be striving to live in a way that qualifies us. Becoming a person of constant good will and feeling peace more consistently can be problematic for a person like me. I looked in the BYU Bookstore and did not find a book titled *Peace for Dummies*. Since I know Jesus is a good example of being a person who possesses good will and enjoys peace in His life 100 percent of the time, I looked for clues in His life that might help me and you on our quest for the same.

My first realization is very simple. Jesus knows who He is. One experience from His life that gives us a bit of insight into this occurred in the temple when Jesus was 12 years old. After celebrating the Passover with His family, Jesus went to the temple to talk to the learned men of the day. His family had left Jerusalem and was on the way back to Nazareth. It wasn't until the family had been traveling for a day that Joseph and Mary discovered Jesus was missing from their numbers and returned to find Him. The worried parents had to travel the day's journey back to Jerusalem, and then it took them an additional two days of searching before they located Him in the temple talking to "the doctors."[13] When Mary and Joseph finally located Jesus in the temple, Mary asked Jesus in a tone I imagine was a little sharp and a lot relieved:

> *Son, why hast thou thus dealt with us? behold, thy father and I have sought thee sorrowing.*
>
> *And he said unto them, How is it that ye sought me?* **wist** *ye not that I must be about my* **Father's** *business?*[14]

My second realization is equally simple and connected to the first. Not only was Jesus clear about who He is, He also understood why

He was here on the earth and who He was to become. The knowledge of Jesus that He was the literal offspring of our Heavenly Father and that His role in life was to bring immortality and the possibility of eternal life to all of His spiritual siblings framed every aspect of Jesus Christ's mortal life. He was so clear about His divinity and His role in our Heavenly Father's plan that every decision Jesus made and every behavior He displayed was consistent with His knowledge. Nothing He ever did or said disqualified Him from being the perfect, sin-free, unblemished sacrificial lamb of the Most High God.

I have sung "I Am a Child of God"[15] since I was a young child, and yet it has taken me longer than Jesus to figure out that as a daughter of God I need to keep my decisions, behaviors, and words consistent with the roles my Father would have me fill on this earth and in eternity.

My son loves animals. At five years of age, two of his favorite places are Hogle Zoo in Salt Lake City and the Monte L. Bean Museum here on campus. Until recently he did not know the official names of those places, and he would distinguish between them by calling one "the live zoo" and the other "the dead zoo." He has informed me that he wants to be a zookeeper when he grows up. He spends hours playing with the toy animals we have in our collection—setting them up, assembling similar animals into family groups, creating safe and comfortable places for them to live and sleep. In his play he is developing skills and trying to act in ways he thinks are appropriate for a role he intends to fulfill at some time in the future.

There are many roles each of us will fulfill during our lives. In addition, we know as sons and daughters of our Father in Heaven that we have the ability to someday become gods and goddesses. Jesus Christ lived His life as our Savior long before He stepped into the Garden of Gethsemane or emerged from the tomb. Even when we think it might be in the distant future, it is not too early for us to develop now the characteristics and skills, like peace and good will, that will help us take on those roles.

It is always exciting at the beginning of each new school year to see new students come to campus. One of the most fulfilling parts of the work we do in Residence Life is to see the progress students make in solidifying their understanding of who they are and then acting according to that understanding. We enjoy being a part of students' lives while they are building their character. I have a special place in my heart for the few students who may stumble a bit and then catch the vision of their great divine potential and blossom.

Over the years of my service at the university I have observed good will through quiet acts of service students do for each other in the halls and in their apartments off campus. On a number of occasions I have been told of groups of students who have banded together to send a student without the means home for the Christmas break. A couple of years ago a close family member of one of our students committed suicide. The student's floor mates gathered and read *Ensign* articles about suicide so they could better support their friend when he returned from the funeral. I know when one student was seriously injured, the people on her floor—some who hardly knew her—gathered quickly to pray for her. The list of these simple acts of good will goes on and on. These students and so many others like them are examples to me of people who understand who they are and are living their lives in a way that qualifies them to feel peace.

While having an understanding of who you are and who you are to become and striving to have good will in your heart will allow you to feel peace, one surefire way to mess it up is to become distracted and to behave in ways that are not congruent with your divine nature.

This brings me to the third realization I want to share today. Once again the lesson is very simple, and again the example I have comes from the life of the Savior. Another way to refer to behaviors that are unbecoming of someone with a divine and royal destiny is through the word *sin*. Jesus Christ successfully avoided sin, and He did it by managing temptation in His life.

Before you discount the possibility of managing temptation and avoiding sin as unique to Jesus because of His divine parentage, allow me to remind you of what He inherited from His mortal mother. From Mary, Jesus inherited the potential for death, both physical and spiritual. Jesus felt temptation: "He suffered temptations but gave no heed unto them."[16] President Howard W. Hunter said, "It is important to remember that Jesus was capable of sinning, . . . but . . . he remained true. . . . He had to retain the capacity and ability to sin had he willed so to do."[17]

Two rather small details from the scriptures provide us with insights on how Christ successfully responded to temptation. In the account of the time Jesus Christ was tempted by Satan, Matthew wrote, "And when the tempter came to him, he said, If thou be the Son of God, command that these stones be made bread."[18] The minor point that I am convinced has critical importance is that Satan approached Christ: "the tempter came to him." Christ was not out looking for Satan.

Then, following the three temptations that Satan exposed our Savior to, Jesus simply dispatched Satan with the words "Get thee hence, Satan."[19] None of the Savior's responses to the temptations engaged Satan in conversation. He did not flirt with the possibility of actually going along with Satan. He did not ask anyone for clarification about how close to the line He could get before a sin would actually be committed and He never claimed it was His right to experience some fun or indulge Himself before He had to get serious about preparing for His future role.

My smallest daughter and I enjoy doing finger plays. One finger play we do over and over is about five little monkeys who swing in the trees teasing Mr. Alligator and jeering, "You can't catch me!" Each of the five monkeys teases Mr. Alligator in turn. In the end of the finger-play, Mr. Alligator is the only one left. We laugh as we end the play about Mr. Alligator, who is "just as full as he could be."

It is not a laughing matter when I learn of students who have felt somehow indestructible and who have teased and flirted with Satan by engaging in behaviors that are not absolutely congruent with who they are and who they are supposed to become.

One student came to BYU from out of state. During high school she had distinguished herself among her friends as an individual with high standards. Then she met some people in Provo who were not unlike the students she had gone to school with back home.

Over time her evening activities became dances and parties where Y Sparkle and BYU brownies were not the refreshments of choice. To fit into this crowd of people, clothing was worn in a more provocative manner. Early on, the rationalization given for the behaviors was that technically she had not broken any of the commandments. As time went on, the flirting with Satan became a more committed relationship.

This young woman was intelligent. Her grades and test scores qualified her for admission into BYU. She had a track record of being a committed member of the Church. She was not exceptionally different from any of us. Intellectual ability and confidence in our moral strength do not prevent us from being the special sort of stupid that lets us think we can tease Satan and not be caught—like the monkeys swinging in the trees.

Sin distracts us and blurs our vision. The young woman lost sight of who she was and who she was to become. She blamed others for her situation, and good will dried up. Her life became void of peace. I lost contact with the young woman when she went home to get her life back on track. It would take effort, the help of her ecclesiastical leader, support from her family, and a commitment on her part to fully utilize the blessing of the Atonement—the ultimate gift of our Redeemer—to restore the feeling of peace in her life.

As you know, sin is not the only distraction we can experience in our lives. At times the hectic nature of our responsibilities, concerns we have, and trials we experience can distract us too. Although there are days we may wish our lives were less chaotic and our responsibilities and pressures would go away, we must be realistic and understand that these things will always be around us. We may wish the world would become a perfect reflection of good will, but we must realize that it is not likely to happen soon. While we strive to live our lives as Jesus did, our efforts will and do fall short and we have need to repent over and over. Chaos, pressures, and sin are part of our lives. The angels knew this when they pronounced peace on the earth more than 2,000 years ago. If we can follow the Lord's example of knowing who we are and living our lives in a way that is congruent with our current status as children of our Eternal Father and our future status as gods and goddesses, we will indeed have good will in our hearts. Hopefully we can do a better job of avoiding sin by removing ourselves from situations where we are flirting with Satan.

Developing an understanding of who we are, learning to live according to that understanding, avoiding sin, and repenting when we fail—and figuring out how to be individuals with good will in our hearts—are all part of the reason we are here on this earth. Jesus Christ came to the earth and is our example in all things; He learned who He was, lived according to that understanding, avoided sin, and was an individual of supreme good will. The Christmas bells Henry Wadsworth Longfellow heard will ring again this year celebrating the birth of our Savior, "The Prince of Peace."[20] We are reminded again of the pronouncement of the heavenly host. That we will have good will in our hearts, that the restrictions will not apply to us, and that we will feel the promised peace now and always is my prayer, in the name of Jesus Christ, amen.

NOTES

1. Luke 2:14.

2. *Funk & Wagnalls Standard College Dictionary*, 1977, s.v. "good will," 576.

3. See William F. Arndt and F. Wilbur Gingrich, *A Greek-English Lexicon of the New Testament and Other Early Christian Literature* (Chicago: University of Chicago Press, 1957), 319.

4. Isaiah 57:21.

5. "Choose the Right," *Hymns*, 1985, no. 239.

6. See Charles C. Calhoun, *Longfellow: A Rediscovered Life* (Boston: Beacon Press, 2004), 228–29.

7. See Calhoun, *Longfellow*, 215–20.

8. See Calhoun, *Longfellow*, 191.

9. See Calhoun, *Longfellow*, 114–18.

10. "I Heard the Bells on Christmas Day," *Hymns*, 1985, no. 214.

11. See Luke 22:50–51, John 18:10–11.

12. Moroni 7:47.

13. Luke 2:42–46.

14. Luke 2:48–49.

15. "I Am a Child of God," *Songbook*, 1995, 2–3.

16. D&C 20:22.

17. Howard W. Hunter, "The Temptations of Christ," *Ensign*, November 1976, 19.

18. Matthew 4:3.

19. Matthew 4:10.

20. Isaiah 9:6.

Finding Answers

—◆—

Joseph Fielding McConkie

Addressing the Saints in Nauvoo on the subject of revelation, the Prophet Joseph Smith said:

> *I am going to take up this subject by virtue of the knowledge of God in me, which I have received from heaven. The opinions of men, so far as I am concerned, are to me as the crackling of thorns under the pot, or the whistling of the wind. I break the ground; I lead the way like Columbus when he was invited to a banquet, where he was assigned the most honorable place at the table, and served with the ceremonials which were observed towards sovereigns. A shallow courtier present, who was meanly jealous of him, abruptly asked him whether he thought that in case he had not discovered the Indies, there were not other men in Spain who would have been capable of the enterprise? Columbus made no reply, but took an egg and invited the company to make it stand on end. They all attempted it, but in vain; whereupon he struck it upon the table so as to break one end, and left it standing on the broken part, illustrating that when he had once shown the way to the new world nothing was easier than to follow it.*[1]

Joseph Fielding McConkie was a BYU emeritus professor of ancient scripture when this devotional address was delivered on 12 December 2006. © *Brigham Young University.*

Having been privileged to have had some rather remarkable mentors—men who have clearly marked the way—and having had a few experiences that might be worth sharing, I will take the occasion this morning to make some suggestions relative to the matter of finding answers.

Like making an egg stand on end, the principles are quite simple. If I can articulate them well enough, it will be as though you always knew them.

LEARNING TO SOLVE YOUR OWN PROBLEMS

It was not long after my graduation from this institution that I found myself in Vietnam. I had been commissioned an officer in the Army of the United States and was serving as an LDS chaplain.

Throughout the country our LDS servicemen were organized into groups that functioned like quorums and moved with their military units. These groups were placed in one of three districts, each of which acted under the direction of a district presidency.

My military unit was base-camped in the southern part of the country. Our district president was an air force chaplain by the name of Farrell Smith. I served as his first counselor. As chaplains we were responsible for meeting the spiritual needs of the military units to which we were assigned and also had the general assignment of looking after our LDS servicemen wherever we might find them.

Time will not permit me to describe the nature of the problems we faced. Suffice it to say, they reached far beyond our experience.

We were extremely pleased when we received word that Victor L. Brown of the Presiding Bishopric was on his way to visit with us. We were to travel with him from one end of the country to the other, meeting with as many of our servicemen's groups as possible.

We quickly made the arrangements; I cite but one example. We needed a pilot who could commandeer either a chopper or fixed-wing craft and be able to fly at a moment's notice.

For such arrangements we bypassed the military chain of command and dealt with a higher authority. The Lord always saw that the right man was in the right place.

Chaplain Smith and I then sat in council together. We made a list of the questions we wanted to ask our visiting authority. We divided them up and committed them to memory.

When the times and places of our meetings were announced, our servicemen came from all over the country. We held meetings on the sides of runways, in bunkers and ditches. We held meetings with the ground rumbling beneath our feet and the sound of large guns thundering around us. In some instances we were even able to meet in small military chapels.

Between meetings, as soon as we were airborne, Chaplain Smith and I would take turns asking Bishop Brown questions. His counsel was wise, but it became more than evident what we were doing, and he called a sharp halt to our question asking.

He said, "Brethren, I am going to tell you a story. You won't like it, but it is a great story."

He then proceeded with his story, and, as he had anticipated, we did not like it.

The story centered around a young man who had a very difficult problem. He did not know what to do, so he visited with his bishop.

The bishop listened carefully and thoughtfully. He asked a few questions to assure that he understood all that was involved. He then confessed that he had no idea what counsel to give but told the young man that he would be meeting with the stake president the next evening and that he would present the matter to him.

The next evening the bishop met with the stake president. He explained the young man's problem. The stake president listened attentively and asked a few questions to assure he understood all that was involved. He then said, "Bishop, I have no idea what to tell you, but tomorrow I will be meeting with a member of the Quorum of the Twelve. I will present the matter to him."

The next day, as he met with the member of the Quorum of the Twelve, the stake president raised the matter. The Apostle listened attentively and asked a few questions to assure that he fully understood what was involved. He then said, "President, I have no idea what to tell you, but this afternoon I will be meeting with President McKay. I will ask him."

That afternoon he met with President McKay and carefully explained the problem. President McKay listened attentively and asked a few questions to assure that he understood all that was involved and then said, "Well, that's his (meaning the young man's) problem, isn't it."

Such was the story. We thought the ending a little abrupt. We had expected a great line, something we could chisel in stone; instead, we got one of those drab old truths that build character but can't get the hair on your arms to stand up.

The story brought an end to our question session and with it the realization that our problems were ours and it was for us to solve them. That is why the Lord placed us there.

The lesson is one that we are generally reluctant to learn. I had a father and two grandfathers who shared a great love of the gospel and who had devoted their lives to its study. They were a marvelous source of understanding.

I have, however, a very distinct memory of the occasion that I went to my father with some gospel questions only to receive the following response: "Look, Junior, you have the same sources available to you as I have to me."

More important than any answers these men gave to my questions was their teaching me how to get answers for myself. They are now gone. Questions continue, as does the confidence that the same sources that were available to them are available to me.

All of you know that we believe in the ministering of angels. You also know that angels will not do for us what we can do for ourselves. For them to do so would be contrary to the order of heaven.

There is a measurable difference between a student coming to my office to seek clarification on something they have read or that was taught in class and the student that comes asking to be taught what they missed because they chose not to come to class or complete the reading assignment.

Would not the same difference exist between those who keep their covenants and those who choose to miss meetings, skip their reading, and ignore assignments while asking God to overlook their neglect in the dispensing of His blessings?

We are generally familiar with the process of revelation announced in section 9 of the Doctrine and Covenants where we are directed to study the matter out in our minds, draw the best conclusion we can, and then bring our best offering to the Lord, asking for His approval while yet being ready to accept His counsel otherwise. The very nature of this process is designed to balance our experience and agency with the wisdom of heaven.

SEEKING THE COMPANIONSHIP OF THE HOLY GHOST

Now let us couple the wise use of agency with the gift of the Holy Ghost. To enhance our understanding of this gift, let us first distinguish it from the Light of Christ, which is given to every soul born into this world.[2] This Light, often referred to as "conscience," enables people to distinguish between right and wrong and entices them to do things that are edifying, enlightening, and uplifting.

Possession of the Light of Christ does not require faith in God or the testimony that Jesus is the Christ. Its purpose, however, is to lead all men to that end.[3]

Revelations from the Holy Ghost are of a higher order, or reach beyond the light and knowledge that is had by the generality of humankind.[4]

Membership in the Church is not requisite to receiving a revelation from the Holy Ghost. Were this the case, no one could obtain the spiritual witness necessary to join the Church.[5]

In fact, such a spiritual confirmation is required of those we refer to as converts before they are baptized and before we lay hands upon their heads and give them the promise of the gift of the Holy Ghost.[6]

We frequently speak of our right to the constant companionship of the Holy Ghost. We are generally left without any explanation as to what this means.

We know that the intent is not to suggest that we stand in a constant deluge of revelation. It is the slothful and unwise servant who has to be commanded in all things.[7]

Perhaps an analogy, one taught me by my father, will help in distinguishing between having received a revelation from the Holy Ghost and our having the gift of the Holy Ghost.

Imagine yourself traveling in the dark of night through very rugged and difficult terrain carefully seeking your way to a place of safety where you will be reunited with your family. Let us also suppose that a flash of lightning momentarily marks the path of safety before you.

The momentary flash of light pointing you in the direction of safety and shelter in our analogy represents a manifestation through the Holy Ghost.

If you then follow the path it marked out, it will lead you to the waters of baptism at the hands of a legal administrator who will, as he confirms you a member of the Church, say, "Receive the Holy Ghost," which means "the gift of the Holy Ghost."

The light by which you now walk embraces the companionship of the Holy Ghost. It is the light of the gospel—or, for some, the gospel in a new light. In either case, it enables you to see that which you could not see before.

It now becomes your privilege to walk, as it were, by the light of day. The light is constant, and, in most instances, the path you are called on to travel is clearly marked. In those instances in which it is not, you are entitled to the necessary vision, impression, or prodding necessary to assure your arrival at the place of safety.

To enjoy the "constant companionship of the Holy Ghost" means, for instance, that, as you fill your assignments as a teacher in the Church (if you are prepared properly), you will be taught things from on high as you teach others.

Such an experience will require more of you than the kind of presentation in which you simply repeat or rearrange the thoughts of others. The fact that every member of the Church is given the gift of the Holy Ghost is the evidence that the Lord wants to reveal things to you and through you.[8]

I have heard my father observe that he learned the gospel by listening to what he was directed to say when he preached the gospel. That experience should be universal among Latter-day Saints.

As you young men lay your hands on the heads of your wives to bless them before they give birth to your children or as you take those children in your arms to give them a father's blessing, if you hold yourself open to them, thoughts and promises will flow into your mind and you will become an instrument for the Lord in conveying or giving His blessing.

As you serve in positions of leadership or trust and seek direction as to who should be called or what should be done, that same Spirit will lead you far beyond your own thought process and mark a course that reaches beyond that which you can see even by the light of day. This is the companionship of which we speak.

WHEN NO SURE ANSWER COMES

There will be some instances in which no sure answer comes. We have a series of revelations in the Doctrine and Covenants in which the Lord tells the early missionaries of this dispensation that there were some matters that were to be left to their discretion. The phrase that is constantly repeated is "it mattereth not unto me."[9]

Brigham Young explained this doctrine:

If I do not know the will of my Father, and what He requires of me in a certain transaction, if I ask Him to give me wisdom concerning any require-ment in life, or in regard to my own course, or that of my friends, my fam-ily, my children, or those that I preside over, and get no answer from Him, and then do the very best that my judgment will teach me, He is bound to own and honor that transaction, and He will do so to all intents and purposes.[10]

ASKING THE RIGHT QUESTION

So it is that in finding answers we must find the balance between agency and inspiration. Building upon this foundation, let me teach you a very fundamental but often overlooked principle relative to getting answers to prayers and to questions that trouble you.

Few things facilitate getting the right answer like asking the right question. Let me illustrate.

A young woman came up to me after a meeting at which I had spoken a few weeks ago. She asked if I could help her with a question dealing with the Old Testament. I told her that I would be willing to try.

She asked the question, and I did not have an idea in the world how to answer it. I told her so and then asked why the answer to such a question was important to her.

She indicated that her husband had raised the issue along with other like questions. Each question he was asking carried with it the spirit of doubt. His questions were intended to challenge, not to build faith.

The real question here is: If I had been able to answer each of the questions with which this man was challenging his wife, would it have accomplished anything more than require him to come up with more questions?

The real question needing answering is: Why was he so anxious to discredit God and show the foolishness of scripture? Perhaps he ought be asked "What commandment is it that you don't want to keep?" or "What blessings would you like to quit receiving?"

I recently received a note from a former student. He requested help in answering questions common to anti-Mormon literature.

I know the answers to these questions, but I also know that my answering them will make no difference whatsoever unless there is a change in the purpose and spirit of those asking them.

My questions are these: Is there really a shortage of evidence that Joseph Smith is a prophet? Are the unanswered questions in the Old Testament the real lion in our path?

I have a letter on my desk from a mother who told me a tragic story about the behavior of a man who had been called as a priesthood leader. "How," she asked, "can I explain to my daughter that callings in this Church are inspired and at the same time explain the behavior of this man?"

While I share her hurt and embarrassment over what took place, I cannot help but wonder if she is not asking the wrong question. Surely her faith and that of her daughter cannot be so fragile that the misdeeds of one man would call the truthfulness of the whole gospel plan into question.

At issue is if our faith should rest in the infallibility of priesthood leaders or on the assurance that if we keep our covenants the Spirit of the Lord will always be our companion.

Again, often what stands between us and answers to our prayers is our failure to ask the right questions. The role of the Holy Ghost is as important in determining what we pray about as it is in bringing the answers we seek.

In the book of James we find the promise that we may ask wisdom of God, but it requires that we do so "in faith, nothing wavering."[11] Of those who "waver," James said, "Let not that man think that he shall receive any thing of the Lord."[12]

Perhaps the greatest revelation of this dispensation was the one Joseph Smith received prompting him to go into the woods and find a place to pray. Having read the injunction in James, he said:

Never did any passage of scripture come with more power to the heart of man than this did at this time to mine. It seemed to enter with great force into every feeling of my heart. I reflected on it again and again, knowing that if any person needed wisdom from God, I did.[13]

Do you see what is taking place here? Joseph was getting a revelation telling him to go get a revelation. The Spirit was directing him in what he asked, and, because the Spirit was his companion in the asking of the question, he could do it with complete faith.

In 3 Nephi, Christ is recorded as saying, "And whatsoever ye shall ask the Father in my name, which is right, believing that ye shall receive, behold it shall be given unto you."[14]

Think of that! We have the sure promise that if we pray in the manner prescribed by Christ and ask for that "which is right," our prayers will be answered.

Our instruction is to pray to the Father in the name of Christ. To pray in Christ's name obligates us to pray as He would pray or to pray in His Spirit. This is true of all that we do in His name.

This principle is affirmed in revelation both ancient and modern. To those of our day, the Lord said: "And if ye are purified and cleansed from all sin, ye shall ask whatsoever you will in the name of Jesus and it shall be done. *But know this, it shall be given you what you shall ask.*"[15]

Again we read, "He that asketh in the Spirit asketh according to the will of God; wherefore it is done even as he asketh."[16]

To those of his day, John the Beloved wrote, "And this is the confidence that we have in him, that, if we ask any thing according to his will, he heareth us."[17]

RETURNING TO VIETNAM

I return to where we began, with two young chaplains in Vietnam. Upon examination, my story is most common—indeed, it is a universal story.

For all of us, growing up includes leaving the security of home and the protective care of loving parents to enter a world full of problems and challenges that reach far beyond the experience that is ours.

In doing so, we would like to have a ready source to tell us how to handle difficult situations. Such is not the Lord's system.

If angels will not do for you what you can do for yourself, be assured that the Holy Ghost will not do it either. It is not the design of heaven that we be rescued from all difficult situations. Rather, it is the system that we grow up and learn to handle them.

The sense of being overwhelmed is very much a part of the journey. The power with which God clothes us in His holy temples does not suppose that the journey we have been called to make will be an easy one.

Nevertheless, the path we seek will always be clearly marked by the covenants we have made and the callings we have received.

It is in the accepting of our lot and moving forward with what the Lord has asked of us that we discover that the Holy Ghost enjoys our company, angels feel constrained to join us, and the heavens open to our vision.

Of such I testify, in the name of Jesus Christ, amen.

NOTES

1. Joseph Smith, *HC* 5:402.
2. See Moroni 7:16; D&C 93:2.
3. See D&C 84:46–48.
4. See 1 Nephi 10:17–19.
5. See Moroni 10:4–5.
6. See D&C 20:37–41.
7. See D&C 58:26–29.
8. Joseph Smith said, "No man can receive the Holy Ghost without receiving revelations. The Holy Ghost is a revelator" (*HC* 6:58).
9. D&C 61:22; 62:5.
10. *JD* 3:205.
11. James 1:5–6.
12. James 1:7.
13. JS—H 1:12.
14. 3 Nephi 18:20.
15. D&C 50:29–30; emphasis added.
16. D&C 46:30.
17. 1 John 5:14.

The Still, Small Voice

———◆———

Sharon G. Samuelson

Welcome to Brigham Young University for the 2007 school year. Hopefully you had a wonderful Christmas holiday as you remembered and honored the birth of our Savior, Jesus Christ. I so enjoy this time of year because it also includes gatherings with those you love—family and friends. These times and others create memories to be remembered and recalled throughout one's lifetime.

One such memory of mine includes an extended family portrait taken several years ago. Whenever someone who has not seen it before views this portrait, a puzzled look appears on the person's face and this question is usually asked: "Why is there a little boy in the picture holding a blue bucket?"

To the viewer, this appears to be rather odd in a formal portrait setting, and the individual's curiosity is piqued. This cute little boy in the picture is my nephew, Jeremy. Jeremy is autistic. His parents brought the bucket to the photographer's studio filled with some of his favorite toys. Having a picture taken with so many people is a

Sharon G. Samuelson, wife of BYU president Cecil O. Samuelson, delivered this devotional on 9 January 2007. © Brigham Young University.

tedious process, and much confusion can arise. Since Jeremy didn't like to be in crowds or in an unstructured environment, his parents wanted him to have something to entertain him until the time came to take the picture. His security and comfort on this occasion was found in clutching firmly his blue bucket, and he would not let it be taken away from him when the time arrived to pose for the picture—even by his lovingly pleading parents. Thus Jeremy has his bucket in the picture, and our family members smile with love for Jeremy when we view the photograph.

During the Savior's ministry, He was asked by His disciples this question: "Who is the greatest in the kingdom of heaven?"[1] In response He

called a little child unto him, and set him in the midst of them,

And said, Verily I say unto you, Except ye be converted, and become as little children, ye shall not enter into the kingdom of heaven.

Whosoever therefore shall humble himself as this little child, the same is greatest in the kingdom of heaven.

And whoso shall receive one such little child in my name receiveth me.[2]

The scriptures also teach us that "a little child shall lead them."[3] Jeremy has taught his family many spiritual lessons, and often the family has felt that he at times was more spiritually in tune than they. May I tell you of one of these times that occurred to me when I was taught by this young boy?

At nine and one-half years of age, Jeremy expressed a desire to be baptized, and so it was arranged to have him baptized at the same time as his younger brother. Jeremy was very excited. As family and friends were waiting in a classroom for their turn to proceed to the font for the baptism to be performed, Jeremy went about greeting everyone with excitement as he repeated to each of us the words "I am going to have the Holy Ghost in me. I am going to be baptized and have the Holy Ghost." My heart was touched as this little boy—who often didn't relate to others in such a way—felt that something very important was to occur in his life that day. He was going to be baptized and then receive the gift of the Holy Ghost, and he was pleased. One may wonder how much Jeremy really understood about baptism, the Holy Ghost, Jesus, and Heavenly Father. However, his parents have had experiences and conversations with Jeremy that testify that he has had spiritual lessons through the Holy Ghost in the ensuing years.

Those of you here today who have been baptized and confirmed members of The Church of Jesus Christ of Latter-day Saints have been given by the laying on of hands by one in authority one of the greatest gifts you can enjoy on earth, the constant companionship of the Holy Ghost, if you but heed the promptings of that Spirit and keep yourselves worthy of its presence. Are you as excited about it as was a little nine-and-one-half-year-old boy? How often do you express gratitude to your Heavenly Father for the great privilege it is for you to have the companionship of one of the members of the Godhead? Do you seek to use this blessing in your lives each and every day?

During the weeks and months ahead in this new school year, you will have many opportunities to make choices and decisions based on your beliefs, values, and desires that will define your integrity, worth, decency, honor, and spirituality. You are blessed with the scriptures; a prophet of the Lord, President Gordon B. Hinckley; Apostles; and righteous models in your families and associates who can provide teachings and examples of true conduct in your lives. Many wonderful blessings await you when you are faithful and serve others and the Lord.

However, sometimes you will run into stumbling blocks in your path. There may be difficult decisions to make, temptations that may seem overwhelming, crises in your faith and feelings of personal worth, or times of sorrow where you find it difficult to find solace. Sometimes you may feel confused and alone in your struggles. At times such as these there is the need for inspiration, understanding, and guidance to assist you as you forge onward in your pursuits.

As our Savior approached the conclusion of His ministry on earth, He spoke to His disciples and members of the Church about leaving them. They had often been in the presence of the Savior, and He had guided, taught, and ministered unto them. They sorrowed at the prospect of Him leaving them. They also feared that they would feel alone and distraught without Him. However, He promised:

I will pray the Father, and he shall give you another Comforter, that he may abide with you for ever. . . .

But the Comforter, which is the Holy Ghost, whom the Father will send in my name, he shall teach you all things, and bring all things to your remembrance, whatsoever I have said unto you.[4]

Just as the Saints at that time were not left alone, the Holy Ghost can abide with you every hour of the day wherever you may be. It can be your constant companion; however, in order to enjoy the benefits of this wonderful gift, you must be worthy to receive it and thus be able to use it in your lives. The Holy Ghost can be a compass to direct you back to your Heavenly Father.

In 1847 the Prophet Joseph Smith appeared to Brigham Young in a dream or vision. Brigham Young asked the Prophet if he had a message for the Brethren. The Prophet said:

Tell the people to be humble and faithful, and be sure to keep the spirit of the Lord and it will lead them right. Be careful and not turn away the small still voice; it will teach you what to do and where to go; it will yield the fruits of the kingdom. Tell the brethren to keep their hearts open to conviction, so that when the Holy Ghost comes to them, their hearts will be ready to receive it.[5]

This is also a message for you today. With this wonderful gift you may know what to do and what not to do to obtain happiness and peace. You can resist temptation, be warned of dangers, and be guided as you make important decisions and solve problems. Every aspect of your lives can be influenced by the presence of the Holy Ghost.

President Boyd K. Packer has taught:

You can never make a serious mistake without being warned. You will never take the wrong road or go around the wrong bend or make the wrong decision without you having been warned. That pattern is the pattern of the Latter-day Saint. You were confirmed a member of the Church, and you had conferred upon you the gift of the Holy Ghost to be a guide and a companion to you, to be a comfort to you. The Holy Ghost is a comforter.[6]

The Holy Ghost can communicate with you if you but seek this communication and are worthy to receive it. Revelation from the Holy Ghost is often described as a "still small voice"[7] and most often comes as words you feel more than hear. How many times have you said, "I had a feeling . . ." If you are in tune with the Spirit, this can be a communication from the Holy Ghost.

You have been taught by our Church leaders and the scriptures that the Holy Ghost will not dwell with a person who does not obey and keep the commandments of our Heavenly Father. As you take the sacrament each Sunday, you promise to obey the Lord's commandments. In the sacrament prayer you are told by the Lord that you can "always have his Spirit to be with [you]"[8] if you keep this promise. Your hearts and minds will be ready to receive the still, small voice and the whisperings of the Spirit if you are worthy.

I have always been confounded by the actions of Laman and Lemuel as described in the Book of Mormon. They rebelled against the Lord and their brother Nephi even though they had been spoken to by an angel and heard his voice from time to time. They even attempted to take Nephi's life. Nephi said to them:

Ye have heard his voice from time to time; and he hath spoken unto you in a still small voice, but ye were past feeling, that ye could not feel his words.[9]

If you are not keeping the Lord's commandments, you will not be able to feel or hear the still, small voice.

The desire of your hearts, I know, is that you are constantly in tune with the Holy Ghost and have this compass to guide and bless you in every aspect of your lives. Our Savior, Jesus Christ, loves you dearly and wants you to be comforted and guided as you strive to gain strong testimonies of Him and to one day return to His presence. He will give you abundant blessings, and it is through the power of the Holy Ghost that you can receive them if you but strive to serve Him and all your brothers and sisters. It is my prayer that all of us keep our hearts open to receive the promptings of the Spirit and use this sacred gift in our lives, and I say this in the name of Jesus Christ, amen.

NOTES

1. Matthew 18:1.

2. Matthew 18:2–5.

3. Isaiah 11:6.

4. John 14:16, 26.

5. *Manuscript History of Brigham Young: 1846–1847*, ed. Elden J. Watson (Salt Lake City: Elden Jay Watson, 1971), 529; 23 February 1847.

6. Boyd K. Packer, "Some Things Every Missionary Should Know," unpublished address, 26 June 2002, new mission presidents' seminar.

7. 1 Nephi 17:45; D&C 85:6.

8. D&C 20:77.

9. 1 Nephi 17:45.

Mixing Reason and Faith

———◆———

Cecil O. Samuelson

It is always a pleasure to be with you as we celebrate the onset of a new year together. This is a wonderful time in our BYU history, in the history of the Church, and even the history of the world. Yes, we are faced with many problems, challenges, and disappointments in our personal and collective lives, and yet with all of the things we might wish were different, there is much evidence that these are the "best of times."

A couple of months ago there was an interesting article in the *Deseret Morning News* that had been reprinted from the *Washington Post*. It was authored by the Reverend John I. Jenkins, president of the University of Notre Dame, and by his provost, Thomas Burish ("Reason and Faith at Harvard," *Washington Post*, 23 October 2006, A21). Their article began with this question: "What should a properly educated college graduate of the early 21st century know?"

I immediately and reflexively asked myself the question "What should a properly educated *LDS* college graduate of the early 21st

———

Cecil O. Samuelson was BYU president when this devotional address was delivered on 9 January 2007. © *Intellectual Reserve, Inc.*

century know?" And, more specifically, "What should a properly educated and motivated Latter-day Saint *BYU* graduate of our day know?"

I shall return to my questions in a few moments. Let me first address the query of our friends from Notre Dame.

They noted that a task force on general education at Harvard University had recently proposed an answer to their question by stating that, among other things, such a graduate should know "the role of religion in contemporary, historical, or future events—personal, cultural, national, or international." To meet this goal, the Harvard committee recommended that every Harvard student be required to take at least one course in the area that the committee described as "Reason and Faith."

My understanding is that this recommendation has been suggested only and has not been enacted. It likely will never be, and Jenkins and Burish acknowledge this.

As reported by the Notre Dame leaders, the Harvard committee found that today's college students struggle with an academic environment that they describe as "profoundly secular." Most would agree with this assessment of Harvard University and perhaps most American institutions of higher education. I doubt our friends at Notre Dame consider that description to be completely accurate of their campus, and I know of no one, thank heaven, who would suggest that to be the case at BYU.

Father Jenkins and Dr. Burish gave a historical perspective that reminds us that secular preeminence has not always been the case at Harvard and other great universities. In fact, most have their roots in and early support from various religious communities. "For centuries," Jenkins and Burish report, "scholars, scientists and artists agreed that convictions of faith were wholly compatible with the highest levels of reasoning, inquiry and creativity."

Sadly, we know that is no longer the case at many places. On the other hand, we gladly proclaim our assertion that faith and reason are both vibrant and integrated at Brigham Young University. For this we are profoundly grateful.

Please make no mistake: I see no effort nor momentum to make BYU's approach to learning the academic model for emulation broadly across this country or any other. What we do see is something of an awakening to the reality that both reason and faith have a place in the academy and that, for many, this is not only true but also appropriate. It increasingly seems to be recognized that religion, in spite of many detractors and critics, is clearly a fact of 21st-century life.

According to Harvard University's own data, over 90 percent of entering Harvard students discuss religion and more than 70 percent attend religious services at least some of the time. The Harvard task force observes that when students get to college, they

often struggle—sometimes for the first time in their lives—to sort out the relationship between their own beliefs and practices, the different beliefs and practices of fellow students, and the profoundly secular and intellectual world of the academy itself. [*Preliminary Report: Task Force on General Education* (Cambridge, Massachusetts: Harvard University Faculty of Arts and Sciences, October 2006), 18; www.fas.harvard.edu/~secfas/Gen_Ed_Prelim_Report.pdf]

Without being unduly critical, I note that this observation from Cambridge, Massachusetts, gives added cogency to the BYU Mission and Aims statements.

Please be certain that the folks at Harvard are not talking about framing secular learning in an environment of sustaining faith such as we strive to achieve at BYU. Let me return again to the words of the Harvard Task Force:

Harvard is no longer an institution with a religious mission, but religion is a fact that Harvard's graduates will confront in their lives both in and after college. We therefore require students to take one course in a category entitled Reason and Faith. Let us be clear [the committee continues]. *Courses in Reason and Faith are not religious apologetics. They are courses that examine the interplay between religion and various aspects of . . . culture and society.* [*Preliminary Report*, 19]

A number of other recent, credible academic studies have reached similarly interesting and somewhat surprising conclusions in contrast to those that subscribe to the "God is dead" school of thinking first rampant in higher education circles decades ago and persisting with some dominance in many American universities today.

The Higher Education Research Institute at UCLA is currently conducting a broad-reaching study of the spiritual life of more than 112,000 American college students representing 236 U.S. institutions. The survey so far has found that 79 percent professed a belief in God, 69 percent claimed to pray, and about three-fourths reported attending religious services at least some of the time ("Reason and Faith at Harvard"; also *The Spiritual Life of College Students: A National Study of College Students' Search for Meaning and Purpose* [Los Angeles: UCLA Higher Education Research Institute, 2004–05], 4; http://spirituality. ucla.edu/spirituality/reports/FINAL%20REPORT.pdf).

Baylor University also recently conducted a national study entitled "The Values and Beliefs of the American Public." They estimate that 85 to 90 percent of Americans "believe in God," over two-thirds pray at least weekly, and half attend church monthly (*American Piety in the 21st Century: New Insights to the Depth and Complexity of Religion in the U.S.* [Waco, Texas: Baylor Institute for Studies of Religion, September 2006], 4; www.baylor.edu/content/services/document. php/33304.pdf).

All of these studies and some others confirm the assertion that many people have strongly held religious and spiritual values. While I personally might not be quite as optimistic as Sir John Marks Templeton, the 1998 recipient of a BYU honorary doctorate and head of the Templeton Foundation, which financed many of the aforementioned studies, his observation does deserve careful consideration:

Of all the encouraging trends that mark the closing years of the twentieth century, none is more heartening or more important than the remarkable spread of spiritual values. [John M. Templeton, *Is Progress Speeding Up?: Our Multiplying Multitudes of Blessings* (Philadelphia: Templeton Foundation Press, 1997), 243]

While we might find all of these observations to be interesting and even comforting, you might well ask, "What does this have to do with us?" I believe a great deal. While we subscribe to, and occasionally glory in, the assertion of Peter that we are "a peculiar people" (1 Peter 2:9), there is so much that we have in common with all of Heavenly Father's children.

I return to the question posed at the outset: "What should a properly educated Latter-day Saint BYU graduate of the early 21st century know?" The answer is both in what we share and in what we have to share.

First, I would assert that the properly educated Latter-day Saint BYU graduate should know what any properly educated college or university graduate should know. Implicit in this assertion is that if we ask more of the BYU graduate in some area, we do not excuse corresponding or compensatory deficits in other areas of what constitutes a proper education. In fact, we aspire explicitly to have our graduates be in the first rank of those deeply and broadly educated in all the dimensions that the academy would deem to be both desirable and essential. You will know that our Aims and Mission statements do not equivocate on this matter.

Second, Brigham Young University and its supporting trustees have the expectation that our Latter-day Saint graduates will also have a deep and profound understanding of and faith in some fundamentals and principles related to our Church and its doctrines. Let me refer to the words of President J. Reuben Clark, Jr., given in 1938 in his "The Charted Course of the Church in Education," with which, hopefully, many of you students and all of the faculty are familiar:

> *In all this there are for the Church and for each and all of its members, two prime things which may not be overlooked, forgotten, shaded, or discarded:*
> *First: That Jesus Christ is the Son of God, the Only Begotten of the Father in the flesh, the Creator of the world, the Lamb of God, the Sacrifice for the sins of the world, the Atoner for Adam's transgression; that He was crucified; that His spirit left His body; that He died; that He*

was laid away in the tomb; that on the third day His spirit was reunited with His body, which again became a living being; that He was raised from the tomb a resurrected being, a perfect Being, the First Fruits of the Resurrection; that He later ascended to the Father; and that because of His death and by and through His resurrection every man born into the world since the beginning will be likewise literally resurrected. This doctrine is as old as the world. Job declared: "And though after my skin worms destroy this body, yet in my flesh shall I see God, whom I shall see for myself and mine eyes shall behold, and not another." (Job 19:26, 27.)

The resurrected body is a body of flesh and bones and spirit, and Job was uttering a great and everlasting truth. These positive facts, and all other facts necessarily implied therein, must all be honestly believed, in full faith, by every member of the Church.

The second of the two things to which we must all give full faith is: That the Father and the Son actually and in truth and very deed appeared to the Prophet Joseph in a vision in the woods; that other heavenly visions followed to Joseph and to others; that the Gospel and the holy Priesthood after the Order of the Son of God were in truth and fact restored to the earth from which they were lost by the apostasy of the Primitive Church; that the Lord again set up His Church, through the agency of Joseph Smith; that the Book of Mormon is just what it professes to be; that to the Prophet came numerous revelations for the guidance, upbuilding, organization, and encouragement of the Church and its members; that the Prophet's successors, likewise called of God, have received revelations as the needs of the Church have required, and that they will continue to receive revelations as the Church and its members, living the truth they already have, shall stand in need of more; that this is in truth the Church of Jesus Christ of Latter-day Saints; and that its foundation beliefs are the laws and principles laid down in the Articles of Faith. These facts also, and each of them, together with all things necessarily implied therein or flowing therefrom, must stand, unchanged, unmodified, without dilution, excuse, apology, or avoidance; they may not be explained away or submerged. Without these two great beliefs the Church would cease to be the Church. [J. Reuben Clark, Jr., "The Charted Course of the Church in Education," talk given at Aspen Grove, 8 August 1938]

In this long quotation from President Clark's foundational address we find an excellent summary of the special or additional things a properly educated Latter-day Saint BYU graduate of the early 21st century should know. I suspect in this regard most of you have already qualified, and I congratulate you. For those who may yet be struggling with any of the dimensions of President Clark's outline, let me suggest that there is no better place than Brigham Young University—together with its student wards, stakes, and other support systems—to find, round out, and qualify for this remarkable knowledge.

As President Spencer W. Kimball taught when he asked Sister Naomi W. Randall to change one word in her wonderful hymn of testimony, "I Am a Child of God" (*Hymns*, 1985, no. 301), more is required of us than just knowing, as vital as knowledge itself is. We must also "do."

What is it that we must do? All of us—students, faculty, staff, and administration—are regularly reminded that as we come to BYU, we "enter to learn; go forth to serve."

We, of course, serve in many and diverse ways and should always do so as we search for appropriate means and approaches to do even more and to do it better. One of the ways that we serve is by sharing what we have learned or polished or enhanced during our stay at BYU. Of course this means that if we have trained in education or engineering, nursing or neurosciences, in law or languages, in business or biology, or in any branch of learning available here at BYU, we apply the best and latest principles of these honored professions in the context of our ethical, gospel, and moral understandings. As we attempt to implement the counsel of the broad mandate of the Restoration scriptures, we commit to making a better world by contributing directly to strong families, communities, congregations, companies, and other vital institutions. Listen to these words of the Lord:

Behold, I will hasten my work in its time. . . .

And I give unto you a commandment that you shall teach one another the doctrine of the kingdom.

Teach ye diligently and my grace shall attend you, that you may be instructed more perfectly in theory, in principle, in doctrine, in the law of the gospel, in all things that pertain unto the kingdom of God, that are expedient for you to understand;

Of things both in heaven and in the earth, and under the earth; things which have been, things which are, things which must shortly come to pass; things which are at home, things which are abroad; the wars and the perplexities of the nations, and the judgments which are on the land; and a knowledge also of countries and of kingdoms. . . .

And as all have not faith, seek ye diligently and teach one another words of wisdom; yea, seek ye out of the best books words of wisdom; seek learning, even by study and also by faith. [D&C 88:73, 77–79, 118]

There is, however, even more that we can and must do. In addition to keeping the Lord's commandments faithfully, we must, as the Apostle Peter taught, "be ready always to give an answer to every man that asketh you a reason of the hope that is in you" (1 Peter 3:15).

All of you who have served as missionaries and, hopefully, the rest of us as well know and appreciate that this is a very delicate and sensitive matter. It calls for decorum, tenderness, and tact. It demands great respect for the feelings, faith, traditions, and values of others. It requires understanding that those not of our Church background and culture often will not see things as we might or reach the same conclusions we do about the same observations and data. It mandates great reverence and respect for all individuals as children of God whatever their individual or current circumstances. It is expected that we not only preach the Golden Rule but also practice it. It asks for patience, long-suffering, forgiveness, and humility. Most of all, to have the opportunity to share the reason for our optimism, faith, and hope, we must live our lives with complete authenticity, including having full congruence of our behaviors and actions with the fundamentals we hold dear.

As we go about contributing in the ways that we have learned to serve while being students at Brigham Young University, we invite the verbal opportunities to share our hope and testimonies. Often it is more important that we can behaviorally bear our witness of these fundamental principles to those who observe and interact with us.

As I stated at the outset in reporting the interesting data on the feelings of so many college students with respect to reason and faith, I believe in many ways there are more with us than against us (see 2 Kings 6:16) and many "who are only kept from the truth because they know not where to find it" (D&C 123:12).

But it is not only in the outside world where we find these kindred souls. Across our campus are those who come seeking one kind of knowledge and find additional, unexpected light. These individuals not only come from the United States but also from around the world. They may be from California or Alabama, New Hampshire or Texas, from Turkey, Russia, Argentina, or from Sri Lanka, China, or Guatemala.

Each of their experiences is unique and personal. Yet there are some common themes. These individuals generally have big smiles across their faces. They are happy. They say they have found something of great worth. Listen to these comments:

"I felt something when I came to BYU. I felt something good like I've never felt before."

"I didn't grow up believing there is a God, but now I have come to know my Heavenly Father. I know He loves me."

"I used to think my life didn't have any particular purpose. Now I know my Heavenly Father has a plan for me."

"People were so kind and friendly. I wanted to know why."

Sometimes it has been the example of great roommates or a caring faculty or staff member. Sometimes it has been the full-time missionaries. In one case it was the little LDS girl next door who many years ago tried to read the Book of Mormon to a young boy as he jumped on her trampoline.

The seeds of faith and light are planted, cultivated, nurtured, and grow bathed in the glow of His tender care—the behavioral and verbal testimony examples of Latter-day Saint BYU students and graduates on campus and around the world.

My prayer and the blessing I invoke upon us at the beginning of another year brimming with potential is that we will reflect regularly on what a properly educated Latter-day Saint BYU graduate of the 21st century will know and do and that we will then continue to get on with the exciting adventure of becoming and helping each other become more authentic examples of such. In the name of Jesus Christ, amen.

Lehi's Dream and You

———◆———

Boyd K. Packer

I asked our records department to tell me how many college-age youth we have in the Church. They responded 1,974,001. Good, I thought, I will speak to the *one.*

You may be here in this congregation or somewhere in any one of 170 countries. You, the one of nearly two million, are in the early morning of your life, while I am in the late evening of mine.

My college life began at Weber College, then a very small junior college. World War II had just ended. Most of the men in our class were recently returned from military service. We were, by and large, more mature than college students of your day. We had been through the war and carried with us many memories. Some of them we held on to; others we were glad to have fade away. We were more serious and did not enter into fun and games as much as you do. We wanted to get on with our lives and knew that education was the key.

Boyd K. Packer was Acting President of the Quorum of the Twelve Apostles of The Church of Jesus Christ of Latter-day Saints when this devotional address was delivered on 16 January 2007. © *Intellectual Reserve, Inc.*

We took the insignias and labels and sometimes even the buttons off our uniforms, mixed them with odds and ends of civilian clothes, and wore them to school. That was all we had to wear.

At military training camps, we had been marched from place to place in formation. Often we would sing marching songs. At college, I attended the Institute of Religion classes. We had our own marching songs. I remember one of them:

A root-tee-toot, a root-tee-toot.
Oh, we are boys of the institute.
We don't smoke, and we don't chew.
And we don't go with girls that do.
Some folks say we don't have fun.
We don't!

Some laughed with us; others laughed at us. Whatever ridicule they intended with their mocking was of no concern to us. We had gained personal testimonies of the gospel. We had decided long since that we would live the gospel and not be ashamed of the Church or the history or any part of it (see Romans 1:16).

The whole focus of our lives in the military had been on destruction. That is what war is about. We were inspired by the noble virtue of patriotism. To be devoted to destruction without being destroyed yourself spiritually or morally was the test of life.

I did not serve a mission during those years. Staying close to the Book of Mormon has, I think, made up for that. That witness had come little by little.

Together, my wife and I made our way through the ordinary challenges of life—getting through school, finding employment, raising a family.

You too live in a time of war, the spiritual war that will never end. War itself now dominates the affairs of mankind. Your world at war has lost its innocence. There is nothing, however crude or unworthy, that is not deemed acceptable for movies or plays or music

or conversation. The world seems to be turned upside down. (See
2 Peter 2:1–22.)

Formality, respect for authority, dignity, and nobility are mocked.
Modesty and neatness yield to slouchiness and shabbiness in dress and
grooming. The rules of honesty and integrity and basic morality are
now ignored. Conversation is laced with profanity. You see that in art
and literature, in drama and entertainment. Instead of being refined,
they become coarse. (See 1 Timothy 4:1–3; 2 Timothy 3:1–9.)

You have decisions almost every day as to whether you will follow
those trends. You have many tests ahead.

As a boy, President Joseph F. Smith, son of Hyrum, came west
in 1848 with his widowed mother. He was called as a missionary to
Hawaii when he was 15 years of age. He spent much of the next four
years alone. He was released in 1857 at the age of 19 (just the age
we call missionaries now). Penniless, he stopped in California to earn
money for warm clothes.

With another man, . . . [Joseph] *took passage in a mail wagon. They
traveled all night, and at daylight stopped near a ranch for breakfast. The
passenger and the mail carrier began to prepare breakfast, while Joseph
went a short distance from camp to* [gather wood and] *look after the horses.
. . . A wagon load of drunken men from Monte came in view, on their road
to San Bernardino to kill the "Mormons," as they boasted.*

*The oaths and foul language which they uttered, between their shooting,
and the swinging of their pistols, were almost indescribable. . . . They were
all cursing the "Mormons," and uttering boasts of what they would do when
they met them. They . . . caught sight of the mail wagon. . . .* [His com-
panion] *and the mail carrier, fearing for their safety, had retired behind the
chaparral, leaving all the baggage and supplies . . . exposed and unprotected.*

Just as [one] *drunken man approached,* [young Joseph F.] *came in
view . . . , too late to hide. . . . The ruffian was swinging his weapon, and
uttering the most blood-curdling oaths and threats ever heard against the
"Mormons." "I dared not run," says* [Joseph F.] *Smith, "though I trembled
for fear which I dared not show. I therefore walked right up to the camp
fire, and arrived there just a minute or two before the drunken desperado,*

who came directly toward me, and, swinging his revolver in my face, with an oath cried out: 'Are you a ——————— "Mormon?"'

[Young Joseph] *looked him straight in the eyes, and answered with emphasis: "Yes, sir'ee; dyed in the wool; true blue, through and through."*

The desperado's arms both dropped by his sides, as if paralyzed, his pistol in one hand, and he said in a subdued . . . voice, offering his hand: "Well, you are the ————— pleasantest man I ever met! Shake. I am glad to see a fellow stand for his convictions." Then he turned and [left]. [Joseph F. Smith, *Gospel Doctrine* (Salt Lake City: Deseret News, 1919), 673–74; see also Joseph Fielding Smith, *Life of Joseph F. Smith: Sixth President of The Church of Jesus Christ of Latter-day Saints* (Salt Lake City: Deseret Book, 1969), 188–89]

Joseph F. Smith became the sixth President of the Church. His son Joseph Fielding Smith, who wrote the account I just gave, became the tenth President of the Church. I knew President Smith well. In 1970, he called me to the Quorum of the Twelve Apostles.

You will not face the kind of test that Joseph F. Smith faced. In ways, your tests are going to be harder.

The Book of Mormon became the cornerstone of my testimony.

In the eighth chapter of 1 Nephi, read about Lehi's dream. He told his family, "Behold, I have dreamed a dream; or, in other words, I have seen a vision" (1 Nephi 8:2).

You may think that Lehi's dream or vision has no special meaning for you, but it does. You are in it; all of us are in it.

Nephi said, "[All scripture is likened] unto us, that it might be for our profit and learning" (1 Nephi 19:23).

Lehi's dream or vision of the iron rod has in it everything a young Latter-day Saint needs to understand the test of life.

Lehi saw:

A great and spacious building (see 1 Nephi 11:35–36; 12:18),
A path following a river (see 1 Nephi 8:19–22),
A mist of darkness (see 1 Nephi 12:16–17),

An iron rod which led through the mist of darkness (see 1 Nephi 11:24–25),

The tree of life, "whose fruit was desirable to make one happy" (1 Nephi 8:10; see 1 Nephi 11:8–9, 21–24).

Read it carefully; then read it again.

If you hold to the rod, you can *feel* your way forward with the gift of the Holy Ghost, conferred upon you at the time you were confirmed a member of the Church. The Holy Ghost will comfort you. You will be able to feel the influence of the angels, as Nephi did, and feel your way through life.

The Book of Mormon has been my iron rod.

Lehi saw great multitudes of people "pressing forward" (1 Nephi 8:21) toward the tree.

The great and spacious building

was filled with people, both old and young, both male and female; and their manner of dress was exceedingly fine; and they were in the attitude of mocking and pointing their fingers towards those who had come at and were partaking of the fruit. [1 Nephi 8:27]

One word in this dream or vision should have special meaning to you young Latter-day Saints. The word is *after.* It was *after* the people had found the tree that they became ashamed, and because of the mockery of the world they fell away.

And after *they had tasted of the fruit they were ashamed, because of those that were scoffing at them; and they fell away into forbidden paths and were lost.* . . .

And great was the multitude that did enter into that strange building. And after *they did enter into that building they did point the finger of scorn at me and those that were partaking of the fruit also;* [that was the test, and then Lehi said] *but we heeded them not.* [And that was the answer.] [1 Nephi 8:28, 33; emphasis added]

Lehi's son, Nephi, wrote:

I, Nephi, was desirous also that I might see, and hear, and know of these things, by the power of the Holy Ghost, which is the gift of God unto all those who diligently seek him. . . .

For he that diligently seeketh shall find; and the mysteries of God shall be unfolded unto them, by the power of the Holy Ghost, as well in these times as in times of old, and as well in times of old as in times to come; wherefore, the course of the Lord is one eternal round. [1 Nephi 10:17, 19]

All of the symbolism in Lehi's dream was explained to his son Nephi, and Nephi wrote about it.

At your baptism and confirmation, you took hold of the iron rod. But you are never safe. It is *after* you have partaken of that fruit that your test will come.

I think now and then of one of our classmates—very bright, good looking, faithful in the Church, and drenched with talent and ability. He married well and rose quickly to prominence. He began to compromise to please the world and please those around him. They flattered him into following after their ways, which were the ways of the world.

Sometimes it is so simple a thing as how you groom yourself or what you wear, such as a young woman teasing her hair endlessly to give the impression that it has not been combed or a young man dressing in slouchy clothes, wanting to be in style.

Somewhere in little things, my classmate's grasp on the iron rod loosened a bit. His wife held on to the rod with one hand and on to him with the other. Finally, he slipped away from her and let go of the rod. Just as Lehi's dream or vision predicted, he fell away into forbidden paths and was lost.

Largely because of television, instead of looking over into that spacious building, we are, in effect, living inside of it. That is your fate in this generation. You are living in that great and spacious building.

Who wrote this incredible vision? There is nothing like it in the Bible. Did Joseph Smith compose it? Did he write the Book of Mormon? That is harder to believe than the account of angels and golden plates. Joseph Smith was only 24 years old when the Book of Mormon was published.

You will be safe if you look like and groom like and act like an ordinary Latter-day Saint: dress modestly, attend your meetings, pay tithes, take the sacrament, honor the priesthood, honor your parents, follow your leaders, read the scriptures, study the Book of Mormon, and pray, always pray. An unseen power will hold your hand as you hold to the iron rod.

Will this solve all your problems? Of course not! That would be contrary to the purpose of your coming into mortality. It will, however, give you a solid foundation on which to build your life. (See Helaman 5:12.)

The mist of darkness will cover you at times so much that you will not be able to see your way even a short distance ahead. You will not be able to see clearly. But you can *feel* your way. With the gift of the Holy Ghost, you can *feel* your way ahead through life. Grasp the iron rod, and do not let go. Through the power of the Holy Ghost, you can *feel* your way through life. (See 3 Nephi 18:25; D&C 9:8.)

We live in a time of war, that spiritual war that will never end. Moroni warned us that the secret combinations begun by Gadianton

are had among all people. . . .

Wherefore, O ye Gentiles [and the term *gentile* in that place in the Book of Mormon refers to us in our generation], *it is wisdom in God that these things should be shown unto you, that thereby ye may repent of your sins, and suffer not that these murderous combinations shall get above you. . . .*

Wherefore, the Lord commandeth you, when ye shall see these things come among you that ye shall awake to a sense of your awful situation, because of this secret combination which shall be among you. [Ether 8:20, 23–24]

Atheists and agnostics make nonbelief their religion and today organize in unprecedented ways to attack faith and belief. They are now organized, and they pursue political power. You will be hearing much about them and from them. Much of their attack is indirect in mocking the faithful, in mocking religion.

The types of Sherem, Nehor, and Korihor live among us today (see Jacob 7:1–21; Alma 1:1–15; Alma 30:6–60). Their arguments are not so different from those in the Book of Mormon.

You who are young will see many things that will try your courage and test your faith. All of the mocking does not come from outside of the Church. Let me say that again: All of the mocking does not come from outside of the Church. Be careful that you do not fall into the category of mocking.

The Lord promised, "If ye are prepared ye shall not fear" (D&C 38:30).

Even Moroni faced the same challenge. He said, because of his weakness in writing,

I fear . . . the Gentiles shall mock at our words.

[And the Lord said to him:] *Fools mock, but they shall mourn; and my grace is sufficient for the meek, that they shall take no advantage of your weakness;*

And if men come unto me I will show unto them their weakness. I give unto men weakness that they may be humble; and my grace is sufficient for all men that humble themselves before me; for if they humble themselves before me, and have faith in me, then will I make weak things become strong unto them. [Ether 12:25–27]

Embedded in that dream or vision is the "pearl of great price" (Matthew 13:46).

Lehi and Nephi saw:

A virgin bearing a child in her arms,
One who should prepare the way—John the Baptist,
The ministry of the Son of God,

Twelve others following the Messiah,
The heavens open and angels ministering to them,
The multitudes blessed and healed,
And the Crucifixion of the Christ.

All of this they saw in dream or vision. And they saw the wisdom
and pride of the world opposing His work. (See 1 Nephi 11:14–36;
see also 1 Nephi 1:9–14.)

And that is what we face now.

Now to you, the one of two million, I speak individually. Just as
the prophets and apostles in times past did, "we talk of Christ, we
rejoice in Christ, we preach of Christ, we prophesy of Christ, . . . that
our children may know to what source they may look for a remission
of their sins" (2 Nephi 25:26).

Angels speak by the power of the Holy Ghost; wherefore, they speak the
words of Christ. Wherefore, I said unto you, feast upon the words of Christ;
for behold, the words of Christ will tell you all things what ye should do.

[And then Nephi added:] *Wherefore, now after I have spoken these*
words, if ye cannot understand them it will be because ye ask not, neither
do ye knock; wherefore, ye are not brought into the light, but must perish
in the dark.

For behold, again I say unto you that if ye will enter in by the way, and
receive the Holy Ghost, it will show unto you all things what ye should do.
[2 Nephi 32:3–5]

You live in an interesting generation where trials will be constant
in your life. Learn to follow the promptings of the Holy Ghost. It
is to be a shield and a protection and a teacher for you. Never be
ashamed or embarrassed about the doctrines of the gospel or about
the standards that we teach in the Church. You always, if you are
faithful in the Church, will be that much different from the world
at large.

You have the advantage of being assured that you can be inspired
in all of your decisions. You have many decisions ahead of you—small

decisions that have to do with getting through school, finding a life's companion, finding an occupation, settling in, raising children in a world that is turned upside down. Your children will be exposed so much more than we were in our generation.

We notice, as we travel about the Church, that our young people are stronger than heretofore. When I hear them speak in conferences and in sacrament meeting, I hear them quote the scriptures, and I hear them protecting the standards. I do not hear the cynical mocking that is typical of those who are not faithful and not truly converted.

We preside over a Church of twelve million-plus and growing. The Church is out in the world. Much of it is international now. Most of the members of the Church, by that standard, live a different life than you do. Many of them do not have the opportunity of going to college, but they live the gospel. And it is a wonderful, powerful thing to see them and to be among them.

As we think of you young Latter-day Saints and think of the Book of Mormon and think of the dream or vision that Lehi had, we see that there are prophecies in there that can be specifically applied to your life. Read it again, beginning with the eighth chapter of 1 Nephi, and read on to the counsel that is given. The Book of Mormon talks about life after death: what happens to the spirit (see Alma 40:11–12) and what happens in the spirit world (see 2 Nephi 2:29; 9:10–13; Alma 12:24). All of the things that you need to know are there. Read it, and make it a part of your life. Then the criticism or mocking of the world, the mocking of those in the Church, will be of no concern to you as it is of no concern to us (see 1 Nephi 8:33). We just move forward doing the things which we are called to do and know that the Lord is guiding us.

I pray the blessings of the Lord upon you in your work. I pray the blessings of the Lord upon you in your life as you move forward from the morning of your life, where you are now, to the late evening of your life, where I am now, that you will know that the gospel of Jesus Christ is true. You will face many great and tumultuous and difficult things in your life, and you will also enjoy great inspiration and joy in your life.

You are better than we were. I have the conviction that against what was surely coming and the prophecies that were given, the Lord has reserved special spirits to bring forth at this time to see that His Church and kingdom are protected and moved forward in the world. As a servant of the Lord, I invoke His blessings upon you and bear testimony to you that the gospel is true, in the name of Jesus Christ, amen.

Pilgrimages

Alvin F. Sherman, Jr.

In 2002 my wife and I directed a Study Abroad program to Madrid. As part of the program's activities we organized a trip to Santiago de Compostela in northern Spain. This city became famous in the Middle Ages when it was assumed to be the resting place for the remains of the Apostle James. As a result it flourished as one of Christianity's most-frequented pilgrimage sites. For pilgrims the Santiago trail symbolized every man's search for forgiveness, identity, and purpose. Because of these strong spiritual corollaries, we felt that it would be good for the students to experience a four-kilometer portion of the trail. We started at the Monte do Gozo, or Mount of Joy—the point at which the pilgrims catch their first glimpse of the city—and walked to the cathedral.

While we walked we conversed with pilgrims—many of them having already traveled hundreds of kilometers on foot. We learned that each one had a unique story and purpose for pursuing their journey. All of them held in common a sense of belonging to a community of believers, a connection to the earth, a place in history, and a spiritual legacy embodied in the trail. Though there were a

Alvin F. Sherman, Jr., was chair of the BYU Department of Spanish and Portuguese when this devotional address was given on 30 January 2007. © *Brigham Young University.*

multitude of reasons for undertaking the journey, the joy the pilgrims experienced at its completion was singular. This fact became clear when we attended the pilgrims' mass in the cathedral and witnessed the humility and gratitude they expressed as they closed this chapter of their life. It became apparent from the look in their eyes and the expression on their face that they would walk away from their experience with renewed hope and a deeper faith. What we noted in their countenance and what they felt upon completing their journey is humankind's universal need to find fulfillment and joy in having reached a desired goal, for God has declared: "This is my work and my glory—to bring to pass the immortality and eternal life of man."[1]

Pilgrimages allow you to pause, to meditate, to listen, and to learn. As a result, you may discover peace, hope, and new possibilities. Key to a successful journey is your attitude. You must be teachable, humble, obedient, selfless, diligent, and persistent. These qualities produce a singleness of heart, mind, and will and prepare you to receive divine instruction.

The Lord taught the Prophet Joseph Smith:

> *And if your eye be single to my glory, your whole bodies shall be filled with light, and there shall be no darkness in you; and that body which is filled with light comprehendeth all things.*[2]

In Proverbs the poet declared, "The path of the just is as the shining light, that shineth more and more unto the perfect day."[3] King David implored, "Wilt not thou deliver my feet from falling, that I may walk before God in the light of the living?"[4] The path of righteousness is always present to those of us who look for it. Unfortunately, many travelers ignore it and are tempted by the easy way. Your success along life's path depends on the choices that you make, whether to walk the "strait" and "narrow" road that leads to eternal joy or to wander the "wide" and "broad" way that brings sorrow. Job was cautioned that the disobedient will "rebel against the light" because "they know not the ways thereof, nor abide in the paths thereof."[5]

In a recent stake conference Elder Donald J. Butler referred to a sign he saw outside of Juneau, Alaska, that read: "Choose your rut, for you will be in it the next 20 miles."

There are two ways that you can see the ruts in your life. There are those ruts that are unproductive, dull, and, most important, mundane. These roads lead nowhere and become traps that inhibit movement and destroy your agency. Some of these ruts you will carve out for yourself throughout a lifetime of passiveness or disobedience; others will be traps laid by the wicked and divisive. On the other hand, there are the ruts that resemble those left by our pioneer forefathers. Those ruts represent the sure, unwavering path that leads to a newness of life and hope.

Along these roads you will meet other travelers. Some of these encounters will be instructive, edifying, and inspiring. Others will weaken your soul by undermining your values and challenging your most sacred beliefs. Where you go and what you do depends on the path you choose and the associations you willingly embrace.

President Spencer W. Kimball warned:

> *In these days directly ahead of you is the decisive decision. Are you going to yield to the easy urge to follow the crowd, or are you going to raise your head above the crowd and let them follow you? Are you going to slip off into mediocrity, or are you going to rise to the heights which your Heavenly Father set for you? You could stand above the crowd and become a leader among your people so that some day they would call your name blessed, or you can follow the usual demands and urges and desires and lose yourself in the herd of millions of folks who do not rise to their potential. The decision is yours and yours only. No one else can fashion and order your life.*[6]

Cleopas and his traveling companion learned this important lesson on the road to Emmaus. While the two men walked and talked of the things that had transpired in Jerusalem after the death of the Savior, the Lord drew near and asked, "What manner of communications are these that ye have one to another, as ye walk, and are sad?"[7]

After Cleopas recapped the events of the day, the Savior began to teach them. He rehearsed to them the scriptures that foretold His mission and death. Both men listened intently, drawn to the stranger and His message. As the small group approached a nearby village, the Savior

made as though he would have gone further.

But they constrained him, saying, Abide with us: for it is toward evening, and the day is far spent. And he went in to tarry with them.

And it came to pass, as he sat at meat with them, he took bread, and blessed it, and brake, and gave to them.

And their eyes were opened, and they knew him; and he vanished out of their sight.

And they said one to another, Did not our heart burn within us, while he talked with us by the way, and while he opened to us the scriptures?[8]

On that road two men traveled and communed with one another. While they walked they met another traveler who opened their eyes that they might see more clearly and understand more deeply eternal truth. They learned on the road to Emmaus that the truth they sought was not to be found solely in the things that they had seen but in the feelings they experienced when touched by the spirit of testimony. During their brief encounter with the Savior, He opened their mind, engaged their spirit, and confirmed the reality of what they had witnessed concerning His life. Not only was the truth confirmed to their mind but to their soul.

Let's consider the Lord's counsel to Oliver Cowdery when he hoped to translate portions of the Book of Mormon. The Lord declared:

You must study it out in your mind; then you must ask me if it be right, and if it is right I will cause that your bosom shall burn within you; therefore, you shall feel that it is right.[9]

Elder Bruce R. McConkie affirmed:

Logic and reason lead truth seekers along the path to a testimony, and they are aids in strengthening the revealed assurances of which a testimony is composed. But the actual sure knowledge which constitutes "the testimony of Jesus" must come by "the spirit of prophecy." This is received when the Holy Spirit speaks to the spirit within men; it comes when the whisperings of the still small voice are heard by the inner man. Receipt of a testimony is accompanied by a feeling of calm, unwavering certainty.[10]

When you open your heart and mind to the whisperings of the Holy Ghost, your spirit vibrates and responds to its promptings. Then, and only then, can true spiritual progress occur as you take that next step along life's path.

Elder Boyd K. Packer declared:

Oh, if I could teach you this one principle! A testimony is to be found *in the* bearing *of it. Somewhere in your quest for spiritual knowledge, there is that "leap of faith," as the philosophers call it. It is the moment when you have gone to the edge of the light and step into the darkness to discover that the way is lighted ahead for just a footstep or two.*[11]

Unfortunately those who reject these whisperings "wander in a wilderness where there is no way. They grope in the dark without light."[12]

As each of you walk the path of life, take care to harmonize the *feeling* of the Spirit with the *doing*. In the Epistle of James we read:

Be ye doers of the word, and not hearers only, deceiving your own selves.

For if any be a hearer of the word, and not a doer, he is like unto a man beholding his natural face in a glass:

For he beholdeth himself, and goeth his way, and straightway forgetteth what manner of man he was.

But whoso . . . continueth therein, he being not a forgetful hearer, but a doer of the work, this man shall be blessed in his deed.[13]

Joseph Smith learned this principle when, feeling the need to satisfy a spiritual longing, he studied the scriptures, found his answer, and then acted on God's promise. He recorded:

After I had retired to the place where I had previously designed to go, having looked around me, and finding myself alone, I kneeled down and began to offer up the desires of my heart to God.[14]

The knowledge he sought came because he studied it out in his mind, exercised faith, and exerted the physical effort required to get his answer. Joseph's answer was a glorious one, and, as a result, he embarked on a path that would lead to revelations, restorations, and the fulfillment of prophecy. Not all of us will experience such great and glorious manifestations of divine intervention, but the Lord has promised the humble seeker of truth:

Ask, and it shall be given you; seek, and ye shall find; knock, and it shall be opened unto you.

For every one that asketh receiveth; and he that seeketh findeth; and to him that knocketh it shall be opened.[15]

In 1 Nephi and 2 Nephi we read the story of Lehi and his family and their journeys in the wilderness. Through Lehi, Sariah, Nephi, Jacob, Laman, and Lemuel, the Lord reveals patterns of behavior that lead either along the path of righteousness or to a path wandering aimlessly toward self-destruction. Key to understanding how they reacted to Lehi, to his visions, and to his teachings is the level of commitment, desire, and obedience individually exercised toward God. Therefore, Lehi's vision of the tree of life provides a significant model—and revelation—regarding the consequences of choice and action on your individual pilgrimage toward salvation.

The core of Lehi's dream centers on the redemption of his children and their eternal progress. This fundamental concept becomes the nucleus of all the subsequent journeys in the Book of Mormon as prophets strove to set their descendants' feet on the true path that leads to salvation.

In Lehi's account a man in white robes motioned to the prophet to accompany him.[16] He led Lehi through "a dark and dreary waste,"[17] yet the prophet trusted the messenger and pressed on in his journey. Lehi declared:

> *And after I had traveled for the space of many hours in darkness, I began to pray unto the Lord that he would have mercy on me, according to the multitude of his tender mercies.*[18]

Soon he entered "a large and spacious field"[19] and saw "a tree, whose fruit was desirable to make one happy."[20] He ate the fruit that was "sweet, above all that [he] ever before tasted" and "white, to exceed all the whiteness that [he] had ever seen"[21] to the point that it "filled [his] soul with exceedingly great joy."[22]

Later in the Book of Mormon, Ammon taught that this joy is the "everlasting light" that is the "everlasting salvation" enjoyed by all those who "are encircled about with the matchless bounty of his love."[23]

In subsequent verses in chapter 8 of 1 Nephi, Lehi described the path that he desired his family to travel. Ultimately, he hoped that they would also eat of the fruit. Lehi also warned his family of the pitfalls that would await them along way.

Integral to Lehi's dream is his description of the travelers moving toward the tree of life. Among them are those who press forward "that they might obtain the path" and who "commence in the path" but are lost in the "mist of darkness" and "lose their way, that they wandered off and were lost."[24] These are those who hear the word and do not understand it, and "then cometh the wicked one, and catcheth away that which was sown in his heart."[25] Others catch "hold of the end of the rod of iron" and "press forward through the mist of darkness, clinging to the rod of iron, even until they . . . come forth and partake of the fruit of the tree."[26] However, they soon "cast their eyes about as if they were ashamed,"[27] being overcome by the contempt of the world, and they fall away to wander along "forbidden paths" and become lost.[28] Indeed, these are those who at first received the word with joy, but when difficulties arose they vacillated in their commitment to the gospel and were offended because of the word.[29]

Finally, Lehi described the faithful who "caught hold of the end of the rod of iron; and . . . press[ed] their way forward, continually holding fast to the rod of iron, until they came forth and fell down [to worship] and partook of the fruit of the tree."[30] This person hears, understands, and applies the word and bears fruit.[31]

The dream introduced a fourth group of travelers made up of those who choose to ignore the rod of iron and, instead, feel their way toward the "great and spacious building."[32] Some of them wander along "strange roads" while others drown "in the depths of the fountain" and are lost from view.[33] This group represents those who hear the word but because of the cares of the world and the deceitfulness of riches close their hearts.[34]

Later, in chapter 15, Nephi expanded on this vision and taught his brothers:

Whoso would hearken unto the word of God, and would hold fast unto it, they would never perish; neither could the temptations and the fiery darts of the adversary overpower them unto blindness, to lead them away to destruction.[35]

As a second witness, Nephi was privileged to see his father's vision. His account elucidates Lehi's experience by providing an interpretation of the signs and symbols found in the dream that can lead the determined traveler to enjoy the fruit of Jesus Christ's infinite Atonement. Because Nephi had sufficient faith to believe, to accept the words of his father, and to take that step forward in his progression, he received a personal witness of the Savior's birth to Mary,"[36] His baptism at the hands of John,[37] the calling of the Twelve Apostles,[38] Christ's miracles,[39] and His Crucifixion.[40] Nephi's vision carried him forward to witness the persecution of the Saints of God[41] and the destruction of his people because of sin.[42] Finally, Nephi saw the restoration of the gospel in the latter days.[43]

Both iterations of the dream blend into a single testimony of the divine nature of humanity's pilgrimage through mortality. As disciples, we are invited to turn our gaze away from worldliness, to hold tight to the revealed word, to receive God's love, and to seek after Jesus Christ, who is our Savior and Redeemer.[44]

Indeed, Nephi has become your exemplar of the humble pilgrim. His willingness to listen to his father and to seek a personal witness of the truth set him apart from his brothers and kept him on the strait and narrow path of righteousness. Because Nephi never doubted, he learned obedience through the recovery of the plates of Laban, patience through affliction and hardship, wisdom when he was commanded to build a ship, and recognition of the reality of priesthood power and authority when he learned to trust in God.

On the other hand, Laman and Lemuel dutifully "followed" their father into the wilderness yet allowed themselves to succumb to petty complaining, jealousy, and rebellion. Because of their unwillingness to learn for themselves the truthfulness of Lehi's words, they undervalued the journey, and, as a result, the physical discomfort they experienced overshadowed the multitude of blessings that awaited them. It is interesting to note that Laman and Lemuel had digressed in their spiritual aptitude to the point that they were unable to recognize God's power to inspire, to direct, and to sustain them. Instead, they fell prey to vanity and pride, which led them into a state of resentment and bitterness.

Elder Neal A. Maxwell warned:

> *Failing to understand the "dealings" of the Lord with His children— meaning His relations with and treatment of His children—is very fundamental. Murmuring is but one of the symptoms, and not the only consequence either; in fact, brothers and sisters, this failure affects everything else!*
>
> *To misread something so crucial constitutes a failure to know God, who then ends up being wrongly seen as unreachable, uninvolved, uncaring, and*

unable—a disabled and diminished Deity, really—about whose seeming limitations, ironically, some then quickly complain.[45]

Nephi told his brothers:

Do ye not remember the things which the Lord hath said?—If ye will not harden your hearts, and ask me in faith, believing that ye shall receive, with diligence in keeping my commandments, surely these things shall be made known unto you.[46]

As Nephi began to wrap up his record and close it with his witness of Christ, he returned to his experience with his father's vision and declared:

After ye have gotten into this strait and narrow path, I would ask if all is done? Behold, I say unto you, Nay; for ye have not come thus far save it were by the word of Christ with unshaken faith in him, relying wholly upon the merits of him who is mighty to save.

Wherefore, ye must press forward with a steadfastness in Christ, having a perfect brightness of hope, and a love of God and of all men. Wherefore, if ye shall press forward, feasting upon the word of Christ, and endure to the end, behold, thus saith the Father: Ye shall have eternal life.[47]

In 1855, Brigham Young, Heber C. Kimball, and Jedediah M. Grant invited Church members to

seek continually unto the Lord for wisdom . . . that when we shall have finished our pilgrimage upon the earth, we may go hence in peace, having wrought righteousness and established justice thereon, and, through having fought the good fight and kept the faith, be prepared to come forth with a glorious resurrection to inherit eternal lives and exaltation.[48]

Last year my stake took the youth to Martin's Cove. Each participant was to trek in the name of either a rescuer or a handcart pioneer. Part of our preparation was to learn as much as we could about their experience. Our goal was to "walk in their footsteps." Through my research I discovered that two of my great-grandfather's brothers had been involved in this pioneer tragedy. Moses Cluff, who had just returned from a mission to England, joined the Hodgett Wagon Company that accompanied the Willie and Martin Handcart Companies. His younger brother, Harvey Cluff, who was only 20 years old, was one of the "valley boys" who formed the first wave of rescuers to meet up with the stranded pioneers. As I learned about their experiences, one interesting detail stood out. Harvey's history reads:

[The] *raging blizzard from the north compelled the relief party to seek shelter some miles down the river where the growth of willows was dense enough to break the force of the wind and afford shelter to animals and some protection to the camp. While encamped in this retired spot, three miles from the road, Harvey was called upon by the captain to take a sign board to the road, in case there were any who might pass along the road and thereby miss the camp. . . . In a few hours after the board was up, two men, Captain Willie and his companion, rode horseback into camp. . . . These two men, without bedding, could not have survived through the night, had they not been directed to the relief camp by the sign board.*[49]

Harvey's obedience and willingness to make the appropriate sacrifice of self not only saved Captain Willie and his companion but facilitated the rescue of all those who were stranded along the trail. Like those who were searching for relief and rescue from the storm, you must scan the horizon for signs along the path that will guide you to shelter and safety. You must press forward with faith, and, by and by, the path will appear and the destination will become evident to you.

My pilgrimage into the Wyoming prairie—through wind, sand, and rain—taught me to appreciate more deeply the faith and endurance of those who embarked on the long and arduous journey that led them to Zion. Throughout the experience I realized more fully that the challenges found along life's journey are often tempered by the rewards you receive because of diligence, persistence, obedience, and all those other qualities that make for a dedicated pilgrim. There was an added blessing that came from the trek. I was allowed to experience briefly the sweetness of peace that comes from completing a journey and enduring to the end.

Paul reminded us:

Let us lay aside every weight, and the sin which doth so easily beset us, and let us run with patience the race that is set before us,

Looking unto Jesus the author and finisher of our faith; who for the joy that was set before him endured the cross, despising the shame, and is set down at the right hand of the throne of God.[50]

The most significant pilgrimage that you will experience in your life will be the one that moves you to seek truth, to exercise faith, and to gain a firm testimony that Jesus is the Messiah, the Son of God, and the Savior and Redeemer of the world.

I testify that you and I are where we should be, marking a path toward our eternal goal. We have been given the charge to improve our minds and deepen our testimony through study, faith, and prayer. Inasmuch as we have accepted this responsibility and have set our foot upon the path of learning, we must make it our primary obligation to prepare ourselves to be effective instruments in the hands of God.

I testify that this gospel is true, that it is the great source of all knowledge. The greatest knowledge of all is that God lives, that Jesus is the Christ, that the gospel has been restored in these latter days through prophets who are divinely called, and that all this is accomplished and sustained by modern-day revelation. I say this in the name of Jesus Christ, amen.

NOTES

1. Moses 1:39.
2. D&C 88:67.
3. Proverbs 4:18.

4. Psalm 56:13.

5. Job 24:13.

6. *TSWK*, 147.

7. Luke 24:17.

8. Luke 24:28–32.

9. D&C 9:8.

10. *MD*, s.v. "testimony," 785.

11. Boyd K. Packer, *"That All May Be Edified"* (Salt Lake City: Bookcraft, 1982), 340; emphasis in original.

12. Job 12:24–25.

13. James 1:22–25.

14. JS—H 1:15.

15. Luke 11:9–10.

16. See 1 Nephi 8:5–6.

17. 1 Nephi 8:7.

18. 1 Nephi 8:8.

19. 1 Nephi 8:9.

20. 1 Nephi 8:10.

21. 1 Nephi 8:11.

22. 1 Nephi 8:12.

23. Alma 26:15.

24. 1 Nephi 8:21–23.

25. Matthew 13:19.

26. 1 Nephi 8:24.

27. 1 Nephi 8:25.

28. 1 Nephi 8:28.

29. See Matthew 13:20–21.

30. 1 Nephi 8:30.

31. See Matthew 13:23.

32. 1 Nephi 8:31.

33. 1 Nephi 8:32.

34. See Matthew 13:22.

35. 1 Nephi 15:24.

36. See 1 Nephi 11:18.

37. See 1 Nephi 11:27.

38. See 1 Nephi 11:29.

39. See 1 Nephi 11:31.

40. See 1 Nephi 11:32–33.

41. See 1 Nephi 11:34–36.

42. See 1 Nephi 12:19–23.

43. See 1 Nephi 13.

44. See John 3:16.

45. Neal A. Maxwell, "Lessons from Laman and Lemuel," *Ensign*, November 1999, 6.

46. 1 Nephi 15:11.

47. 2 Nephi 31:19–20.

48. "Thirteenth General Epistle" (29 October 1855), in James R. Clark, comp., *Messages of the First Presidency*, 6 vols. (Salt Lake City: Bookcraft, 1966–75), 2:187.

49. *The Cluff Family Journal* (Provo: Cluff Family Reunion, 1899–1904), 169–70.

50. Hebrews 12:1–2.

A Reservoir of Living Water

David A. Bednar

Sister Bednar and I are grateful to meet with you tonight. As we travel the earth, we especially appreciate opportunities to gather with and learn from faithful young people like you. Tonight I pray for the assistance of the Holy Ghost as we worship together and seek in unity to be taught from on high (see D&C 43:16).

I want to begin by asking a simple question. What is the most valuable substance or commodity in the world? We might initially think that gold, oil, or diamonds have the greatest worth. But of all the minerals, metals, gems, and solvents found on and in the earth, the most valuable is water.

Life springs from water. Life is sustained by water. Water is the medium required to perform the various functions associated with all known forms of life. Our physical bodies are approximately two-thirds water. Whereas a person can survive for many days or even weeks without food, an individual will usually die in only three or four days without water. Most of the world's great centers of

David A. Bednar was a member of the Quorum of the Twelve Apostles of The Church of Jesus Christ of Latter-day Saints when this fireside address was delivered on 4 February 2007. © *Intellectual Reserve, Inc.*

population are situated near sources of fresh water. Simply stated, life could not exist without the availability of and access to adequate upplies of clean water.

LIVING WATER

Given the vital role of water in sustaining all forms of life, the Savior's use of the term "living water" is supernally significant. As described in the fourth chapter of John, Jesus and His disciples passed through Samaria as they were traveling from Judea to Galilee. In the city of Sychar they stopped at Jacob's well:

> *There cometh a woman of Samaria to draw water: Jesus saith unto her, Give me to drink.*
>
> *(For his disciples were gone away unto the city to buy meat.)*
>
> *Then saith the woman of Samaria unto him, How is it that thou, being a Jew, askest drink of me, which am a woman of Samaria? for the Jews have no dealings with the Samaritans.*
>
> *Jesus answered and said unto her, If thou knewest the gift of God, and who it is that saith to thee, Give me to drink; thou wouldest have asked of him, and he would have given thee living water.*
>
> *The woman saith unto him, Sir, thou hast nothing to draw with, and the well is deep: from whence then hast thou that living water? . . .*
>
> *Jesus answered and said unto her, Whosoever drinketh of this water shall thirst again:*
>
> *But whosoever drinketh of the water that I shall give him shall never thirst; but the water that I shall give him shall be in him a well of water springing up into everlasting life.* [John 4:7–11, 13–14]

The living water referred to in this episode is a representation of the Lord Jesus Christ and His gospel. And as water is necessary to sustain physical life, so the Savior and His doctrines, principles, and ordinances are essential for eternal life. You and I need His living water daily and in ample supply to sustain our ongoing spiritual growth and development.

THE SCRIPTURES ARE A RESERVOIR OF LIVING WATER

The scriptures contain the words of Christ and are a reservoir of living water to which we have ready access and from which we can drink deeply and long. You and I must look to and come unto Christ, who is "the fountain of living waters" (1 Nephi 11:25; compare Ether 8:26, 12:28), by reading (see Mosiah 1:5), studying (see D&C 26:1), searching (see John 5:39; Alma 17:2), and feasting (see 2 Nephi 32:3) upon the words of Christ as contained in the holy scriptures. By so doing, we can receive both spiritual direction and protection during our mortal journey.

The Church of Jesus Christ of Latter-day Saints has a sacred stewardship to preserve the written revelations in purity and in safety (see D&C 42:56)—this precious reservoir of living water. A monumental work was accomplished by the Church in the 1970s and 1980s and resulted in the edition of the scriptures we enjoy today with extensive footnotes, cross-references, and additional study aids, maps, and information.

As the updated scriptures were first introduced to the members of the Church in the early 1980s, Elder Boyd K. Packer prophesied:

> *With the passing of years, these scriptures will produce successive generations of faithful Christians who know the Lord Jesus Christ and are disposed to obey His will.*
>
> *The older generation has been raised without them, but there is another generation growing up.* [CR, October 1982, 75; or "Scriptures," *Ensign*, November 1982, 53]

Twenty-four years have passed since Elder Packer spoke those words. And the generation to which he was referring is seated tonight in Church buildings all across the globe! He was talking about you, and he was talking about me. The vast majority of you have only known the scriptures as we have them today. Please keep that fact in mind as I continue to quote Elder Packer:

The revelations will be opened to them as to no other in the history of the world. Into their hands now are placed the sticks of Joseph and of Judah. They will develop a gospel scholarship beyond that which their forebears could achieve. They will have the testimony that Jesus is the Christ and be competent to proclaim Him and to defend Him. [*CR*, October 1982, 75; or "Scriptures," 53]

Not only are we blessed to have these scriptures so readily available to us today, but we also have the responsibility to use them consistently and effectively and to drink deeply from the reservoir of living water. I believe this generation of youth is more immersed in the scriptures, more deeply acquainted with the words of the prophets, and more prone to turn to the revelations for answers than any previous generation. But we still have a great distance to travel along the strait and narrow path—more to learn, more to apply, and more to experience.

OBTAINING LIVING WATER FROM THE SCRIPTURAL RESERVOIR

I now want to review with you three basic ways or methods of obtaining living water from the scriptural reservoir: (1) *reading* the scriptures from beginning to end, (2) *studying* the scriptures by topic, and (3) *searching* the scriptures for connections, patterns, and themes. Each of these approaches can help satisfy our spiritual thirst if we invite the companionship and assistance of the Holy Ghost as we read, study, and search.

Reading a book of scripture from beginning to end initiates the flow of living water into our lives by introducing us to important stories, gospel doctrines, and timeless principles. This approach also enables us to learn about major characters in the scriptures and the sequence, timing, and context of events and teachings. Reading the written word in this way exposes us to the breadth of a volume of scripture. This is the first and most fundamental way of obtaining living water.

Studying by topic typically follows, grows out of, and builds upon our reading of the scriptures from beginning to end. For example, as we read the Book of Mormon we may identify and seek to find answers to important doctrinal and practical questions such as these:

- What is faith in the Savior?
- Why is faith in Jesus Christ the first principle of the gospel?
- Why and how does faith in the Redeemer lead to repentance?
- How does the Atonement strengthen me to do things in my daily life that I could never do with my own limited capacity and in my own strength?

Focusing upon such questions and studying by topic, using the Topical Guide and index to the triple combination, allow us to dig into and explore the depth of the scriptures and obtain a much richer spiritual knowledge. This approach increases the rate at which living water flows into our lives.

Both reading from beginning to end and studying by topic are prerequisites to the third basic method of obtaining living water from the scriptural reservoir. Whereas reading a book of scripture from beginning to end provides a basic breadth of knowledge, studying by topic increases the depth of our knowledge. *Searching* in the revelations for connections, patterns, and themes builds upon and adds to our spiritual knowledge by bringing together and expanding these first two methods; it broadens our perspective and understanding of the plan of salvation.

In my judgment, diligently searching to discover connections, patterns, and themes is in part what it means to "feast" upon the words of Christ. This approach can open the floodgates of the spiritual reservoir, enlighten our understanding through His Spirit, and produce a depth of gratitude for the holy scriptures and a degree of spiritual commitment that can be received in no other way. Such searching enables us to build upon the rock of our Redeemer and to withstand the winds of wickedness in these latter days.

I want to emphasize an essential point. You might initially assume that a person must have extensive formal education to use the methods I am describing. This assumption simply is not correct. Any honest seeker of truth, regardless of educational background, can successfully employ these simple approaches. You and I do not need sophisticated study aids and should not rely extensively upon the spiritual knowledge of others. We simply need to have a sincere desire to learn, the companionship of the Holy Ghost, the holy scriptures, and an active and inquiring mind.

The Prophet Joseph Smith taught that we should

search the Scriptures—search the revelations which we publish, and ask your Heavenly Father, in the name of His Son Jesus Christ, to manifest the truth unto you, and if you do it with an eye single to His glory, nothing doubting, He will answer you by the power of His Holy Spirit. You will then know for yourselves and not for another. You will not then be dependent on man for the knowledge of God. [HC 1:282]

If you and I will ask, seek, and knock (see Matthew 7:7), always keeping ourselves worthy to learn from the Spirit, then the gates of the spiritual reservoir will open to us and the living water will flow. I witness, I testify, and I promise that this is true.

Let me briefly explain and provide examples of what I mean by connections, patterns, and themes.

CONNECTIONS

A connection is a relationship or link between ideas, people, things, or events, and the scriptures are full of connections. Consider the relationship between the Eternal Father and His Son, Jesus Christ (see Mosiah 15:1–9); between mercy and grace (see 2 Nephi 9:8); between clean hands and a pure heart (see Psalm 24:4); between a broken heart and a contrite spirit (see 3 Nephi 9:20); between the wheat and the tares (see D&C 101:65); between knowledge and intelligence (see D&C 130:18–19); between justification and sanctification (see D&C 20:30–31); between sheep and goats (see Matthew 25:32–33); between immortality and eternal life (see Moses 1:39); and countless others. Prayerfully identifying, learning about, and pondering such connections—the similarities and differences, for example—

is a primary source of living water and yields inspired insights and treasures of hidden knowledge.

As I have read each of the standard works from beginning to end and studied different topics, I noticed that the word *understanding* was commonly described in relation to the heart. Two verses in the Book of Mormon illustrate this connection:

"Ye have not applied your *hearts* to *understanding;* therefore, ye have not been wise" (Mosiah 12:27; emphasis added).

"And the multitude did hear and do bear record; and their hearts were open and they did *understand* in their *hearts* the words which he prayed" (3 Nephi 19:33; emphasis added).

I find it most interesting in these and many other verses that understanding is linked primarily to the heart. Note that we are not explicitly counseled to apply our minds to understanding. Obviously, we must use our minds and our rational capacity to obtain and evaluate information and to reach appropriate conclusions and judgments. But perhaps the scriptures are suggesting to us that reason and "the arm of flesh" (D&C 1:19) are not sufficient to produce true understanding. Thus, understanding, as the word is used in the scriptures, does not refer solely or even primarily to intellectual or cognitive comprehension. Rather, understanding occurs when what we know in our minds is confirmed as true in our hearts by the witness of the Holy Ghost.

The spiritual gift of revelation most typically operates as thoughts and feelings put into our minds and hearts by the Holy Ghost (see D&C 8:2–3, 100:5–8). And as testimony and conviction move from our heads to our hearts, we no longer just have information or knowledge—but we begin to understand and seek after the mighty change of heart. Understanding, then, is the result of revelation; it is a spiritual gift, it is a prerequisite to conversion, and it entices us to more consistently live in accordance with the principles we are learning.

This revealed insight about the relationship between the heart and understanding has greatly influenced my approach to gospel learning and study, has affected positively the way Sister Bednar and I teach our children and grandchildren, and has impacted my priesthood service.

PATTERNS

A pattern is a plan, model, or standard that can be used as a guide for repetitively doing or making something. And the scriptures are full of spiritual patterns. Typically, a scriptural pattern is broader and more comprehensive than a connection. In the Doctrine and Covenants we find patterns for preaching the gospel (see D&C 50:13–29), for avoiding deception (see D&C 52:14, 18–19), for constructing temples (see D&C 115:14–16), for establishing cities (see D&C 94), for organizing priesthood quorums (see D&C 107:85–100) and high councils (see D&C 102:12), and for a variety of other purposes. Identifying and studying scriptural patterns is another important source of living water and helps us become acquainted and more familiar with the wisdom and the mind of the Lord (see D&C 95:13).

As I have both read from beginning to end and studied topics in the Doctrine and Covenants, I have been impressed with a pattern that is evident in many of the Lord's responses to the questions of missionaries. On a number of occasions in 1831, various groups of elders who had been called to preach the gospel desired to know how they should proceed and by what route and manner they should travel. In revelations given through the Prophet Joseph Smith, the Lord respectively counseled these brethren that they could travel on water or by land (see D&C 61:22), that they could make or purchase the needed vehicles (see D&C 60:5), that they could travel all together or go two by two (see D&C 62:5), and that they could appropriately travel in a number of different directions (see D&C 80:3). The revelations specifically instructed the brethren to make these decisions "as seemeth you good" (D&C 60:5; 62:5) or "as it is made known unto them according to their judgments" (D&C 61:22). And in each of these instances the Savior declared, "It mattereth not unto me" (D&C 60:5, 61:22, 62:5, 63:40; see also 80:3).

The Lord's statement that such things "mattereth not unto me" initially may seem surprising. Clearly, the Savior was not saying to these missionaries that He did not care about what they were doing. Rather, He was emphasizing the importance of putting first things first and focusing upon the right things—which, in these instances, were getting to the assigned field of labor and initiating the work. They were to exercise faith, use good judgment, act in accordance with the direction of the Spirit, and determine the best way to travel to their assignments. The essential thing was the work they had been called to perform; how they got there was important but was not essential.

What a remarkable pattern for you and for me to apply in our lives. Jesus Christ knows and loves us individually. He is concerned about our spiritual development and progress, and He encourages us to grow through the exercise of inspired, righteous, and wise judgment. The Redeemer will never leave us alone. We should always pray for guidance and direction. We should always seek for the constant companionship of the Holy Ghost. But we should not be dismayed or discouraged if answers to our petitions for direction or help do not necessarily come quickly. Such answers rarely come all at once. Our progress would be hindered and our judgment would be weak if every answer was given to us immediately and without requiring the price of faith, work, study, and persistence.

The pattern I am describing is illustrated succinctly in the following instruction to those early missionaries:

> *I, the Lord, am willing, if any among you desire to ride upon horses, or upon mules, or in chariots, he shall receive this blessing, if he receive it from the hand of the Lord, with* a thankful heart in all things.
>
> *These things remain with you to do* according to judgment and the directions of the Spirit.
>
> *Behold, the kingdom is yours. And behold, and lo,* I am with the faithful always. *Even so. Amen.* [D&C 62:7–9; emphasis added]

The principal issues in this episode are not horses, mules, or chariots; rather, they are gratitude, judgment, and faithfulness. Please note the basic elements in this pattern: (1) a thankful heart in all things; (2) act according to judgment and the directions of the Spirit; and (3) the Savior is with the faithful always. Can we begin to sense the direction and assurance, the renewal and strength that can come from following this simple pattern for inspired and righteous judgment? Truly, scriptural patterns are a precious source of living water.

The most demanding judgments we ever make are seldom between good or bad or between attractive and unattractive alternatives. Usually, our toughest choices are between good and good. In this scriptural episode, horses, mules, and chariots may have been equally effective options for missionary travel. In a similar way, you and I also might identify at various times in our lives more than one acceptable opportunity or option that we could choose to pursue. We should remember this pattern from the scriptures as we approach such important decisions. If we put essential things first in our lives—things such as dedicated discipleship, honoring covenants, and keeping the commandments—then we will be blessed with inspiration and strong judgment as we pursue the path that leads us back to our heavenly home. If we put essential things first, we "cannot go amiss" (D&C 80:3).

THEMES

Themes are overarching, recurring, and unifying qualities or ideas, like essential threads woven throughout a text. Generally, scriptural themes are broader and more comprehensive than patterns or connections. In fact, themes provide the background and context for understanding connections and patterns. The process of searching for and identifying scriptural themes leads us to the fundamental doctrines and principles of salvation—to the eternal truths that invite the confirming witness of the Holy Ghost (see 1 John 5:6). This approach to obtaining living water from the scriptural reservoir is the most demanding and rigorous; it also yields the greatest edification and spiritual refreshment. And the scriptures are replete with powerful themes.

For example, the Book of Mormon came forth in this dispensation to "the convincing of the Jew and Gentile that Jesus is the Christ, the Eternal God, manifesting himself unto all nations" (Book of Mormon title page). The central and recurring theme of the Book of Mormon is the invitation for all to "come unto Christ, and be perfected in him" (Moroni 10:32). The teachings, warnings, admonitions, and episodes in this remarkable book of scripture all focus upon and testify of Jesus the Christ as the Redeemer and our Savior.

Let me provide a few additional examples of important themes using scriptures from the Book of Mormon:

"If . . . the children of men keep the commandments of God he doth nourish them, and strengthen them, and provide means whereby they can accomplish the thing which he has commanded them" (1 Nephi 17:3).

"Press forward with a steadfastness in Christ" (2 Nephi 31:20).

"Men are, that they might have joy" (2 Nephi 2:25).

"In the strength of the Lord thou canst do all things" (Alma 20:4).

"Wickedness never was happiness" (Alma 41:10).

If you promise not to laugh, I will tell you about one of the simple ways I search for scriptural themes. I do not advocate or recommend that you use the same approach; different people use different methods with equal effectiveness. I am simply describing a process that works well for me.

In preparation for a recent speaking assignment, I was impressed to talk about the spirit and purposes of gathering. I had been studying and pondering Elder Russell M. Nelson's recent conference message on the principle of gathering (see *CR*, September–October 2006, 83–87; or "The Gathering of Scattered Israel," *Ensign*, November 2006, 79–82), and the topic was perfectly suited to the nature of and setting for my assignment (see "The Spirit and Purposes of Gathering," address delivered at a BYU–Idaho devotional, 31 October 2006; www.byui.edu/Presentations/Transcripts/Devotionals/2006_10_31_Bednar.htm).

I recognized that I had much to learn from the scriptures about gathering. So I identified and made copies of every scripture in the standard works that included any form of the word *gather.* I next read each scripture, looking for connections, patterns, and themes. It is important to note that I did not start my reading with a preconceived set of things for which I was looking. I prayed for the assistance of the Holy Ghost and simply started reading.

As I reviewed the scriptures about gathering, I marked verses with similar phrases or points of emphasis, using a colored pencil. By the time I had read all of the scriptures, some of the verses were marked in red, some were marked in green, and some were marked in other colors.

Now, here comes the part that may make you laugh. I next used my scissors to cut out the scriptures I had copied and sorted them into piles by color. The process produced a large pile of scriptures marked with red, a large pile of scriptures marked with green, and so forth. I then sorted the scriptures within each large pile into smaller piles. As a first grader I must have really liked cutting with scissors and putting things into piles!

The results of this process taught me a great deal about the principle of gathering. For example, I learned from examining my large piles that the scriptures describe at least three key aspects of gathering: the *purposes* of gathering, the *types and places* of gathering, and the *blessings* of gathering.

I noted that some of the primary *purposes* of gathering are to worship (see Mosiah 18:25), to receive counsel and instruction (see Mosiah 18:7), to build up the Church (see D&C 101:63–64), and to provide defense and protection (see D&C 115:6). In studying about the *types and places* of gathering, I discovered that we are gathered into eternal families (see Mosiah 2:5), into the restored Church (see D&C 101:64–65), into stakes of Zion (see D&C 109:59), into holy temples (see Alma 26:5–6), and into two great centers: old Jerusalem (see Ether 13:11) and the city of Zion or New Jerusalem (see D&C 42:9; Articles of Faith 1:10). I was grateful to learn that edification (see

Ephesians 4:12–13), preservation (see Moses 7:61), and strength (see D&C 82:14) are some of the *blessings* of gathering.

Through this process I gained an even deeper appreciation for the spirit of gathering as an integral part of the restoration of all things in the dispensation of the fulness of times. I will not take the time now to recount the other things I learned about gathering; my purpose here is to briefly illustrate one way of searching for scriptural themes.

THE BLESSINGS WE CAN RECEIVE

The blessings of knowledge, understanding, revelation, and spiritual exhilaration that we can receive as we read, study, and search the scriptures are marvelous. "Feasting upon the word of Christ" (2 Nephi 31:20) is edifying, exciting, and enjoyable. The word is good, "for it beginneth to enlarge my soul; yea, it beginneth to enlighten my understanding, yea, it beginneth to be delicious to me" (Alma 32:28). "Behold they are written, ye have them before you, therefore search them" (3 Nephi 20:11), and they "shall be in [you] a well of water springing up into everlasting life" (John 4:14).

In my personal reading, studying, and searching over a period of years, I have focused many times upon the doctrine of the Atonement of Jesus Christ. No event, knowledge, or influence has had a greater impact upon me during my 54 years of mortality than repeatedly reading about, studying in depth, and searching for connections, patterns, and themes related to the doctrine of the Atonement. This central, saving doctrine, over time, gradually has distilled upon my soul as the dews from heaven; has influenced my thoughts, words, and deeds (see Mosiah 4:30); and literally has become for me a well of living water.

LEHI'S VISION

The importance of reading, studying, and searching the scriptures is highlighted in several elements of Lehi's vision of the tree of life.

Father Lehi saw several groups of people pressing forward along the strait and narrow path, seeking to obtain the tree and its fruit. The members of each group had entered onto the path through the gate of repentance and baptism by water and had received the gift of the Holy Ghost (see 2 Nephi 31:17–20). The tree of life is the central feature in the dream and is identified in 1 Nephi 11 as a representation of Jesus Christ. The fruit on the tree is a symbol for the blessings of the Savior's Atonement. Interestingly, the major theme of the Book of Mormon, inviting all to come unto Christ, is central in Lehi's vision. Of particular interest is the rod of iron that led to the tree (see 1 Nephi 8:19). The rod of iron is the word of God.

In 1 Nephi 8, verses 21 through 23, we learn about a group of people who pressed forward and commenced in the path that led to the tree of life. However, as the people encountered the mist of darkness, which represents the temptations of the devil (see 1 Nephi 12:17), they lost their way, they wandered off, and they were lost.

It is important to note that no mention is made about the rod of iron in these verses. Those who ignore or treat lightly the word of God do not have access to that divine compass which points the way to the Savior. Consider that this group obtained the path and pressed forward, exhibiting a measure of faith in Christ and spiritual conviction, but they were diverted by the temptations of the devil and were lost.

In verses 24 through 28 of chapter 8 we read about a second group of people who obtained the strait and narrow path that led to the tree of life. This group pressed forward through the mist of darkness, clinging to the rod of iron even until they did come forth and partake of the fruit of the tree. However, as this second group of people was mocked by the occupants of the great and spacious building, they were ashamed and fell away into forbidden paths and were lost. Please notice that this group is described as *clinging* to the rod of iron.

It is significant that the second group pressed forward with faith and commitment. They also had the added blessing of the rod of iron, *and they were clinging to it!* However, as they were confronted with persecution and adversity, they fell away into forbidden paths and were lost. Even with faith, commitment, and the word of God, this group was lost—perhaps because they only *periodically* read *or* studied *or* searched the scriptures. Clinging to the rod of iron suggests to me only occasional "bursts" of study or irregular dipping rather than consistent, ongoing immersion in the word of God.

In verse 30 we read about a third group of people who pressed forward continually holding fast to the rod of iron until they came forth and fell down and partook of the fruit of the tree. The key phrase in this verse is "continually holding fast" to the rod of iron.

The third group also pressed forward with faith and conviction; however, there is no indication that they wandered off, fell into forbidden paths, or were lost. Perhaps this third group of people *consistently* read *and* studied *and* searched the words of Christ. Perhaps it was the constant flow of living water that saved the third group from perishing. This is the group you and I should strive to join.

What meaneth the rod of iron which our father saw, that led to the tree?

And I said unto them that it was the word of God; and whoso would hearken unto the word of God, and would hold fast *unto it, they would never perish; neither could the temptations and the fiery darts of the adversary overpower them unto blindness, to lead them away to destruction.* [1 Nephi 15:23–24; emphasis added]

What, then, is the difference between clinging and holding fast to the rod of iron? Let me suggest that holding fast to the iron rod entails the prayerful and consistent use of all three of the ways of obtaining living water that we have discussed tonight.

And it came to pass that I beheld that the rod of iron, which my father had seen, was the word of God, which led to the fountain of living waters, or to the tree of life. [1 Nephi 11:25]

Each of these approaches—reading from beginning to end, studying by topic, and searching for connections, patterns, and themes—is edifying, is instructive, and provides an intermittent portion of the Savior's living water. I believe, however, that the regular use of all three methods produces a more constant flow of living water and is in large measure what it means to hold fast to the rod of iron.

Through normal activity each day, you and I lose a substantial amount of the water that constitutes so much of our physical bodies. Thirst is a demand by the cells of the body for water, and the water in our bodies must be replenished daily. It frankly does not make sense to occasionally "fill up" with water, with long periods of dehydration in between. The same thing is true spiritually. Spiritual thirst is a need for living water. A constant flow of living water is far superior to sporadic sipping.

Are you and I daily reading, studying, and searching the scriptures in a way that enables us to hold fast to the rod of iron—or are you and I merely clinging? Are you and I pressing forward toward the fountain of living waters—relying upon the word of God? These are important questions for each of us to ponder prayerfully.

As we conclude tonight, we will sing together the hymn "The Iron Rod." Indeed, this song of the righteous will be a fervent and poignant prayer (see D&C 25:12). May we have ears to hear the lessons this hymn teaches.

I witness of Jesus Christ and of the power of His word and of Him as the Word. He is the Son of the Eternal Father, and I know that He lives. I testify that holding fast to the rod of iron will lead to His living water. As His servant, I invoke this blessing upon you: that your desire and capacity to hold fast to the rod of iron will be enlarged, that your faith in the Savior will increase and replace your fears, and that as you drink deeply from the scriptural reservoir you will come to know Him. May we ever remember that

when temptation's pow'r is nigh,
Our pathway clouded o'er,
Upon the rod we can rely,
And heaven's aid implore.
["The Iron Rod," *Hymns*, 1985, no. 274]

In the sacred name of Jesus Christ, amen.

Faith, Family, and Friendship

———◆———

Peter M. Johnson

Good morning, my brothers and sisters. Let me begin by telling you a little about myself. In the process I will share with you my testimony of the gospel of Jesus Christ as well as the three key ingredients we need to ensure happiness and peace in this life and give us a taste of what life will be like in our heavenly home.

I grew up in the Queens borough of New York City. New York City is a wonderful place that is full of excitement and entertainment. As a youth I was heavily involved with rap music, and my brother and I belonged to a rap group called CBS. No, it was not the television station. The acronym CBS stood for Can't Be Stopped. We thought the name was cool.

We traveled throughout the city performing at wedding receptions, high school dances, and block parties. During the summer months different rap groups would visit the neighborhood park to perform free concerts. Most of the youth involved with rap visited the parks to listen and, at times, compete with the other rap

Peter M. Johnson was an assistant professor of accounting at BYU when this devotional address was given on 6 February 2007. © Brigham Young University.

groups. Often, however, these free concerts attracted drug deals and promoted random violence.

It was during the summer of my 14th year that a random violent event occurred—which I will not go into—that provided me an opportunity to leave New York City and changed the course of my life forever.

During that time I was fortunate that my mother decided to send the family money and invited all of the children to come live with her in Hawaii. The money came at the right time, and that week I purchased a one-way ticket to Hawaii.

When I arrived in Hawaii, I quickly recognized its many differences from New York City—the ocean's clear blue water and the fresh cool breeze at night. I also recognized the many different nationalities and cultures. After my first day of attending Mililani High School, I came home and told my mother that it had felt like I was representing Africa at a United Nations meeting.

During the first few weeks of high school, the basketball coach noticed that I was one of the tallest young men on campus, and he invited me to try out for the basketball team. While living in New York I had not played much basketball. I enjoyed baseball and was on the bowling team, but I had never played on a basketball team. I believe it was because of my height that I started on the varsity team as a sophomore.

We won three basketball games that year, and everyone in the community was excited because it was three more games than the team had won the year before. In my junior year we won six games, and by the time I was a senior we had won 14 games and we became the Western Division champions, which advanced us to the Hawaii state play-offs. Because of my successful senior year, I was recruited to play basketball for BYU–Hawaii. All I knew about BYU–Hawaii was that it was a church school similar to Notre Dame or a St. Mary's University.

At the start of the fall semester I was instructed by my academic advisor that I needed to take several religion courses to graduate from BYU–Hawaii. For my first semester I decided to take a New

Testament course, and for the first time I began to understand in part the importance of a Savior. While living in New York I had been a converted Muslim. The Islamic faith regards Jesus Christ as a great man or prophet, similar to Moses or Abraham. I had not realized the importance of Jesus Christ and His atoning sacrifice until I read about His life in the Gospel of Luke. I studied how the Savior healed the sick, raised the dead, and made the blind to see and the deaf to hear.

Imagine for a minute that we all lived during the time of the Savior and that we watched from a distance as He called His apostles and performed many miracles, including feeding the 4,000. Imagine that we also watched as He took upon Him the sins of the world.

In Luke 22:39 it reads, "And he came out, and went, as he was wont, to the mount of Olives; and his disciples also followed him." The word *wont* means "usually." When the Savior wanted to be alone, He often visited the Mount of Olives and similar places to pray.

The scripture continues:

And when he was at the place, he said unto [His apostles], *Pray that ye enter not into temptation.*

And he was withdrawn from them about a stone's cast, and [He] *kneeled down, and prayed.* [Luke 22:40–41]

Picture in your mind the Savior instructing His apostles to pray to overcome temptation and then His withdrawing Himself "from them about a stone's cast"—around 30 to 40 yards. He then knelt down to pray, saying, "Father, if thou be willing, remove this cup from me: nevertheless not my will, but thine, be done" (Luke 22:42).

At this moment I believe the Savior knew that He would take upon Him the sins of the world; nevertheless, He asked the Father if there was another way that this sacrifice could be made. If not, His response was, "Not my will, but thine, be done."

And there appeared an angel unto him from heaven, strengthening him.

And being in an agony he prayed more earnestly: and his sweat was as it were great drops of blood falling down to the ground. [Luke 22:43–44]

The Savior felt the pain of our sins. You know how it feels when you have made a mistake and your heart begins to ache. The Savior felt our heartaches and our feelings of guilt and anguish. He took upon Him the sins of all mankind—my sins, your sins, the sins of those who lived before us, and the sins of those who will live after us. The pain was so great that it caused the Savior, even Jesus Christ, to bleed from every pore of His body (see Mosiah 3:7, D&C 19:18). Well, you know the rest of the story. Judas betrayed the Savior with a kiss and Jesus suffered more pain before He was nailed to the cross. The Savior suffered death so that we might have life.

As the fall semester progressed, I was introduced to the missionaries. They visited my dorm room on a regular basis. I remember playing my rap music on my boom box, and I would ask the missionaries if they wanted me to turn the music down. For a long time I thought my music was the reason the missionaries came by my dorm room so often. It was not until I served my own mission that I learned that missionaries are not allowed to listen to music.

After about a week of daily visits, the missionaries asked if I wanted to take the missionary discussions. My first discussion with them was in the library on the BYU–Hawaii campus, and they showed me the video *The First Vision.* The movie talked about Joseph Smith and how at the age of 14 he felt confused about the many different religions. He wanted to learn the truth and to understand Heavenly Father's plan more fully. Young Joseph searched the scriptures and read in James 1:5 that "if any of you lack wisdom, let him ask of God." This scripture touched young Joseph, and he decided to exercise his faith and to ask God to direct him to the truth (see JS—H 1:9–13).

Joseph Smith went into a grove of trees and knelt to pray. As he prayed he saw a marvelous light, and in the midst of that light young Joseph saw our Heavenly Father and Jesus Christ (see JS—H 1:14–20). As I watched this video, I felt in my heart it was true.

Joseph Smith exercised faith, trusted in the Lord, and received the answer to his prayer.

The missionaries continued to teach me the remainder of the fall semester. It was fun and I learned a lot, but I had no desire to join the Church.

The next semester I again met with my college advisor and was again instructed to take a religion course. I decided to take the Book of Mormon course. I had no doubt about the possibility of additional scriptures because as a Muslim I had studied the Holy Koran.

My Book of Mormon instructor was Brother Gary Smith of the School of Business. As the course began I started to read about Nephi and how as a young man he listened to the Lord. And when Father Lehi instructed his sons to return to Jerusalem for the brass plates, Laman and Lemuel complained whereas Nephi simply said:

I will go and do the things which the Lord hath commanded, for I know that the Lord giveth no commandments unto the children of men, save he shall prepare a way for them that they may accomplish the thing which he commandeth them. [1 Nephi 3:7]

Nephi exercised faith, trusted in the Lord, and obtained the brass plates.

I read about King Benjamin and how he served the people with all his heart, might, mind, and strength. He loved the people he served and, more important, he loved the Lord. During his last days upon the earth King Benjamin built a tower so he could teach his people many things pertaining to the kingdom of God. King Benjamin stated:

I tell you these things that ye may learn wisdom; that ye may learn that when ye are in the service of your fellow beings ye are only in the service of your God. [Mosiah 2:17]

King Benjamin served his people as we must serve one another. King Benjamin exercised faith, trusted in the Lord, and brought peace to an entire nation.

I read on in 3 Nephi of how the resurrected Lord visited the people on the American continent. The Savior was introduced by His Father:

> *Behold my Beloved Son, in whom I am well pleased, in whom I have glorified my name—hear ye him. . . .*
>
> *And it came to pass that he stretched forth his hand and spake unto the people, saying:*
>
> *Behold, I am Jesus Christ, whom the prophets testified shall come into the world.*
>
> *And behold, I am the light and the life of the world; and I have drunk out of that bitter cup which the Father hath given me, and have glorified the Father in taking upon me the sins of the world, in the which I have suffered the will of the Father in all things from the beginning.* [3 Nephi 11:7, 9–11]

The Lord told the people:

> *Arise and come forth unto me, that ye may thrust your hands into my side, and also that ye may feel the prints of the nails in my hands and in my feet, that ye may know that I am the God of Israel, and the God of the whole earth, and have been slain for the sins of the world.* [3 Nephi 11:14]

The Savior—my Savior, the resurrected Lord—extends His hands of mercy and love to all who will come unto Him. The Savior. My Brother. My Friend. I stopped reading.

It was near the end of winter semester. I completed my finals and was preparing to return home to the other side of the island. My scholarship did not cover the spring term, and I was prepared to work for the spring and summer to save some money for the fall semester. On the day I was prepared to leave campus, I received a note in my mailbox from Brother Gary Smith, my Book of Mormon teacher.

He wanted to see me. I returned to my dorm room, where I received another note stating Brother Gary Smith wanted to see me. I thought to myself, "Why would he want to see me? Will Brother Smith give me an F grade for religion? No one ever fails religion."

I dropped by his office, and the secretary mentioned that Brother Smith was at the Seasider, a mini-café on campus. I found him, and, as we talked, Brother Smith proceeded to tell me how I knew the Church was true and that it was time for me to join the Church. I looked at him amazed, and I wondered what he had been drinking.

He continued and said, "From what I'm about to tell you, either one of two things will happen. You will join the Church right away or it will take you awhile." He quoted a scripture in Ether that states:

*And now, I, Moroni, would speak somewhat concerning these things;
I would show unto the world that faith is things which are hoped for and
not seen; wherefore, dispute not because ye see not, for ye receive no witness
until after the trial of your faith.* [Ether 12:6]

I thought, "What does this scripture have to do with me?"

Brother Smith explained that he believed I was waiting for some type of miracle or vision to take place before I would join the Church. He said, "You need to act upon what you already know to be true before you will receive a greater witness. 'Wherefore, dispute not because ye see not, for ye receive no witness until after the trial [or exercise] of your faith.'"

Brother Smith was right. I thought, "Why can't I receive a vision like the Prophet Joseph Smith?" I wanted a greater witness. Well, it took me awhile to join the Church.

I returned to the other side of the island and started to hang out with my friends. Toward the end of the summer I began to feel somewhat empty, confused, and uncertain. I was missing school and the wonderful feelings I had felt at BYU–Hawaii. I knew something was wrong because I could not wait to return to school.

Two weeks before school was to begin, I received a phone call from Coach Ken Wagner. Coach Wagner was the assistant coach at BYU–Hawaii, and during that summer he had received the head coaching job at Dixie College in St. George, Utah.

He asked if I wanted to play for him at Dixie College. I said yes. That first year I did not play basketball; I redshirted. This gave me the time to watch the Mormons. As I watched, I noticed that at least three types of Mormons seemed to exist.

The first type is similar to you: students who attend institute and seminary and take religion classes on a regular basis. Their personalities glow, and they always seem to have smiles on their faces. When tough times come upon them, they know whom they can trust and that the Lord will help.

The second type of Mormons are the ones who realize that they are away from home for the first time and no one will know what they are doing. They party and get involved in immoral relationships. They believe they are having fun when in their hearts they feel unhappy. They do not have the "glow."

The third type of Mormons are the ones who "sit on the fence," unsure about who they are. When the winds of temptation blow their way, they seem to follow in that direction. They look confused more than anything else.

As I noticed these types of Mormons, I thought, "Peter, what type of Mormon do you want to be?" I wanted to be just like Rick West, my first roommate at BYU–Hawaii and a returned missionary; Bob Barnes, a teammate at Dixie College and a great friend; and Coach Wagner, who had helped me to understand the importance of family. They had the glow.

I thought, "If I am going to be a Mormon, I must learn how they date." So I enrolled in an institute class called Dating and Courtship. And I guess the other 28 male students in the class thought the same as I did.

Soon afterward, a good friend, Trudy Smith, began to take the missionary discussions. She invited me to attend with her. This time the sister missionaries taught me about The Church of Jesus Christ of Latter-day Saints. As you know, sister missionaries teach the gospel differently than do the elders. After each discussion they would cry as they shared their testimonies, and they wanted so much to hug me but realized that it was against mission rules. Toward the end of the discussions they asked me to do something the elders had not. They asked me to fast and to pray about the truthfulness of the gospel. I was familiar with fasting. As a Muslim, we fasted during the month of Ramadan, a sacred time for worship.

I fasted, and when I was done, I returned to my dorm room at Dixie College, knelt down on my knees, and simply asked, "Heavenly Father, is the Book of Mormon the word of God? And is Joseph Smith a prophet?"

No, I did not receive a vision or a visit from an angel. I felt warmth in my heart, a feeling I had felt many times before—a feeling I had felt when I attended BYU–Hawaii and took Brother Smith's Book of Mormon class. It was the same feeling I had felt when I saw the movie about Joseph Smith. This time, however, the feeling of warmth came when I was by myself, and I knew it came from God. He answered my prayer. I had a testimony.

I told the missionaries that I wanted to be baptized, but first I wanted to return to Hawaii so my mother could witness my joining the Church. I thought that as soon as I got off the plane I would find the missionaries and join the Church. Well, that did not happen. I started to hang out with my old friends, and I returned to my old habits. Toward the end of the summer the old feelings of uncertainty and confusion returned.

In August 1986 I was at home in my room, and I decided to read the Bible. I read in John, "If ye love me, keep my commandments" (John 14:15). I knew I loved my mother; she is a source of strength in my life. I knew I loved my family, but did I love God?

I knelt down to pray and told my Heavenly Father for the first time that I loved Him. Later that day I was on my way to the gym to play basketball when I noticed two missionaries riding their bikes. I almost ran them over! They pulled to the side of the road, and I asked them to come by my home that night. They thought it was a miracle. The next week I was baptized a member of The Church of Jesus Christ of Latter-day Saints.

I returned to Dixie College that fall and played my sophomore year. We had a great team. We won 32 games and lost only three. I was recruited by several NCAA Division I universities, but I decided to postpone my college education to serve a mission. I was called to serve in Alabama. In Alabama I met people and families who exercised their faith and trusted in the Lord. Because of their faith, their lives were blessed.

One such individual was Sister Eva Oryang from Uganda, Africa. While living in her home country she had held a top political office and served as a prominent member of the government. However, in the summer of 1988 government officials of Uganda received several death threats, and Sister Oryang feared for her life. She left Uganda and arrived in Tuskegee, Alabama, where her oldest son was attending Tuskegee University. After two weeks of living in the United States, she became discouraged and very depressed. She had left a few of her children and a husband back in Africa, and she was unsure as to when her family would be together again.

Sister Oryang had learned of God back in her country and had faith in Him. One night she prayed. She prayed all night until the next morning, and all she said in her prayer was this: "Heavenly Father, I know I need a church. Will you please send me the right church first?"

In the morning there was a knock on the door. Her daughter answered the door and returned to her mother's room. "Mother, you have visitors."

Sister Oryang thought to herself, "I am a stranger in this country. How can I have visitors?" Seeing the young men at the door, she thought, "America is a strange place. Parents send their children outdoors with names on their shirts."

The missionaries introduced themselves. Sister Oryang told them, "I have just finished my prayers, and I asked the Lord to send me the right church." Of course the missionaries smiled with joy and stated that they *were* representatives of the right church.[1]

As Sister Oryang led the way into the living room, there was another knock on the door. It was a minister of another faith who lived across the street. He had been watching the family for the past week and thought this would be a good time to visit. Comparing this older gentleman to the missionaries, Sister Oryang wondered, "How can these young boys tell me anything about God?"

She led the minister into the kitchen. As he sat down, there was another knock at the door. Two older sisters of yet another faith had been proselytizing in the area and decided to knock on the Oryangs' door!

Sister Oryang thought, "I have just finished my prayer, and I asked the Lord to send me the right church *first*." She said good-bye to the minister and the two other sisters and listened intently to the missionaries. Within weeks Sister Oryang joined The Church of Jesus Christ of Latter-day Saints. Other family members soon joined the Church as well.

Before the Oryang family joined the Church, the Tuskegee Branch had about 10 members attending each Sunday. Following Sister Oryang's conversion—and through her example of faith and testimony—the branch grew in just nine months from 10 to more than 60 people attending church. And her son David became president of the Tuskegee Branch a few years later.

Sister Oryang, like others, was blessed with the fullness of the everlasting gospel—a gift she shared with many. She understood the influence and the power of the Holy Ghost and how it helps to change lives and bring people closer to our Heavenly Father. I worked with Sister Oryang following her conversion, and she helped me understand the three key ingredients necessary to ensure happiness and peace in this life and give us a taste of what life will be like in our heavenly home.

The key ingredients are faith, family, and friendship.

The first ingredient, faith, is essential for us to obtain the power necessary to understand the love that our Heavenly Father has for us and His desire for our success. Faith is the power that moves us to repent and instills in us the desire to improve. Exercising faith allows us to overcome discouragement and heartache as we recognize that the Savior suffered in the Garden of Gethsemane so that the suffering and pain we feel at times can be relieved and peace restored.

There is a difference between having faith and exercising faith. Having faith denotes a belief in the Savior; exercising faith requires action. When we exercise faith, we allow our belief to guide us to pray, to read and study the scriptures, to repent, and to keep the commandments of God. It is through exercising faith that our belief, knowledge, and love for the Savior grow and thereby strengthen us.

The second ingredient is family. Having a solid family relationship is imperative in helping us to understand the principles of forgiveness, service, and selflessness. President Spencer W. Kimball, our 12th president of the Church, suggested that it is through families that we master the teachings of the gospel of Christ. He stated:

Spirituality is . . . nurtured in our actions of patience, kindness, and forgiveness toward each other and in our applying gospel principles in the family circle. Home is where we become experts and scholars in gospel righteousness, learning and living gospel truths together.[2]

Families come in all shapes and sizes. Some children are raised in a single-parent home, some are adopted, and some are taught and raised by grandparents and other relatives. I was raised by a single parent. My mother always taught me to have faith, and she helped me to understand the workings of God in our lives.

Now I am married and have been adopted into Stephanie's family. I continue to learn a great deal from my in-laws and how important grandparents are in raising and teaching our children.

The third ingredient is friendship. President Larry Gibson, president of the Highland Utah West Stake, defines a friend as "one who is attached to another by affection, by esteem, and by respect. It is these attributes that lead to a desire to be with a friend and seek to promote prosperity and happiness."[3] Good friends provide support and guidance.

In April 1997 general conference, President Hinckley, our beloved prophet, declared that every member of the Church needs three things:

"a friend, a responsibility, and nurturing with 'the good word of God' (Moroni 6:4)."[4] Later he suggested that becoming a friend is probably the most difficult. To get outside our comfort zone and to extend a hand of friendship is challenging. It takes time to develop friendships—but this is the time we need to take.

At some point we will all be tested. It is a part of life. When those times come—and they will come—it is a great feeling to know you have a friend at school, at work, or in your ward to show you love, to listen to your concerns, to be an example of goodness, and to testify of truth. These are the attributes of friendship. The Savior called us His friends when He said, "Greater love hath no man than this, that a man lay down his life for his friends" (John 15:13). And in Proverbs it states, "A friend loveth at all times" (Proverbs 17:17). We need to take the time to become friends. There are those whom you associate with who need your friendship and support.

Brothers and sisters, I know God lives. I know Jesus is the Christ, the Son of God, and the Only Begotten of the Father—our Redeemer, our Savior, and our Friend. I know we have a living prophet, even Gordon B. Hinckley, and this is the Lord's Church upon the face of the earth.

We have been given much; therefore we must give of ourselves and incorporate and strengthen faith, family, and friendships. Doing so can ensure happiness and peace in this life and help us begin to understand, in part, what life will be like in our heavenly home.

My friends, take full advantage of the Lord's goodness. His arms of mercy and love are extended, and all are invited to come. For the Lord has said:

Come unto me, all ye that labour and are heavy laden, and I will give you rest.

Take my yoke upon you, and learn of me; for I am meek and lowly in heart: and ye shall find rest unto your souls.

For my yoke is easy, and my burden is light. [Matthew 11:28–30]

The Savior loves you and me. In the name of Jesus Christ, amen.

NOTES

1. The missionaries who knocked on the Oryangs' door that morning were Elder David Steab and his companion. They taught and subsequently baptized the Oryang family in 1988. Peter Johnson served in Tuskegee, Alabama, from September 1988 to May 1989—after the Oryangs were members of the Church. It was during this time that the branch grew from 10 to more than 60 people attending sacrament meeting on a consistent basis.

2. Spencer W. Kimball, "Therefore I Was Taught," *Ensign*, January 1982, 3.

3. Highland 27th Ward Conference, Highland Utah West Stake, 14 January 2007.

4. Gordon B. Hinckley, "Converts and Young Men," *Ensign*, May 1997, 47.

Personal Ministry: Sacred and Precious

Bonnie D. Parkin

I guess you are wondering why I wore this red jacket. My hope is that it will remind you that tomorrow is Valentine's Day. So, on this day before Valentine's Day, I've been wondering: "How's your heart?" If your heart hasn't already been promised to someone, think about doing it. And remember, your mother doesn't count!

I'd like to begin with a story.

My daughter-in-law's mother, Susan, was a wonderful seamstress. President Kimball lived in their ward. One Sunday, Susan noticed that he had a new suit. Her father had recently returned from a trip to New York and had brought her some exquisite silk fabric. Susan thought that fabric would make a handsome tie to go with President Kimball's new suit. So on Monday she made the tie. She wrapped it in tissue paper and walked up the block to President Kimball's home.

On her way to the front door, she suddenly stopped and thought, "Who am I to make a tie for the prophet? He probably has plenty of them." Deciding she had made a mistake, she turned to leave.

Bonnie D. Parkin was Relief Society general president of The Church of Jesus Christ of Latter-day Saints when this devotional address was given on 13 February 2007. © *Intellectual Reserve, Inc.*

Just then Sister Kimball opened the front door and said, "Oh, Susan!"

Stumbling all over herself, Susan said, "I saw President Kimball in his new suit on Sunday. Dad just brought me some silk from New York . . . and so I made him a tie."

Before Susan could continue, Sister Kimball stopped her, took hold of her shoulders, and said: "Susan, never suppress a generous thought."

Susan didn't have an assignment to make that tie. She wasn't hired to do so. Despite feeling a bit hesitant, she did it because it *felt* right. Susan had a quiet sense of mission to serve others. I was also the beneficiary of such service. Her service went beyond any calling because it lasted throughout her life. Never suppressing a generous thought became a part of her *personal* ministry.

Some years ago, at the conclusion of a Utah Board of Higher Education meeting, Elder Neal Maxwell submitted his resignation. He said he needed to do so to make time for his personal ministry. Most of the board members assumed he was referring to his apostleship. However, he explained that his personal ministry was different than his apostleship. His personal ministry was to comfort fellow cancer patients.

We often speak about the Savior's ministry. But have you ever wondered if *you* have a personal ministry? I have.

What is personal ministry? Each of us has a personal ministry. I believe we received our personal ministry in the premortal world. It was divinely given and lasts a lifetime.

I hope all of you are excited to study the teachings of President Kimball in Relief Society and priesthood this year. I love what he taught when he said:

Remember, in the world before we came here, faithful women were given certain assignments while faithful men were foreordained to certain priesthood tasks. While we do not now remember the particulars, this does not alter the glorious reality of what we once agreed to. You are accountable for those things which long ago were expected of you just as are those we sustain as prophets and apostles![1]

How can we know what was entrusted to us at that time? As we accept callings and love and obey the Lord, our personal ministry unfolds. It is a sacred and precious thing. It embraces the people who come and go across the path of our life. It extends beyond our temporary callings as presidents, counselors, secretaries, teachers, and so on. It is illuminated by our patriarchal blessings. And while each of our ministries is unique, they allow us to become extensions of the Lord's love.

The Holy Ghost is key to pursuing our personal ministry. I pray that the Spirit will attend us in these moments together and that we will each have a greater desire to minister personally to others.

It's so important to realize that every interaction we have is an opportunity to minister, to nurture. You can minister to someone right now. Tell the person sitting next to you "Thank you for sitting by me." And if no one's sitting by you, pop over next to someone and tell them thanks.

"To minister" is defined as attending to the needs and wants of others. The Bible Dictionary adds, "The work of the ministry is to do the work of the Lord on the earth—to represent the Lord among the people."[2]

Ministering involves extending charity—that pure love of Christ—to others, one person at a time. By doing so, we offer a kind, generous, peaceful, and pure heart. Opportunities to minister may come within the formal stewardship of a calling or assignment, or they may come as we spontaneously extend ourselves to someone in need. I believe these words of Elder Maxwell:

Our impact is less likely to emanate from the pulpit—more often it will occur in one-to-one relationships, or in small groups where we can have an impact on an individual.[3]

Such ministering follows the scriptural admonitions that should govern our every interaction with all of our brothers and sisters: "Be gentle unto all men, apt to teach, patient."[4] "See that ye love one another with a pure heart fervently."[5] As we offer such Christlike service to those around us, we and they are blessed and feel His love.

Most ministering opportunities are spontaneous, not planned in advance. Much of the Savior's ministering seemed almost incidental, happening while He was on His way to somewhere else—while He was doing something else. Chapter 9 of the Gospel of Matthew is an amazing illustration of that.

Early in the chapter, the Savior disembarked a ship. A man with palsy was brought to Him. Jesus stopped and healed him. Then Jesus had a discussion with the Pharisees and a man interrupted, saying his daughter had died. So Jesus left to assist the man. On His way, a woman touched His garment. Jesus healed her. He continued on His way and raised the girl from the dead. As He departed her home, two blind men followed Him, and He healed them. As He continued on His way, He cast the devil from a man possessed. All of this took place in one chapter! He gave us the example of ministering *as He went*.

Just as a doctor comes to heal the sick, Jesus came to heal the sinner. When the Pharisees criticized Him for spending time with sinners, He responded, "They that be whole need not a physician, but they that are sick." Then He said, "Go ye and learn what that meaneth, I will have mercy."[6] Had they simply watched Him ministering as He went, they would have learned what He meant. They would have seen His mercy. When we are merciful to others, we can feel at one with the Savior in that moment.

President Hunter taught:

We have the responsibility to learn of him, the things he taught and the things he did during his earthly ministry. Having learned these lessons we are under commandment to follow his example.[7]

Like Him, we can go and do likewise if our hearts are open to those opportunities.

Just as ministering doesn't always need to be planned, it doesn't need to be spectacular. It is something we can do every day in natural, comfortable ways. Mother Teresa suggested that we "do small things with great love."

My sister Joyce called our 98-year-old Aunt Leona and asked, "What can I do for you?"

Aunt Leona didn't even hesitate but said, "Oh, I would just love a note in the mail when you have a minute."

That's pretty simple. Who do you know that needs a note?

While we were serving in London, we received a missionary from another mission. During his first interview he told my husband, Jim, that he did not like the Brits and did not want a British companion. Jim had prayed about the companionship and had felt impressed to put this missionary with one of the hardest-working missionaries—who also just happened to be British. Although that British missionary never complained about his new companion, he later told us it was a difficult time. Nonetheless, he served his companion in small ways: he made him breakfast, ironed his shirts, even shined his shoes. At the conclusion of his mission, I asked the missionary who had not wanted to serve with a Brit who his favorite companion had been. It was no surprise—it was his British companion.

I've heard remarkable stories of how you BYU students, faculty, and staff minister to each other. Listen for the common threads as I share three experiences.

I was a little apprehensive and nervous when I moved into a new apartment. Of the girls in the apartment, two were sisters and the others were already good friends. I worried about fitting in. To complicate matters, their interests and strengths were my weaknesses: they could make bread from scratch, bake pies, and run a household. Their uniforms for these activities were their well-worn aprons, which hung prominently on the kitchen wall. Then, as I was moving in, I noticed a sewing machine on the kitchen table. I was shocked. They even did their own sewing!

Well, they must have read me very easily because I was soon presented with my very own apron that they had sewn just for me. It didn't seem like ministering, but that blue apron symbolized their extended friendship, and it made me feel welcome. They helped me gain confidence in the kitchen—but, more lasting, they helped me through their examples. They included me in their circle as they gave of themselves. I still have and use that blue apron in my kitchen as I try to open my home and heart to others around me.[8]

The second experience is from a BYU graduate:

As a sophomore, I had a roommate named Krista. She ministered to me by just being a loyal and kind friend. She asked about my life and always listened. She noticed what my talents were and suggested a field of work I never would have considered—the next 15 years of my life were altered because she noticed my skills and abilities and I took her advice related to a career. She could have noticed my inabilities and weaknesses—maybe she did, but she never commented on them. She just helped me be the best person I could by believing in me.[9]

The last experience tells of a professor's impact:

I was a research assistant for a professor who taught me how to run statistics software, how to cull themes out of qualitative data, and how to patiently comb through survey responses. But he also shared with me faith-filled personal experiences and stories about his family. He lived his values and always remembered which things were most important in life. He inspired me to want to sing more and laugh more and appreciate life often, even in its extremities. When I came to his office to work, I always left edified. He ministered to me even though I wasn't doing a stellar job for him because I was so busy and stressed out with school. He looked at the situation and saw the most important thing in it. And that thing was not the work. It was a person who needed hope and faith in a challenging time of life.[10]

One common thread I see in these stories is people who followed the Savior's admonition: "Feed my lambs. . . . Feed my sheep."[11]

Isn't it wonderful that there is so much flexibility in *how* we minister to each other? I hope you can see that all our personal interactions provide us with opportunities to minister.

President Hinckley said:

Believe in yourselves. Believe in your capacity to do some good in this world. God sent us here for a purpose, and that was to improve the world in which we live. The wonderful thing is that we can do it.[12]

We can often learn more about our personal ministry *through* our callings. I hope all of you are visiting teachers or home teachers. Look at these assignments with new eyes. They are great opportunities to minister to each other. Do you know the hearts of those you visit? Do you spend time with them? Do you listen and give them the great gift of knowing they have been heard and understood? It takes time and energy, but it is so important! I testify that as you seek for inspiration, you will not only know how best to serve others but will better understand your own personal ministry.

Let me give you an example. Elder Maxwell talked the talk, but he also walked the walk. Aileen Figuerres, who currently serves on the Relief Society General Board, shared this story:

Elder Maxwell oversaw the Asia North Area while my husband, Cyril, presided over the Japan Fukuoka Mission. Each time we saw the Maxwells, they would ask if there was anything they could do for us when they returned to Utah. However, we never wanted to burden such busy people with extra things to do.

While we were in Japan, our daughter Dawn was a new BYU student. One day she was called to the front desk of her dorm to find Elder and Sister Maxwell waiting. [Wouldn't that be a surprise!] They knew she was away from us and brought her a potted plant for her room and a book by Elder Maxwell. He humbly and humorously suggested that she could read it if she was ever having difficulty falling asleep. They chatted with her, told her about what we were doing, and offered her the name and phone number of their daughter who lived nearby in case Dawn ever needed assistance.

But this was not the end of their ministering to a young college student. During the Christmas holidays Dawn received a call to make sure she had somewhere to go. Sister Maxwell even invited her to the MTC to hear Elder Maxwell speak.

Their ministering was a blessing to Dawn and to us, her parents, who thought about her and worried about her as we lived half a world apart from each other.

Have you ever been the recipient of someone's ministering? Do you welcome or resist when others try to minister to you? Does it make you feel like a "project"? Sometime ago in our ward priesthood meeting, one of the brethren mentioned that the compassionate service leader in Relief Society had said there were ward members who did not want to be projects. This made it difficult for the sisters to serve them. My husband raised his hand and said if it would help, he did not mind being a project. So if the sisters wanted to bring him some meals when I was out of town, that would be okay. Unfortunately for Jim, they thought he was just kidding.

Jim, will you share your favorite story of learning to receive?

Jim Parkin: Once when Bonnie was the ward Relief Society president, an unusual thing happened. She was sick and could not go to church. She gave me careful instructions for preparing Sunday dinner. I put the roast in the pan with potatoes and carrots and celery around it, with the proper seasoning, and placed it in the oven. The boys and I were stoked, as it was our favorite Sunday dinner.

When we returned from church, the house smelled of that wonderful roast beef fragrance. I went to Bonnie's bedside for further instructions. She told me to put the roast and all the trimmings on serving dishes and take it to another family in the ward.

All I could say was: "What will we eat?"

She said, "Diana heard I was sick, and she's bringing us dinner."

Remembering the wonderful roast I had just soloed on, I said, "Well, how about we eat our dinner and give Diana's dinner to that other family?"

Bonnie responded, "No! We need to learn to receive as well as to give."

That lesson has served me well, and I have taught it on many occasions. But it still hasn't gotten me any extra dinners from the Relief Society!

Bonnie Parkin: Thanks, honey. What I know is that personal ministry must begin in our homes—and apartments.

Don't deny others the blessings of service. Allowing them to minister to us is another form of ministering. Personal ministry helps us feel the love of the Lord and come unto Him. Alma taught us that we entered into a covenant with the Lord at the time of our baptism. We specifically committed *"to bear one another's burdens, that they may be light; . . . and . . . mourn with those that mourn; . . . and comfort those that stand in need of comfort."* As we minister to each other, Alma promised that the Lord would "pour out his Spirit more abundantly upon [us]."[13] Thus, when we serve one another, we are individually blessed.

A young couple took Alma's words to heart. They learned that a woman in their BYU ward had been diagnosed with advanced leukemia. They opened their hearts to her, her husband, and their young daughter. Listen to what this couple did. They contributed the money they would have spent on Christmas to this family to help defray their mounting medical bills, and they visited the wife in the hospital, read to her, and brought small gifts to cheer her.

Six months after the diagnosis, this mother died. The young couple had planned to move east to pursue professional opportunities following graduation. They decided to delay their move so that they could help this newly widowed father while he completed law school. When the father went to class, the young couple cared for his two-year-old daughter. They planned a surprise birthday party for this dad, and, with help from the ward, they kept the meals coming.

I can't imagine that such extended service was easy for either this young couple or the widowed father.

Love and relationships—simply and profoundly—are what personal ministry is all about. President Hinckley said:

Our mission in life, as followers of the Lord Jesus Christ, must be a mission of saving. . . .

If we are to build that Zion of which the prophets have spoken and of which the Lord has given mighty promise, we must set aside our consuming selfishness. We must rise above our love for comfort and ease, and in the very process of effort and struggle, even in our extremity, we shall become better acquainted with our God.[14]

We can become better acquainted with Heavenly Father through prayer. Personal ministry can answer prayers. We can offer a daily prayer that enlists the help of the Lord Jesus Christ as we ask: "Help me to be the answer to someone's prayer today." The Lord consistently answers this prayer as we tune our eyes and ears to discerning the needs of those around us.

The prayers of one missionary's parents were answered by the personal ministry of another. A missionary arrived in a foreign mission and was struggling with discouragement. He said he couldn't take it and wanted to come home. His parents and others tried to encourage him but to no avail. At a reception during a training session, this distraught father mentioned his son's struggle to a priesthood leader.

The following week an envelope arrived at the parents' home. Inside was a copy of a letter that had been sent to their son. The letter had been typed on a typewriter and very tenderly addressed to the discouraged elder. It was several pages long, full of encouragement and the writer's own missionary experiences about faith and sticking to it. The letter was warm, loving, thoughtful, personal, and signed, "Sincerely, your brother, President Gordon B. Hinckley." Shortly after this, the elder wrote his parents to say he was staying. He became a mighty power for good among the people of his mission.[15]

It is motivating to think that in spite of President Hinckley's many responsibilities and his age, he is actively involved in personal ministry. As I attend the board meetings of the Church Educational System, I am moved and touched when it is President Hinckley's turn to pray: He prays for each of you that you will be blessed with faith and testimony in Jesus Christ. As you increase your faith and testimony, you answer a prophet's prayers.

We become the hands of our Savior as we do His work. In a missionary zone conference we discussed being the answer to someone's prayers. One pair of missionaries went home and prayed that evening and the next morning that they would be the answer to someone's prayers. The next morning they walked down the high street, and a man came running out of a hotel. He asked if they had a copy of the Book of Mormon—and they did! He explained he was a member attending a business conference. He was worried about some personal problems, and, as he prayed, he received the impression that his answer was in the Book of Mormon. But he did not have one with him. That morning he was sitting in the hotel restaurant. He suddenly had the impression to go immediately to the front of the hotel, where he saw the missionaries, who provided him with the answer to his prayer.

Asking to be an answer to someone's prayer has a powerful impact. There are sacred, quiet experiences for those who participate with the Lord in answering prayers. As we go about listening, watching, and feeling for the answer to those prayers—even in the midst of our busy schedules—I testify that our earthly ministry unfolds by revelation and divine empowerment. Our testimonies, faith, and feelings of connectedness to the Lord expand in amazing, unexpected ways.

And we can increase that participation with the Lord through prayer and even fasting for others. This helps us become aware of the great power the Lord grants us to make a difference for our brothers and sisters. In short, we can initiate and partake in small miracles on behalf of others—miracles that we are uniquely prepared to do, and that *only* we can do.

Wherever and whenever we are ministering, we are sharing God's love. Then, as He always does, both the giver and the receiver are blessed. May I suggest that finding your personal ministry begins with making a decision about a consistent way of being: a way that seeks to nurture, to be entirely helpful—not just now and again, but always. Ultimately, it is a decision to further consecrate ourselves to the Lord, to more fully take upon ourselves His name—to do as He did. Making this decision deepens our connectedness to one another and to the Lord. Such a responsive way of being is who we really are—from before this life.

I'd like to share part of a letter from someone who experienced this connection with another and with the Lord:

Dear Sister Parkin,

We fly quite a bit, and when we got our boarding passes, we had been upgraded to first class. This has never happened before, and may not again, but it was a little exciting.

As I was getting on the plane, I saw to my left a young woman in military uniform. The thought immediately came to me, "You need to give her your seat." It was quite a strong impression, and one I could not ignore. So, not being totally obedient, I went to my seat and put my bag down and sat down. I could not sit there though, and I walked back to talk to the stewards. I told them I wanted to give my seat to someone I had seen while getting on. Then I went back to get my bag.

I stood by the stewards until this young woman boarded the plane, and I pointed her out. They stopped her and informed her that I wanted to give her my seat. She was very appreciative, and I told her that I appreciated all she did for our country and I was happy to do this. I found out her seat assignment and went back and settled in.

About halfway through the flight this young woman came back to my seat and thanked me again. She kept calling me ma'am and telling me how grateful she was for this kindness. Then she handed me a little piece of paper and walked back to her seat. The note said, "Ma'am, I just wanted to say thank you so much! You helped me out in my hour of need. This soldier is forever thankful for your kindness. I am heading home to attend my mother's funeral. She passed away yesterday in a car accident. I thought God left me and punished me for something, but through this He gave me an angel to help my travel. Thank you. Here is a little something that helped me out. Now I'm passing it to you." Enclosed with the note was a little metal cross that said, *"God loves you."*

The letter concludes:

I am so grateful that I listened to the Holy Ghost and acted on that prompting. I don't know her name or where she was going. I really only know that she was a soldier. But I know that Heavenly Father knows her name and where she was going and that she was hurting. He wanted her to know that He loves her and was comforting her at this difficult time. I know that Heavenly Father loves me, too, and that He trusts me. It was such a simple thing to do. I guess that is what most service is—very simple things.[16]

My dear brothers and sisters, we are each called to reach out to others—most of the time it happens through simple acts of kindness, one to one. These are the events that really matter!

Our personal ministry is sacred and precious. It allows us to become an extension of the Lord's love. It embraces all who cross our path. What are those things you can do for another person that only you can do? I invite you to find out.

As you leave the Marriott Center today, you will have immediate opportunities to practice your personal ministry. Please, never suppress a generous thought.

God bless you to follow your promptings, and, as you do, I promise that He will expand your heart to become more like His. My heart has expanded as I have ministered and been ministered to. It's in those ministering moments that I know that God loves me, and I testify that He also loves you and pray that you can feel His love daily. I testify that Jesus is the Christ. I know this for myself. In the sacred name of Jesus Christ, amen.

NOTES

1. Spencer W. Kimball, "The Role of Righteous Women," *Ensign*, November 1979, 102.

2. Bible Dictionary, s.v. "ministry," 732.

3. Neal A. Maxwell, *"A More Excellent Way": Essays on Leadership for Latter-day Saints* (Salt Lake City: Deseret Book, 1967), 74.

4. 2 Timothy 2:24.

5. 1 Peter 1:22.

6. Matthew 9:12–13.

7. *The Teachings of Howard W. Hunter,* ed. Clyde J. Williams (Salt Lake City: Bookcraft, 1997), 40.

8. Personal correspondence.

9. Personal correspondence.

10. Personal correspondence.

11. John 21:15–17.

12. Gordon B. Hinckley, San Diego youth and young adult firesides, March 1996, reported in "'Strengthen Belief in God and Self,' Prophet Counsels," *Church News*, 30 March 1996, Z3.

13. Mosiah 18:8–10; emphasis added.

14. Gordon B. Hinckley, "Our Mission of Saving," *Ensign*, November 1991, 59.

15. See Eric B. Shumway, "Unto the Least of These," BYU–Idaho devotional, 1 April 2003; www.byui.edu/Presentations/Transcripts/Devotionals/2003_04_01_Shumway.htm.

16. Personal correspondence.

Hold Fast to the Words of the Prophets

Neil L. Andersen

Thirty-three years ago, while a student at Brigham Young University, I had a small role in an evening fireside like the one we are holding tonight. The speaker was President Spencer W. Kimball, and I found myself walking next to him as he moved toward the entry coming into the Marriott Center. I asked him if he ever became nervous standing before such a large assembly. With a smile, he responded: "Brother Andersen, you know that the scriptures say, 'If ye are prepared ye shall not fear' (D&C 38:30). I am trembling from my head to my toes." Tonight I know how he felt.

I express my love and respect for each of you seated here and for you who are gathered across the world. I know of your goodness and devotion to the gospel, your faith and hope for the future, and your desire to please your Heavenly Father. I pray that the Lord's Spirit will bless my words and your understanding.

Neil L. Andersen was a member of the Presidency of the Seventy of The Church of Jesus Christ of Latter-day Saints when this fireside address was given on 4 March 2007. © *Intellectual Reserve, Inc.*

HOLD FAST TO THE IRON ROD

I want to tell you of the Lord's guiding hand in our meeting tonight. During the early days of January I worked to organize and outline what I would present to you. Knowing that Elder David A. Bednar was scheduled to speak to you in February, I asked him if he had finalized the subject he would address.

I was taken aback when he responded that his talk was about holding fast to the iron rod. It was the exact title I had chosen for my talk. The choir was already practicing this beautiful number that they have just shared with us.

As Elder Bednar and I discussed the messages we had prepared, it was evident that we had approached the subject differently. Elder Bednar thought for a moment and said: "The Lord loves the young adults of the Church. There is purpose in this. This is a message the Lord wants delivered." I determined to proceed.

Then, just a week later and before Elder Bednar's talk, President Boyd K. Packer, acting president of the Quorum of the Twelve Apostles, gave a BYU devotional address he entitled "Lehi's Dream and You."[1] He too included in his talk what it means to hold fast to the iron rod.

My brothers and sisters, this is a subject the Lord wants you to think about.

You will remember from the talks of President Packer and Elder Bednar, and from your own study of the Book of Mormon, the key elements of Lehi's dream of the tree of life. Elder Bednar taught us that the tree of life, identified as the love of God, is a representation of Jesus Christ and that the joy and happiness received by partaking of the fruit of the tree symbolizes the blessings of the Savior's Atonement (see 1 Nephi 8:10; 11:8–9, 21–24).[2]

There was also a great and spacious building (see 1 Nephi 11:35–36, 12:18). President Packer's talk opened my mind to new ways of thinking about this part of the dream.

Also in the dream were mists of darkness (see 1 Nephi 12:16–17)—representing the temptations of the devil—that obscured the pathway (see 1 Nephi 8:19–22) leading to the tree. Finally, there was an iron rod (see 1 Nephi 11:24–25)—representing the word of God—allowing one to successfully pass through the mists of darkness and arrive at the tree.

The choir sang so beautifully:

Hold to the rod, the iron rod;
'Tis strong, and bright, and true.
The iron rod is the word of God;
'Twill safely guide us through.[3]

How we loved hearing it sung in Spanish and Portuguese as well, and how we wish we could hear it in all the languages of those who are listening to us tonight.

Nephi promised us that "whoso would hearken unto the word of God, and would hold fast unto it, . . . would never perish; neither could the temptations . . . of the adversary overpower them . . . , to lead them away to destruction" (1 Nephi 15:24).

The iron rod *is* the word of God. I like to think of it in this way: The word of God contains three very strong elements that intertwine and sustain one another to form an immovable rod. These three elements include, first, the scriptures, or the words of the ancient prophets. You will remember Elder Bednar's piercing question of last month: "Are you and I daily reading, studying, and searching the scriptures in a way that enables us to hold fast to the rod of iron?"[4]

The second element of the word of God is the personal revelation and inspiration that comes to us through the Holy Ghost. President Packer said it this way:

If you hold to the rod, you can feel *your way forward with the gift of the Holy Ghost. . . .*

. . . Grasp the iron rod, and do not let go. Through the power of the Holy Ghost, you can feel *your way through life. (See 3 Nephi 18:25; D&C 9:8.)*[5]

My subject tonight is the third element, a critical addition intertwining with the other two. This third part of the iron rod represents the words of the living prophets. We must also hold fast to the word of God as delivered by the living prophets. My prayer is that from our time together tonight we will increase our attentiveness to what the living prophets are teaching, accelerate our response to what we are learning, and deepen our understanding of what it means to *hold fast* to their words.

THE WORDS OF THE LIVING PROPHETS

Many years ago, President George Q. Cannon, then a member of the First Presidency, said:

We have the Bible, the Book of Mormon and the Book of Doctrine and Covenants; but all these books, without the living oracles and a constant stream of revelation from the Lord, would not lead any people into the Celestial Kingdom of God. This may seem a strange declaration to make, but strange as it may sound, it is nevertheless true.

Of course, these records are all of infinite value. They cannot be too highly prized, nor can they be too closely studied. But in and of themselves, with all the light that they give, they are insufficient to guide the children of men and to lead them into the presence of God. To be thus led requires a living Priesthood and constant revelation from God to the people according to the circumstances in which they may be placed.[6]

Of course we who are here tonight love President Gordon B. Hinckley, the two counselors in the First Presidency, and the Quorum of the Twelve Apostles. But in acknowledging our love and our loyalty, I would ask, "Could our attention to the counsel and the teaching of these Brethren be more active, searching, and responsive?"

Think how you would respond to the following questions: Could you tell me the names of the three members of the First Presidency and the names of each of those who comprise the Quorum of the

Twelve? These are the 15 men you and I sustain as prophets, seers, and revelators.

If we were to hold up a picture of these Brethren, would you recognize each of them? We rarely pay close attention to someone we do not recognize or know.

Could you share with me the counsel given by the First Presidency and the Quorum of the Twelve Apostles from last October's general conference? And could you identify the concerns of President Hinckley, President Monson, and President Faust in the First Presidency messages of the *Ensign* and *Liahona* during the first three months of this year?

Perhaps more important, could you share with me a recent decision where you changed something in your life because of counsel received from one of these 15 men?

The reasons our answers to these questions are so important rest in the calling and responsibility of the First Presidency and the Twelve Apostles. Whenever the Lord's Church has been established, the Lord has called prophets and apostles. The Savior said, "Ye have not chosen me, but I have chosen you, and ordained you" (John 15:16). To these men that ordination brings a spiritual power and a solemn responsibility—a power to know and to testify and a responsibility to teach and to bless. It also brings a responsibility and a promise to us. We have the responsibility to listen and to follow, and we have a promise that blessings will come as we believe and act on their words.

When the Lord called twelve disciples in the Americas after His Resurrection, He taught the people this: "Blessed are ye if ye shall give heed unto the words of these twelve whom I have chosen from among you to minister unto you, and to be your servants" (3 Nephi 12:1). In our day, in a very difficult time, the Lord promised the Saints: "If my people will hearken unto my voice, and unto the voice of my servants whom I have appointed to lead my people, behold, verily I say unto you, they shall not be moved out of their place" (D&C 124:45).

This is the Lord's pattern. He calls 15 men from "the ordinary pursuits of life"[7] and endows them with the keys and power to guide and direct us. We are not forced to obey; there is no compulsion. But if we will be attentive to their words, if we will be responsive and willing to change our behavior as the Holy Ghost confirms their counsel, we will not be moved out of our place—meaning we will hold fast to the iron rod and will forever remain safely on the path leading to the tree of life.

How do we seek out and hold fast to the counsel of the living prophets? Let's consider the question by thinking more deeply about the three words we use in sustaining these men—*prophets, seers,* and *revelators.*

PROPHETS

First, the word *prophet.* The Apostle John said that "the testimony of Jesus is the spirit of prophecy" (Revelation 19:10). Prophets testify of Christ. Their sure witness of the living Christ is one of the greatest blessings to the Church and to the world. The Lord declared that these men are to be "special witnesses of the name of Christ in all the world" (D&C 107:23). Above all else, their voices are raised in testimony of His divinity and His reality. This witness, born in their discipleship and tempered in their ordination, can have a significant influence on our own feelings.

Their testimonies are expressed simply, allowing the Holy Ghost to carry the witness into our hearts. For example, we may hear them testify with such words as these: "As surely as I know that I am here and you are there, I know that Jesus is the Christ. He lives!"[8] Or, "Mine is the certain knowledge that Jesus is our divine Savior, Redeemer, and the Son of God the Father. I know of his reality by a sure perception so sacred I cannot give utterance to it."[9]

While these statements are powerful, it is the accompanying spiritual confirmation that burns in our hearts and strengthens us.

Explaining the role of angels, Mormon taught:

And the office of their ministry [the ministry of angels] *is . . . to prepare the way among the children of men, by declaring the word of Christ unto the chosen vessels of the Lord, that they may bear testimony of him.*

And by so doing, the Lord God prepareth the way that the residue of men may have faith in Christ, that the Holy Ghost may have place in their hearts. [Moroni 7:31–32]

The First Presidency and the Quorum of the Twelve Apostles are the Lord's chosen vessels.

Our own faith in the Savior grows and develops through the times and seasons of our lives. There may be moments of doubt or discouragement when we feel as though we are enveloped in the mists of darkness. Do not underestimate what we each can receive from the solemn, sure testimony of the Savior borne by His special witnesses. That witness, received in a spirit of faith, will strengthen us in moments of difficulty and give us a firm footing as we move along the path toward the tree of life. Hold fast to the words of the prophets. Ponder them. Believe them. Trust them. Follow them.

Let me give you an example. A young married friend of mine lost his little daughter in a tragic accident. In the months that followed, with the loneliness, the asking "why," and the sadness, doubt began to enter his life. He told me that he wasn't sure what he believed anymore. I suggested to him that in this difficult time he might want to yield to his doubts a little less and trust the words of the Savior and the Savior's chosen vessels a little more. My friend pored over the scriptures, the promises of the Savior, and the bold, reassuring witness of the living prophets. He held fast to their sure testimony of the Savior when his own seemed to falter. He held fast to the iron rod. With time, the darkness dissipated, the tree came back into view, and he partook of the precious fruit of the Atonement.

SEERS

Next, what is a *seer?* In the Book of Mormon, Ammon explained the role of a seer to King Limhi:

But a seer can know of things which are past, and also of things which are to come, and by them shall all things be revealed, . . . and hidden things shall come to light, and things which are not known shall be made known by them. [Mosiah 8:17]

Look at this beautiful picture [a partial photo of blue water and shoreline]: What do you see? Wouldn't you love to be canoeing in this peaceful setting? Doesn't it look appealing?

What if your view was suddenly enlarged and you saw this [a full photo showing the same water pouring over a waterfall]: The canoe ride would be very different from what you first perceived.

Spiritually, seers see the wider view. They see what we sometimes cannot see. Their words and counsel help us see the larger view. If we heed their counsel, holding fast to the iron rod, we will be safe.

Let me give you an example. President Hinckley has spoken strongly about the blessings of tithing. He speaks frequently to the General Authorities on this subject. He has said:

We can pay our tithing. This is not so much a matter of money as it is a matter of faith. . . .

I urge you, . . . every one of you, to take the Lord at His word in this important matter.[10]

We reiterate the promise of the Lord given anciently through the prophet Malachi that he will open the windows of heaven upon those who are honest with him in the payment of their tithes and offerings, that there shall not be room enough to receive the promised blessings.[11]

In the fall of 2001 three of the Twelve were in Brazil at the same time, and each taught the promises of an honest tithing. A few months later a young college student in São Paulo was put to the test. She was working and going to school. Here are her words, which were shared by President Hinckley:

> *The university in which I studied had a regulation that prohibited the students* [who had not paid all their fees] *from taking tests. . . .*
> *I . . . faced serious financial difficulties. It was a Thursday when I received my salary. When I figured the monthly budget, I noticed that there wouldn't be enough to pay* [both] *my tithing and my university. I would have to choose between them. The bimonthly tests would start the following week, and if I didn't take them I could lose the school year. I felt great agony. . . . My heart ached. I had a painful decision before me, and I didn't know what to decide.*

Through prayer she determined that she would trust in the Lord and in the words of the prophets. On Sunday she paid her tithing. The next day she sought a way to be able to take her tests but could not find a solution. She then explained what happened:

> *The working period was ending when my employer approached and gave the last orders of the day. . . . Suddenly, he halted, and . . . asked, "How is your college?" I was surprised. . . . The only thing I could answer . . . was, "Everything is all right!" He looked thoughtfully at me and bid farewell again. . . .*
> *Suddenly the secretary entered the room, saying that I was a very fortunate person! When I asked her why, she simply answered: "The employer has just said that from today on the company is going to pay fully for your college and your books. Before you leave, stop at my desk and inform me of the costs so that tomorrow I can give you the check."*

The student then explained her feelings:

> *After* [the secretary] *left, crying and feeling very humble, I knelt exactly where I was and thanked the Lord for His generosity. I . . . said to Heavenly Father that He didn't have to bless me so much. I only needed the cost of one month's installment, and the tithing I had paid on Sunday was very small compared to the amount I was receiving! During that prayer the words recorded in Malachi* [and declared so often by the prophets and apostles] *came to my mind: "Prove me now herewith, saith the Lord*

of hosts, if I will not open you the windows of heaven, and pour you out a blessing, that there shall not be room enough to receive it" (Mal. 3:10).[12]

Clouded in the mists of darkness, the decision was difficult; the outcome was unsure. But she held fast to the iron rod. Her faith in the Lord and in the Lord's prophets was confirmed. While all experiences may not be so immediate in their resolution, the promises for those who honestly keep the law of tithing are absolutely certain.

I have heard President Thomas S. Monson say to returned missionaries, "There is one way you will always stay active in the Church—always be honest in your payment of tithing." What a beautiful promise!

REVELATORS

Finally, a *revelator.* "The English word *revelation* is translated from a Greek word *apocalypse*, meaning to make known or uncover."[13] As revelators, the First Presidency and the Quorum of the Twelve Apostles make known the Lord's specific concerns for us and what we need to do to respond. Moreover, with so many choices and decisions available to us, revelators help direct our attention to what is most important in our journey through mortality. They help us focus.

In August 2005 President Hinckley invited us to read the Book of Mormon prior to the end of the year. He helped us focus our discretionary time toward what the Lord would have us do. As often accompanies the invitations of prophets, a promise was included by President Hinckley—a promise that I'm sure is as true today as when he said it in August 2005. He said this:

Without reservation I promise you that if each of you will observe this simple program, regardless of how many times you previously may have read the Book of Mormon, there will come into your lives and into your homes an added measure of the Spirit of the Lord, a strengthened resolution to walk in obedience to His commandments, and a stronger testimony of the living reality of the Son of God.[14]

Were we not blessed just as the prophet promised?

One sister from the Ukraine wrote: "Every morning I asked that the Holy Ghost be my companion so He could enlighten my mind. A miracle occurred: the Book of Mormon was opened to me anew. I received answers to questions I had had for years." A brother from Germany wrote: "Because I studied longer each day, I made connections I had never made before. The Book of Mormon truly is full of testimonies of Jesus Christ. Because of the Spirit I felt, my own testimony of my Redeemer increased."[15]

And how about this comment from a young family in Utah: "We wondered if our four-year-old was even listening [when we read the Book of Mormon], but then one day when asked why his room was so messy, he replied, 'Someone has been plundering in there!'"[16]

Here is another example of the role of a revelator. President Hinckley has strongly counseled you, the young adults of the Church, to pursue as much education as possible. In October general conference he said: "I call your attention to another matter that gives me great concern. In revelation the Lord has mandated that this people get all the education they can. He has been very clear about this."[17]

What is the great concern? Education. Who has been very clear about this? The Lord. Who is revealing this to you? His prophet. And, yes, he is speaking to you.

If you come from a family that has few resources for education, you may be unsure about what this means for you. When you are unsure, hold fast to the iron rod. Trust the words of the prophet! The answers will come.

In some parts of the world, such as in the United States and Europe, it may mean that you need to sell your automobile or live in more humble circumstances in order to stay enrolled or return to school. In other areas of the world the sacrifice may be greater. In some countries the Perpetual Education Fund may be able to help. In almost all cases it will require faith, trusting in the Lord and in the Lord's prophet—holding fast to the iron rod—as you find your way. If you are not sure how to follow the specific counsel of the prophet, pray with all your heart and discuss your concerns with your parents and with your bishop. While it will require patience and faith, I promise you that answers will come and a way will be opened to you.

I have seen answers come to many young people of faith in Latin America. Thousands are holding fast to the iron rod, trusting in President Hinckley, and pursuing their education.

Prophetic direction flows from each member of the First Presidency and the Quorum of the Twelve Apostles, all of whom we sustain as prophets, seers, and revelators. If we had time, we could review the counsel from each of them.

Let me give you an example of counsel from one of the Twelve. Nearly two years ago Elder Dallin H. Oaks addressed you in an evening like we are sharing tonight. You will remember that he caught your attention when he raised the issue of dating rather than "hanging out." He said:

> *My single young friends, we counsel you to channel your associations with the opposite sex into dating patterns that have the potential to mature into marriage, not hanging-out patterns that only have the prospect to mature into team sports like touch football.*[18]

Now, the important question: What did you do following his talk? Did anything change? Elder Henry B. Eyring gave this warning:

> *The failure to take prophetic counsel lessens our power to take inspired counsel in the future. . . .*
>
> *Every time in my life when I have chosen to delay following inspired counsel or decided that I was an exception, I came to know that I had put myself in harm's way. Every time that I have listened to the counsel of prophets, felt it confirmed in prayer, and then followed it, I have found that I moved toward safety.*[19]

How do your actions over the past two years show that you are holding fast to the iron rod? Those who responded positively and promptly to Elder Oaks's counsel surely found that the blessings of heaven followed. Let me read from a letter sent to Church head-quarters from a couple in Arizona more than a year after his talk:

Your remarks have had a lasting impact on our lives. . . .

. . . Your direct and clear counsel helped us realize that dating was an opportunity to get to know one another better and not an immediate commitment to a long-term relationship or marriage.[20]

The result was that they *were* married in May in the Washington D.C. Temple.

I would like to invite my wife, Kathy, who has taught these principles so well to our family, to share her feelings about the importance of the words of the prophets.

REMARKS FROM SISTER KATHY ANDERSEN

My dear brothers and sisters, I had an experience about 20 years ago that made a deep impression on me. We were living in Florida. We had taken our children to the stake center to listen to general conference together. A short time later we received our conference edition of the *Ensign* magazine in the mail. We decided that for family home evening each week we would study one of the conference talks given by a member of the First Presidency or the Quorum of the Twelve Apostles.

Our children were young, but they were old enough to read, and we wanted each member of the family to have a copy of the talks so that we could read and study and mark them together. We didn't have a store in Florida where we could purchase additional *Ensign* maga-zines, so I took the copy that we had received in the mail to our local copy center and made copies of the talks for our family.

When I finished, I took the copies to the cashier, who tabulated the cost of the copies I had made and announced to me that I owed approximately $50. I am embarrassed to say that I felt a little bit sick at my stomach. And I thought, "That is a lot of money to pay to make copies of these talks for our children." Then, brothers and sisters, this thought pierced my heart: "What is it worth to you and your family to have the words of God's prophets?"

I knew then, but I know with even greater certainty now, that it is worth everything to us and to our family. It is worth everything to you and to your future families. Of this I bear testimony in the name of Jesus Christ, amen.

"AS IF FROM MINE OWN MOUTH"

It is a marvelous blessing to be married to a person who has pure and uncompromising faith. I love you, Kathy, and am grateful for you.

In one month we will have the opportunity to participate in a general conference of the Church and hear the messages of the men we have spoken about tonight. General conference is a time to pause from what we are doing, to listen to the Lord's servants, and to prayerfully set our course for the months ahead. Please consider these questions:

- Have I clearly marked general conference on my calendar so that I will be able to listen to each of the sessions available to me?
- How will I prepare myself during this coming month so that I will be spiritually ready to receive the messages?

And, as general conference concludes, we might ask:

- What specific impressions came to me during the conference?
- What necessary changes will I make in my life?

The iron rod *is* the word of God. The scriptures, the words of the living prophets, and the gift of the Holy Ghost are powerful in their ability to keep us safe. Let us hold fast to the words of the prophets. Let us hold fast to the iron rod.

I would like to conclude with an experience we had in March 2000. Sister Andersen and I were invited to attend the temple dedication in Albuquerque, New Mexico. I knew that I would be asked to speak and that my remarks should be brief.

We entered the celestial room dressed in white. President Hinckley sat in the middle chair with a member of the Twelve on his right and with me on his left. As we reverently awaited the first session, I felt a distinct and specific impression that I should adjust the remarks I had prepared. The impression came: "Speak of the keys. Speak of the keys."

I quickly turned to the scriptures to locate the passages that explain the keys of the priesthood being returned to the earth. Then—and I can remember it as if it were yesterday—a powerful spiritual feeling came into my mind and heart. The feeling that burned within me was this: "He who sits next to you holds all the priesthood keys upon the earth. He who sits next to you holds all the priesthood keys upon the earth."

I took a deep breath. I looked over at President Hinckley. I could not deny the powerful manifestation of the Spirit. I thought of this scripture:

> *For his word ye shall receive, as if from mine own mouth. . . .*
>
> *For by doing these things the gates of hell shall not prevail against you; yea, and the Lord God will disperse the powers of darkness from before you, and cause the heavens to shake for your good.* [D&C 21:5–6]

God, our Heavenly Father, lives and loves us. His Only Begotten Son, Jesus Christ, is our Savior. He is resurrected. He lives. Together They appeared to the Prophet Joseph Smith. President Gordon B. Hinckley is the Lord's anointed prophet today, vested with all the priesthood keys upon the earth. I so testify in the name of Jesus Christ, amen.

NOTES

1. See Boyd K. Packer, "Lehi's Dream and You," BYU devotional address, 16 January 2007.

2. See David A. Bednar, "A Reservoir of Living Water," fireside address given at BYU, 4 February 2007.

3. "The Iron Rod," *Hymns*, 1985, no. 274.

4. Bednar, "A Reservoir."

5. Packer, "Lehi's Dream"; emphasis in original.

6. George Q. Cannon, *Gospel Truth*, sel. Jerreld L. Newquist, 2 vols. (Salt Lake City: Deseret Book, 1974), 1:323. Relative to the importance of living prophets, President Wilford Woodruff, the fourth president of the Church, said: "If we had before us every revelation which God ever gave to man; if we had the Book of Enoch; if we had the untranslated plates before us in the English language; if we had the records of the Revelator St. John which are sealed up, and all other revelations, and they were piled up here a hundred feet high, the church and kingdom of God could not grow, in this or any other age of the world, without the living oracles of God" (*The Discourses of Wilford Woodruff*, sel. G. Homer Durham [Salt Lake City: Bookcraft, 1946], 53).

7. Boyd K. Packer, *CR*, October 1996, 5; or "The Twelve Apostles," *Ensign*, November 1996, 6.

8. Boyd K. Packer, *CR*, April 2000, 9; or "The Cloven Tongues of Fire," *Ensign*, May 2000, 9.

9. James E. Faust, *CR*, April 1995, 83; or "Heirs to the Kingdom of God," *Ensign*, May 1995, 63.

10. Gordon B. Hinckley, *CR*, October 1985, 110; or "Let Us Move This Work Forward," *Ensign*, November 1985, 85.

11. Gordon B. Hinckley, *CR*, April 1984, 69; or "The Miracle Made Possible by Faith," *Ensign*, May 1984, 47.

12. Gordon B. Hinckley, *CR*, April 2002, 85–86; or "We Walk by Faith," *Ensign*, May 2002, 73–74.

13. Bible Dictionary, s.v. "revelation," 762.

14. Gordon B. Hinckley, "A Testimony Vibrant and True," *Ensign*, August 2005, 6.

15. Tatyana Vyshemirskaya and Dagmar Leiß, in "Something Remarkable: Testimonies of the Blessings," *Ensign*, December 2006, 17.

16. Buxton family, in "Taking the Challenge," *Ensign*, December 2006, 14.

17. Gordon B. Hinckley, *CR*, September–October 2006, 66–67; or "Rise Up, O Men of God," *Ensign*, November 2006, 60.

18. Dallin H. Oaks, "The Dedication of a Lifetime," CES fireside for young adults, Oakland, California, 1 May 2005.

19. Henry B. Eyring, *CR*, April 1997, 33; or "Finding Safety in Counsel," *Ensign*, May 1997, 25.

20. Letter dated 19 November 2006.

Precious Precepts of Truth

———◆———

William A. Barrett

What a blessing it is to be here at BYU—to sing, study, and worship under the light of the restored gospel and to be guided by prophets, seers, and revelators! I am deeply grateful for that, and grateful today to be surrounded by superb faculty, extraordinary students, parents, friends, and family—including my brothers Robert and Wayne Barrett, both of whom are also professors here at BYU.

I was privileged to teach a Book of Mormon class last semester, which I count as one of the greatest experiences I have had in the 20 years I've been here at BYU. While grading a student's paper from that class, I was prompted with some thoughts that I would like to share with you here today.

"NEARER TO GOD"

Joseph Smith said:

I told the brethren that the Book of Mormon was the most correct of any book on earth, and the keystone of our religion, and a man would get nearer to God by abiding by its precepts, than by any other book.[1]

———

William A. Barrett was a BYU professor of computer science when this devotional address was given on 6 March 2007. © *Brigham Young University.*

Since I am, by nature, an experimental scientist, I wanted to see if that statement was true. So I performed "an experiment upon [the] words."[2] To conduct the experiment, I kept a daily Book of Mormon journal. Each morning I would read and ponder a verse and then write about it—sometimes only part of a verse, because the Book of Mormon is so rich. Sometimes I would write a paragraph and sometimes two to three pages. It took me several handwritten journals and five years to get through 2 Nephi. The meaning of many verses would not yield themselves to a single reading—such as those in the Isaiah chapters. Often, multiple prayerful readings and ponderings were necessary, following which often came the sweet, tutoring influence of the Spirit as I would write. And I would find myself learning from what was being written.[3] I would also try to teach and apply what I read and what I wrote.

What was the result of this experiment? Not only did it get me nearer to God, but the catalyzing influence of the Book of Mormon taught me to listen to and learn from the Spirit and to treasure the precious precepts and freshwater doctrine that flow unimpeded from its pages. It has also cultivated a love for the Book of Mormon that will never fade. I read from it every day. In short, I'm hooked!

"PRECEPT UPON PRECEPT"

I remember reading one morning the words of Nephi found in 2 Nephi 28:30, where Nephi wrote:

For behold, thus saith the Lord God: I will give unto the children of men line upon line, precept upon precept, here a little and there a little; and blessed are those who hearken unto my precepts, and lend an ear unto my counsel, for they shall learn wisdom; for unto him that receiveth I will give more; and from them that shall say, We have enough, from them shall be taken away even that which they have.[4]

And I wrote the following:

Our ever-so-generous Heavenly Father does not penuriously withhold precious precepts from us. He is not stingy but is giving. But He does not want to drown us in doctrine or give us more than we can handle. Rather, He gives us "line upon line, precept upon precept, here a little and there a little," measuring carefully what we can handle, what we can assimilate, making sure that we absorb and respond to that which we have been given before pouring more upon us. What a gracious and kind Heavenly Father we have!

My writing prompted me to ask the question I began with: Why and how are we blessed when we hearken to His precepts and lend an ear to His counsel? And the answers began to flow.

First, our Father's divine laws are packaged in precious precepts taught by His Son. For example, "Blessed are the peacemakers, for they shall be called the children of God."[5] And those who make peace with God, with their neighbor, and with themselves *are* blessed—with an increased measure of the Spirit in their lives, with happiness, and with greater knowledge and purpose. Thus, "when we obtain any blessing from God, it is by obedience to that law upon which it is predicated."[6] The law, in this particular example, is to live in peace. The precept is that blessings come from living the law. *The perceptive come to learn and love the predicates of the precepts.*

A motivating precept for those at BYU might be: "Whatever principle of intelligence we attain unto in this life, it will rise with us in the resurrection."[7] Perhaps this precept can be generalized: Whatever principle of testimony, devotion, and worthiness I attain unto before my mission will rise with me in the mission field. Whatever principle of obedience, diligence, and selfless service I attain unto during my mission will rise with me when I return. Whatever principle of kindness, gentleness, and charity I attain unto before marriage will rise with me in my family life. And maybe even, for us here now: Whatever measure of work, effort, and understanding I attain unto during this semester will rise with me in finals week.

A second reason why we are blessed when we hearken to His precepts and lend an ear to His counsel is that those who receive and act on the precepts of God receive more. And, since each precept brings with it attendant blessings, receiving more precepts brings more blessings.[8] Thus to the list of precious precepts we may add the *precept of perpetuation*, since one precept, acted upon, begets another. This is not quite the precept of *perpetual precepts*, since it is incumbent upon us to act, but it is close.

Third, in addition to the blessings attached to a given precept, and the promise of more to come, there is a bonus blessing. That is that the compounding and knitting together of precious precepts yields compounded blessings, just as with compounded interest. The quantum mechanics of both precepts and blessings rubbing against each other also produce a quantum leap in gratitude and joy, in faith and humility, and in the ability to perceive the higher-level precepts that flow from the interleaving of precept with precept and blessing with blessing. Such weaving produces genuine wisdom and, when woven by the Lord, becomes part of the tapestry of our lives.

So in this verse *more* really does mean more—more than we have room to receive, because such precepts and blessing are forever growing so that we can forever grow, because that too is woven into the fabric of our divine nature. Thus when we say "we've had enough," we cease to grow and begin to shrink from the endowment attendant to our being sons and daughters of God. Such shrinking not only curtails growth but causes a spiraling decline and unraveling of the compounded precepts and blessings we once enjoyed. In such shrinking I do not believe that our kind Father snatches back that which we have with anger or disgust or retribution, for His hand is ever "stretched out still," but I do believe His heart breaks a little, and often a lot, when we are not willing to receive that which we might have received.[9] And being an all-wise Heavenly Father, He will not burden us with precepts and blessings we are not prepared to receive. As the Master Gardener, He *titrates the soil of our soul* in a mercifully measured way, "line upon line, precept upon precept, here a little and there a little," not because He is not giving—quite the opposite. It is so that little by little we can one day receive all that He has.[10] Because His love for us is perfect, He will not drown us with perfect precepts or blessings if we are not prepared to receive them—*whether they are being dispensed with an eyedropper or a fire hose.*

LEARNING PRECEPTS FROM LIFE'S EXPERIENCES

Life in general is a grand experiment in learning correct precepts. Allow me to illustrate this with an example from my childhood. When I was 10 years old, I was out in the country at my grandmother's house sledding with my two brothers on New Year's Day. It was a beautiful Currier and Ives setting as we stood at the top of the hill gazing down over the pasture covered in white with a beautiful, clear stream angling across the bottom. As in a Norman Rockwell painting, I hopped on my Flexible Flyer and told my brother Wayne to hop on top. My artistic brother, Robert, remained at the top of the hill to capture the magic moment in his memory as down the hill we went. As we leveled out at the base of the hill, I performed the hard-rudder-right maneuver to avoid the impending stream. The sled disregarded my instructions, and into the icy stream we went.

Undaunted, we dragged ourselves back into the house, took a hot bath, put on some warm, dry clothes, and went out again. As we approached the top of the hill again, I hopped on the sled and invited my older but now somewhat more cautious brother to hop on board. I thought to myself, "This really should have worked." And down we went again. But as we neared the stream, age gave way to discretion and, discretion being the better part of valor, my older brother bailed on me. (After all, he is a mathematician, and he had a "proof by example.") As for me—and, as you might suspect—the flexible steering mechanism again failed me, and again I plummeted into the icy stream. Alone. However, this time a stick from the brush went through my cheek, and we had to go find someone to sew it up, or else I would have been out there a third time. Even though it "really should have worked," the laws of physics said otherwise. But perhaps some useful precepts can be drawn—even from failed experiments.

For one, overwhelming momentum overrides small course corrections: a vital lesson to remember in sledding as well as in personal relationships when you are alone with someone late at night—a potential slippery slope and a pattern for heartache; a reminder that if we fail to follow divinely established patterns of conduct and morality, as taught by living prophets, the momentum of the moment may inflict mortal wounds, robbing us of virtue, happiness, and peace of mind. Small course corrections each week as we partake of the sacrament and each morning and night as we kneel before our Heavenly Father, remembering Him who was wounded for our transgressions, will prevent us from taking on the debilitating wounds that delay or destroy our scheduled patterns of personal progress and our future rendezvous with happiness. Such spiritual corrections are vital because the adversary also has patterns and plans by which he tries to destroy us—patterns that fuel the vain and foolish precepts of men. But, for us, a better pattern is: Don't be alone with someone late at night. Instead, allow small course corrections to guide your momentum rather than the other way around. Such careful thinking and behavior, if practiced daily and exercised thoughtfully, will allow us to one day steer our immortal souls to "the right hand of God in the kingdom of heaven."[11]

THE GOSPEL EMBRACES ALL TRUE PRECEPTS

Clearly, discovering *all* true precepts from personal experience can be hazardous. As a practical matter, you have to be willing to learn from others, since there isn't time to perform all of the experiments or make all of the mistakes yourself. This is why the restored gospel is placed within our grasp and why we are here at BYU. Discovering true precepts in faith, in science, in the arts, in great literature, or in whatever course of study is a great adventure. I am confident that our Father in Heaven does not differentiate true precepts based on their perceived domain.

Brigham Young taught:

Our religion is simply the truth. It is all said in this one expression—it embraces all truth, wherever found, in all the works of God and man that are visible or invisible to mortal eye.[12]

Yet, having said that, we must still labor for and search for true precepts like the woman who, if she lost a piece of silver, would "light a candle, and sweep the house, and seek diligently till she find it."[13] Sometimes students wring their hands, cross their fingers, and hope that their answer to a problem is right, even when the answer is hollow or not well thought out. Such flawed thinking can also lead to bad results when it comes to life's real problems regarding relationships, finances, or other personal choices. In contrast, I am convinced that those who really love the truth care more about finding correct answers and about what is really right than they care about vacuous answers that are expedient or acceptable. The world already offers too many solutions of this kind. Life's real reward for genuine solutions to real problems is an exclamation point, not a check mark!

Henry Eyring, a noted chemist and father to Elder Henry B. Eyring, stated:

> *The significant thing about a scientist is this: he simply expects the truth to prevail because it* is *the truth. He doesn't work very much on the reactions of the heart. In science, the thing* is, *and its being so is something one cannot resent. If a thing is wrong, nothing can save it, and if it is right, it cannot help succeeding.*[14]

Brigham Young stated that "truth is calculated to sustain itself; it is based upon eternal facts and will endure, while all else will sooner or later perish."[15]

So, whether in the lab, in the classroom, or in the scriptures, we search for true principles and precepts with dogged determination. Whether in sledding or in science, we search for answers with tenacity and faith that we will find a solution.

I've often told my own children that my idea of heaven is being trapped in a room with a handful of bright students and some problems that are so difficult you don't even know how to articulate them. They often respond by saying, "Hmmm, that kind of sounds like the other place to me."

But when we have paid the price, needed answers to tough problems come as sudden bursts of ideas and intelligence, bringing elegant, high-level insights—the unmistakable signature of the Spirit—but in His own time and in His own way. The best ideas always come from the Spirit. The rest we just labor and muddle over and try to make work. The following examples illustrate some of our current muddling:

1. In computer graphics we create models of real-world objects so that they can be animated and placed in movies. In our lab we do this by extracting points from photographs and then connecting the dots to describe the object geometry. By assigning the right color to these points, a realistic model is created. Just as correctly connecting points here result in a believable model, so connecting the "points" of true precepts helps us to see "things as they really are, and . . . as they really will be."[16]

2. With about 2.5 billion document images in the granite mountain vault, automated handwriting recognition has become an important problem in family history because it helps us more efficiently identify names and information for temple work. We approach this problem using pattern-recognition algorithms coupled with human training. Finding and recognizing ancestors not only helps us find ourselves but also helps us recognize the unfolding patterns and precepts in our own lives.

3. Our recent research in the medical domain makes use of globally optimal algorithms to accurately extract anatomy from medical scans. Just as a global understanding of object properties in medical imaging allows proper and timely diagnosis, so seeing our own inner parts through the lens of precious precepts from the restored gospel will help us not only see who we currently are but what we ultimately must become.

As we try to understand secular knowledge, we do the best we can—the best we can surmise with what we know. But it changes. Keep that in mind as you learn. We don't repudiate ideas just because they are from men, but, as we muddle along, we winnow and sift for the truth, weighing what we learn carefully in the balance of restored truth and subjecting it to the light of the restored gospel. If a precept is true, it fits within the gospel framework. It is a piece of the puzzle. And if we will search and study by faith, the spiritual dimensions of all the precepts that we learn will become more evident to us, and thereby enhance our faith.

PRECEPTS OF GOD VERSUS PRECEPTS OF MEN

Nephi warned us about the precepts of men that will prevail in our day. He used phrases such as "contend one with another"; "eat, drink, and be merry"; "lie a little"; and "take . . . advantage of [others]." He described these as "false and vain and foolish doctrines."[17] Thus another instructive experiment that enhances spiritual knowledge is to identify a precept of men and then discover the contrasting precept of God, or vice versa. For example:

- The precepts of men tell us that we must see before we can believe. Nephi teaches us that we must believe before we can see.[18]
- The precepts of men teach that resources are scarce—that you must get *all* you can *while* you can. Scriptural precepts teach us that "there is enough and to spare."[19]
- Men's precepts urge a makeover in the image of the world. Alma urges a makeover in the image of God.[20]
- Men teach to believe in nothing; hope for nothing; endure nothing; and "live without God in the world."[21] But we believe all things, hope all things, endure all things, and find abundant life through Him.[22]
- Men's ways are to hide or cover sins because "no one will know."[23] God's way is for us to "confess . . . and forsake" sins so that He *can* "remember them no more."[24]
- The precepts of men speak of being beaten "with a few stripes" but ultimately being saved without ever having to change, without ever overcoming self or the world, without ever changing our hearts or feeling the peace and joy of repentance and forgiveness—without ever becoming like Him.[25] But by accepting our Savior's stripes for

us[26] and repenting "in the depths of humility,"[27] we can overcome ourselves and the world.[28]

The precepts of men will ultimately fail. The precepts of God will endure forever.[29]

PRECEPTS THAT GET US NEARER TO GOD

A year or so ago I conducted another experiment. I began to write down a list of precepts that I felt were unique to the Book of Mormon. Several hours and several pages later I knew that I had only just begun. Allow me to close where I began, by sharing a few of the precepts from the Book of Mormon that have become precious, personal precepts to me and that get me nearer to God.

- Nephi's "I will go and do"[30] reminds us that it is in the *going* and *doing* that we not only find that the Lord provides a way but we find *the way* itself. And in following that way we also find ourselves drawing nearer to Him.
- Lehi's "opposition in all things"[31] helps me understand and cope with life's triumphs and tragedies. It helps me remember that I chose to choose and that is why I am here. And it helps me remember, too, that our Savior had agency too but gave it away for you and for me, allowing His will to be swallowed up in the will of the Father as He suffered, bled, and died for me. And that I can never forget. And it draws me nearer to Him.
- Jacob's "infinite atonement"[32] brings me nearer to God because it lets me know that I can be forgiven and become clean again and have my guilt swept away. It draws me nearer to God because it helps me understand how very comprehensive the *infinite* Atonement of Jesus Christ truly is as He suffered for every broken bone and every broken heart. It helps me understand that His *infinite* suffering was born out of His *infinite* love for you and for me and that we are of *infinite* worth because an *infinite* price was paid for us!

- Saved by grace, "after all we can do"[33] reminds me that some of the most precious precepts are found in pondering the "parentheticals."

- From cover to cover, the Book of Mormon teaches me that Jesus Christ is and was the long-promised Messiah, the Holy One of Israel, our Savior and Redeemer, the Lamb of God, the Son of God.[34] Understanding His premortal identity, His long-suffering with the children of Israel, and the very personal love He showed to the Nephites helps me remember that He who has "graven [us] upon the palms of [His] hands"[35] cannot forget us but is in this for the long haul. And seeing His endurance helps me endure a little longer too.

- And, finally, enduring to the end[36] gets me nearer to Him—because it is at the end I will find Him!

ABIDING IN HIM—THE ONLY TRUE PRECEPT

It is both the reading and abiding that gets us nearer to God, and that allows us to accept His invitation to come unto Him and be saved because we cannot be saved in ignorance. We cannot receive all that our Father has without understanding all that He is and does. And so we perform the ultimate experiment by planting the seed in our own hearts. We nourish it with patience and faith until it becomes "a tree, springing up in [us] unto everlasting life,"[37] throwing out a branch of charity here and virtue there and overcoming the natural man in the process. Through His incomparable Atonement, Christ offers to us the fruit of the tree if we will fall down and partake of it.[38] And if we do, then "when he shall appear we shall be like him, for we shall see him as he is."[39] We will not only get nearer to Him spiritually but nearer to being like Him, and you can't get any nearer than that.

Elder Holland taught that to "abide" means "'to remain, to stay' . . . but stay *forever.*"[40] If we will abide in these precepts, they will abide in us. More important, if we will abide in these precepts, we will abide in Him whose precepts these are, and *He* will abide in us[41]—"permanently, unyieldingly, steadfastly, [and] forever."[42]

Thus Christ, of whom the Book of Mormon bears witness, is the ultimate precept. It is of Him that our lives must bear witness as we accept His invitation to come unto Him and become like Him.[43] And it is of Him and His living reality that I bear witness. In the name of Jesus Christ, amen.

NOTES

1. *HC* 4:461.

2. Alma 32:27.

3. See A. Theodore Tuttle, "Teaching the Word to the Rising Generation," address to religious educators, 10 July 1970, BYU; full talk printed in *Charge to Religious Educators*, 2d ed. (Salt Lake City: The Church of Jesus Christ of Latter-day Saints, 1982), 129–32.

4. 2 Nephi 28:30; emphasis added.

5. Matthew 5:9; see also 3 Nephi 12:9.

6. D&C 130:21.

7. D&C 130:18.

8. See Alma 12:10.

9. See D&C 88:33.

10. See D&C 84:38.

11. Helaman 3:30.

12. *JD* 10:251.

13. Luke 15:8.

14. Henry Eyring, *Reflections of a Scientist* (Salt Lake City: Deseret Book, 1983), 7; emphasis in original.

15. *JD* 14:115.

16. Jacob 4:13.

17. 2 Nephi 28:4–9.

18. See 1 Nephi 4:6, 11:1.

19. D&C 104:17; see also D&C 49:19.

20. See Alma 5:14.

21. Mosiah 27:31.

22. See Articles of Faith 1:13; also John 10:10.

23. See D&C 121:37, Isaiah 29:15, 2 Nephi 28:9, Luke 12:3, D&C 1:3.

24. D&C 58:43 and 42.

25. 2 Nephi 28:8.

26. See Isaiah 53:5.

27. 2 Nephi 9:42, Mosiah 4:11.

28. See D&C 63:47, 64:2.

29. See Moroni 7:46–47.

30. 1 Nephi 3:7.

31. 2 Nephi 2:11; see also verse 15.

32. 2 Nephi 9:7.

33. 2 Nephi 25:23.

34. See 1 Nephi 10:4, 13:40, 22:12; 2 Nephi 1:10; Mosiah 3:8; Helaman 14:12.

35. 1 Nephi 21:16.

36. See 2 Nephi 31:20.

37. Alma 33:23; see also Alma 32:33, 40–41.

38. See 1 Nephi 8:30.

39. Moroni 7:48, 1 John 3:2; see also Ephesians 4:13.

40. Jeffrey R. Holland, "Abide in Me," *Ensign,* May 2004, 32; emphasis in original.

41. See John 15:4.

42. Holland, "Abide," 32.

43. See 3 Nephi 27:27, Moroni 10:32.

Be a Missionary All Your Life

Quentin L. Cook

I consider it a great privilege and responsibility to be given this opportunity to speak to you. After I received this assignment from the First Presidency, I asked President Samuelson what I should talk about.

He said, "You are the executive director of the Missionary Department. Why don't you talk about missionary work?"

I have decided to follow his counsel.

You are a magnificent sight! Many of you are recently returned from full-time missions. Many of you will soon be full-time missionaries. I hope all of you are committed to being lifelong missionaries.

Some feel this is a difficult time to do missionary work. A Gallup Poll three weeks ago found 46 percent of Americans view "Mormons" unfavorably, 11 percent don't know who we are, and 18 percent think of polygamy when our name is mentioned.[1]

Let's put this in perspective. In 1842 John Wentworth, editor of the *Chicago Democrat*, wrote to Joseph Smith requesting information about the Church. The Church had been organized 12 years earlier

Quentin L. Cook was a member of the First Quorum of the Seventy of The Church of Jesus Christ of Latter-day Saints when this devotional address was given on 13 March 2007. © *Intellectual Reserve, Inc.*

and had just over 20,000 members. The Prophet Joseph replied and concluded his response by using the Standard of Truth as a preface to what we know today as the Thirteen Articles of Faith.

As I tour missions, many missionaries memorize the Standard of Truth. It conveys in a concise way what must be accomplished. As I recite it, I invite those of you who know it to say it with me:

No unhallowed hand can stop the work from progressing; persecutions may rage, mobs may combine, armies may assemble, calumny may defame, but the truth of God will go forth boldly, nobly, and independent, till it has penetrated every continent, visited every clime, swept every country, and sounded in every ear, till the purposes of God shall be accomplished, and the Great Jehovah shall say the work is done.[2]

Who is going to help achieve this? You and your generation!

I believe with all of my heart that we are on the threshold of the most significant missionary success to date. Let me share two accounts of those who have been converted in the recent past.

The conversion of Jordan Vajda, a fine young man who had been a Catholic priest, is instructive. When he was in grade school he had Latter-day Saint friends in his class who shared with him their love of the gospel. At age 13 he found an offer from the Church for a free Book of Mormon. He sent for it, and two sister missionaries responded. They were surprised that he was only 13 and had requested the Book of Mormon. He was impressed with what they taught and what he felt, but after discussions with his family, he decided to become a priest in the Catholic Church. As he prepared to be a priest, he remained interested in The Church of Jesus Christ of Latter-day Saints.

He studied at the Graduate Theological Union in Berkeley, California. He became acquainted with many who take the position we are not Christians, but he also associated with the students at the Latter-day Saint institute of religion at Berkeley. He decided to write a master's thesis on why certain people maintain that we are not Christians. Two of the issues he addressed in his master's thesis were:

1. The nature of God and our belief that God the Father and His Son Jesus Christ are the two separate individuals the Prophet Joseph beheld in the First Vision.

2. Exaltation and our belief in eternal progression—that we can progress to live with and be like God.

He compared these doctrinal issues with Pre–Nicene Creed early Christian writers and determined that there was significant support for the position of the Church of Jesus Christ. He concluded in his master's thesis, which has since been published by the Foundation for Ancient Research and Mormon Studies:

> *Ironically, those who would excoriate Mormons for believing in the doctrine of exaltation actually agree with them that the early church experienced a "great apostasy" on fundamental doctrinal questions.*[3]

This was primarily an academic pursuit. He became a priest in the Dominican order and had assignments in Arizona and then at the University of Washington. There he came in contact with our missionaries.

After being taught by missionaries and praying sincerely, he received inspiration that he should resign as a Catholic priest and be baptized and confirmed into the Church of Jesus Christ. His letter of resignation expressed his love and appreciation for the Catholic Church and then stated:

> *But why am I doing what I am doing? To put it most simply: I have found a fuller truth and goodness and beauty in The Church of Jesus Christ of Latter-day Saints. After years of study and reflection, I have come to believe that the LDS Church is the only true and living Church of Jesus Christ, guided and led by living apostles and prophets.*
>
> *I believe that Joseph Smith is a prophet of God, called and ordained for this, the dispensation of the fullness of times. I love the Book of Mormon; I believe it to be the word of God for us in these latter days.*
>
> *I can no longer deny my feelings, my heart, my conscience. I cannot deny the confirming witness of the Holy Ghost which has come after much*

prayer and soul-searching. At this point in my life, at this moment, as I look forward to and prepare for my convert baptism, I have found a happiness greater than I ever imagined possible.[4]

This good man is completely active in the Church, has been to the temple, teaches the Gospel Doctrine class in his ward, and has a management position in a hospital in Seattle.

The gospel truly changes people's lives. Last month I met the missionaries who taught a family of five in South Carolina last year. The father of this wonderful African-American family was born and raised in Newark, New Jersey. His father had abandoned his mother when he was very young. He said his "angel mother" worked hard every day of her life to keep them from being homeless. He cannot remember one fun day as a child or as a teenager. He stated, "Other than the love of my mother, I felt very much alone in this world." He served in the navy on the aircraft carrier *Kitty Hawk*, where he learned discipline, organization, and order. He subsequently met and married his sweetheart, and they have three children. They came in contact with the missionaries, and he subsequently wrote:

The missionaries taught us to pray. They taught us about the Restoration. They taught us about revelation and truth. As they bore their testimonies, my heart became softened and I saw in their eyes the truth of what they said. In my whole life I have never seen such sincerity and love. On May 5, 2006, my family was baptized into The Church of Jesus Christ of Latter-day Saints.

Now I really do believe that I have found my place in this world.[5]

He has received the Melchizedek Priesthood, he baptized his eight-year-old daughter two weeks ago, and the family is planning on going to the temple this May to be sealed for time and all eternity.

Listen carefully to the requirements for baptism as set forth in D&C 20:37:

All those who humble themselves before God, and desire to be baptized, and come forth with broken hearts and contrite spirits, and witness before the church that they have truly repented of all their sins, and are willing to take upon them the name of Jesus Christ, having a determination to serve him to the end, and truly manifest by their works that they have received of the Spirit of Christ unto the remission of their sins, shall be received by baptism into his church.

When you think of the two accounts I recited and realize that there were over 270,000 wonderful converts who met the requirements for baptism last year, you get some idea of the significance of missionary work.

These two accounts emphasize the great joy that comes into the lives of new converts.

People all over the world are seeking permanent happiness. The prominent magazine *The Economist*, in its holiday double issue, featured "happiness" on its cover and as its lead story. In one article it noted that increased national economic success had not increased happiness. "Happiness . . . has hardly changed over 50 years. . . . Rich countries do not get happier as they get richer."[6]

Happiness has little to do with material wealth. Nor does permanent happiness come from entertainment or fun and games. Instead of being diversions from an otherwise productive life, these pursuits have become all-consuming to many people.

The lead article on happiness in *The Economist* quoted Adam Smith, the father of capitalism, as questioning: "How many people ruin themselves by laying out money on trinkets of frivolous utility?"[7]

Unfortunately, much of what is available today is not just frivolous but also morally reprehensible.

Contrast this with those who prepare for baptism with a broken heart and a contrite spirit.

We all face problems and challenges. The rain falls on the just and the unjust, but those who accept the gospel and live righteously have a wonderful promise in D&C 59:23: "But learn that he who doeth the works of righteousness shall receive his reward, even peace in this world, and eternal life in the world to come."

Peace in this life does not come from merely pursuing worldly objectives. Eternal life, especially exaltation, does not come from pursuing merely worldly objectives.

Our challenge is to share the joyous, eternally significant gospel with our brothers and sisters so they can find peace and happiness and exaltation.

With this in mind, how can we be effective missionaries?

First: Be a missionary all your life.

President David O. McKay taught that every member is a missionary, and it is as true today as when it was first declared.

President Gordon B. Hinckley has said it this way: "Great is our work, tremendous is our responsibility in helping to find those to teach. The Lord has laid upon us a mandate to teach the gospel to every creature."[8]

The Prophet Joseph Smith declared, "After all that has been said, the greatest and most important duty is to preach the Gospel."[9]

Second: Overcome feelings of hesitancy or inadequacy.

The account of the first missionary to serve outside of North America in this dispensation is inspiring.

In June of 1837, in the Kirtland Temple, the Prophet Joseph Smith whispered to Heber C. Kimball that "the Spirit of the Lord" had spoken that Heber should "go to England and proclaim my Gospel, and open the door of salvation to that nation."[10]

At the time Heber C. Kimball was 36 years old. He had been a member of the Church for five years and an Apostle for two years. He had a wife and small children, and he was the first missionary called to serve outside of North America.

A financial panic had swept over the country and the Church in 1837. It was not an auspicious time for Joseph or Heber to commence such a project. But, as Joseph said, "the Spirit of the Lord" had directed the action.

Heber recorded his reaction: "O, Lord, I am a man of stammering tongue, and altogether unfit for such a work; how can I go to preach in that land."[11]

Almost everyone who attempts missionary work feels inadequate in some way. The idea of such a mission was almost more than Heber could bear, but his faith and obedience prevailed. He stated:

> However, all these considerations did not deter me from the path of duty; the moment I understood the will of my Heavenly Father, I felt a determination to go at all hazards, believing that He would support me by His almighty power, and endow me with every qualification that I needed; . . . I felt that the cause of truth, the Gospel of Christ, outweighed every other consideration.[12]

Just think of the challenge of being a missionary and opening a new country without members, church buildings, a mission home, or any funds.

Despite these feelings of inadequacy, Elder Kimball worked hard and was very humble. He and his companions were very successful.

Third: Do not be discouraged because missionary work is hard.

The New Testament tells of the Apostle Paul's visit to Athens. Paul wanted to proclaim the message of the resurrected Christ. Certain philosophers invited Paul to Mars Hill. Acts 17:21, speaking of Paul's audience, states: "For all the Athenians and strangers which were there spent their time in nothing else, but either to tell, or to hear some new thing."

Doesn't that sound like the world we live in now? When the Athenians realized that Paul was speaking of the risen Savior, some of them mocked him, and the more polite but still not interested said, in verse 32, "We will hear thee again of this matter." The situation in our own day is not a lot different. Missionaries experience this kind of rejection every day.

Elder Jeffrey R. Holland of the Quorum of the Twelve, in speaking about how hard missionary work is and has been, said:

I am convinced that missionary work is not easy because salvation is not a cheap experience. Salvation never was easy. We are The Church of Jesus Christ, this is the truth, and He is our Great Eternal Head. How could we believe it would be easy for us when it was never, ever easy for Him?[13]

Fourth: Be a good example and take every opportunity to share the gospel.

Paul counseled Timothy, "Be thou an example of the believers, in word, in conversation, in charity, in spirit, in faith, in purity."[14] It is not enough to preach the gospel. One must also live the gospel. Very often people are receptive to being taught because they have had a positive experience with a Church member.

I know one BYU graduate who is a great example, loves people, loves the Lord, and has a great desire to be everyone's friend and share the gospel.

He points out that there is a mirror quality to conversation. If we talk about the weather, people respond by talking about the weather. If we talk about sports, they respond by talking about sports. This friend says he asks people he meets about their school and listens intently. After they respond by asking him about his school, he tells them about BYU and then shares his testimony of the gospel. Then, in a positive way, he offers to let them learn more from the missionaries. He has been very successful in sharing the gospel. He has also remained on excellent terms with his friends who do not respond to his challenge because he genuinely loves them and is interested in them.

One sister in France who is a great missionary talks every day about the joy she receives in teaching Primary children and ends up having many gospel conversations and many referrals for the missionaries.

Elder Clayton M. Christensen, who is a professor at Harvard Business School and an Area Seventy, indicated:

I have learned to use terms that associate me with Mormonism in my conversations—comments about my mission to Korea, my children's

*missions, my assignments in the Church, my having attended Brigham
Young University, and so on. These comments open the door for a conversation
about the Church. Most who notice that I have opened this door choose
not to walk through it. A few do, however, usually saying, "So you're a
Mormon?" I then ask if they'd like to learn more about us.*[15]

The First Presidency and Quorum of the Twelve are the missionary committee of the Church and oversee all aspects of missionary work. President Hinckley became president of the Church 12 years ago yesterday—March 12, 1995. Under his prophetic guidance a great deal has been accomplished. Let me give you some numbers describing what has happened during those 12 years:

• Approximately 387,750 missionaries have entered the mission field, which represents almost 40 percent of the missionaries who have ever served in this dispensation.
• About 3,400,000 converts have been baptized, which is the equivalent of more than one-fourth of the total current membership of the Church.
• The total number of missions in the Church has increased from 303 to 347.
• The number of converts increased by almost 30,000 in 2006.
• Retention as measured by sacrament meeting attendance, priesthood ordinations, and tithing faithfulness has increased significantly.

I am very enthusiastic about where we are at this time in missionary work. But, as President Hinckley always counsels the Brethren, "We can still do better."

Preach My Gospel: A Guide to Missionary Service was first introduced in October 2004. President Hinckley commenced this effort in an address to all General Authorities. He called for the missionaries to learn the doctrine and teach the principles by the Spirit in their own words and avoid rote recitations of the discussions. The First Presidency subsequently "raised the bar" on missionary worthiness standards and instructed the Missionary Executive Council to bring forth the new guide to missionary service.

Every member of the First Presidency and Quorum of the Twelve participated to a significant degree. The Missionary Executive Council, under the direction of Elder M. Russell Ballard, and the Missionary Department were inspired in their efforts. It literally felt like the windows of heaven were opened and the Lord's inspiration poured out to bring forth this great resource.

I was deeply touched when President Boyd K. Packer, acting president of the Quorum of Twelve, speaking of *Preach My Gospel*, said, "It was designed beyond the veil and put together here."[16]

Over 1.4 million copies of *Preach My Gospel* have been acquired by members of the Church. I hope you will all become familiar with this great missionary guide. It will help strengthen you to live worthily to receive sacred temple ordinances. For you young men, it will help prepare you for mission service. For you sisters, it will help you apply doctrine in a future role as a wife or mother, and, if you choose to serve a full-time mission, you will be prepared to preach the gospel.[17]

There are great blessings, including eternal joy, in helping to bring souls unto Christ.[18]

Among the blessings of being a full-time missionary are the lifelong relationships you develop with missionary companions. Let me share one account with you that will help those of you who have not served missions to understand this better. This is from a letter a junior companion wrote to his senior companion who had trained him 33 years earlier. I quote in part:

> *I want you to know how much you have meant to me as I have often thought of you over the years since we served together 33 years ago. You have been one of the guiding influences in my life.*
>
> *I appreciated you keeping all the mission rules. . . .*
>
> *I remember a particularly cold and rainy day. It was about a half hour before the time to go back to the apartment. It had been raining all day, and I was wet and tired. We had stopped our bikes on the corner of an intersection. . . . We had done everything on the list we had prepared that morning;*

there was nothing else to be done. You looked at your watch, which showed a half hour left in our day. Then you looked over at me. I knew what you were thinking. I knew you were trying to decide whether or not to go home. After all, we were both wet, and we were far from our apartment. I tried to look as cold and as tired as I possibly could in the hopes that I could sway you in your decision.

"Let's knock on the doors of the houses on this street," you said. With that, we spent one more half hour in the rain and cold. And with that, you taught a new missionary what it meant to keep the mission rules. . . .

From that moment on, when I wanted to go home early I didn't! The blessings earned in those last few minutes of every day resulted in at least two conversions that I had while laboring later in my mission. I think it might be appropriate for you to list me *among your converts. I love you, Elder.*[19]

Other blessings of serving a mission are having the opportunity of being nurtured under the guidance of a mission president who has been called by inspiration; developing gospel knowledge and study habits that will serve you well throughout your life; and achieving the enormous strength that comes from doing something that is very challenging. Having increased faith in the Lord Jesus Christ and the restoration of His gospel is a most significant blessing.

But the most important reason for going on a mission and being committed to missionary work throughout your life is because it is doctrinally what the Savior has asked us to do.

The last chapters of Matthew, Mark, and Luke; the last two chapters of John; and the first eight verses of Acts contain the only New Testament accounts of the risen Christ. Suppose for a minute that you had been a disciple of the Savior during His life here on earth. Suppose you had believed His teachings. Can you imagine how wonderful it would have been to actually behold the risen Lord? Can you imagine how attentive you would have been to His message?

There may have been other things the risen Lord taught that were not recorded, but the overwhelming message in each of the accounts was to preach His gospel.

The next-to-last verse in Matthew is a good example: "Go ye therefore, and teach all nations, baptizing them in the name of the Father, and of the Son, and of the Holy Ghost."[20]

We could go to almost any part of the Book of Mormon for the same message. Think of Alma and his lifelong commitment to bring souls unto repentance even when he was the head of state.

What about missionary work in this dispensation?

I am particularly impressed with section 112 of the Doctrine and Covenants. It was the only revelation recorded in the Doctrine and Covenants for 1837, and it was received on the same day the gospel was first publicly preached in England—which was the first time the gospel was preached outside of North America (July 23, 1837). Elder Kimball's wife, Vilate, sent him a letter that summer in 1837. She wrote, in part:

> *I know not where to begin to write or what to say to you first for the multitude of thoughts that rush upon my mind. You see I have filled a good part of my sheet with a revelation which I thought would be more interesting to you than anything else I could write. I copied it from Elder [Thomas] Marsh's book as he wrote it from Joseph's mouth.*[21]

There is much that could be said about section 112, but verse 21 is particularly significant for those preparing to serve missions. It states:

> *And again, I say unto you, that whosoever ye shall send in my name, by the voice of your brethren, the Twelve, duly recommended and authorized by you, shall have power to open the door of my kingdom unto any nation whithersoever ye shall send them.*

That describes our missionaries today. Every missionary is called to serve by the prophet and assigned to a field of labor by one of the Twelve Apostles.

As I see missionaries all over the world—including here in North America—teaching investigators in so many languages, it is inspiring to reflect on D&C 90:11:

For it shall come to pass in that day, that every man shall hear the fulness of the gospel in his own tongue, and in his own language, through those who are ordained unto this power.

Missionary work is not just one of the 88 keys on a piano that is occasionally played; it is a major chord in a compelling melody that needs to be played continuously throughout our lives if we are to remain in harmony with our commitment to Christianity and the gospel of Jesus Christ.

My specific challenge to each of you is to make a commitment to be a missionary for the rest of your life.

I interviewed a new missionary a few months ago who had been a member for just over a year. He had just arrived in the mission field. He told me how his friend, who was a Latter-day Saint, had gone on a mission and then referred his name to the missionaries in his hometown. Those missionaries then taught and baptized him.

If you look at your group of friends back home, there are many who would respond to the gospel if you would have the faith to share the message of the Restoration with them.

What we desperately need is for member-missionary work to become a way of life—for the Savior's mandate to share the gospel to become part of who we are.

I pray that this generation of leaders here at BYU, along with your colleagues across the world, will follow the Savior's counsel and the prophetic counsel of all of the prophets of this dispensation to preach the gospel throughout your lives.

I would like to echo and reaffirm the words of Alma the Younger as recorded in Alma 5:45:

And this is not all. Do ye not suppose that I know of these things myself? Behold, I testify unto you that I do know that these things whereof I have spoken are true.

I bear my personal witness of the divinity of Jesus Christ, that Joseph Smith is the prophet of this dispensation and that missionary work is divinely appointed and the lifeblood of the Church, in the sacred name of Jesus Christ, amen.

NOTES

1. *Americans' Views of the Mormon Religion,* poll conducted by the Gallup News Service, February 22–25, 2007; http://galluppoll.com/content/default.aspx?ci=26758; see also "Opinions Are Diverse on 'Those Mormons,'" *Deseret News,* 3 March 2007, A01.

2. *HC* 4:540.

3. Jordan Vajda, *"Partakers of the Divine Nature": A Comparative Analysis of Patristic and Mormon Doctrines of Divinization,* Occasional Papers, no. 3 (Provo: Foundation for Ancient Research and Mormon Studies, 2002), 57.

4. Jordan Vajda, letter of 21 June 2003 to Very Reverend Roberto Corral, OP.

5. Personal correspondence to missionaries, unpublished.

6. "Economics Discovers Its Feelings," *The Economist* 381, no. 8509 (23 December 2006–5 January 2007): 34.

7. "Happiness (and How to Measure It)," *The Economist,* 13.

8. Gordon B. Hinckley, "Find the Lambs, Feed the Sheep," *Ensign,* May 1999, 107.

9. Joseph Smith, *HC* 2:478.

10. Joseph Smith, in Orson F. Whitney, *Life of Heber C. Kimball* (Salt Lake City: Bookcraft, 1945), 104.

11. Heber C. Kimball, in Whitney, *Life,* 104.

12. Heber C. Kimball, in Whitney, *Life,* 104.

13. Jeffrey R. Holland, "Missionary Work and the Atonement," *Ensign,* March 2001, 15; emphasis in original.

14. 1 Timothy 4:12.

15. Clayton M. Christensen, "My Ways Are Not Your Ways," *Ensign*, February 2007, 58.

16. Boyd K. Packer, "One in Thine Hand," address delivered at mission presidents' seminar, Provo Missionary Training Center, 22 June 2005, 4.

17. See Richard G. Scott, "Now Is the Time to Serve a Mission!" *Ensign*, May 2006, 87–90.

18. See D&C 18:15.

19. Personal correspondence between two missionaries, unpublished; emphasis in original.

20. Matthew 28:19.

21. Vilate Kimball, Letter to Heber C. Kimball, 6 September 1837, Heber C. Kimball correspondence, 1837–1852, Church History Library; text modernized.

Live Right Now

———◆———

Gerrit W. Gong

Brothers and sisters, isn't language interesting? For example, a bus station is where a bus stops. A train station is where a train stops. On my desk is a work station. It is where . . .

At church we hope those who sit on the stand understand how long we can stand to sit.

When they grow on vines, blackberries when green are red. Wireless BlackBerries when read in class make green instructors blue.

The title of my talk—Live Right Now—also has dual meaning. "Live right now" can mean "live—right now." It can also mean "live right—now." Both meanings testify to the supernal blessings of choice—what the scriptures call "moral agency" (D&C 101:78).

"Live—right now" doesn't mean eat, drink, and be merry for my class project isn't due until tomorrow! It means that, while we learn from the past and plan for the future, we make decisions in the present. The nature of mortality is we live—right now.

Gerrit W. Gong was assistant to the president for Planning and Assessment at Brigham Young University when this devotional address was given on 20 March 2007. © Brigham Young University.

"Live right—now" is also key to joy in both time and eternity. The metrics of faith, repentance, covenants, and receptiveness to the Holy Ghost are all and always tied to our living righteously. Today's choices shape tomorrow's decisions.

Choice is as eternal as we are. Our opportunity to exercise moral agency in mortality is one of God's great gifts. Yet we make many of life's most important choices before we are constitutionally qualified to run for Congress (age 25)! Faith, marriage, career—these and other important decisions loom as large as an 18-wheeler barreling toward you at breakneck speed, and you have the uneasy feeling objects in the rearview mirror are even larger than they appear.

Choices—we may put them off but we can't escape them. Choices reveal, define, and refine us. We have the gift of the Holy Ghost. When we make mistakes—and we all do—there is always a way back. And the way back is the way forward. The Savior's Atonement helps us see the Lord's promises fulfilled in our lives.

As part of living right now, let me speak in turn about choice, promptings, and promises.

CHOICE

First, choice.

I once substituted in a teenage Sunday School class. These were good kids, but they challenged me as I walked in. "Brother Gong," they said, "Sunday School is boring. We've heard everything before."

I thought for a moment, then asked, "Have you ever talked about the quintessential existential dilemmas of moral agency?"

The class said, "Huh?"

I asked if they were willing to learn together.

They were, so we did.

Quintessential means in a "pure and most concentrated form"; *existential* means "grounded in the experience of existence"; and *dilemma*—well, you know a dilemma means "a problem involving a difficult choice."

So quintessential existential dilemmas (QEDs, for short) are the challenges inherent in making life's most important and defining choices. The terminology may be new, but the dilemmas essential to real choice are as old as the Fall. Maybe new words can help us think more deeply about our choices as we seek to live right in the right now.

Please remember mortality involves, well, real choices! "There is an opposition in all things" (2 Nephi 2:11) so we can act for ourselves, being enticed by the one (sweet) or the other (bitter) (see 2 Nephi 2:15–16). The remarkable truth "Adam fell that men might be; and men are, that they might have joy" (2 Nephi 2:25) assures us existential choice need not engender forlornness, anguish, and despair (as described by Jean-Paul Sartre) but, ultimately, the joy for which men and women are.

Let's consider four illustrative examples of what I mean by QEDs.

First QED: We are enjoined to "be anxiously engaged in a good cause" (D&C 58:27) but not to run faster than we have strength (see Mosiah 4:27; D&C 10:4). Often everything happens at once: big class assignment, family home evening, service project, extra work shift—and the cute guy or girl on the second row in American Heritage finally smiled shyly and asked if you could get together. How do we diligently do all things "in wisdom and order" (Mosiah 4:27)?

Another QED: We know we should pray but may not know what to pray for. The scriptures instruct that we "must not perform any thing unto the Lord save in the first place [we] shall pray unto the Father in the name of Christ, that he will consecrate [our] performance unto [our good]" (2 Nephi 32:9). Yet the scriptures also remind us we do not know "what we should pray for as we ought" (Romans 8:26). Left on our own, we quickly discover "there is none that doeth good, no, not one" (Psalm 14:3; see also Moroni 10:25, Matthew 19:17, Mark 10:18).

We do understand neither waiting to be told all things nor doing everything on our own leads to happiness. Those who wait for absolute inspiration find themselves paralyzed, sometimes susceptible to deception from uninspired sources. Those who never seek Heavenly Father's inspiration sometimes get what they thought they wanted. You know the expression: "Be careful what you ask for."

Choosing to trust in God takes faith. The best guide of all as we seek to choose faith in every footstep is the whisperings of the Holy Spirit. Teaches President Boyd K. Packer:

> *Once you really determine to follow that guide, your testimony will grow and you will find provisions set out along the way in unexpected places, as evidence that someone knew that you would be traveling that way.* ["Spiritual Crocodiles," *Ensign*, May 1976, 31]

On occasion, in unexpected places, I have been grateful—as you have been—to find such provisions.

A third kind of QED reflects our sincere desire to submit our will to Heavenly Father. How do we say "Thy will be done" and truly mean "I want what He wants"?

Remember the great prophet Abraham? He was told he would miraculously have a son and then commanded to sacrifice that son.

While they were traveling together in the Holy Land, Professor Truman Madsen once asked President Hugh B. Brown:

> *"Why . . . was Abraham commanded to go to Mount Moriah and offer his only hope of posterity."*
>
> *It was clear that* [President Brown], *nearly ninety, had thought and prayed and wept over that question before.* [President Brown] *finally said, "Abraham needed to learn something about Abraham."* [Truman G. Madsen, *The Highest in Us* (Salt Lake City: Bookcraft, 1978), 49]

Happily, most choices are not Abrahamic tests. But mortal choices let us learn and choose something about ourselves. In a sense, mortality is the ultimate "choose your own adventure." Each choice opens new opportunities to choose and closes others.

As we choose the Lord and obey His commandments, we come to understand and accept His will. Indeed, as we *reconcile* [our]*selves to the will of God, and not to the will of the devil and the flesh;* [we] *remember, after* [we] *are reconciled unto God, that it is only in and through the grace of God that* [we] *are saved.* [2 Nephi 10:24]

In chapter 10 of Helaman, Nephi became so faithful and obedient the Lord promised, "All things shall be done unto thee according to thy word, for thou shalt not ask that which is contrary to my will" (Helaman 10:5; see also D&C 46:30).

Each semester our student stake executive secretary and clerks schedule many temple recommend interviews. Over the years Vince Shrader, Clinton Sandy, Hyrum Wright, Jeremy Johnson, Paul Orgill, Stephen Ricks, Andrew McNabb, and others have served faithfully. I love meeting all our members, including happily engaged couples.

May I share something I've observed about what makes happy couples happy? Happy couples CTR the DTR. They Choose The Right in Defining The Relationship. They let the spiritual lead the physical. In ways small and large, whether just starting to date, courting, or during their engagement, happy couples set distinct, appropriate bounds before marriage that bless all aspects of their lives—now and later. Living right now makes possible living happily later.

In interviews I sometimes say, "My purpose as your priesthood leader in asking these questions—about testimony, tithing, the law of chastity, etc.—is not to keep you from entering the temple. It is to help you know that when you are in the house of the Lord you are worthy to receive every blessing pronounced upon you."

The Lord wants us to qualify for every blessing. Indeed, "There is a law, . . . And when we obtain any blessing from God, it is by obedience to that law upon which it is predicated" (D&C 130:20–21).

Never underestimate seemingly small decisions. This includes how we choose to dress, speak, or otherwise portray ourselves.

In a Sunday School class in our student stake, I asked, "Do you protect your credit card and financial identity?" Every hand went up. I then asked, "Do you protect your spiritual identity in how you dress, speak, or portray yourself online?" I invited volunteers to share their MySpace or Facebook profiles. Would you feel comfortable showing your profile in Sunday School—or on the big screen at this devotional?

What would your parents or bishop, or your current or future spouse or children, think about you spiritually if they saw the profile you use today?

By the way, many employers now review profiles of and other online information about prospective employees before hiring them. Many screen names are functional or fun. But how would an employer feel about hiring winkydink cutiepie pinkygirl hotty14 to write important legal briefs? Would they hire hotstuff dabomb rm34 to put a mature face on the firm's new regional office?

Life doesn't stop while we wait for answers. As a member of our student stake put it, "The pioneers received inspiration as the wagon wheels turned." Remember the Lord's counsel:

Let us cheerfully do all things that lie in our power; and then may we stand still, with the utmost assurance, to see the salvation of God, and for his arm to be revealed. [D&C 123:17]

President Gordon B. Hinckley's life is a testimony of how to both pray and work. "Get on your knees and ask for help, and then get up and go to work, and you'll be able to find your way through almost any situation," he says. His good advice for university students and for all of us is also, "If you go to bed at 10:00 and get up by 6:00 a.m., things will work out for you." (In Sheri L. Dew, *Go Forward with Faith: The Biography of Gordon B. Hinckley* [Salt Lake City: Deseret Book, 1996], 167.)

My wife, Susan, and I courted across two hemispheres. She was teaching in Provo. I was studying at Oxford University in England while trying to learn everything I could about her from across the Atlantic Ocean. Call it "distance education" of the best kind. It's one reason I can honestly say I earned a PhD in international relations.

Both Susan and I knew what we wanted, but we also sought the Lord's confirming inspiration.

I prayed many times before I found the right way to ask the right question in a way that felt right for me. It was not just "Should I marry Susan?" That is, "Please tell me what to do." It was also to say humbly, "I want to ask Susan to marry me. Please confirm this decision, which I have made with all my heart." We waited and listened with faith for His quiet confirmation—answers that come according to each varied circumstance.

During his final visit to BYU, Elder Neal A. Maxwell quoted lines of verse given him by Professor John Sorenson. The verses describe

a great stallion at full gallop in a meadow, who—
at his master's voice—seizes up to a stunned but instant halt. . . .
. . . only the velvet ears
prick forward, awaiting the next order.
[Mary Karr, "Who the Meek Are Not," *Atlantic Monthly* 289, no. 5 (May 2002), 64]

Said Elder Maxwell, "Do you see a new picture of meekness being at 'full gallop' but with 'velvet ears'?" (Neal A. Maxwell, "Blending Research and Revelation," remarks at BYU President's Leadership Council meeting, 19 March 2004).

A fourth quintessential existential dilemma: How do I distinguish between promptings of the Spirit and my own personal feelings? In this month's *Ensign*, Elder Dallin H. Oaks reminds us humility precedes inspiration (see "Humility Precedes Inspiration," *Ensign*, March 2007, 61; quoted from Oaks, "I Have a Question," *Ensign*, June 1983, 27).

Humbly seeking inspiration while fully obeying all the commandments will help us determine if we are attracted to that cute girl or guy by spiritual prompting or as a response to a Madison Avenue perfume or aftershave. It can help us know when we are giving or receiving a priesthood blessing that what we are saying or hearing is not only what our own heart may earnestly want (or not want) but is in fact the will, mind, word, and voice of the Lord (see D&C 68:3–4).

By definition, QEDs involve real choices. We choose not only between good and evil but often between good and good. Happily, we are not alone as we seek to live right now.

PROMPTINGS

Promptings from Heavenly Father through the Holy Ghost can help us live right now. I am grateful Heavenly Father respects perfectly our agency and at the same time—in circumstances and at times He knows best—also prompts and guides us.

In the spirit of a devotional, let me briefly share four personal experiences where promptings taught me how the Lord will guide us as we make our own best choices while seeking inspiration.

First, promptings sometimes open unanticipated opportunities to help others.

With us here today is a wonderful woman who shared this experience. She arrived at her local supermarket and felt prompted to enter through a different door than the one she normally used. She found herself in a less familiar section of the store.

There she couldn't help overhearing a conversation. It went something like this.

"Can't we get jam? I like jam with peanut butter. Besides, you chose last time."

"Maybe so, but we need more protein. Cold cuts have more protein than jam."

Two young men wearing white shirts and name tags and holding a small calculator were confronting a tight missionary food budget. While cold cuts or jam may not constitute a classic quintessential existential dilemma, the dilemma of choosing cold cuts or jam was real.

The generous woman said, "Elders, please put both the cold cuts and jam in your basket. I would be so happy if you would let me pay for your food this week."

She told me, "I was glad Heavenly Father prompted me to go through a different door and allowed me to help those faithful elders in a small way."

Second, promptings sometimes come when our hearts go out to someone else.

While serving as a branch president in another country, I interviewed for baptism a young man with a strong testimony. He had traveled many miles over many hours on a trip I knew he could probably afford to make only once.

As we discussed the law of chastity, he hung his head. "I want to be baptized," he said, "but I am living with someone and we're not married."

As my heart went out to him, an impression came. It was very clear: "Ask him what he means by being married." I said, "Please tell me what you mean by being married."

He said, "Well, we went down to the government office and registered as a married couple, but we didn't have money for a family wedding banquet."

"Wait! You are married in the government's eyes, and not married only in the sense you haven't had a family wedding banquet?"

"Yes," he said, "we are legally married."

That worthy young husband was baptized. As I recall, there was later even a family wedding banquet.

Third, promptings sometimes comfort or prepare us for things Heavenly Father knows are coming.

Some years ago I awoke one morning with a clear but curious impression: I should use frequent-flier miles to upgrade my parents' airplane tickets for their visit to our family in Virginia. I had the tickets upgraded, then forgot completely about it.

During the visit my father was very tired one afternoon but wanted to go with me as I ran errands. Although I thought he should really stay and rest, I happily agreed for us to run the errands together. Somewhere between the laundry and the grocery store, I had a quiet feeling my father would not visit again.

A few months later I was attending a business conference in Kyoto, Japan, when I received word my father had unexpectedly died. I cried for many days. But, as I looked back, I realized I had been lovingly prepared in advance. Earlier small promptings regarding plane tickets and running errands later provided great comfort.

Fourth, promptings sometimes come at the very instant we need them to help us address questions important to someone else.

Once, in a country with customs and beliefs different from those of the U.S., I was riding in a car with a fine leader of another religion. He said, "Dr. Gong, I have a test for you."

I thought he was joking, but he wasn't. I thought he would move to another topic, but he didn't. He was quite serious.

"Imagine you are traveling in my country," he said. "You are invited inside a very humble home. You're offered a small glass of lime juice to drink. What do you do?"

At first I wondered if he were testing whether I dared drink the local juice. His was a more difficult question than that.

I knew the family was offering their best. I thought, perhaps I should thank the family but not drink the lime juice. This would acknowledge their generosity but not consume the precious juice. But might they feel insulted that I thought their offering too little or not good enough?

Alternatively, I thought maybe I should thank the family and drink the juice. This would acknowledge their generosity but could be awkward if they felt obliged to bring more juice—which they might not have. All this went through my mind in a flash.

"So what do you think?" my host asked again.

I was silent for a minute. Then, with a prayer in my heart, I opened my mouth, not yet knowing what I would say. It was then it came. What I said surprised us both.

"I would thank the family profusely," I said. "Then I would drink part of the juice and say, 'Your generosity is so great, I am unable to finish.'"

He clapped his hands. "You understand the hearts of my people," he said warmly. In a way that surprised and moved me, it mattered to this great leader that someone understood.

Sometimes it is "right now," in the instant, that we learn things important to someone else (see D&C 100:6).

I share these personal examples—which we each have in our lives—to testify Heavenly Father loves us more and knows us better than we do ourselves. We can seek the guiding whisperings of the Holy Spirit. We can be grateful on occasion for pre-positioned provisions along our path. We can "gallop with velvet ears." And we can make our best decisions knowing—on occasions and in circumstances He determines—His promptings will bless us and those around us by opening choices we would not otherwise have known.

PROMISES

As we make our best choices and follow guiding promptings in a consistent effort to live right now, we unlock the Lord's promises in our lives.

One of the Lord's promises is that His Son will be our Savior and Redeemer.

Human choices are inevitably incomplete and incorrect, and they often have unintended, or even sometimes destructive consequences.

Human choices require atonement.

We have all had experiences where we tried to be helpful and weren't. I once arrived early for priesthood meeting. Thinking I could help ready our classroom, I erased the blackboard dense with writing. As he began our lesson, our dedicated instructor said, with surprise but without criticism, "I came early and put our lesson on the board, but somehow it's been erased." The class turned out fine, but I remember the forbearance of our priesthood teacher who, incidentally, is today's U.S. Senate majority leader.

That's a simple example. What about the roommate who inadvertently hurts the tender feelings of another roommate in a way that causes her to stop coming to church? What about the friend who accidentally fatally injures his best friend in a car accident?

In each of our lives things happen that make us stop and consider what is most important. A heart attack, a near drowning, a suicide— the sudden jolt of death, injury, or major changes make us seek at-one-ment. At these tender moments, the four things that matter most find expression as "thank you," "I love you," "please forgive me," and "I forgive you" (Ira Byock, *The Four Things That Matter Most* [New York: Free Press, 2004], 3).

Each of these phrases is an echo of the Atonement. In each we feel our Savior's love for us as we extend His love and forgiveness to others. Each eases pain, offers hope and comfort, and reconciles injustices and hurts that come from living in a world of sticks and stones.

And we don't have to wait for death or trauma. The Savior's Atonement can infuse our role relationships, experiences, and knowledges right now. Our lives become richer, more peaceful, and more whole as we say with all our hearts "thank you," "I love you," "please forgive me," and "I forgive you."

Atonement ultimately comes because of our Savior's "infinite and eternal," "great and last sacrifice" (Alma 34:13–14). He knows "according to the flesh how to succor his people" (Alma 7:12). He can heal us. He can comfort and bless those hurt by our mistakes, by our imperfect choices.

As we always remember Him and keep His commandments and always have His Spirit to be with us (see D&C 20:77), we recognize another great scriptural promise:

Every soul who forsaketh his sins and cometh unto me, and calleth on my name, and obeyeth my voice, and keepeth my commandments, shall see my face and know that I am. [D&C 93:1]

Face matters. We face the facts. We *Face the Nation.* As the musical based on Victor Hugo's *Les Misérables* concludes, Eponine, Fantine, and Jean Valjean sing together "To love another person is to see the face of God" (*Les Misérables,* finale, act 2 [French lyrics, Alain Boublil; English lyrics, Herbert Kretzmer; music, Claude-Michel Schönberg]).

Do you know the scriptures contain by one count some 635 references to *face* and some 22 references to *face-to-face?* This includes precious accounts where great prophets including Moses, Abraham, Jacob, Enoch, the brother of Jared, Moroni, and the Prophet Joseph Smith all saw and spoke with God "face to face."

Elder David A. Bednar recently testified, "The scriptures contain the words of Christ and are a reservoir of living water." He taught us how to read, study, search, and feast upon the words of Christ ("A Reservoir of Living Water," fireside address, 4 February 2007). I am grateful I can seek and ponder connections, patterns, and themes such as "face" and "face-to-face."

In our day some say an unknowable God has no face. Some say God must not exist because scientific measures do not detect Him. Some say God exists only as an idea or spirit. How blessed we are to know He has a name, a voice, a face (see D&C 93:1), indeed, "a body of flesh and bones [only glorified]; the Son also" (D&C 130:22).

We approach our Heavenly Father in prayer in the name of Jesus Christ. To me, this too is a wonderful quintessential existential dilemma. We do not presume overfamiliarity as we speak of or with our Heavenly Father. But neither do we so fear His glory and perfection that we mistakenly think Him unapproachable or distant. He invites us to come to Him, and we do so on bended knee as His children.

"We know that, when he shall appear, we shall be like him; for we shall see him as he is" (1 John 3:2).

CONCLUSION

Let me conclude by offering five suggestions for how we can live right now:

1. Ponder your patriarchal blessing. Notice where Heavenly Father may give specific direction and where He gives only general guidance and expects you to learn how to make righteous choices.

2. Ask yourself, Are there things in my life I should start, stop, or continue doing? Seemingly small actions or attitudes carried on over time can set important long-term trajectories. "Out of small things proceedeth that which is great" (D&C 64:33).

3. Study the lives of the great prophets, including Abraham. Ask how you increase your understanding, trust, and experience with the

Lord so as to be prepared for challenges and opportunities in your life.

4. Review circumstances in which you received guiding promptings and how you responded to those promptings.

5. Count your many blessings. Look for ways to add "thank you," "I love you," "please forgive me," and "I forgive you" to your daily life.

May we raise our faces toward the promised day when we shall see His face and know that He is, as He encircles us in His eternal arms of mercy and safety (see Alma 5:33, 34:16; see also 3 Nephi 9:14).

Our journey complete, we will then see no longer "through a glass, darkly; but . . . face to face" (1 Corinthians 13:12), knowing as we are known, grateful for choices, promptings, and promises that invite us, with a fullness of joy, to live right now.

In the name of Jesus Christ, amen.

Preparing for That Which Is to Come

Richard O. Cowan

I have had the rare privilege of teaching at BYU for nearly 46 years—a dream that I feared might never be realized because of my being blind. Today I would like to share some lessons gleaned from what I have taught as well as some others from my own life. Specifically, I would like to talk about the progress of the Church until the time I joined the BYU faculty in 1961, what has happened since that time, what lies ahead, and what our individual roles should be in preparing "for that which is to come" (D&C 1:12). I pray that the Spirit will be with us, that we might truly "understand one another, [be] edified and rejoice together" (D&C 50:22).

Today is April 3—a significant date in our history. Let's go back 171 years to April 3, 1836. Just one week earlier, at Kirtland, Ohio, the Saints had dedicated their first temple. They had to overcome poverty and persecution as they built the House of the Lord, and truly their sacrifice did bring "forth the blessings of heaven."[1] In the dedicatory service and meetings that followed during the next

Richard O. Cowan was a BYU professor in the Department of Church History and Doctrine when this devotional address was given on 3 April 2007. © *Brigham Young University.*

few days, many present saw visions or spoke in tongues. Joseph Smith's history declared that "this was a time of rejoicing long to be remembered."[2]

These spiritual events reached a climax on Easter Sunday, April 3. After the day's services had been concluded, Joseph Smith and Oliver Cowdery knelt in prayer. They were in the Melchizedek Priesthood pulpits, a "veil" or canvas curtain having been lowered to seclude them from the rest of the room. Joseph recorded that the Savior appeared and accepted the recently dedicated temple and promised, "I will manifest myself to my people in mercy in this house." The Lord prophesied that "the hearts of thousands and tens of thousands shall greatly rejoice" because of the blessings made known in this temple "and the fame of this house shall spread to foreign lands" (D&C 110:7, 9, 10).

Keys restored by other heavenly messengers on this same occasion have supported different activities of the Church over the years. The keys of gathering brought by Moses (see D&C 110:11) have been linked with missionary work. Significantly, the Church's first overseas mission—to Britain—was opened in 1837, just one year after Moses came.

And on the same day in 1836 Elijah the prophet restored keys that would "turn the hearts of the fathers to the children, and the children to the fathers" (D&C 110:15). The years immediately following his visit witnessed an upsurge of interest in family history, with important genealogical associations being organized both in Europe and America at this time. Elijah's keys are commonly associated with temple ordinances and work for the dead; these practices, incidentally, were not restored in Kirtland but rather at Nauvoo.

After Joseph Smith introduced baptism for the dead, the Saints at Nauvoo eagerly went into the Mississippi River to perform this ordinance. Then, in 1842, the Prophet gave the endowment to selected faithful Saints. Elder James E. Talmage described it as a "course of instruction"[3] tracing our progress from the time of the Creation until when we return to God's presence and emphasizing our need to live by high gospel ideals. In his journal Joseph Smith recorded that he had communicated the priesthood keys and principles by which the Saints could ascend into the presence of God.[4] At about this same time the first couples were married or sealed for eternity. This ordinance promises some of the loftiest blessings the gospel offers.

Even after the Martyrdom of Joseph Smith in 1844, the Saints at Nauvoo completed their temple. About 5,000 Saints received their eagerly anticipated endowment blessings. On February 3, 1846, however, Brigham Young urged the Saints to prepare to leave Nauvoo immediately before the enemies could hedge up the way, promising to build other temples after they had reached the mountains. Noting the people's "anxiety" to receive their temple ordinances, he agreed to continue another few days.[5] When I think of the eagerness of those early Saints to receive their temple blessings, I wonder if we take our easy access to temples for granted.

Following the pioneers' epic exodus, the number of temples continued to grow. The original two temples were lost, but four new ones were built in Utah during the second half of the nineteenth century. This total doubled during the first half of the twentieth century as temples were built in Hawaii, Alberta, Arizona, and Idaho. Note that it took half of a century to add just four temples. The pace surely has quickened more recently.

As I grew up in Southern California, we eagerly looked forward to the time when we would have a temple there. The annual stake temple excursions to St. George or Mesa were spiritual highlights during my youth. I was in high school when the Los Angeles Temple was announced; I was proud to show a copy of the *Church News* with an architect's rendering of the temple to friends and even teachers—although, as far as I knew, I was the only Latter-day Saint at our school. I anxiously followed the various stages of temple construction before leaving for my mission. Two and one-half years later I was released just in time to attend the temple's dedication. During the 1950s the Church also dedicated its first "overseas temples" in Switzerland, New Zealand, and England.

During this same time education had been a major component in the Church's work of "perfecting the Saints" (see Ephesians 4:12).

Brigham Young Academy, founded in 1875, was the first of about 30 of these Church-sponsored high schools. As college-level courses were added, its name was changed in 1903 to Brigham Young University. During the early twentieth century seminaries and institutes provided part-time religious education to a growing number of high school and college students. With the success of these programs the Church decided during the later 1920s to close most of its schools. In 1930, however, Church leaders explained three reasons why they were keeping BYU. First, it would be a place for training teachers. (This is still one of the largest majors on campus.) Second, faithful scholars at a Church university could interpret the discoveries of science and the results of research in the light of gospel truths. And, third, the high standards of its students would be a light to the world.[6]

The Lord has exhorted us, "Arise and shine forth, that thy light may be a standard for the nations" (D&C 115:5). In 1930 BYU had only about 2,000 students, but enrollment would explode during the years just after World War II. In more recent times, BYU performing groups, successful athletic teams, and the favorable impression students give to visitors to our campus have enabled you students to truly be a light to the world. I remember President Merrill J. Bateman here in the Marriott Center speaking about the positive impact of what he called "BYU families" on Church units and activities worldwide.[7] Keep up the good work!

In 1961, when I joined the BYU faculty, the Church only had about 1.75 million members. There were only 13 temples in service. BYU's student body was about 11,000, and there were still many temporary buildings left over from the postwar boom. Now let's consider the important strides forward that I have witnessed during the years I have been here at BYU. I remember hearing something Dallin H. Oaks said at an Annual University Conference when he was president at BYU:

Often . . . I have stood at the window of my office, looking out across the northern part of the campus to the Language Training Mission and

the temple. I tell the visitors who share this sight that these three institu-
tions—university, mission, and temple—are the most powerful combination
of institutions on the face of the earth. They make this place unique in all
the world.[8]

When I came to BYU two of these three elements were not yet
present: There was no MTC and there was no temple. Gratefully I
have witnessed not only growth here on campus but the addition of
these other two institutions as well.

Interestingly, the beginnings of what would become the MTC
took place during the same semester that I started teaching here. On
December 4, 1961, I had the opportunity of attending the inaugural
meeting of what was then called the Missionary Language Institute
when the first 29 elders arrived. Then, in 1976, the first phase of
the current MTC complex was dedicated by President Spencer W.
Kimball. Once again it was my opportunity to be present at this
meeting. I heard him challenge the missionaries to learn their languages well and later teach them to their children because these skills
would be important to the growing worldwide Church. During the
three decades since that day, over a half million elders and sisters who
received their orientation here have gone all over the world to share
the marvelous message of the gospel.

Returning to the subject of temples, I was a member of the BYU
Sixth Stake presidency in 1967 when we were invited to a special
meeting. Hugh B. Brown and N. Eldon Tanner, counselors in the
First Presidency, announced plans to build the Provo Temple. Two
years later I had the interesting experience of attending the temple
groundbreaking. Once again with great interest I closely followed the
construction of a temple. Then, during the open house, I helped prepare Braille floor plans and organize a special tour for those who were
visually impaired.

The temple's dedication on February 9, 1972, was a special experience. President Joseph Fielding Smith presided. In his dedicatory
prayer, among other things, he petitioned, "Let that great temple
of learning, the Brigham Young University, . . . be prospered to the

full. Let Thy enlightening power rest upon those who teach and those who are taught."[9] As a BYU faculty member, I was and am grateful for that blessing. As we left the temple, we were so moved by the Spirit that we didn't feel like speaking until we were outside. The dedicatory proceedings were carried by closed circuit to several large auditoriums here on campus. Many students told me how those attending here in the Marriott Center had the unusual and impressive experience of seeing thousands of people exiting this huge arena in reverent silence.

For the next quarter of a century the Provo Temple was the most productive in the Church in terms of endowments for the dead. During that period these ordinances were performed for over 12 million persons—approximately equal to the present worldwide membership of the Church. I, like many thousands of BYU students, have been blessed with the privilege of going to the House of Lord and being strengthened and guided by the sacred ordinances and the Lord's Spirit there.

The Provo Temple was only the 15th in the Church. Since its dedication the number of temples has continued to grow. New kinds of temples have been designed to meet special needs. A recent article in the *Ensign* described what happened when President Gordon B. Hinckley could not find a place to build a temple in crowded Hong Kong. He was inspired to have the existing mission office removed and to have a larger building designed that would incorporate sacred temple facilities as well as the public offices and a chapel.[10] Another new kind of temple came about in Vernal, Utah, when the old stake tabernacle, no longer in use, was remodeled into a beautiful temple. In like manner, the historic Latter-day Saint chapel in Copenhagen, Denmark, has been transformed into a temple. (I have shared with my Church history classes the inspirational stories of how missionaries gathered at this chapel as they were evacuated from Germany and Czechoslovakia at the outbreak of World War II.) A combination of these two concepts was seen when a temple was constructed on the upper floors of the Church building in downtown Manhattan.

Forty-seven temples were in service when Gordon B. Hinckley became President of the Church in 1995. Still, he was anxious to take temples to the people in an even greater way. Last November I had the opportunity to visit the Mormon colonies in northern Mexico and to learn firsthand from the Saints about a special and significant event that transpired there. As President Hinckley participated in the 1997 centennial celebration of the Juárez Academy, he was impressed with the faithfulness of the Saints there. Though few in number, they have provided countless missionaries and over a hundred mission presidents. While riding back to El Paso, President Hinckley pondered the idea of building smaller temples. When he dedicated the Colonia Juárez Temple two years later, he gratefully acknowledged:

It was here in Northern Mexico, that Thou didst reveal the idea and the plan of a smaller temple, complete in every necessary detail, but suited in size to the needs and circumstances of the Church membership in this area of Thy vineyard.[11]

Since then, more than 60 of these small temples have been built on every continent. The most recent, temple number 124, was dedicated in Helsinki, Finland.

During my time at BYU the Church has continued to grow worldwide. From 1 million members in the pioneer centennial year of 1947, membership grew to 10 million in the sesquicentennial year of 1997—a tenfold increase during that half century. In this latter year, for the first time, more than half of all Church members lived outside of the United States. At the general conference this past weekend the Church reported that its membership now stands at nearly 13 million. With this growth in membership and with the multiplication of temples internationally, the Lord's declaration that the fame of the Kirtland Temple should be known throughout the earth certainly has been fulfilled.

Now let us turn to a consideration of what is to be accomplished in the future. Prophecy indicates that the Lord's kingdom will continue to roll forth until it fills the earth (see Daniel 2:24–45). But there will be challenges and difficulties to overcome. The Lord has commanded, "Prepare ye, prepare ye for that which is to come, for the Lord is nigh" (D&C 1:12). The Master counseled His New Testament disciples, "Watch" and "Be ye also ready: for in such an hour as ye think not the Son of man cometh" (Matthew 24:42, 44).

An experience I had as a missionary brought this lesson home to me. It was a Saturday morning in Laredo during August. We were expecting the mission president's first counselor the following day to conduct a district conference. I went out early to do some cleanup in front of our chapel. (I had to do this work early to avoid the heat later in the day.) My companion was working inside on some reports. Two other missionaries chose to sleep in. At about 6:30 a car drove up, and out stepped not the president's counselor whom we expected the next day but the mission president himself! He had come unannounced to look at some property we were buying. In subsequent weeks he went around the mission speaking about the Second Coming and likening it to his visit to Laredo when he found two elders working and two sleeping. (I'm grateful I hadn't decided to sleep in on that particular morning!)

How must we prepare? I have learned that there are three main sources of guidance to which we may turn. Interestingly, President Neil L. Andersen of the Seventy emphasized these same three channels at his CES fireside talk here in the Marriott Center a month ago. The first is personal direction through the Spirit. President Heber C. Kimball warned, "There will be a great sifting time, and many will fall; for I say unto you there is a *test*, a TEST, a TEST coming, and who will be able to stand?" He then answered his own question: "The time will come when no man nor woman will be able to endure on borrowed light. Each will have to be guided by the light within himself. If you do not have it, how can you stand?"[12] Sometime after the Martyrdom, Brigham Young saw Joseph Smith in vision. The Prophet instructed his successor: "Be careful and not turn away the small still voice; it will teach you what to do and where to go."[13]

We often think of revelation guiding the Church only during the days of Joseph Smith or of the pioneers. I am grateful to have been able to teach about evidence of divine guidance in our own day as well. During his 1921 tour of missions around the world, Elder David O. McKay was directed to a secluded garden in Beijing where he could offer a special prayer. Another time he was prompted to leave a volcano overlook just before it crumbled into the lava below. And in Jerusalem he was prompted to take a particular train that enabled him to meet the man with whom he would tour the Armenian Mission.

Matthew Cowley, president of the New Zealand Mission, instructed his missionary assistant to keep his bags packed so they could leave immediately whenever directed by the Spirit to members who needed help. Elder Norman Seibold was prompted to get off trains at certain stations as he sought to locate fellow missionaries needing help during the evacuation from Germany at the outbreak of World War II.

Inspiration was also evident in President Hinckley's selection of the site for a temple in Guayaquil, Ecuador. After inspecting a half dozen sites, he was impressed to return to the first one and this time go beyond a row of trees and an area of swampy ground. There they found a dirt road leading to a hill overlooking the whole city. As the group stood looking down, tears filling their eyes, they "knew that a prophet had found the site for the temple."[14]

Often it has been necessary to "go forward with faith" as did Nephi when he went to retrieve the brass plates, not knowing how the desired goal could be accomplished (see 1 Nephi 4:6). At a devotional assembly here in the Marriott Center, Elder Glen L. Rudd related how he drove into a large Caribbean city to find a member who had requested a blessing; even though he didn't have her address, he was prompted to park in a spot that turned out to be right in front of her home.

I have had to do the same thing. During my second year of college my bishop and I filled out my mission papers, not knowing if I could be called with my disability. I did have the privilege to serve, and that experience has had a far-reaching impact on my life. Enjoying the special spirit at a small district conference attended by one of the General Authorities, I was impressed that I should make teaching at BYU my life's work. While in the mission I also met a certain sister missionary, Dawn Houghton, who would become my eternal companion. Together we had to "go forward with faith." On our way back to California after attending general conference, we decided to get married even though I would be in graduate school and Dawn would need to work to support us. When I reached home, I found a telegram waiting that notified me that I had been awarded a Danforth Fellowship that would take care of all our expenses through my receiving the PhD. Blessings don't always come so quickly!

From my study of Church history as well as from my own experience, I have learned that these blessings often come only following diligent effort. For example, the Lord has instructed that He will give us a witness of the truth only after we have studied out the matter in our own mind (see D&C 9:7–9). Only after Henry Burkhart had repeatedly requested permission for East German Saints to go to Switzerland for temple blessings did the Communist leaders offer the possibility of building a temple right there in the German Democratic Republic. Likewise, after the Cowan family had seemingly done everything possible to trace our ancestry in Scotland, a friend who was helping us with research was inexplicably attracted to an ordinary-looking book in an English secondhand bookstore. It was on an upper shelf so high that he couldn't read its title. When the clerk climbed a ladder to retrieve the book, it turned out to be a history of the very parish from which the Cowans came. We anticipate it will provide the clues we need. Similarly, it was following months of hard work and sacrifice that we had the totally unexpected experience of being presented an award by President Eisenhower at the White House.

I have also learned, however, that inspiration and guidance do not always come just when we would like it. Through Isaiah, the Lord has reminded us, "My thoughts are not your thoughts, neither are your ways my ways" (Isaiah 55:8).

The scriptures have been a second source of comfort and direction as the Saints have sought to prepare "for that which is to come." Of course the impact of James 1:5 on Joseph Smith and the Restoration of the gospel is well known. Three passages have particularly strengthened me:

In Ether 12:27 Moroni assured us that the Lord allows us to have weakness so that we might become humbled and that if we have faith in Christ He can transform weaknesses into strengths.

A Latter-day revelation suggests a close relationship between the Lord and His servants when He promised: "I will go before your face. I will be on your right hand and on your left, and my Spirit shall be in your hearts, and mine angels round about you, to bear you up" (D&C 84:88).

Then I have taken comfort from the Lord's instruction: "Be thou humble; and the Lord thy God shall lead thee by the hand, and give thee answer to thy prayers" (D&C 112:10).

Our living prophets have been a third major source of direction. Truly, "We thank thee, O God, for a prophet / To guide us in these latter days."[15] General conferences became important to me early on. As members of our Southern California ward returned from conference, they brought phonograph recordings of selected talks that were played in sacrament meetings. Then, when I was in high school, I rode to Utah and attended sessions in the Tabernacle with my dad. Now I enjoy attending priesthood sessions at the Conference Center with my own two sons.

We have just concluded a great conference. As I prepared this devotional talk, I gained a greater appreciation for what the General Authorities go through as they prepare their talks. Elder Boyd K. Packer taught the following concerning general conference:

The servants of the Lord will counsel us. You may listen with anxious ears and hearts, or you may turn that counsel aside. . . . What you shall gain will depend not so much upon their preparation of the messages as upon your preparation for them.[16]

Hopefully we prepared ourselves spiritually to receive the inspired messages from our divinely appointed leaders. Now we should implement Elder Harold B. Lee's counsel:

As the Latter-day Saints go home from this conference, it would be well if they consider seriously the importance of taking with them the report of this conference and let it be the guide to their walk and talk during the next six months. These are the important matters the Lord sees fit to reveal to this people in this day.[17]

Speaking to college students, Elder Spencer W. Kimball counseled:

I hope you will get your copy of the [conference messages] *and underline the pertinent thoughts and keep it with you for continual reference. No text nor volume outside of the standard works of the Church should have such a prominent place on your personal library shelves.*[18]

In conclusion, I am grateful to testify that the priesthood keys restored on the third of April 171 years ago have enabled the Lord's work to progress throughout the earth and that He is guiding His Church today. May we ponder our personal part in helping the Lord's kingdom to roll forth. May we profit from the blessings of the temple and from guidance through the Spirit, inspiration from the scriptures, and leadership from our living prophets as we prepare for the Lord's return. These things I pray in the name of Jesus Christ, amen.

NOTES

1. "Praise to the Man," *Hymns*, 1985, no. 27, verse 4.

2. Joseph Smith, *HC* 2:392.

3. James E. Talmage, *The House of the Lord* (Salt Lake City: Bookcraft, 1962), 99.

4. See Joseph Smith, *HC* 5:2; 3 May 1842.

5. Brigham Young, *HC* 7:579.

6. See Joseph F. Merrill, "Brigham Young University, Past, Present, and Future," *Deseret News*, 20 December 1930, section 2 (Christmas News), p. 3.

7. Merrill J. Bateman, "A Zion University," BYU devotional address, 9 January 1996.

8. Dallin H. Oaks, "A House of Faith," BYU Annual University Conference address, 31 August 1977, 8.

9. Joseph Fielding Smith, 9 February 1972, in "Dedication Prayer of Provo Temple," *Church News*, 12 February 1972, 5; also "Provo Temple Dedicatory Prayer," *Ensign*, April 1972, 31.

10. See Monte J. Brough and John K. Carmack, "How the Hong Kong Temple Came to Be," *Ensign*, December 2006, 59–61.

11. Gordon B. Hinckley, dedicatory prayer of the Colonia Juárez Chihuahua Mexico Temple, 6 March 1999, in "This Is a Day Long Looked Forward To," *Church News*, 13 March 1999, 7.

12. Orson F. Whitney, *Life of Heber C. Kimball* (Salt Lake City: Bookcraft, 1967), 446, 450.

13. *Manuscript History of Brigham Young: 1846–1847*, ed. Elden J. Watson (Salt Lake City: Elden Jay Watson, 1971), 529; 23 February 1847.

14. Sheri L. Dew, *Go Forward with Faith: The Biography of Gordon B. Hinckley* (Salt Lake City: Deseret Book, 1996), 481.

15. "We Thank Thee, O God, for a Prophet," *Hymns*, 1985, no. 19.

16. Boyd K. Packer, "Follow the Brethren," BYU devotional address, 23 March 1965; emphasis in original; also Boyd K. Packer, "That All May Be Edified" (Salt Lake City: Bookcraft, 1982), 244.

17. Harold B. Lee, *CR*, April 1946, 68; also "Living in the Bonds of Brotherhood," *Improvement Era* 49, no. 5 (May 1946): 283.

18. Spencer W. Kimball, *TSWK*, 523.

"Don't Miss the Miracle"

Catherine H. Black

Many years ago I discovered a book of poetry entitled *In the Stillness Is the Dancing*. Within the pages of this book is a poem entitled "Don't Miss the Miracle," compiled from the essay "If I Had Three Days to See," written by Helen Keller in 1933. I would like to begin my address today by sharing this poem with you:

I, who cannot see, find hundreds of things
to interest me through mere touch.
I feel the delicate symmetry of a leaf.
I pass my hands lovingly
about the smooth skin of a silver birch,
or the rough shaggy bark of a pine . . .
I feel the delightful, velvety texture of a flower,
and discover its remarkable convolutions;
and something of the miracle of Nature
is revealed to me.

Catherine H. Black was a BYU professor of dance when this devotional address was given on 10 April 2007. © *Brigham Young University.*

Occasionally, if I am very fortunate,
I place my hand gently on a small tree and feel
the happy quiver of a bird in full song . . .
At times my heart cries out with longing
to see these things.
If I can get so much pleasure from mere touch,
how much more beauty must be revealed
by sight.
Yet, those who have eyes apparently see little.
The panorama of color and action
which fills the world is taken for granted . . .
It is . . . a great pity that, in the world of light,
the gift of sight
is used only as a mere convenience rather than
as a means of adding fullness to life.
[Mark Link, *In the Stillness Is the Dancing* (Niles, Illinois: Argus
Communications, 1972), 36–37]

What does it mean to see? *Webster's Encyclopedic Unabridged Dictionary of the English Language* lists 25 definitions for the word *see* ([New York: Gramercy Books, 1989], 1290). The first is "to perceive with the eyes; look at." Being both blind and deaf, according to this definition Helen Keller indeed could not see. However, according to other Webster definitions of the word, which include "to perceive," "discern," "recognize," "have insight," and "understand intellectually or spiritually," Helen Keller not only saw very clearly but, through her writing, admonished us to do the same.

Within the myriad of experiences we encounter every day, how much does each of us really see? How much do we allow the light that illuminates our world to permeate our beings? To what degree do we allow light to enlighten?

What is light? Again I turn to *Webster's Encyclopedic Unabridged Dictionary of the English Language* (828), which defines *light* as "that which makes things visible or affords illumination." In the first chapter of John we are told:

*In the beginning was the Word, and the Word was with God, and the
Word was God.*

The same was in the beginning with God.

*All things were made by him; and without him was not any thing made
that was made.*

In him was life; and the life was the light of men. [John 1:1–4]

Speaking to the people in the temple in Jerusalem, Jesus said,
"I am the light of the world: he that followeth me shall not walk in
darkness, but shall have the light of life" (John 8:12).

The Bible Dictionary tells us:

*The light of Christ is just what the words imply: enlightenment,
knowledge, and an uplifting, ennobling, persevering influence that comes
upon mankind because of Jesus Christ. For instance, Christ is "the true light
that lighteth every man that cometh into the world" (D&C 93:2; John
1:9). The light of Christ fills the "immensity of space" and is the means
by which Christ is able to be "in all things, and is through all things, and
is round about all things." It "giveth life to all things" and is "the law by
which all things are governed." It is also "the light that quickeneth" man's
understanding (see D&C 88:6–13, 41).* [Bible Dictionary, s.v. "light of
Christ," 725]

At the recent funeral of Dr. W. Ralph Andersen, BYU professor
emeritus of botany and range science, I was inspired by excerpts from
his journal that were read by several of his children. Brother Andersen
deeply contemplated the concept of light and truth and seeing with
spiritual eyes. He believed that it was the duty of each of us to use our
God-given personal authority to seek to know God and to do so by
kindling our own light and then walking in that light. The brighter
the light, the clearer the vision.

The gift of life and the gift of light are inseparably connected.
And quality of life is directly proportional to the degree to which we
use the gift of light—not, as Helen Keller says, "as a mere convenience" but "as a means of adding fullness to life." Doing so allows

us to not miss the many miracles in our lives that, in rewarding our faith, demonstrate to us that God knows us as individuals and loves us. When we turn ourselves over to Him and let Him direct our paths, we are blessed with the peace that comes from the realization that whatever we experience in life is as it was meant to be.

I would now like to share with you a few examples of occasions when I have been fortunate to perceive the hand of the Lord in my destiny. It is my hope that they will serve to rekindle within you memories of and gratitude for your own similar encounters with Him as He has directed your paths in the past. It is also my hope that they will inspire each of us to strive to sharpen our perceptions and help us rejoice in the evidence of God's hand in our lives as our various futures unfold.

The first example relates to the passing of my mother in October 1994. Our immediate family (Mom, Dad, my younger sister, Barbara, and I) had gathered for the weekend at my sister's home in Calgary, Alberta, Canada, to celebrate Mom and Dad's golden wedding anniversary. Although their anniversary was on October 20th, we decided to celebrate it the weekend before—from October 14th through the 16th—because I was choreographing a musical at BYU that was scheduled to open shortly after October 20, and I needed to be back in Utah with enough time to fulfill my professional obligations.

My sister and I prepared a weekend full of surprises for our parents, beginning with four gold-colored, helium-filled balloons with Happy 50th Anniversary printed on them, each balloon symbolizing each one of us. These we tied to a banister just inside my sister's front door to greet our parents when they arrived. We enjoyed the most wonderful time that weekend that we had ever spent together as a family.

It was important to my sister and me that our parents have a final surprise on the actual date of their anniversary. This, we decided, should be a bouquet of Peace roses, a variety that Mom had chosen as her wedding flowers. As we proceeded to order these flowers, we learned that that particular variety no longer existed, but there was one that was very close—yellow with a tinge of pink around the top of the petals—and they had to be ordered from Holland. No problem. We ordered one-and-a-half dozen of them to be delivered to our parents' home in Edmonton, Alberta, on the 20th. As soon as we hung up the phone, I regretted not having thought quickly enough to order 20 roses to symbolize the date of the anniversary. However, we decided to leave the order as we had placed it. And that was that.

Early in the morning of October 17th, the day we had designated for my parents and me to return to our respective homes, Mom suffered a severe stroke that ultimately took her life just after midnight on October 19th, one day short of the 50th anniversary. When we arrived home from the hospital that night, one of the four balloons on the banister, out of helium, was lying limp at the base of the other balloons.

The flowers from Holland suddenly became funeral flowers and were rerouted to Calgary for the private funeral we held there on the 20th. When the flowers arrived at the funeral home, there were not 18 roses but in fact 20. And during the ceremony one rose began to wilt. By the time we took the flowers back to my sister's home, that one flower had significantly withered, leaving 19—for us symbolic of the date my mother passed away. A mere coincidence? I choose to think not. For us it was the Lord's arms around us, telling us in His own way that it was time for our wife and mother to return to Him and that all was well.

My second example concerns my father, Michael Herbut, who passed away in August 1999. Throughout his life Dad liked to buy things. Shortly before he died he purchased several rosebushes from a catalog and, since he had no garden of his own, bequeathed them to my sister. Although Alberta *is* Wild Rose Country, domestic roses are very hard to grow there. But my sister wanted to try, and that spring I went up to help her plant the rosebushes. Being a good gardener, she did all she could to assure that the roses would survive. And they did, for a while, in what she named the Michael Herbut Rose Garden. The summer after Dad passed away, while I was visiting my sister, one of the rosebushes was coming into bloom. It was at least the second season that the bush had flowered. Never before had a flower on that bush been anything but pure yellow. At this particular time, however, the rose that was blooming was tinged with pink around the top of the petals, and subsequently the yellow flowers on this bush continued to bloom with pink edges. A tender miracle? I think so.

My final example has unfolded throughout my lifetime and as a result will be considerably longer than the previous two. In August 1972 I was hired on a one-year appointment as a faculty member in the Department of Dance at Brigham Young University. I was not yet a member of The Church of Jesus Christ of Latter-day Saints. It was an interesting year. The students were as full of light and conviction then as now—unofficial missionaries who were grounded in their faith, lived what they believed, and extended themselves to me with love, respect, and caring. Although I was not what one would call a "golden convert," their efforts did bear fruit, and I was baptized on August 18, 1973.

As a child I had grown up in the Russian Orthodox faith and attended Divine Liturgy on Sundays at St. Barbara's Cathedral in Edmonton. The service was delivered in the Russian language, which I did not understand because my parents, like so many children of immigrants at that time, chose not to speak their heritage language anywhere, in favor of English and of assimilation into Canadian culture. There were understandable reasons for this.

My mother often related stories of unkind words and deeds she and other members of her family experienced throughout their lives because they were "different." Growing up, I was also occasionally a recipient of similar unkind acts. While I was a junior high school student, each class member was routinely required, during a roll call of sorts, to state aloud from their desk their ethnic heritage. For those of us with German and Russian ancestry it was not a particularly joyful activity as our classmates followed our declarations with taunts of "Nazi" or "Commie."

I hated those days. I would come home from school in tears, begging my mother, "Couldn't I *please* say I'm Ukrainian?" But even though she was reliving her pain through mine, she would always say the words I wished were not true: "No, Catherine. We are not

Ukrainian. We are Russian." The one goal I had in life was to some-day marry a man with an Anglo-Saxon surname—like Brown, or White, or Green!

Although I was ashamed of my heritage, I did believe in God, and I wanted to do what was right, so I attended church regularly, even though I did not understand a word of what was being said throughout the service.

As a freshman at the University of Alberta, I began to receive gentle promptings to study the Russian language. The reason for this eluded me, but I listened, took a beginning Russian course, and—not being especially talented at language learning (then or now)—shortly after having completed the course, promptly forgot virtually everything I had been taught. Why did I need to learn Russian?

I finished undergraduate school, worked for two years to save money for graduate school, enrolled at the University of Utah, enjoyed the two years I spent there very much, learned a great deal about modern dance, and graduated. I knew that since I was not an American citizen I needed to return to Canada, which I was not quite ready to do because I wanted to hone the dance skills I had just acquired before returning home to a more "pioneering" environment. I investigated and discovered something called a practical training visa, which allowed international students to remain in the United States for up to 18 months to practice skills they had learned in school by being employed in a discipline-related field. I resolved that the first university position offered to me in the United States would be the one I would accept. That position was offered by BYU. Thanks to the efforts of Clayne Jensen—then dean of the College of Physical Education—my practical training visa was renewed every year for four years until I met and married a wonderful widower from New Zealand who had a vibrant and talented young daughter—*and* a green card. Because he had a green card, I was able to obtain one, and my "year" at BYU has turned into 34 years and still counting.

Almost immediately upon becoming a member of the Church, the Spirit of Elijah began to burn deeply within me. I not only faced the fact that I had Russian ancestry but began to embrace it. I became overwhelmingly grateful for all of the sacrifices that both sets of grandparents had made in eking out a better existence for themselves and their posterity in a new land.

I started studying Russian again—between babies and BYU obligations—learning and forgetting and learning again. I cannot tell you how many times I asked myself, "Why am I doing this? This is crazy. I don't have anyone with whom to speak the language. It must be so that I can read genealogical records someday—if I can ever gain access to them from behind the Iron Curtain."

Meanwhile, in the summer of 1989, a wonderful opportunity was made available to me. I was invited to accompany the BYU International Folk Dance Ensemble on their tour to Russia, Poland, and England. As the plane touched down at the Sheremetyevo International Airport in Moscow, I remember thinking, "We could just as well be landing somewhere on the Canadian prairies. It looks exactly the same." No wonder so many Slavic people settled in western Canada at the beginning of the 20th century. They must have felt a measure of security in the midst of geographically familiar surroundings, in spite of the many hardships they had to face.

My mother's father had always wanted to return to Russia for a visit before he died, but unfortunately that never happened. For me, going to Russia with the folk dancers was going back for him. I thought about him continually the entire time I was there. I loved being surrounded by the Russian people and their culture. And I got to practice the language! But something told me that the real purpose for my learning Russian had not yet been fulfilled.

In my excitement to experience Russia, I had completely underplayed my pending opportunity to experience the people and culture of Poland—until I remembered that my father's parents had been born in what today is Poland. I wondered if the folk dancers would be performing anywhere near where these grandparents grew up. As I looked at the map, I remember the following rapidly developing chain of thoughts: (1) Hmmm, interesting, not too far; (2) I wonder if there would be any way I could work it out to get to their villages;

(3) No, I HAVE to find a way to get there; (4) No matter what, I WILL find a way!

The plane landed in Warsaw. We boarded a bus that had been reserved to take us to Mr gowo in the north of Poland. I was sitting in the front seat across from the driver when our tour guide, Danuta, boarded the bus with a clipboard in her hands. As she was looking over the ensemble roster, I heard her say, "Cathy Black."

Sitting directly in front of her, I responded, "That's me."

To which she replied, "I see you are from Canada. I worked in Montreal for two years learning English."

The two of us bonded immediately.

After just a few hours with the Folk Dance Ensemble, Danuta noticed that there was something special about the group compared to others she had been assigned in the past. She said that the performers and leaders were not self-centered, that they were kind and polite to each other, and that they did not ask for anything unless they really needed it.

One of the things we did ask for was a room—one that we could use for a church meeting the next morning. Danuta procured the room and asked whether guests could attend this church meeting. Of course the answer was yes, and she was warmly encouraged to join us, which she did. It was a beautiful testimony meeting during which Danuta was moved to tears a number of times. Following the meeting I gave her my triple combination, and she immediately began to read about Joseph Smith. The next day we boarded the bus back to Warsaw. At the end of that journey Danuta informed us that we would have a different guide to accompany us to the Carpathian Mountains in southeastern Poland and that she would come the next day to say good-bye to us.

Before she left that day I explained to her my obsession about going to visit my grandparents' villages and asked her if there would be any way that she might help me do so. Danuta took down the last names of my ancestors and the names of their villages and told me she would see me tomorrow.

As had been the case in Russia, 1989 was also a very difficult time economically for Poland. Shelves were bare of essential merchandise, and having a telephone, let alone a car, was a luxury. When Danuta arrived to meet us at the bus the next day, she had acquired a car, a driver, and two contacts she had called who agreed to meet with me in the Carpathian Mountains. One of these people was a priest and the other a gentleman by the name of Mieczysław Herbut, who said that he was sure we were not related because he came from a different part of Poland than my grandparents. Pressing him, Danuta asked if he would be willing to meet with me anyway, in spite of his reservations. He said he would.

We were scheduled to meet at a restaurant in Nowy Sącz. Danuta, our driver, and I arrived first and visited while we waited for Mr. Herbut. As he walked through the door, tears welled up in my eyes. Let me show you two photos—one of Mieczysław Herbut and one of my father, Michael Herbut. This is one miracle that nobody could miss! Even more uncanny than the remarkable physical resemblance of these two men was the identical nature of their mannerisms. It was absolutely unbelievable! After receiving the photograph of my father, Mieczysław, who learned English during World War II while a German prisoner of war, wrote to my father informing him that he knew he had discovered a twin brother. The two men continued to correspond with each other until Mieczysław's death in the mid-1990s. Although we have not yet been able to verify a genetic relationship between these two men, I am working on it.

In addition to visiting my grandparents' villages and meeting with people there, Danuta and I searched genealogical records, and I was able to add a generation to my family tree. Since then Danuta has joined the Church, has become proficient in genealogy, and has helped many Americans find their Polish ancestors. By searching Polish records on my behalf, she has helped me access several generations to add to my family tree. In 2005 she was called to codirect the newly created LDS Warsaw Family History Center. I never cease to marvel at the privilege that has been mine to have been part of this amazing series of events.

And there is yet another dimension to this story. On the 1989 trip we discovered that the family names on my father's side were not in fact Russian names but belonged to a Slavic minority population known as Lemkos, who had identified themselves as Russians at the time my grandparents left for North America. This discovery has resulted in a serious academic research agenda for me, which has included trips back to Poland for the express purpose of studying the dance and rituals of the Lemko people.

In the latter part of the 1990s the prompting to study Russian arose yet again. This time I hired a tutor to speak with me once a week over several months. Then, on Sunday, March 19, 2000, while reading a front-page feature article in the *Deseret News* entitled "The Orphans of Vladivostok," I was overcome by the desire to adopt a Russian orphan. I shared my thoughts with my husband, positive he would say, "We're too old." We were almost empty nesters. To my surprise he replied, "Why not?" As we discussed it further, we decided that it would be best for us to adopt two children rather than one and that we would like them to be sisters between the ages of six and 10.

We had never before talked about adoption of any kind; we did not even know where to begin. We decided to start by contacting our adult children to seek their approval. That obtained, we were led, through a series of timely events, to an agency specializing in Russian adoptions. Interestingly, one of the directors of the agency told us that on the very weekend that I was reading the article in the *Deseret News*, they had e-mailed their contact in Russia to ask if they could get two or three more children, whom they felt certain they could place. They were told that two sisters, ages seven and eight, had just been approved for adoption.

We were able to afford this adoption because of an inheritance left to us following my father's passing. The first piece of physical documentation we received concerning the children was a photograph. One of the little girls bore a striking resemblance to my mother's youngest sister. The photograph was followed by written information about the girls. In it we discovered that the one who looked so much like my mother's sister also had the same birthday as my father. When we discovered the girls' surname, it turned out that it was the very name that my parents had planned to give my sister had she been a boy. These, and other similar "coincidences"—some too personal to share—made it clear to my husband and me beyond a shadow of a doubt that these two beautiful children were meant to be part of our family.

Although the process was anything but smooth, miracles continued to happen, and in late October 2000 the judge in Russia pounded her gavel and those two little Russian sisters became legally ours. It was wonderful to have basic Russian language skills to be able to help ease the girls into their new environment. As they have become fluent in English, my promptings to learn Russian have stilled, and I am at peace in knowing what the ultimate purpose was for which I needed to know the language.

The longer I live, the more deeply I appreciate my relationship with the Lord. I marvel that He knows me, cares about me, and literally leads me, guides me, and walks beside me every step of the way— just as He does for each of you (see "I Am a Child of God," *Hymns*, 1985, no. 301). There are evidences of His presence all around us, just waiting to be discovered and acknowledged. What joy and peace we can receive from the recognition of the many miracles in our lives! May we strive constantly not to miss them but to see them clearly is my prayer in the name of Jesus Christ, amen.